WORDS THEIR WAY®

WORD STUDY IN ACTION • TEACHER RESOURCE GUIDE

W9-CAV-576

Glenview, Illinois

Boston, Massachusetts

Chandler, Arizona

Upper Saddle River, New Jersey

ALWAYS LEARNING

PEARSON

Acknowledgment
We thank Michelle Picard and Allison Meadows of Arlington County Public Schools, Virginia, for their contributions to this effort. The contributions they made for a custom printing of *Words Their Way*®: *Word Study in Action* for their school system created the momentum for this developmental edition.

Copyright © 2012 Pearson Education, Inc., or its affiliates. All Rights Reserved. Printed in the United States of America. This publication is protected by copyright, and permission should be obtained from the publisher prior to any prohibited reproduction, storage in a retrieval system, or transmission in any form or by any means, electronic, mechanical, photocopying, recording, or likewise. For information regarding permissions, write to Rights Management & Contracts, One Lake Street, Upper Saddle River, New Jersey 07458.

Words Their Way is a trademark in the U.S. and/or other countries, of Pearson Education, Inc., or its affiliates.

ISBN-13: 978-1-4284-3144-7
ISBN-10: 1-4284-3144-6
23 22 21   20 19 18 17

Contents

Program Overview..2

Program Authors 3

Program Components...4

Developmental Stages 6

Scope and Sequence 8

From Assessment to Instruction.........................10

Walk Through a Lesson..14

Getting Started 16

Follow-Up Routines...20

Ten Principles of Word Study 22

Meeting Individual Differences 24

Word Study with English Language Learners.......25

School-Home Connection.....................................26

Word Study Implementation Checklist.................27

Research Base 28

Research Base References....................................30

Emergent-Early Letter Name

Overview 32

Concept Sorts

Sort 1   Concept Sort **Fruit/Not a Fruit** 36

Sort 2   Concept Sort **Animal/Not an Animal** 37

Sort 3   Concept Sort **Shapes** 38

Sort 4   Concept Sort **Food, Clothes, Toys** 39

Sort 5   Concept Sort **Clothes** 40

Sort 6   Concept Sort **Food** 41

Rhyming Sorts

Sort 7   Rhyming Sort **Nose, Knees, Hair, Head** 42

Sort 8   Rhyming Sort **Clock, Fly, Pan** 43

Sort 9   Rhyming Sort **Bug, Mop, Beet** 44

Sort 10   Rhyming Sort **Jar, Crate, Bell, Grape** 45

Sort 11   Rhyming Sort **Pairs I** 46

Sort 12   Rhyming Sort **Pairs 2** 47

Sort 13   Rhyming Sort **Colors** 48

Beginning Consonants

Sort 14   Beginning Sounds **b, m** 49

Sort 15   Beginning Sounds **r, s** 50

Sort 16   Beginning Sounds **b, m, r, s** 51

Sort 17   Letter Recognition **Bb, Mm, Aa** 52

Sort 18   Letter Recognition **Rr, Ss, Ee** 53

Sort 19   Beginning Sounds **t, g** 54

Sort 20   Beginning Sounds **n, p** 55

Sort 21   Beginning Sounds **t, g, n, p** 56

Sort 22   Letter Recognition **Tt, Gg, Ee** 57

Sort 23   Letter Recognition **Nn, Pp, Ii** 58

Sort 24   Beginning Sounds **c, h** 59

Sort 25   Beginning Sounds **f, d** 60

Sort 26   Beginning Sounds **c, h, f, d** 61

Sort 27   Letter Recognition **Cc, Hh, Ii** 62

Sort 28   Letter Recognition **Ff, Dd, Aa** 63

Sort 29   Beginning Sounds **l, k** 64

Sort 30   Beginning Sounds **j, w, q** 65

Sort 31   Beginning Sounds **l, k, j, w** 66

Sort 32   Letter Recognition **Ll, Kk, Oo** 67

Sort 33   Letter Recognition **Jj, Ww, Qq** 68

Sort 34   Beginning Sounds **y, z, v** 69

Sort 35   Ending Sounds **t, x** 70

Sort 36   Letter Recognition **Yy, Zz, Vv** 71

Sort 37   Letter Recognition **Tt, Xx, Uu** 72

Digraphs

Sort 38   **s, h,** and **Digraph sh** 73

Sort 39   **c, h,** and Digraph **ch** 74

Sort 40   **h** and Digraphs **sh** and **ch** .75

Sort 41   Digraphs **th, wh** 76

Sort 42   Digraphs **sh, ch, wh, th** 77

Letter Name

Overview 78

Beginning Consonants

Sort 1   Beginning Consonants **b, m, r, s** 82

Sort 2   Beginning Consonants **t, g, n, p** 83

Sort 3   Beginning Consonants **c, h, f, d** 84

Sort 4   Beginning Consonants **l, k, j, w** 85

Sort 5   Beginning Consonants **y, z, v** .86

Same Vowel Word Families

Sort 6   Word Families **-at, -an** 87

Sort 7   Word Families **-ad, -an** 88

Sort 8   Word Families **-ap, -ag** 89

Sort 9   Word Families **-ad, -ap, -ag** 90

Sort 10   Word Families **-op, -ot, -og** 91

Sort 11   Word Families **-ip, -ig, -ill** 92

Sort 12   Word Families **-ug, -ut, -un** 93

Sort 13   Word Families **-et, -eg, -en** 94

Sort 14   Word Families **-ed, -et, -eg, -ell** .95

Digraphs and Blends

Sort 15   Consonant Digraphs **ch, sh** 96

Sort 16   Consonant Digraphs **th, wh** 97

Sort 17   Consonant Digraphs **sh, ch, wh, th** 98

Sort 18   Beginning Consonants and Blends **s, t, st** 99

Sort 19   Consonant Blends **sp, sk, sm** 100

Sort 20   Consonant Blends **sc, sn, sw** 101

Sort 21   Consonant Blends **pl, sl, bl, fl** 102

Sort 22   Consonant Blends **cr, cl, fr, gl, gr** 103

Sort 23   Consonant Blends **pr, tr, dr, br** 104

Sort 24   Beginning Sounds **k, wh, qu, tw** 105

Mixed Vowel Word Families

Sort 25   Mixed Vowel Word Families **-at, -ot, -it** 106

Sort 26   Mixed Vowel Word Families **-an, -in, -en, -un** 107

Sort 27   Mixed Vowel Word Families **-ad, -ed, -ab, -ob** 108

Sort 28   Mixed Vowel Word Families **-ap, -ip, -op, -up** 109

Sort 29   Mixed Vowel Word Families **-ag, -eg, -ig, -og, -ug** 110

Sort 30   Mixed Vowel Word Families **-ill, -ell, -all** 111

Sort 31   Mixed Vowel Word Families **-ack, -ick, -ock, -uck** 112

Sort 32   Mixed Vowel Word Families **-ash, -ish, -ush** 113

Sort 33   Mixed Vowel Word Families **-ang, -ing, -ong, -ung** 114

Sort 34   Mixed Vowel Word Families **-ank, -ink, -unk** 115

Short Vowels

Sort 35   Short Vowels **a, o** 116

Sort 36   Short Vowels **i, u** 117

Sort 37   Short Vowels **e, i, o, u** 118

Sort 38   Short **a, i** Words With Beginning Blends 119

Sort 39   Short **e, o, u** Words With Beginning Blends 120

Sort 40   Short **a, e, i** Words With Beginning Digraphs 121

Sort 41   Short Vowel Words With Beginning Blends 122

Sort 42   Short Vowel Words With Final Blends 123

Sort 43   Short Vowel Words With Final Digraphs 124

Sort 44   Short Vowels **a, e, i, o, u** 125

Preconsonantal Nasals

Sort 45   Preconsonantal Nasals **-ng, -mp** 126

Sort 46   Preconsonantal Nasals **-nt, -nd, -nk** 127

r-Influenced Vowels

Sort 47   Short **o** and **or** 128

Sort 48   Short **a** and **ar** 129

Contractions

Sort 49   Contractions 130

Within Word Pattern

Overview 132

Short and Long Vowels

Sort 1   Short and Long **a** (Pictures) 136

Sort 2   Short **a** (CVC) and Long **a** (CVCe) 137

Sort 3   Short and Long **i** (Pictures) 138

Sort 4   Short **i** (CVC) and Long **i** (CVCe) 139

Sort 5   Short and Long **o** (Pictures) 140

Sort 6   Short **o** (CVC) and Long **o** (CVCe) 141

Sort 7   Short and Long **u** (Pictures) 142

Sort 8   Short **u** (CVC) and Long **u** (CVCe) 143

Sort 9   Short and Long **e** (Pictures) 144

Sort 10   Review Short Vowel (CVC) and Long Vowel
(CVCe) Patterns 145

Other Common Long Vowel Patterns

Sort 11   Short **a** (CVC) and Long **a** (CVCe and CVVC-**ai**) 146

Sort 12   Short **a** (CVC) and Long **a** (CVCe, CVVC-**ai**,
and Open Syllable-**ay**) 147

Sort 13   Short **o** (CVC) and Long **o** (CVCe and CVVC-**oa**) 148

Sort 14   Short **o** (CVC) and Long **o** (CVCe, CVVC-**oa**,
and CVV-**ow**) 149

Sort 15   Long **o** (CVCe, CVVC-**oa**, CVV-**ow**, VCC) 150

Sort 16   Short **u** (CVC) and Long **u** (CVCe and CVVC) 151

Sort 17   Short **u** (CVC) and Long **u** (Open Syllable-**ew** and -**ue**) 152

Sort 18   Short **e** (CVC) and Long **e** (CVVC) 153

Sort 19   More Short **e** (CVC and CVVC) and Long **e** (CVVC) 154

Sort 20   Review CVVC Patterns **ai, oa, ee, ea** 155

Sort 21   Short **i** (CVC) and Long **i** (CVCe, VCC-**igh**, and CV Open
Syllable-**y**) 156

Sort 22   Long **i** (CVCe, VCC-**igh**, CV Open Syllable-**y**, iCC) 157

r-Influenced Vowels

Sort 23   **r**-Influenced Vowel Patterns **ar, ir, or, ur** 158

Sort 24   **r**-Influenced Vowel Patterns **ar, are, air** 159

Sort 25   **r**-Influenced Vowel Patterns **er, ear, eer** 160

Sort 26   **r**-Influenced Vowel Patterns **ir, ire, ier** 161

Sort 27   **r**-Influenced Vowel Patterns **or, ore, oar** 162

Sort 28   r-Influenced Vowel Patterns **ur, ure, ur-e** 163

Sort 29   Review of **ar**, Schwa Plus **r**, and **or** 164

Diphthongs and Other Ambiguous Vowels

Sort 30   Diphthongs **oi, oy** 165

Sort 31   Vowel Digraph **oo** 166

Sort 32   Diphthongs **ou, ow** 167

Sort 33   Ambiguous Vowels **aw, au** 168

Sort 34   Ambiguous Vowels **wa, al, ou** 169

Complex Consonant Clusters

Sort 35   Final /k/ Sound Spelled **ck, ke, k** 170

Sort 36   Silent Beginning Consonants **kn-, wr-, gn-** 171

Sort 37   Consonant Digraphs Plus **r**-Blends and **squ-** 172

Sort 38   Triple **r**-blends **scr-, str-, spr-** .173

Sort 39   Hard and Soft **c** and **g** 174

Sort 40   Word Endings **-dge, -ge** 175

Sort 41   Word Endings **-ce, -ve, -se** 176

Sort 42   Word Endings **-tch, -ch** 177

Homophones

Sort 43   Long **a** Homophones #1 178

Sort 44   Long **a** Homophones #2 179

Sort 45   Short and Long **i** Homophones .180

Syllables and Affixes

Overview 182

Compound Words

Sort 1   Compound Words 186

Sort 2   More Compound Words 187

Sort 3   Plural Endings **-es, -s** 188

Inflected Endings

Sort 4   Unusual Plurals 189

Sort 5   Adding **-ing** to Words With VC and VCC Patterns 190

Sort 6   Adding **-ing** to Words With VCe and VVC Patterns 191

Sort 7   Review of Inflected Ending **-ing** 192

Sort 8   Adding **-ed** (Double/No Change) 193

Sort 9   Adding **-ed** (Double/e-Drop/No Change) 194

Sort 10   Adding **-ed** to Words With VC, VCe, VVC,
and VCC Patterns 195

Sort 11   Unusual Past-Tense Words 196

Open and Closed Syllables

Sort 12   Syllable Juncture in VCV and VCCV Patterns 197

Sort 13   More Syllable Junctures in VCV and VCCV Patterns 198

Sort 14   Open and Closed Syllables in VCV Patterns 199

Sort 15   Syllable Juncture in VCV and VVCV Patterns 200

Sort 16   Syllable Juncture in VCCCV and VV Patterns 201

Sort 17   Open and Closed Syllables and Inflected Endings 202

Sort 18   Plural Endings: Final **-y** 203

Sort 19   Adding Inflected Endings **-s, -ed,** and **-ing** to
Words With Final **-y** 204

Accented Syllables

Sort 20   Long **a** Patterns in Accented Syllables 205

Sort 21   Long **i** Patterns in Accented Syllables 206

Sort 22   Long **o** Patterns in Accented Syllables 207

Sort 23   Long **u** Patterns in Accented Syllables 208

Sort 24   Long and Short **e** Patterns in Accented Syllables 209

Sort 25   Review Long Vowel Patterns in Accented Syllables 210

Sort 26   Ambiguous Vowels **oy/oi** and **ou/ow** in Accented Syllables 211

Sort 27   Ambiguous Vowels **au/aw/al** in Accented Syllables 212

Sort 28   **r**-Influenced **a** in Accented Syllables 213

Sort 29   **r**-Influenced **o** in Accented Syllables .214

Sort 30   Words With **w** or **/w/** Before the Vowel 215

Sort 31   /ər/ Spelled **er, ir, ur** in First Syllables 216

Sort 32   /ər/ and **r**-Influenced **e** Spelled **er, ear, ere, eer**
in Accented Syllables 217

Unaccented Syllables

Sort 33   Unaccented Final Syllable **-le** 218

Sort 34   Unaccented Final Syllable /əl/ Spelled **-le, -el, -il, -al** 219

Sort 35   Unaccented Final Syllable /ər/ Spelled **-er, -ar, -or** 220

Sort 36   Agents and Comparatives 221

Sort 37   Final Syllables /ər/ Spelled **-cher, -ture, -sure, -ure** 222

Sort 38   Unaccented Final Syllable /ən/ Spelled **-en, -on, -an, -ain** .223

Sort 39   Unaccented Initial Syllables **a-, de-, be-** 224

Consonants

Sort 40   Initial Hard and Soft **c** and **g** 225

Sort 41   Final **-s** and Soft **c** and **g** 226

Sort 42   More Words With **g** 227

Sort 43   /k/ Spelled **-ck, -ic, -x** 228

Sort 44   /qw/ and /k/ Spelled **qu** 229

Sort 45   Words With Silent Consonants 230

Sort 46   Words With **gh** and **ph** 231

Prefixes and Suffixes

Sort 47   Prefixes **re-, un-** 232

Sort 48   Prefixes **dis-, mis-, pre-** 233

Sort 49   Prefixes **ex-, non-, in-, fore-** 234

Sort 50   Prefixes **uni-, bi-, tri-,** and Other Numbers 235

Sort 51   Suffixes **-y, -ly, -ily** 236

Sort 52   Comparatives **-er, -est** 237

Sort 53   Suffixes **-ness, -ful, -less** 238

Homophones and Homographs

Sort 54   Homophones 239

Sort 55   Homographs 240

Derivational Relations

Overview 242

Prefixes and Suffixes

Sort 1   Prefixes **pre-, fore-, post-, after-** 246

Sort 2   Review Suffixes **-ness, -ful, -less** 247

Sort 3   Adding **-ion** (With No Spelling Change) 248

Sort 4   Adding **-ion** and **-ian** (With No Spelling Change) 249

Sort 5   Adding **-ion** (With e-Drop and
Spelling Change) 250

Sort 6   Adding **-ion** (With Predictable
Changes in Consonants) 251

Sort 7   Consonant Alternation: Silent and Sounded 252

Sort 8   Vowel Alternation: Long to Short .253

Sort 9   Vowel Alternation: Long to Short or /ə/ 254

Sort 10   Adding Suffixes: Vowel Alternation
(Accented to Unaccented) 255

Sort 11   Adding the Suffix **-ity:** Vowel Alternation
(/ə/ to Short) 256

Sort 12   Adding Suffixes: Vowel Alternation
(With Spelling Change) 257

Sort 13   Adding the Suffix **-ation:** Vowel Alternation
(With Spelling Change) 258

Sort 14   Examining Multiple Alternations 259

Sort 15   Greek and Latin Number Prefixes
mono-, bi-, tri- 260

Sort 16   Greek and Latin Prefixes **inter-, sub-, over-** 261

Sort 17   Number Prefixes **quadr-, tetra-, quint-, pent-, dec-** 262

Greek and Latin Roots

Sort 18   Latin Word Roots **spect, port** 263

Sort 19   Latin Word Roots **dic, aud** 264

Sort 20   Latin Word Roots **rupt, tract, mot** 265

Sort 21   Latin Word Roots **ject, man, cred** 266

Sort 22   Latin Word Roots **vid/vis, scrib/script** 267

Sort 23   Latin Word Roots **jud, leg, flu** 268

Sort 24   Greek and Latin Elements **-crat/-cracy, -arch/-archy** 269

Sort 25   Latin Word Roots **spire, sist, sign** 270

Sort 26   Greek and Latin Elements **cap, ped, corp** 271

Sort 27   Greek and Latin Word Roots **sect, vert/vers, form** 272

Sort 28   Greek and Latin Word Roots **onym, gen** 273

Sort 29   Greek and Latin Word Roots **voc, ling, mem, psych** 274

Sort 30   Prefixes **intra-, inter-, intro-** 275

Sort 31   Predictable Spelling Changes **ceiv/cep,
tain/ten, nounce/nunc** 276

Advanced Spelling-Meaning Patterns

Sort 32   Adding Suffixes **-ent/-ence, -ant/-ance #1** 277

Sort 33   Adding Suffixes **-ent/-ence, -ant/-ance #2** 278

Sort 34   Adding Suffixes **-able, -ible** 279

Sort 35   Adding the Suffix **-able**
(With e-Drop and No Spelling Change) 280

Prefix Assimilation

Sort 36   Prefix Assimilation: Prefixes **in-, im-, il-, ir-** 281

Sort 37   Prefix Assimilation: Prefixes **com-, col-, con-** 282

Sort 38   Prefix Assimilation: Prefixes **ob-, ex-, ad-, sub-** 283

Program Overview

For years, teachers have been using *Words Their Way®: Word Study for Phonics, Vocabulary, and Spelling Instruction*, now in its fifth edition, to teach students phonics, spelling, and vocabulary. This hands-on approach to word study teaches students to look closely at words to discover the spelling patterns, syllable structures, and spelling-meaning connections of English orthography that are needed for reading and writing. Students learn to examine, manipulate, and categorize words while focusing their attention on the critical features of the words—their sound, spelling, and meaning. *Words Their Way®: Word Study in Action, Developmental Model*, presents this powerful word study approach in a ready-to-use format for your classroom.

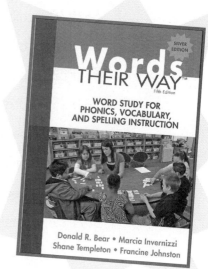

Words Their Way: Word Study in Action Developmental Model

Words Their Way®: Word Study in Action, Developmental Model, covers the five developmental stages of word study: Emergent-Early Letter Name, Letter Name, Within Word Pattern, Syllables and Affixes, and Derivational Relations. There is a student book available for each developmental stage.

The heart of the program is the **sort**, the process of grouping words or pictures that represent sounds into specific categories. Sorting includes teacher-directed instruction as well as independent learning. The teacher begins by demonstrating the sort. Later, as students sort on their own, they make discoveries and generalizations about the conventions of English orthography.

The sequence of the developmental program is based on the alphabet, spelling patterns, and meaning principles that have been observed in students' spelling development. *Words Their Way®: Word Study in Action, Developmental Model*, provides the following important hands-on experiences:

- Comparing and contrasting words by sounds so that students can categorize similar sounds and associate them consistently with letters, letter combinations, syllable patterns, and spelling conventions. For example, words spelled with the CVC pattern (*mad, snap, glass*) are compared with words spelled with the CVCe pattern (*made, flake, whale*).

- Comparing and contrasting words by spelling patterns associated with a sound. For example, words spelled with *oi* (*join, soil, coin*) are compared with words spelled with *oy* (*joy, annoy, toy*).

- Categorizing words and word parts by meaning, use, and part of speech. For example, adjectives ending in *-y* (*chilly, misty, breezy*) are compared to adverbs ending in *-ly* (*quickly, quietly, smoothly*).

Program Authors

Donald R. Bear is director of the E. L. Cord Foundation Center for Learning and Literacy and professor in the College of Education at the University of Nevada, Reno. He and preservice, Master's, and doctoral students teach and assess children who struggle to learn to read and write. Dr. Bear has been involved in innovative professional development grants, and with colleagues has developed assessments used in school districts throughout the country. He is involved in numerous studies that examine literacy development, including studies of orthographic development in different and second languages.

Marcia Invernizzi is the Henderson Professor of Reading Education at the Curry School of Education and director of the McGuffey Reading Center at the University of Virginia where she teaches the clinical practicum, doctoral seminars in reading research, and word study. She is formerly an English and reading teacher and is the principal author of Phonological Awareness Literacy Screening (PALS).

Francine Johnston is an associate professor in the School of Education at the University of North Carolina at Greensboro, where she coordinates the reading program. She taught in public schools for sixteen years as a first-grade teacher and reading specialist. She is interested in how children learn to identify and spell words and the relationship between those.

Shane Templeton is Foundation Professor of Literacy Studies at the University of Nevada, Reno. A former classroom teacher at the primary and secondary levels, he has focused his research on developmental word knowledge in elementary, middle, and high school students. He is a consultant with school districts across the country and several State Departments of Education. Since 1987, he has been a member of the Usage Panel of *The American Heritage Dictionary*.

Program Components

Words Their Way®: Word Study in Action, Developmental Model supports the routines established in *Words Their Way: Word Study for Phonics, Vocabulary, and Spelling Instruction,* 5th Edition, by providing the materials you need for each sort in a ready-to-use format. Picture and word cards, sorting grids, interactive whiteboard technology, game boards, and reading materials that contain the same spelling patterns students sorted are all provided.

Words Their Way: Word Study in Action, Developmental Model contains the following components:

Each developmental level of the program features a consumable **Student Book**. The Student Book contains a four-page lesson for each sort, including picture and/or word cards for students to cut out and a grid onto which students sort and glue or tape the picture or word cards. Each lesson also contains a written activity that gives students practice in the element that corresponds to the lesson's sort. An **envelope** is provided for students to store their picture or word cards for the week. A convenient self-stick strip allows the envelope to be attached to the inside back cover of the Student Book.

The **Big Book of Rhymes** contains a poem for each sort in the Emergent-Early Letter Name, Letter Name, and Within Word Pattern developmental stages. Words in the poems reflect the word features covered in the corresponding sort. High-interest, engaging illustrations accompany each poem and can be used to foster discussion.

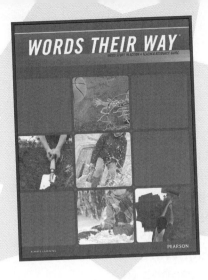

A comprehensive **Teacher Resource Guide** provides both instructional and content support to implement and manage an effective word study program. The first portion of the Teacher Resource Guide gives background and information about *Words Their Way* and how to implement it in your classroom. An overview of each developmental level, which includes the assessments for that level, precedes the lesson pages that provide specific information about teaching each sort.

The **Whiteboard Activities DVD-ROM** enables interactive learning about the feature for each sort:

- **Rhymes** from the Big Book of Rhymes for Emergent-Early Letter Name, Letter Name, and Within Word Pattern can be displayed for teaching concepts of print and words for working with words that exemplify the focus of the sort.
- The **whiteboard drag-and-drop** ability can be used to demonstrate the feature of the sort and allow students to practice the sort themselves in an interactive, enjoyable way.
- The **writing sort** is the page from the Student Book that allows students to practice the word features through writing.

The **Teacher Resource CD-ROM** contains a variety of materials that can be printed and integrated into classroom word-study instruction for interactive learning:

- **Picture or word cards** can be used to demonstrate each sort in each developmental level.
- **Games** give students additional practice for the word features taught in each sort.
- **Rhymes** from the Big Book of Rhymes for Emergent-Early Letter Name, Letter Name, and Within Word Pattern can be printed out for students to take home to read with family members.
- **Blank templates** allow you and your students to create your own sorts and games.

Each sort in Emergent-Early Letter Name, Letter Name, and Within Word Pattern is aligned to a corresponding little book from the *Words Their Way Library*. Each book links to the word features in the sort. Stories are age-appropriate and appealing.

Developmental Stages

The methodology of *Words Their Way: Word Study for Phonics, Vocabulary, and Spelling Instruction* reflects a progression of stages that describe students' spelling behavior as they move from one level of word knowledge to the next. The stages cited in the book make it easier to understand and recognize the basic strategies that students use to spell. In *Words Their Way: Word Study in Action*, these stages have been adapted to correspond to the five specific levels of spelling: Emergent-Early Letter Name, Letter Name, Within Word Pattern, Syllables and Affixes, and Derivational Relations.

Emergent-Early Letter Name During this stage, children learn to recognize and write the letters of the alphabet. They play with the sounds in words and letters. Through most of the stage, children sort pictures by rhyme and beginning sounds. By the end of the stage, children begin to match picture cards to the words that represent their names.

Letter Name At the beginning of this stage, students apply the alphabet principles primarily to consonants. By the end of the stage, students are able to represent most short vowel patterns, consonant digraphs, and consonant blends correctly. In this level, students sort pictures and/or words by beginning consonants, digraphs, and blends, and by word families.

Stages of Spelling in *Words Their Way*

Examples	▶ Emergent	▶ Letter Name (Alphabetic)
bed		*b bd bad*
ship		*s sp sep shep*
float		*f ft fot flot float*
train		*t trn jran tan charn tran*
cattle		*c kd cat cadol*
cellar		*s slr salr celr*
pleasure		*p pjr plasr plager*
confident		
opposition		

Within Word Pattern Students at the beginning of this stage spell most one-syllable, short vowel words correctly. Then students move away from the sound-by-sound approach of the letter name and begin to include patterns or chunks of letter sequences that relate to sound and meaning. In this level, students begin to sort words by long vowel patterns.

Syllables and Affixes Spelling By this stage, students already spell most one-syllable short and long vowel words correctly. The focus of instruction shifts to multisyllabic words and patterns. In *Words Their Way: Word Study in Action*, students sort words by specific vowel combinations, inflected endings (including plurals, *-ing*, and *-ed*), and vowel patterns in accented and unaccented syllables. Students study how syllables divide in words with open syllables (*cli/mate, trea/ty, re/act*) and closed syllables (*sup/ply, clos/et, hun/dred*).

Derivational Relations At the beginning of this stage, students will be able to spell most words correctly. In this stage, students sort words by pattern and meaning, with an emphasis on meaning and related word parts. They discover how spelling preserves meaning even when there are changes in sound (for example, the *e* in *compete* shifts in sound from a long vowel to a schwa in *competition*). After common prefixes and suffixes are studied, students will begin to examine the meanings of bases and roots and the classical origin of polysyllabic words. In this level, students will study suffixes with vowel alternations, as well as Greek and Latin word roots (such as *sect, vert,* and *form*) to expand their word knowledge.

Within Word Pattern	Syllables and Affixes	Derivational Relations

bed

ship

flowt   floaut   flote   float

teran   traen   trane   train

catel   catol   cattel   cattle

saler   celer   seler   celler   *seller   cellar*

plejer   pleser   plesher   *plesar   plesher   plesour   plesure   pleasure*

confadent   confiedent   confedent   confendent   confident

opasishan   oppasishion   opositian   oposision   opposition

7

Scope and Sequence

The following chart shows the skills presented in *Words Their Way®: Word Study in Action*. The first column lists the word features. The subsequent columns indicate the *Words Their Way* level or levels at which the word features are covered.

Features	Emergent-Early Letter Name	Letter Name	Within Word Pattern	Syllables and Affixes	Derivational Relations
Concept Sorts and Rhyming Sorts	•				
Beginning Sounds	•				
Letter Recognition (Uppercase and Lowercase)	•				
Ending Sounds **t, x**	•				
Consonant Digraphs **sh, ch, th, wh**	•	•			
Beginning Consonants **b, m, r, s, t, g, n, p, c, h, f, d, l, k, j, w, y, z, v**		•			
Short Vowel Word Families **at, an, ad, an, ap, ag, op, ot, og, ip, ig, ill, ug, ut, un, et, eg, en, ed, ell**		•			
Consonant Blends **sp, sk, sm, sc, sn, sw, pl, sl, bl, fl, cr, cl, fr, gl, gr, pr, tr, dr, br**		•			
Mixed Vowel Word Families		•			
Short Vowels **a, e, i, o, u**		•			
Short Vowel Words with Beginning Blends and Digraphs		•			
Short Vowel Words with Final Blends and Digraphs		•			
Preconsonantal Nasals **ng, mp, nt, nd, nk**		•			
Contractions		•			
Short Vowel Pattern CVC			•		
Long Vowel Pattern CVCe			•		
Long Vowels and Vowel Pairs **ai, ay, oa, ow, ew, ue, ee, ea, igh**			•		
r-Influenced Vowel Patterns, Schwa Plus **r**		•	•	•	
Diphthongs **oi, oy, ou, ow**			•	•	
Vowel Digraph **oo**			•		
Ambiguous Vowels **aw, au, wa, al, ou**			•	•	
Final /k/ Spelled **-ck, -ke, -k**			•		
Silent Consonants **kn, wr, gn**			•		
Triple **r**-Blends **scr, str, spr**			•		
Hard and Soft **c** and **g**			•		
Word Endings **-dge, -ge, -tch, -ch**			•		
Word Endings **-ce, -ve, -se**			•		
Homophones			•	•	
Compound Words				•	
Plural Endings **-s, -es** and Unusual Past Tense Words				•	
Inflected Endings **-ing, -ed**				•	

	Emergent-Early Letter Name	Letter Name	Within Word Pattern	Syllables and Affixes	Derivational Relations
Syllable Junctures				•	
Open and Closed Syllables and Inflected Endings				•	
Plural Endings: Final **-y**				•	
Adding Inflected Endings **-s, -ed,** and **-ing** to Words with Final **-y**				•	
Long Vowel Patterns in Accented Syllables				•	
Words with **w** or /w/ before the Vowel				•	
Unaccented Final Syllable /əl/ Spelled **-le, -el, -il, -al**				•	
Unaccented Final Syllable /ər/ Spelled **-er, -ar, -or**				•	
Agents and Comparatives				•	
Final Syllables /ər/ Spelled **-cher, -ture, -sure, -ure**				•	
Unaccented Final Syllable /ən/ Spelled **-en, -on, -an, -ain**				•	
Unaccented Initial Syllables **a-, de-, be-**				•	
Final **-s** and Hard and Soft **c** and **g**				•	
/k/ Spelled **-ck, -ic, -x**				•	
/qw/ and /k/ Spelled **qu**				•	
Words with **gh** and **ph**				•	
Prefixes r**e-, un-, dis-, mis-, pre-, uni-, bi-, tri-**				•	•
Prefixes **ex-, non-, in-, fore-**				•	•
Suffixes **-y, -ly, -ily**				•	
Suffixes **-ness, -ful, -less**				•	•
Comparatives **-er, -est**				•	
Homographs				•	
Adding **-ion** and **-ian**					•
Consonant Alternation: Silent and Sounded					•
Vowel Alternation					•
Adding Suffixes **-ity, -ation**: Vowel Alternation					•
Greek and Latin Prefixes **mono-, bi-, tri-, inter-, sub-, over-**					•
Number Prefixes **quadr-, tetra-, quint-, pent-, dec-**					•
Latin Word Roots **spect, port, dic, aud, rupt, tract, mot, ject, man, cred, vid/vis, scrib/script, jud, leg, flu, -spire, -sist, -sign**					•
Greek and Latin Elements **-crat/-cracy, -arch/-archy, cap, ped, corp**					•
Greek and Latin Word Roots **sect, vert/vers, form, onym, gen, voc, ling, mem, psych**					•
Prefixes **intra-, inter-, intro-**					•
Predictable Spelling Changes **ceiv/cep, tain/ten, nounce/nunc**					•
Adding Suffixes **-ent/-ence, -ant/-ance, -able, -ible**					•
Prefix Assimilation: Prefixes **in-, im-, il-, ir-, com-, col-, con-, ob-, ex-, ad-, sub-**					•

From Assessment to Instruction

Effective teaching cannot begin until you understand what students already know about words and what they're ready to learn. Likewise, instructional adjustments cannot be made until you evaluate the results of your teaching. One way to learn about students' development is to observe their reading and writing. Additionally, assessment should include an informal qualitative spelling inventory. Together, reading, writing, and spelling inventories provide a rich collection of information to understand students' knowledge of orthography.

1. Administer a Spelling Inventory

Spelling inventories are made up of words specially chosen to represent a variety of spelling features or patterns at increasing levels of difficulty. (See right for an example.) The words in spelling inventories are designed to show students' knowledge of key spelling features that relate to the different spelling stages. Students take an inventory as they would a spelling test, but they do not study the words in advance. Use the results of the inventory to obtain a general picture of a student's development.

1. Analyze Student's Spelling

Use a feature guide, like the one on p. 11, to analyze students' spellings. This analysis will help you identify what orthographic features students know and what they are ready to study as well as their approximate stage; a feature guide can help you determine a starting place for appropriate instruction. Look at the sample feature guide on the next page. This student missed two features under Other Vowels. This is the place to begin instruction for him.

Spelling Inventory

Word	Student Spelling	Word Correct
1 bed	bed	✓
2 ship	ship	✓
3 when	when	✓
4 lump	lump	✓
5 float	float	✓
6 train	train	✓
7 place	place	✓
8 drive	drive	✓
9 bright	brite	
10 shopping	shoping	
11 spoil	spoyle	
12 serving	serving	✓
13 chewed	chooed	
14 carries	caryes	
15 marched	martched	
16 shower	showers	
17 bottle	bottel	
18 favor	faver	
19 ripen	rippin	
20 cellar	selar	
21 pleasure	pleascher	
22 fortunate	forchunate	
23 confident	confdant	
24 civilize	sivulise	
25 opposition	opozishun	

Feature Guide

Student's Name: *Jake Fisher* Teacher *T. Atkinson* Grade *5* Date *September*

Words Spelled Correctly: *9*/25 Feature Points: *43*/62 Total: *52*/87 Spelling Stage: *Late Within Word Pattern*

SPELLING STAGES →	EMERGENT LATE	LETTER NAME—ALPHABETIC					WITHIN WORD PATTERN			SYLLABLES AND AFFIXES			DERIVATIONAL RELATIONS			
		EARLY	MIDDLE	MIDDLE	LATE	LATE	EARLY	MIDDLE	LATE	EARLY	MIDDLE LATE		EARLY	MIDDLE		
Features →		Consonants Initial	Consonants Final	Short Vowels	Digraphs	Blends	Common Long Vowels	Other Vowels	Inflected Endings	Syllable Junctures	Unaccented Final Syllables		Harder Suffixes	Bases or Roots	Feature Points	Words Spelled Correctly
1. bed		b✓	d✓	e✓											3	1
2. ship			p✓	i✓	sh✓										3	1
3. when				e✓	wh✓										2	1
4. lump		l✓		u✓		mp✓									3	1
5. float			t✓			fl✓	oa✓								3	1
6. train			n✓			tr✓	ai✓								3	1
7. place						pl✓	a-e✓								2	1
8. drive			v✓			dr✓	i-e✓								3	1
9. bright						br✓	igh *i-e*								1	
10. shopping				o✓	sh✓				pping						2	
11. spoil						sp✓	oi *oy*								1	
12. serving							er✓	ving✓							2	1
13. chewed					ch✓		ew *oo*	ed✓							2	
14. carries							ar✓	ies	rr						1	
15. marched					ch✓		ar✓	ed✓							3	
16. shower					sh✓		ow✓			er✓					3	
17. bottle									tt✓	le					1	
18. favor									v✓	or					1	
19. ripen										pen						
20. cellar									ll✓	ar✓					1	
21. pleasure												ure	pleas✓		1	
22. fortunate							or✓					ate✓	fortun		2	1
23. confident												ent	confid			
24. civilize												ize	civil			
25. opposition												tion	pos			
Totals		7/7	5/5	5/5	6/6	7/7	4/5	5/7	3/5	2/5	2/5		1/5	1/5	43	9

11

3. Form Groups

Experience has shown that when students study a particular orthographic feature, it is best if they are in groups with students who are ready to benefit from the same word study. Use the assessment information you gathered in steps 1 and 2 to form your groups. You can organize your groups by using a classroom composite form and/or a spelling-by-stage classroom organization chart as shown below.

Spelling-by-Stage Organization Chart

Spelling Stages	EMERGENT			LETTER NAME			WITHIN WORD PATTERN			SYLLABLES AND AFFIXES			DERIVATIONAL RELATIONS		
	EARLY	MIDDLE	LATE	EARLY	MIDDLE	LATE	EARLY	MIDDLE	LATE	EARLY	MIDDLE	LATE	EARLY	MIDDLE	LATE
							Josh B. Dominique	Beth	Jamie Zac						
							Dustin Ian	Craig	Daniel						
							Emily	Melanie	Eric						
							Brennan	Melissa	Sara						
								Josh							
								Paula							
								Erik							
								Josh C.							
								Joshua							
								Sarah							
								Cliff							
								Camille							

4. Monitor Student Progress

Brief, ongoing assessment alerts you to adjust the content and pacing of instruction in order to meet students' needs and to arrange additional instruction for students who may need extra help. Here are four ways you can monitor progress.

Spell Checks

Spell Checks are provided in *Words Their Way®: Word Study in Action.* They can be used

- to fine-tune placement.
- as a pretest for a spelling feature or prior to instruction to determine what students already know.
- as a posttest after instruction to determine what students have learned.
- as a delayed posttest administered several weeks after instruction to determine what students have retained over time.

Spelling Inventories

Students may be given the same spelling inventory three times during the year to assess progress and to determine whether changes need to be made in grouping or instructional focus. You may use the same spelling inventory each time in order to compare progress on the same words. Remember that students should not study the words on the inventory before you administer it. In between administrations of the spelling inventories, use the Spell Checks to monitor progress within and across stages.

Weekly Spelling Tests and Unit Tests

You can use weekly tests at most grade levels as a way to monitor mastery of the studied features and to send a message to students and parents alike that students are accountable for learning to spell the words they have sorted. Students will usually be very successful on these weekly tests when they are appropriately placed for instruction. However, if they are incorrectly spelling more than a few words, you may need to adjust your instruction. You may also want periodically to give a review test or unit test without asking students to study in advance to test for retention. Simply select a sample of words from previous lessons and call them aloud as you would for any spelling test.

Qualitative Spelling Checklist

You may use a qualitative spelling checklist to identify progress through the stages of spelling development based on students' use of specific spelling features in their writing. You can find a qualitative spelling checklist in Appendix A of *Words Their Way: Word Study for Phonics, Vocabulary, and Spelling Instruction, 5th ed.*

See Chapter 2 of *Words Their Way: Word Study for Phonics, Vocabulary, and Spelling Instruction, 5th ed.,* for a comprehensive explanation of spelling inventories, feature guides, and grouping students.

Expectations for Student Progress

Spell Checks, spelling inventories, and qualitative checklists are used to identify students' developmental stages, to determine the features that need instruction, and to form and reform instructional groups. At the same time, teachers need to set long-term goals and objectives for student growth within grade levels.

- Articulate end-of-grade expectations in terms of stages of development as shown in the chart below.
- Know the typical range of development within grade levels so you can provide additional instruction and intervention for students who lag below that range.
- Know where students must be at the end of the year if they are to succeed in subsequent grades and meet state standards in reading and writing.

GRADE LEVEL	TYPICAL SPELLING STAGE RANGES WITHIN GRADE	END-OF-YEAR SPELLING STAGE GOAL
K	Emergent—Letter name–alphabetic	Middle letter name–alphabetic
1	Late emergent—Within word pattern	Early within word pattern
2	Late letter name—Early syllables & affixes	Late within word pattern
3	Within word pattern—Syllables & affixes	Early syllables & affixes
4	Within word pattern—Syllables & affixes	Middle syllables & affixes
5	Syllables & affixes—Derivational relations	Late syllables & affixes
6 +	Syllables & affixes—Derivational relations	Derivational relations

Spelling Stage Expectations by Grade Level

Walk Through a Lesson

For each sort in *Words Their Way: Word Study in Action, Developmental Model,* there is an easy-to-follow lesson. A lesson plan for Emergent-Early Letter Name, Letter Name and Within Word Pattern is shown on this page. A lesson plan for Syllables and Affixes and Derivational Relations is shown on the next page.

Objectives identify the skill covered and describe what students accomplish in the lesson.

A list of **Materials** lets you see at a glance where to find each component used in the lesson.

The **pictures and/or words** in the lesson are clearly identified.

Bonus Words Many lessons at the first three developmental stages include additional words that coordinate with the sort generalization for more practice.

Introduce/Model

Use the whiteboard DVD-ROM or CD-ROM word cards to introduce and model the sort.

Read a Rhyme occurs at the first three developmental stages. Read a poem from the *Big Book of Rhymes.* Children identify and discuss words in the poem that align with the sort.

Practice the Sort

Students complete and check their sorts and explain the generalization used to sort.

Apply

Students demonstrate what they have learned by completing a writing activity.

A **Game** presents a fun way for students to apply the sort generalization. Games can be printed out from the CD-ROM.

Little Books are available at the first three developmental stages. They provide both shared and independent reading with a book that aligns with the sort as well as opportunities for word hunts.

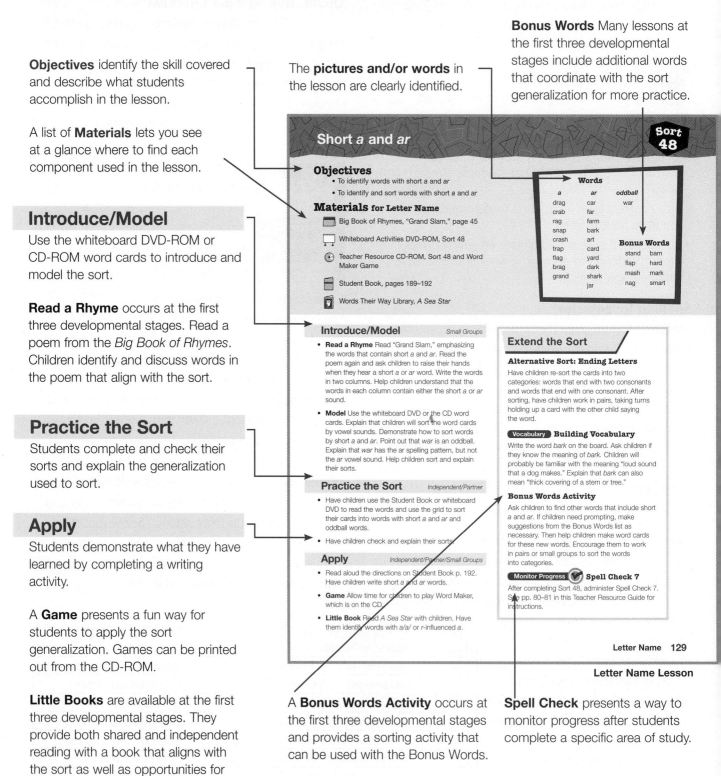

A **Bonus Words Activity** occurs at the first three developmental stages and provides a sorting activity that can be used with the Bonus Words.

Spell Check presents a way to monitor progress after students complete a specific area of study.

14

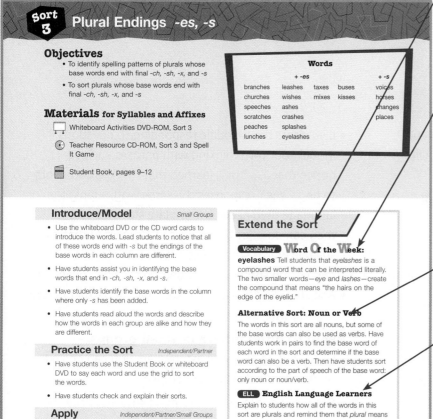

Extend the Sort

A variety of activities provides students with more practice and reinforcement of the sort generalization.

Word of the Week presents explicit vocabulary instruction for one of the words in the sort.

Building Vocabulary, as shown on the facing page, occurs at the first three developmental stages. It provides meanings for unfamiliar words and pictures and suggests a strategy to help students understand words they don't know.

An **Alternative Sort** provides another way for students to sort their picture/word cards.

English Language Learners notes present extra support for vocabulary in context, unfamiliar sounds, and other concepts that English language learners may find difficult.

Teacher Tips are suggestions designed to aid in areas such as instruction, assessment, and classroom management.

(within image) Sort 3 — Plural Endings -es, -s

Objectives
- To identify spelling patterns of plurals whose base words end with final -ch, -sh, -x, and -s
- To sort plurals whose base words end with final -ch, -sh, -x, and -s

Materials for Syllables and Affixes
- Whiteboard Activities DVD-ROM, Sort 3
- Teacher Resource CD-ROM, Sort 3 and Spell It Game
- Student Book, pages 9–12

Words

+ -es				+ -s
branches	leashes	taxes	buses	voices
churches	wishes	mixes	kisses	horses
speeches	ashes			changes
scratches	crashes			places
peaches	splashes			
lunches	eyelashes			

Introduce/Model *Small Groups*
- Use the whiteboard DVD or the CD word cards to introduce the words. Lead students to notice that all of these words end with -s but the endings of the base words in each column are different.
- Have students assist you in identifying the base words that end in -ch, -sh, -x, and -s.
- Have students identify the base words in the column where only -s has been added.
- Have students read aloud the words and describe how the words in each group are alike and how they are different.

Practice the Sort *Independent/Partner*
- Have students use the Student Book or whiteboard DVD to say each word and use the grid to sort the words.
- Have students check and explain their sorts.

Apply *Independent/Partner/Small Groups*
- Read aloud the directions on Student Book p. 12. Have students change the singular words to plurals by adding -s or -es.
- **Game** Allow time for students to play Spell It, which is on the CD.

188 Syllables and Affixes

Extend the Sort

Vocabulary Word Of the Week:
eyelashes Tell students that *eyelashes* is a compound word that can be interpreted literally. The two smaller words—*eye* and *lashes*—create the compound that means "the hairs on the edge of the eyelid."

Alternative Sort: Noun or Verb
The words in this sort are all nouns, but some of the base words can also be used as verbs. Have students work in pairs to find the base word of each word in the sort and determine if the base word can also be a verb. Then have students sort according to the part of speech of the base word: only noun or noun/verb.

ELL English Language Learners
Explain to students how all of the words in this sort are plurals and remind them that *plural* means "more than one." Have students identify and then underline each base word. Challenge them to use each plural and its singular base word in sentences, such as: *I ride a bus to school. Sometimes the buses are late.*

Teacher Tip
Remind students that most singular nouns are made plural by adding -es or -s. However, they should always look at and think about the ending of a base word before choosing -es or -s.

Syllables and Affixes Lesson

Getting Started

One of the benefits of the *Words Their Way: Word Study in Action* program is that all of the components you need for instruction are easily accessible. Grab your Student Book and turn to the corresponding lesson in this Teacher's Resource Guide. The list of materials in the lesson will tell you exactly what you need. Decide where students will work. Remember space is needed for group work, individual work, and partner work.

Establish Routines

Following are recommendations for how to set up routines that will facilitate the transition into fully differentiated small-group word study.

Demonstrate the sorting routines for the whole group.

- Start with some whole-class sorts that will be relatively easy for everyone in the class. Use a teacher-directed closed sort (see p. 17) for maximum support so you can model and offer explicit directions.

- Teach students the basic routines that you want them to apply. Role-play buddy activities such as blind sorts or writing sorts (see p. 20) by having students observe as you partner with a child, demonstrating how to lead the sort and how to take turns. Show students how to cut words out quickly and neatly.

Teach students how to talk about the sorts.

- Students will need to be shown how to think about words, how to reflect, and how to form generalizations.

- Use open-ended questions to promote critical thinking.

- If students have trouble responding to questions, model your own thinking with phrases such as "I notice that . . . ." or "I learned that . . . ." Ask students to begin their responses the same way; supply the language they need to formulate statements until they can do it for themselves. ("We learned that two-syllable words sometimes have double letters in the middle and short vowel sounds in the first syllable.")

- Ask students to practice talking with a partner before sharing with the group.

Begin to differentiate in small groups.

- Once routines are well established, you can begin to work with small groups of students.

- Because your lowest performing students need the most help, create that group first. Observe how students sort, how they do on Spell Checks, and how they work together.

- Modify groups as needed.

Introduce student-centered sorts.

- With experience, students gain skill and independence, which makes it easier for you to manage the groups in a more timely fashion.

- Model how to do both closed and open student sorts (see p. 19) before you assign them to students.

Introduce Sorts

Instruction in word study should follow a gradual release model that begins with teacher modeling and explicit explanations and moves to guided practice and then to independent work. When students begin a new sort, you will need to decide how best to introduce those words so that students are led to form generalizations about how a word feature works. Introductory lessons can range from teacher-directed sorts to student-centered sorts done independently. You will also need to decide on the level of support to provide. Different levels of support are described on the following pages and summarized in the Continuum of Support for Introducing Word Sorts chart on p. 18.

Teacher-Directed Closed Sorts

The highest level of support and explicit instruction is offered in teacher-directed closed sorts. Teachers define the sort categories in advance, using key words and/or headers and through modeling they make it clear how to conduct the sort. For example, in a beginning sound phonics sort, you might model like this: "*Shhhhoe, shhhhell.* I hear the same sound at the beginning of *shoe* and *shell*, so I'm going to put the picture of the shell under *shoe*. They both begin with /sh/, the sound made by the letters *s-h*." After modeling several words this way, gradually release the task to students' control as they finish the sort under your supervision.

As you work with students, discuss the characteristics of the words in each column and develop a generalization based on the selected feature. Students may then sort independently or in pairs under your guidance. Carefully monitor this practice and provide corrective feedback.

The teacher-directed sort includes the following four components.

1. **Demonstrate** Introduce the sort by identifying the pictures or words, establishing the categories, and modeling how to sort.
2. **Sort and Check** Model how to check the sort by reading down each column to listen for a sound or look for the pattern.
3. **Reflect** Guide students to form a generalization by comparing the words or pictures in each column and verbalizing what the words or pictures have in common.
4. **Extend** After group demonstrations, sorting, and reflection, students participate in a number of activities at centers, with partners, as seatwork, and for homework to reinforce and extend their understanding. Follow-up Routines to extend the sort are described on pp. 20–21.

Teacher-Directed Sort: Guess My Category

When children are comfortable with sorts, introduce Guess My Category, which is a variation of the teacher-directed sort. Set up key words or pictures as in a closed sort, but do not offer any explanation of the sort categories. Rather, it will be up to students to develop hypotheses about how the words or pictures in each category are alike. Begin by sorting two or three pictures or words into each group. When you pick up the next picture or word, invite someone to guess where it will go. Continue doing this until all the pictures or words have been sorted. After sorting, check the sort and guide a generalization as you would for the teacher-directed closed sort.

Continuum of Support for Introducing Word Sorts

	FOR NOVICE SORTERS OR TO INTRODUCE NEW FEATURES		FOR EXPERIENCED SORTERS OR TO ASSESS	
	Teacher-Directed Closed Sort	*Teacher-Directed Guess My Category*	*Student-Centered Closed Sort*	*Student-Centered Open Sort*
Materials	One set of words for group to focus on using a pocket chart, overhead, interactive whiteboard, or other method. Students bring their own set of words already cut apart to the group or are given a set at the end of group work to take back to their seats to cut apart and sort.		Students get their own set of words with key words and/or headers.	Students get their own set of words with no key words or headers.
Introduce the Sort	Read through all the words and talk about any that students might not know. Introduce each category with a header and a key word and explicitly describe the features students are to look for.	Read through the words and talk about any that are unfamiliar. Set up the categories with key words but do not describe the feature or put up headers.	Read through the words and talk about any that are unfamiliar. Students can also do this on their own, putting aside any words they don't know to discuss and sort later.	Students work on their own to read through words and put aside any words they don't know.
Sorting	Demonstrate how to sort two or three words in each category and describe explicitly why each word goes there. Students help to complete the sort and justify their placements.	Model by sorting several words in each category but do not explain the reasons. Students are then invited to try sorting the rest of the words.	Students use headers and key words to set up categories and sort independently.	Students determine categories and sort their own words. They explain to you or each other why they sorted as they did.
Check and Reflect	Model how to check the columns and create a generalization with student help. Be ready to model as needed to summarize what the sort has revealed. Sort again at this point if time allows to reinforce the features and reflect once more.	Ask students to describe the features in each category and then check each column. Create a generalization with students' help. Supply headers at this point or label key words.	Call group together or check in individually for students to describe the features and talk about any unfamiliar words. Everyone checks.	"Close" the sort. Establish key words so everyone sorts the same way. Check and talk once more about generalizations. Supply or label headers.
Sort Individually	Students sort their own set of words in the group under your supervision or at their seats. Monitor, remind students to check, and ask each student to state generalizations.	Students sort their own set of words using the key words and headers in the group or independently. Monitor and check in during or after students sort.		

Student-Centered Sorts

Student-Centered Closed Sort In a closed sort, students are provided with a set of words as well as the headers and key words. Students sort the words independently. They have some support, but students must still read each word and think about sounds and patterns as they make their own decisions about where to sort.

Student-Centered Open Sort The open sort demands the highest level of independent effort and thought because students are not given any clues to the categories or features—only a set of words to sort. Pass out a printout of words that has no headers or key words and ask students to create their own categories. Students can be asked to compare their categories with a partner to begin the reflection part of the lesson and come up with their own generalizations before sharing with the larger group.

Follow-Up Routines

To reinforce generalizations and students' memory of words, to connect to reading and writing, and to build speed and accuracy, you can assign students a variety of follow-up activities as described here.

Repeated Sorts

To become fluent readers, students must achieve fast, accurate recognition of words in context. The words they encounter in context are made of the same sounds, patterns, and meaning units they examine out of context, in word study. In order to achieve automaticity in word recognition, students should do a picture or word sort many times. By sorting a few times individually and with partners after a group lesson and by taking their words home to sort several times for homework, students will sort the same words six to eight times.

Buddy Sorts

In a buddy sort, students sort together, read the words or name the pictures in each column to check the sort, and then discuss the generalization covered by the sort. Sorting can take place in tandem, side by side with two sets of words, or alternating turns, with one set of words. Two sorts that work well with buddies are **blind sorts** and **blind writing sorts,** which are described below.

Blind Sorts

In a blind sort, headers or key words are used to establish categories, and the teacher or a partner shuffles the word cards and calls each word aloud without showing it. The student indicates the correct category by pointing to or naming the header. The response is checked and corrected immediately when the printed word is revealed and put in place. Buddies can work together by taking turns either reading the words or indicating where they should go. Model how to do a blind sort as a group activity before expecting students to work together productively.

Writing Sorts

In a writing sort, you write key words or headers to label each category. Then a student sorts individually according to the categories by copying a previous sort done with word cards or by turning over one word at a time from his or her collection and writing it down. Writing words into categories demands that students attend to the sounds or patterns of letters and think about how those characteristics correspond to the key word, picture, or pattern.

Blind Writing Sorts

In a blind writing sort, students write each word in the correct category before seeing the word. Students must rely on the sound they hear in the word as well as their memory for the letters associated with it, cued by the key word. This sort is important for students who need to attend less to visual patterns and more to sounds. Blind writing sorts can help identify what words need more attention and can serve as a pretest for the final assessment. Blind writing sorts done with a buddy or for homework are a good way to prepare for a weekly test. Writing sorts are also an instructionally sound way to construct spelling tests. Key words are written and then students write and sort the words as they are called.

Word Hunts

Word hunts help students see the connection between spelling words and reading words. In word hunts, students hunt through their reading and writing for words that are additional examples of the sound, pattern, or meaning unit they are studying. Before students are expected to do word hunts, model the activity. Word hunts can be conducted in small groups, with partners, or individually for seatwork or homework.

Brainstorming

Brainstorming might be considered a word hunt through one's own memory. You may ask for more words that rhyme with *cat,* words that describe people ending in -*er,* or words that have *spir* as a root. Brainstorming may also be used to introduce a sort by asking students for words that have particular sounds, patterns, or roots and writing them on the board. The words may be written in categories as they are given or categories might be determined by discussion.

Speed Sorts

Students are highly motivated to practice sorts in preparation for speed sorts. Some teachers do speed sorts as a quick whole-class activity by displaying a timer or simply calling the seconds aloud from the classroom clock. Students set up their headers and then shuffle the rest of their words. When you say "go," everyone begins to sort. As they finish, students record their times. After checking, the speed sort may be repeated immediately as well as on other days so students can attempt to beat their own times. Students may also be paired to time each other.

Draw and Label/Cut and Paste

Drawing and labeling pictures is particularly useful for teaching emergent and letter-name spellers initial consonant sounds. Some teachers provide paper that has been divided into columns headed by a key letter and/or picture, with each column divided into boxes. Students brainstorm other words that start with the same sounds, illustrate a word in a box under the appropriate key letter and/or picture, and then label the picture.

Draw and Label is also a good activity at other levels. Multiple meanings for words such as *block* can be illustrated, for example, as a toy, a section of a neighborhood, and a sports play. Homophones such as *bear* and *bare* are made more memorable through drawings. Even advanced spellers in the Derivational Relations stage might illustrate the meanings of words such as *spectacles, spectators*, and *inspector*.

A variation of Draw and Label is Cut and Paste, which is like a word hunt using pictures instead of words. It is especially appropriate for emergent and letter-name spellers. Students hunt through old catalogs and magazines for pictures beginning with a certain sound and then cut out the pictures and paste them in the appropriate column. They then label the pictures.

Word Study Notebook

Word study notebooks provide a built-in, orderly record of activities and progress. Following are suggested activities.

- *Write the word sort.* Students write the words into the same categories developed during hands-on sorting using the same key words or headers. They may also write the generalization of the sort.

- *Select five to ten words to draw and label.* Even older students enjoy the opportunity to illustrate words with drawings that reveal their meanings. Encourage students to think about multiple meanings of even simple words such as *park* and *yard*.

- *Word operations.* Students change a letter (or letters) of a selected word to make new words. For example, starting with the word *black*, a student might substitute other consonant blends or digraphs to generate *stack, quack, track,* and *shack*. Students studying more complex words might substitute prefixes, suffixes, or roots—for example, using *graph* to generate *autograph, biography, photograph,* and *photography*.

- *Select five to ten words to use in sentences.* Challenge students to use two or more words from their sort, especially derivationally related words. (I will need new *spectacles* to *inspect* the *spectacular* new *specimens*.)

- *Record words from word hunts.* Students add new words from their reading and writing to the sorts in their notebooks.

- *Record times from speed sorts.* When students are timed early in the week and then again after repeated sorting, they are likely to show improvement.

- *Record a blind writing sort.* Led by a partner or the teacher, a blind writing sort is a written record of student knowledge.

Ten Principles of Word Study

1. Look for what students use but confuse.

Students cannot learn things they do not already know something about. By examining students' invented spellings, instruction can be planned to help students understand the features they are using but confusing, rather than those they totally neglect. Take your cue from the students. Look to see what features are consistently present and correct to figure out what the students already know. Look for those features that students sometimes use incorrectly and use those features to target their word study instruction.

2. A step backward is a step forward.

Once you have determined the areas in which students need instruction, take a step backward and build a foundation. Contrast something new with something that is already known, and remember that it is important that students experience success. For example, students who are ready to learn long-vowel patterns, which are unfamiliar, should begin by sorting short-vowel sounds, which are familiar. Taking a step backward is the first step forward in word study instruction.

3. Use words students can read.

Students should analyze words that they know how to pronounce. It is easier to look across words for consistent patterns when the words are easy to pronounce. Known words can come from any and all sources students can read, including, but not limited to, recent reading selections such as stories, poems, and phonics readers. When possible, choose words students can read out of context.

4. Compare words that "do" with words that "don't."

To learn what a crow looks like, it helps to see a hawk or a cardinal, not another crow. In defining what something *is*, it is also important to know what it is *not*. Contrasts are important in helping students build categories. Students' spelling errors give clues about what contrasts will help them sort out their confusions. For example, a student who is spelling *stopping* as *stoping* will benefit from a sort that includes words with consonants that are doubled before adding *-ing*, as well as those that do not take double letters.

5. Sort by sight *and* sound.

Words are examined both by the way they sound and how they are spelled. Too often students focus on visual patterns without also considering how words are alike in sound.

6. Begin with obvious contrasts.

When students begin the study of a new feature, choose key words or pictures that are distinctive. For example, do not begin examining initial consonants by comparing *m* and *n*. They are too similar in sound and appearance. It is better at first to contrast *m* with something totally different—*s*, for example—and then work toward finer distinctions.

7. Don't hide exceptions.

Exceptions take place when students generalize. Do not hide these exceptions. By placing these "exception" words into a category of their own, new patterns are sometimes found. Looking at long vowel patterns, students find exceptions like *give, have,* and *love,* which each have *-ve.* They form a small but consistent pattern of their own.

8. Avoid rules.

Rules with many exceptions are discouraging and teach children nothing. Learning about English spelling forces students to think about sound and pattern at the same time in order to find consistencies in spelling. Students find these consistencies on their own and make generalizations, but it is the teacher's job to structure tasks to get students into the habit of looking at words, asking questions, and searching for order.

9. Work for automaticity.

Accuracy in sorting is not enough; accuracy and speed are the clear signs of mastery. This automaticity leads to the fluency needed for strong reading and writing skills. As they practice, students will move from caution to fluency in their sorting. Keep sorting until they do.

10. Return to meaningful texts.

After sorting, students need to return to meaningful texts to hunt for other examples to add to their sorts. This activity supports adding more words, including more difficult vocabulary, to their sorts.

Meeting Individual Differences

Recognizing that students in your classroom are at different developmental stages of word study as well as at different levels within a particular stage, will help you differentiate instruction for them. In addition to having them work with sorts at their developmental level, you can meet individual differences by adjusting the pace of instruction, making sorts easier, and making sorts harder.

Adjust Pacing

The pacing of the sorts in *Words Their Way: Word Study in Action, Developmental Model* is designed for average growth. However, because all students do not work at the same speed, you can adjust pacing in these ways.

- If students catch on quickly, move at a faster pace. Spend fewer days on a series of sorts or skip some sorts altogether.
- If students are not keeping up, slow down the pace. Do this by spending more time on the sorts. You can also create additional sorts using the pictures and words in the program.

Making Sorts Easier

Following are suggestions for those students who need more help with word study.

- When beginning a new unit of study, have students sort with fewer categories. As students become adept at sorting, increase the number of categories in a sort.
- If an example word is unfamiliar to students, use one that is easier and familiar to students.
- Provide additional example words for a category.
- If there are unfamiliar words in the sort, put them at the end so that known words are the first to be sorted.
- Eliminate "oddballs," the words that do not fit the targeted letter-sound or pattern feature, from the sort.
- At the first three developmental levels, do not include the Bonus Words.
- Review sorts when necessary.

Making Sorts Harder

Following are suggestions for those students who need a more challenging word study routine.

- Add more difficult words to the sort. For example, adding words with blends and digraphs (*black, chest, trunk*) to a short vowel sort is more challenging than simple words such as *tap* and *set.*
- Have students suggest additional words that fit the targeted spelling feature.
- Do fewer follow-up activities.
- Skip sorts that review.

Word Study with English Language Learners

Many challenges face students learning to read and write in a new language. However, it is important to remember that although students are new to English, they do have proficiency in another language. In addition, two students who are the same age and speak the same home language may be on different levels with word study, just as English-speaking students might be.

When you form groups for word study, consider students' developmental levels, but also take into account whether or not students are English learners who need additional language support. For students to benefit from hearing each other speak, form heterogeneous language groups so that you have a range of oral proficiency in your small groups; at other times group together students who are the least proficient in oral English skills in order to help them build those skills.

At the early stages of language learning, picture sorts are most appropriate for English learners. Concept sorts with pictures or objects are the least demanding. When doing picture sorts for sounds, keep in mind that students need to know the names of enough pictures to demonstrate the sound relationship being sorted. Always name the pictures before the sort begins and have students repeat the picture names.

When moving on to word sorts, ensure that students are making oral-written language connections by reading the words aloud. Go over all the words before sorting, pronouncing them and talking about their meanings. Continue saying the words aloud during the sort. It is also important for English learners to say the words aloud as they sort; this ensures that students connect spelling patterns to what they hear in spoken words.

With *Words Their Way: Word Study in Action, Developmental Model*, here are additional ways you can support English language learners.

- Provide explicit vocabulary instruction.
- Pronounce picture names and words before, during, and after sorting. Explain word meanings, and use words in sentences that give strong context for the meaning.
- Have students illustrate words with simple drawings to remind them of meanings.
- Provide additional picture support for words in sorts to help English learners build background knowledge and vocabulary.
- Check for understanding of sorting words as you meet with students.
- Encourage students' frequent oral use of the sort words.
- Have students use the words orally in sentences or phrases, depending on their proficiency.
- Incorporate multimodal strategies, such as chanting, tapping, and movement.
- Pair English learners with English-speaking partners in buddy activities.
- Set a tone that will encourage English learners to ask questions about words whose meanings or pronunciations they do not know.

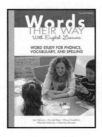

See *Words Their Way® with English Language Learners: Word Study for Phonics, Vocabulary, and Spelling Instruction*, 2nd ed., for more comprehensive information about English language learners and additional activities.

School-Home Connection

Classrooms are busy places and many teachers find it difficult to devote a lot of time to word study, so homework can provide additional practice time. A letter such as the one below is a good way to encourage parents to become involved in their children's spelling homework. Parents are often firm believers in the importance of spelling because it is such a visible sign of literacy. Unfortunately, invented spelling is often a scapegoat because some people associate the acceptance of it with a lack of instruction and a lack of expectation of accuracy in children's writing. Communicate clearly to parents that their children will be held responsible for what they have been taught. Homework assignments also help parents see what is being taught in phonics and spelling.

Dear Parents,

Your child will be bringing home a collection of spelling words that have been introduced in class. Your child is expected to do these activities to ensure that the words and the spelling principles they represent are mastered. These activities have been modeled and practiced in school, so your child can teach you how to do them.

• Remind your child to *sort the words* into categories like the ones we did in school. Your child should read each word aloud during this activity. Ask your child to explain to you why the words are sorted in a particular way—what does the sort reveal about spelling in general? Ask your child to sort the words a second time as fast as possible. You may want to time him or her.

• Do a *blind sort* with your child. Lay down a word from each category as a header and then read the rest of the words aloud. Your child must indicate where the word goes without seeing it. Lay it down and let your child move it if he or she is wrong. Repeat if your child makes more than one error.

• Assist your child in doing a *word hunt*, looking in a book he or she has already read, for words that have the same sound, same pattern, or both. Try to find two or three for each category.

• Do a *writing sort*. As you call out the words in random order, your child should write them in categories. Call out any words your child misspells a second or even third time.

Thank you for your support. Together we can help your child make valuable progress!

Sincerely,

Word Study
Implementation Checklist

	Yes	No
Is your small-group instruction differentiated and developmentally appropriate?		
Are your word study materials well organized and accessible?		
Do your word study lessons include teacher modeling?		
Do you use teacher talk that will help students scaffold their thinking and facilitate self-correction?		
Do you set up instruction so that students become familiar with your word study routines?		
Do your word study routines facilitate the discovery of how words work through hands-on exploration and student discussion?		
Do you help students develop and articulate hypotheses about how words work?		
Do you guide students to develop automaticity in decoding and encoding words?		
Does your instruction help students deepen their understanding of word meanings?		
Do you help students extend and transfer their learning about how words work to other reading and writing activities?		
Do you promote the use of word study folders or notebooks in order for students to record their thinking about words?		
Do you guide students to become purposefully engaged?		

Research Base

The *developmental* model of word study is grounded in investigations of the spelling system of English and of learners' developing knowledge of this system. English spelling is more logical than traditionally believed (Henderson & Templeton, 1986; Johnston, 2001; Templeton, 2011; Venezky, 1999). Over time, learners develop understanding of this logic through the examination of sound, pattern, and meaning in spelling. Insight into the developmental nature of spelling development began with the landmark work of Charles Read and Edmund Henderson and his students at the University of Virginia (Read, 1971, 1975; Henderson, 1981; Henderson & Beers, 1980). These early studies, together with the continuing work of Henderson's students and of other researchers, provide the foundation for an approach to word study that is developmentally grounded and pedagogically solid (Bear, Invernizzi, Templeton, & Johnston, 2012; Templeton & Bear, 1992; Invernizzi & Hayes, 2004). In English as well as in a number of other languages, learners follow a developmental progression that builds on the progressive understanding of letter-sound relationships, within-word and between-syllable patterns, and meaning.

Research	Findings	Put into Action with *Words Their Way*
Berninger, Abbott, Nagy, & Carlisle, 2009; Ehri, 2005; Henderson & Templeton, 1986; Hughes & Searle, 1997; Invernizzi & Hayes, 2004, 2010; Leong, 2000; Schlagal, 1992; Seymour, 1992; Taft, 2003; Templeton & Bear, 1992; Templeton & Morris, 1999, 2000	Most learners acquire knowledge of orthography following a predictable progression from *sound* or *alphabetic* structure through *pattern* and *meaning*.	At each level of *Words Their Way in Action – The Developmental Model*, the spelling patterns and the words selected to represent them correspond to students' level of understanding. In addition to pattern, word selection is based on frequency of occurrence and degree of word familiarity.
Clarke, 1988; Beers & Henderson, 1977; Ehri & Roberts, 2006; Flanigan, 2007; Henderson, 1981; Invernizzi, Justice, Landrum, & Booker, 2005; Oulette & Sénéchal, 2008; Read, 1971, 1977	Emergent and Beginning Readers' learning of letters and use of that knowledge through spelling reflects a systematic logic and should be encouraged by teachers. These early spelling efforts are powerful contributors to the development of phonemic awareness.	Emergent and Early Letter Name sorts and activities support and extend children's dawning understanding of beginning and ending consonants as well as a *concept of word in text*, a critical benchmark in the development of full phonemic awareness.
Bear, Templeton, & Warner, 1991; Morris, Nelson, & Perney, 1986; Morris, Blanton, Blanton, Nowacek, & Perney, 1995; Sterbinsky, 2007; Townsend, Bear, & Templeton, 2009; Townsend, Bear, & Templeton, 2010; Townsend, Burton, Bear, & Templeton, 2010	Well-constructed qualitative spelling inventories are good predictors of students' reading proficiency and vocabulary knowledge.	Initial and ongoing assessments in *Words Their Way* determine the most appropriate patterns and words each student should examine.
Berninger, Vaughan, Abbott, Brooks, Begay, Curtin, Byrd, & Graham, 2000; Bourassa & Treiman, 2008; Ehri & McCormick, 1998; Graham, Harris, & Chorzempa, 2002; Hayes, 2004; Invernizzi, Rosemary, Juel, & Richards, 1997; Iversen & Tunmer, 1993; Joseph & McCachran, 2003; Kirk & Gillon, 2009; McCandliss, Beck, Sandak, & Perfetti, 2003; Morris, Blanton, Blanton, Nowacek, & Perney, 1995; Santa & Hoien, 1999; Santoro, Coyne, & Simmons, 2006; Scott, 2000; Templeton, 2004; Worthy & Invernizzi, 1989; Zutell, 1998	Providing word study for below-level students that is matched to their developmental level is significantly more effective than attempting to support those students' learning of on-level words and patterns. This holds for learning disabled students as well.	Initial and ongoing progress monitoring provides support for appropriate and effective differentiation of word study for students.

Research	Findings	Put Into Action With _Words Their Way_
Abbott, 2001; Joseph, 2000, 2002; Juel & Minden-Cupp, 2000; Weber & Henderson, 1989; Santa & Hoien, 1999; White, 2005	Word sorting activities provide more engaging as well as long-lasting learning than traditional approaches to spelling. Comparing and contrasting single-syllable words according to letter/spelling patterns strongly supports the connections among sound and spelling. These connections in turn support more automatic application to spelling and reading words.	Beginning with Emergent learners and continuing through the Letter Name-Alphabetic and Within Word Pattern developmental levels, _word sort_ or categorization activities each week provide _hands-on_ and _minds-on_ opportunities to examine words and word patterns from a variety of perspectives, leading to the necessary breadth and depth of orthographic understanding.
Carlo, August, McLaughlin, Snow, Dressler, Lippman, Lively, & White, 2004	Comparing and contrasting two-syllable and multisyllabic words according to syllable patterns or meaning-based units strongly supports connections among sound, spelling, and meaning. These connections support more automatic reading and spelling, as well as the learning of the meaning of unfamiliar words encountered in print.	For students at the Syllables and Affixes or Derivational Relations developmental levels, examining words from a variety of perspectives over one or two weeks develops understanding of more advanced orthographic patterns as well as morphological analysis strategies. These understandings in turn support the development of vocabulary knowledge.
Bear, 1989, 1991, 1992; Berninger, Vaughan, Abbott, Brooks, Begay, Curtin, Byrd, & Graham, 2000; Carlisle & Stone, 2005; Conrad, 2008; Ehri, 1997, 2005; Ehri & Wilce, 1987; Gill, 1992; Johnston, 1998; Nunes & Bryant, 2009; Zutell, 1992; Zutell & Rasinski, 1989	There is a reciprocal relationship between reading or decoding words—identifying them in print—and spelling or encoding words in writing. Orthographic knowledge significantly predicts beginning readers' acquisition of sight words and the development of fluency.	At each level, words that represent appropriate developmental features support the growth of students' underlying _orthographic_ knowledge, which in turn is applied in the decoding of unfamiliar words. Activities will engage students in applying this knowledge in context.
Bowers & Kirby, 2010; Carlisle, 2000, 2010; Derwing, Smith, & Wiebe, 1995; Ehri & Rosenthal, 2007; Fowler & Lieberman, 1995; Henry, 1989, 1993; Larkin & Snowling, 2008; Larsen & Nippold, 2007; Nagy, Diakidoy, & Anderson, 1993; Nunes & Bryant, 2006; Reichle & Perfetti, 2003; Rosenthal & Ehri, 2008; Templeton, 1979, 1989, 1992, 2004b; Templeton & Scarborough-Franks, 1985; White, Power, & White, 1989	Orthographic knowledge facilitates vocabulary knowledge through spelling-meaning connections or _morphological_ analysis.	Beginning in the Syllables and Affixes stage and expanding considerably in the Derivational Relations stage, activities engage students in exploring the processes of word formation involving affixes, bases, and roots.
Bear & Shen, 2000; Bear, Templeton, Helman, & Baren, 2003; Carlo, August, McLaughlin, Snow, Dressler, Lippman, Lively, & White, 2004; Helman, 2004	In developing understanding of the relationship between print and spoken language, learners in most languages follow the same progression: sound to pattern to meaning. With appropriate support, guidance, and pacing, English learners are able to apply their knowledge of word structure in their home language to the understanding of word structure in English.	Alternate or additional sorting activities and vocabulary development, together with teacher tips, are provided.

Research Base References

Abbott, M. (2001). Effects of traditional versus extended word-study spelling instruction on students' orthographic knowledge. *Reading Online, 5*(3).

Bear, D. (1989). Why beginning reading must be word-by-word. *Visible Language, 23*(4), 353–367.

Bear, D. (1991). "Learning to fasten the seat of my union suit without looking around": The synchrony of literacy development. *Theory into Practice, 30*(3), 149–157.

Bear, D. R. (1992). The prosody of oral reading and stage of word knowledge. In Templeton, S. & Bear, D. (Eds.), *Development of orthographic knowledge and the foundations of literacy: A memorial Festschrift for Edmund H. Henderson* (pp. 137–189). Hillsdale, NJ: Lawrence Erlbaum.

Bear, D. R., Invernizzi, M., Templeton, S., & Johnston, F. (2012). *Words their way: Word study for phonics, vocabulary, and spelling* (5th ed.). Boston: Pearson/Allyn & Bacon.

Bear, D. R., & Shen, H. H. (2000). Development of orthographic skills in Chinese children. *Reading and Writing: An Interdisciplinary Journal, 13,* 197–236.

Bear, D. R., Templeton, S., & Warner, M. (1991). The development of a qualitative inventory of higher levels of orthographic knowledge. In J. Zutell & S. McCormick (Eds.), *Learner factors/teacher factors: Issues in literacy research and instruction* (Fortieth yearbook of the National Reading Conference; pp. 105–110). Chicago, IL: National Reading Conference.

Beers, J. W., & Henderson, E. H. (1977). A study of developing orthographic concepts among first graders. *Research in the Teaching of English, 11,* 133–148.

Berninger, V. W., Abbott, R. D., Nagy, W., & Carlisle, J. (2009). Growth in phonological, orthographic, and morphological awareness in grades 1 to 6. *Journal of Psycholinguistic Research. 39*(2), 141–163.

Berninger, V. W., Vaughan, K., Abbott, R. D., Brooks, A., Begay, K., Curtin, G., Byrd, K., & Graham, S. (2000). Language-based spelling instruction: Teaching children to make multiple connections between spoken and written words. *Learning Disability Quarterly, 23,* 117–35.

Bourassa, D., & Treiman, R. (2008). Morphological constancy in spelling: A comparison of children with dyslexia and typically developing children. *Dyslexia, 14,* 155–169.

Bowers, P. N., & Kirby, J. R. (2010). Effects of morphological instruction on vocabulary acquisition. *Reading and Writing: An Interdisciplinary Journal. 23*(5), 515–537.

Carlisle, J. F. (2000). Awareness of the structure and meaning of morphologically complex words impact on reading. *Reading and Writing, 12,* 169–190.

Carlisle, J. F. (2010). Effects of instruction in morphological awareness on literacy achievement: An integrative review. *Reading Research Quarterly, 45*(4), 464–487.

Carlisle, J. F., & Stone, C. A.. (2005). Exploring the role of morphemes in reading. *Reading Research Quarterly, 40* (4), 428–449.

Carlo, M.S., August, D., McLaughlin, B., Snow, C. E., Dressler, C., Lippman, D. N., Lively, T. J., & White, C. E. (2004). Closing the gap: Addressing the vocabulary needs of English-language learners in bilingual and mainstream classrooms. *Reading Research Quarterly, 39*(2), 188–215.

Clarke, L. K. (1988). Invented versus traditional spelling in first graders' writing: Effects on learning to spell and read. *Research in the Teaching of English, 22.* 281–309.

Conrad, N. J. (2008). From reading to spelling and spelling to reading: Transfer goes both ways. *Journal of Educational Psychology, 100* (4), 869–878.

Derwing, B. L., Smith, M. L., Wiebe, G. E. (1995). On the role of spelling in morpheme recognition: Experimental studies with children and adults. In L. B. Feldman (Ed.), *Morphological aspects of language processing* (pp. 3–27). Hillsdale, NJ: Lawrence Erlbaum Associates.

Ehri, L. C. (1997). Learning to read and learning to spell are one and the same, almost. In C. A. Perfetti, L. Rieben, & M. Fayol (Eds.), *Learning to spell: Research, theory, and practice across languages* (pp. 237–269). Mahwah, NJ: Lawrence Erlbaum Associates.

Ehri, L. C. (2005). Learning to read words: Theory, findings, and issues. *Scientific Studies of Reading, 9* (2), 167–188.

Ehri, L. C., & McCormick, S. (1998). Phases of word learning: Implications for instruction with delayed and disabled readers. *Reading & Writing Quarterly, 14,* 135–163.

Ehri, L. C., & Roberts, T. (2006). The roots of learning to read and write: Acquisition of letters and phonemic awareness. In D. K. Dickinson & S. B. Neuman (Eds.), *Handbook of early literacy research* (vol. 2, pp. 113–131). New York: The Guilford Press.

Ehri, L. C. & Rosenthal, J. (2007). Spellings of words: A neglected facilitator of vocabulary learning. *Journal of Literacy Research, 4,* 389–409.

Ehri, L. C. & Wilce, L. (1987). Does learning to spell help beginners learn to read words? *Reading Research Quarterly, 22,* 47–65.

Flanigan, K. (2007). A concept of word in text: A pivotal event in early reading acquisition. *Journal of Literacy Research, 39*(1), 37–70.

Fowler, A. E., & Liberman, I. Y (1995). The role of phonology and orthography in morphological awareness. In L. B. Feldman (Ed.), *Morphological aspects of language processing* (pp. 157–188). Hillsdale, NJ: Lawrence Erlbaum Associates.

Gill, J. T. (1992). The relationship between word recognition and spelling. In S. Templeton & D. R. Bear (Eds.), *Development of orthographic knowledge and the foundations of literacy: A memorial Festschrift for Edmund H. Henderson* (pp. 79–104). Hillsdale, NJ: Erlbaum.

Graham, S., Harris, K. R., Chorzempa, B.F. (2002). Contribution of spelling instruction to the spelling, writing, and reading of poor spellers. *Journal of Educational Psychology, 94,* 669–686.

Helman, L. (2004). Building on the sound system of Spanish. *The Reading Teacher, 57,* 452–460.

Helman, L. A. & Bear, D. R. (2007). Does an established model of orthographic development hold true for English learners? In D. W. Rowe, R. Jimenez, D. L. Compton, D. K. Dickinson, Y. Kim, K. M. Leander, and V. J. Risko (Eds.), *56th Yearbook of the National Reading Conference* (pp. 266–280).

Helman, L. A., Bear, D. R., Templeton, S., Invernizzi, M., & Johnston, F. (2011). *Words their way with English learners* (2nd ed.). Boston: Pearson/Allyn & Bacon.

Henderson, E. H. (1981). *Learning to read and spell: The child's knowledge of words.* DeKalb, IL: Northern Illinois Press.

Henderson, E. H., & Beers, J. (Eds.) (1980). *Developmental and cognitive aspects of learning to spell: A reflection of word knowledge.* Newark, DE: International Reading Association.

Henderson, E. H., & Templeton, S. (1986). A developmental perspective of formal spelling instruction through alphabet, pattern, and meaning. *Elementary School Journal, 86,* 305–316.

Henry, M. K (1989). Children's word structure knowledge: Implications for decoding and spelling instruction. *Reading and Writing, 1,* 135–152.

Henry, M. K. (1993). Morphological structure: Latin and Greek roots and affixes as upper grade code strategies. *Reading & Writing, 5,* 227–241.

Hughes, M., & Searle, D. (1997). *The violent "e" and other tricky sounds: Learning to spell from Kindergarten through grade 6.* Portsmouth, NH: Stenhouse.

Invernizzi, M. (1992). The vowel and what follows: A phonological frame of orthographic analysis. In S. Templeton, & D. R. Bear (Eds.), *Development of orthographic knowledge and the foundations of literacy: A memorial Festschrift for Edmund H. Henderson* (pp. 105–136). Hillsdale, NJ: Lawrence Erlbaum Associates.

Invernizzi, M., & Hayes, L. (2004). Developmental-spelling research: A systematic imperative. *Reading Research Quarterly, 39,* 216–228.

Invernizzi, M., & Hayes, L. (2010). Word recognition. In D. Allington & A. McGill-Franzen (Eds.), *Handbook of reading disabilities.* Newark, DE: International Reading Association.

Invernizzi, M., Justice, L., Landrum, T., & Booker, K. (Winter, 2005). Early literacy screening in kindergarten: Widespread implementation in Virginia. *Journal of Literacy Research, 36,* 479–500.

Invernizzi, M., Rosemary, C., Juel, C., & Richards, H. C. (1997). At-risk readers and community volunteers: A 3-year perspective. *Scientific Studies of Reading, 1,* 277–300.

Iversen, S., & Tunmer, W. (1993). Phonological processing skills and the Reading Recovery program. *Journal of Educational Psychology, 85,* 112–126.

Johnston, F. R. (1998). The reader, the text, and the task: Learning words in first grade. *The Reading Teacher, 51,* 666–675.

Johnston, F. R. (2000). *Word learning in predictable text. Journal of Education Psychology, 92,* 248–255.

Johnston, F. R. (2001). The utility of phonic generalizations: Let's take another look at Clymer's conclusions. *The Reading Teacher, 55,* 132–143.

Joseph, L. M. (2000). Developing first graders' phonemic awareness, word identification and spelling: A comparison of two contemporary phonic instructional approaches. *Reading Research and Instruction, 39,* 160–169.

Joseph, L. M. (2002). Facilitating word recognition and spelling using word boxes and word sort phonic procedures. *School Psychology Review, 31*(1), 122–129.

Joseph, L. M., & McCachran, M. (2003). Comparison of a word study phonics technique between students with moderate to mild mental retardation and struggling readers without disabilities. *Education and Training in Developmental Disabilities, 38,* 192–199.

Juel, C, & Minden-Cupp, C. (2000). Learning to read words: linguistic units and instructional strategies. *Reading Research Quarterly, 35,* 458–492.

Kieffer, M. J., & Lesaux, N. K. (2007). Breaking down words to build meaning: Morphology, vocabulary, and reading comprehension in the urban classroom. *Reading Teacher, 61*(2), 134–144.

Kirk, C., & Gillon, G. (2009). Integrated morphological awareness intervention as a tool for improving literacy. *Language, Speech, & Hearing Services in Schools, 40* (3), 341–351.

Larkin, R. F., & Snowling, M. J. (2008). *Morphological spelling development. Reading & Writing Quarterly, 24,* 363–376.

Larsen, J. A., & Nippold, M. A. (2007). Morphological analysis in school-age children: *Dynamic assessment of a word learning strategy. Language, Speech, and Hearing Services in Schools, 38,* 201–212.

Leong, C. K. (1998). Strategies used by 9- to 12-year-old children in written spelling. In C. Hulme & R. M. Joshi (Eds.), *Reading and spelling: Development and disorders* (pp. 421–432). Mahwah, NJ: Lawrence Erlbaum Associates.

McCandliss, B., Beck, I., Sandak, R., & Perfetti, C. (2003). Focusing attention on decoding for children with poor reading skills: Design and preliminary tests of the word building intervention. *Scientific Studies of Reading, 7,* 75–103.

Morris, D. Blanton, L., Blanton, W. E., Nowacek, J., & Perney, J. (1995). Teaching low-achieving spellers at their "instructional level." *Elementary School Journal, 96,* 163–178.

Morris, D., Blanton, L., Blanton, W., & Perney, J. (1995). Spelling instruction and achievement in six classrooms. *Elementary School Journal, 96,* 145–162.

Nagy, W., Diakidoy, I., & Anderson, R. (1993). The acquisition of morphology: Learning the contribution of suffixes to the meaning of derivatives. *Journal of Reading Behavior, 25,* 155–170.

Nunes, T., & Bryant, P. (2006). *Improving literacy by teaching morphemes.* London: Routledge.

Nunes, T., & Bryant, P. (2009). *Children's reading and spelling: Beyond the first steps.* London: Chichester, West Sussex, UK: Wiley-Blackwell.

Ouellette, G. P., & Sénéchal, M. (2008). A window into early literacy: Exploring the cognitive and linguistic underpinnings of invented spelling. *Scientific studies of reading, 12*(2), 195–219.

Read, C (1971). Pre-school children's knowledge of English phonology. *Harvard Educational Review, 41,* 1–34.

Read, C. (1975). *Children's categorizations of speech sounds in English* (Research Report No. 17). Urbana, IL: National Council of Teachers of English.

Reichle, E. D., & Perfetti, C. A. (2003). Morphology in word identification: A word-experience model that accounts for morpheme frequency effects. *Scientific Studies of Reading, 7*(3), 219–237.

Rosenthal, J., & Ehri, L. C. (2008). The mnemonic value of orthography for vocabulary learning. *Journal of Educational Psychology,* 100(1), 175–191.

Santa, C. M., & Hoien, T. (1999). An assessment of Early Steps: A program for early intervention of reading problems. *Reading Research Quarterly, 33,* 338–355.

Santoro, L. E., Coyne, M. D., & Simmons, D. (2006). The reading-spelling connection: Developing and evaluating a beginning spelling intervention for children at risk of reading disability. *Learning Disabilities Research & Practice, 21,* 122–133.

Schlagal, R. (1992). Patterns of orthographic development into the intermediate grades. In S. Templeton & D. R. Bear (Eds.), *Development of orthographic knowledge and the foundations of literacy: A memorial Festschrift for Edmund H. Henderson* (pp. 31–52). Hillsdale, NJ: Lawrence Erlbaum Associates.Scott, C. M. (2000). Principles and methods of spelling instruction: Applications for poor spellers. *Topics in Language Disorders, 20,* pp. 66–82.

Seymour, P. (1992). Cognitive theories of spelling and implications for instruction. In C. M. Sterling & C. Robson (Eds.), *Psychology, spelling, and education* (pp. 50–70). Clevedon, UK: Multilingual Matters, Ltd.

Sterbinsky, A. (2007). *Words their way spelling inventories: Reliability and validity analyses.* Memphis, TN: Center for Research in Educational Policy, University of Memphis.

Taft, M. (2003). Morphological representation as a correlation between form and meaning. In E. G. H. Assink & D. Sandra (Eds.), *Reading complex words: Cross language studies* (pp. 113–137). New York: Kluwer Academic.

Templeton, S. (1979). Spelling first, sound later: The relationship between orthography and higher order phonological knowledge in older students. *Research in the Teaching of English,* 13, 255–264.

Templeton, S. (1989). Tacit and explicit knowledge of derivational morphology: Foundations for a unified approach to spelling and vocabulary development in the intermediate grades and beyond. *Reading Psychology, 10,* 233–253.

Templeton, S. (1992). Theory, nature, and pedagogy of higher-order orthographic development in older students. In S. Templeton & D. R. Bear (Eds.), *Development of orthographic knowledge and the foundations of literacy: A memorial Festschrift for Edmund H. Henderson* (pp. 253–277). Hillsdale, NJ: Lawrence Erlbaum Associates.

Templeton, S. (2004). Instructional approaches to spelling: The window on students' word knowledge in reading and writing. In L. Wilkinson & E. Silliman (Eds.), *Language and literacy learning: Collaboration between speech language pathologists and classroom teachers* (pp. 273–291). New York: Guilford Press.

Templeton, S. (2004). The vocabulary-spelling connection: Orthographic development and morphological knowledge at the intermediate grades and beyond. In J. F. Baumann & E. J. Kame'enui (Eds.), *Vocabulary instruction: Research to Practice* (pp. 118–138). New York: Guilford Press.

Templeton, S. (2011). Teaching spelling in the English/language arts classroom. In D. Lapp & D. Fisher (Eds.), *The handbook of research on teaching the English language arts* (3rd ed.) (pp. 247–251). IRA/NCTE: Erlbaum/Taylor Francis.

Templeton, S., & D. R. Bear (Eds.). (1992). *Development of orthographic knowledge and the foundations of literacy: A memorial festschrift for Edmund H. Henderson.* Hillsdale, NJ: Lawrence Erlbaum Associates.

Templeton, S., & Morris, D. (2000). Spelling. In M. Kamil, P. Mosenthal, P. D. Pearson, & R. Barr (Eds.), *Handbook of Reading Research: Vol. 3* (pp. 525–543). Mahwah, NJ: Lawrence Erlbaum Associates.

Templeton, S., & Scarborough-Franks, L. (1985). The spelling's the thing: Older students' knowledge of derivational morphology in phonology and orthography. *Applied Psycholinguistics, 6,* 371–389.

Townsend, D., Bear, D. R., & Templeton, S. (2009). The role of orthography in academic word knowledge and measures of academic achievement for middle school students. Paper presented at the annual meeting of the National Reading Conference, Albuquerque, New Mexico, December.

Townsend, Burton, Bear, & Templeton (2010). The role of morphological awareness of academic words for academic achievement. Paper presented at the annual meeting of the American Educational Research Association, Denver, Colorado, May.

Townsend, D., Bear, D. R., & Templeton, S. (2010). Academic Vocabulary Spelling Inventory. In S. Templeton, F. Johnston, D. Bear & M. Invernizzi, Vocabulary their way: Word study for middle and secondary students. Boston: Pearson/Allyn & Bacon.

Weber, W. R., & Henderson, E. H. (1989). A computer-based program of word study: Effects on reading and spelling. *Reading Psychology, 10,* 157–171.

White, T. G. (2005). Effects of systematic and strategic analogy-based phonics on Grade 2 students' word reading and reading comprehension. *Reading Research Quarterly, 40*(2), 234–255.

White, T., Power, M., & White, S. (1989). Morphological analysis: Implications for teaching and understanding vocabulary growth. *Reading Research Quarterly, 24,* 283–304.

Worthy, M. J., & Invernizzi, M. (1989). Spelling errors of normal and disabled students on achievement levels one through four: Instructional implications. *Bulletin of the Orton Society, 40,* 138–149.

Zutell, J. (1992). An integrated view of word knowledge: Correlational studies of the relationships among spelling, reading, and conceptual development. In S. Templeton & D. Bear (Eds.), *Development of orthographic knowledge and the foundations of literacy: A memorial Festschrift for Edmund H. Henderson* (pp. 213–230). Hillsdale, NJ: Lawrence Erlbaum.

Zutell, J. (1998). Word sorting: A developmental spelling approach to word study for delayed readers. *Reading & Writing Quarterly, 14,* 219–238.

Emergent-Early Letter Name

The Emergent-Early Letter Name stage of literacy development is a period in which young children imitate and experiment with the forms and functions of print. Emergent and Early Letter Name readers are busy navigating their way to literacy, learning about directionality, the distinctive features of print, and how these correlate with oral language. The Emergent-Early Letter Name stage lies at the beginning of a lifetime of learning about written language.

Types of Sorts in Emergent-Early Letter Name
- Concept Sorts
- Rhyming Sorts
- Beginning Consonants
- Letter Recognition
- Consonant Digraphs

Characteristics of Emergent Learners

Emergent learners are found mostly in preschool, kindergarten, and the beginning of first grade.

Emergent Learners

- may not write at all or they may write with scribbles, letter-like forms, or random letters.

- lack concept of word. Emergent learners cannot read in the conventional sense, but can follow along in simple, predictable text with the support of memory and pictures. It is from such pretend reading that they begin to develop a concept of word. **Concept of word** is the ability to match spoken words to printed words as demonstrated by the ability to point to the words of a memorized text while reading.

- pretend to read and write.

- may have well-developed language skills and know a great deal about stories and books; others may not.

- lack letter-sound correspondence.

Characteristics of Early Letter Name Learners

Early Letter Name learners are found mostly in kindergarten and the beginning of first grade.

Early Letter Name-Alphabetic Learners

- spell beginning, end, and prominent sounds in words, for example *B* or *BD* for *bed*.

- are developing a rudimentary concept of word in text, which means they can use initial consonants to locate words on the page, but easily get off track with two-syllable words.

- confuse letter-sound matches when the name of the letter suggests a different sound *(y, g, h)* or because the sounds are articulated similarly *(p/b, t/d, f/v, g/k)*.

- collect sight words.

Teacher Tips

- If children are using letters to represent the initial sounds of words (spelling *cat* as *K* or *baby* as *BB*), they are moving into the Early Letter Name-alphabetic stage, but will still benefit from many of the activities in the Emergent-Early Letter Name stage.

- It is not necessary for children to develop a certain amount of oral language before learning the alphabet or seeing printed words tracked in correspondence to speech. Children can develop oral language, learn about stories, and learn about words, sounds, and the alphabet simultaneously as teachers model reading and writing and encourage children to imitate and experiment.

Focus of Instruction

- The concept sorts are an excellent way to introduce children to sorting. They can learn the process of sorting using familiar objects while extending their thinking and vocabulary.

- The rhyming sorts allow children to participate in phonological awareness activities. Rhyme awareness activities prompt children to play with words and to begin to focus on speech sounds. Use a familiar book or poem to talk about rhyming words, including the *Big Book of Rhymes*, which has a rhyme to introduce each sort.

- The beginning consonant sounds sorts enable children to focus on beginning consonant sounds and to learn about the alphabet, uppercase and lowercase letters, and font variations. Young readers must learn to recognize letters despite the variation in letter styles that abound in the world of print.

- Finally, the digraph sorts introduce children to the digraphs *sh, ch, th,* and *wh*.

The concept sorts, rhyme sorts, and initial sound sorts at this level may be integrated and revisited. Children can begin to sort by sounds at the same time they are learning to identify letters and track print. Adjust the sequence to fit your reading program and to meet children's needs.

Pace of Instruction

Make adjustments in the pace of instruction to meet the needs of children. For children who catch on quickly, move to a faster pace by spending fewer days on a series of sorts or by skipping some sorts altogether. For example, some children may not need to complete every concept or rhyming sort. Conversely, you may find it necessary to slow down the pace for some children by expanding lessons. To slow the pace, provide another opportunity for guided practice in a small group and ask students to repeat the sorts and games.

All children in the Emergent-Early Letter Name stage should participate in the beginning consonant activities, but some children will be able to handle a faster pace with more categories. The Spell Checks can help you determine the focus and pace of instruction. Spend more time on instruction and provide more practice for children who are not on track for meeting end-of-year goals.

You may have children who have already mastered rhyme and/or initial consonant sounds. Modifying the pace and using flexible small groups allows you to avoid teaching them what they already know and to spend more time on features that need instruction.

Word Study Routines

Shared Reading The *Big Book of Rhymes* provides a way to introduce the sort in a meaningful context and provides poems that focus on the features for word study. Here are steps for sharing the rhyme.

- Point to and read the title of the poem and talk about the illustration.

- Point to the words as you read the poem aloud and then discuss it. Reread the poem several times, pausing before rhyming words at the end of lines to invite student participation. The rhyme can also be used to point out features of print such as left-to-right orientation, return sweep, capital letters, and punctuation.

- Encourage children to read along with you after the first reading. With some children you might focus on just two lines at a time. Call on volunteers to point to the words as they recite from memory.

- Draw attention to words, depending on the feature being studied that week. Ask children to identify rhyming words or words that begin with certain letters or sounds. For example, *This rhyme has several words that begin with* m. *Here is the word* Mandy. *It begins with a capital* M. *Can you find other words that begin with* m? *Yes,* mess *and* mop *also begin with* m.

Introduce the Sort There are several options for introducing the sort. Here are the basic steps for a teacher-directed sort.

• Say *Here are some pictures we are going to sort. Let's name them together.* Take time to talk about any word whose meaning might be unfamiliar.

• Introduce the key pictures that will serve as headers for the sorting columns and model how to sort. Explain how you are going to sort and why. *Today we are going to sort by the first sound. Here is a bear.* Bear *starts with /b/. Listen to the first sound in* bear, /b/. *Here is a mouse.* Mouse *starts with /m/. Listen to the first sound in* mouse, /m/. *Let's see if we can find other pictures to put under these headers. Here is a bone.* Bone *and* bear *begin with the same bound, /b/, so I'm going to put the bone under the bear.*

• Sort at least one picture for each category as you model your thinking. Continue to sort, gradually involving children by letting them select a picture to place into a category and explaining why it goes there.

• Once all the pictures are sorted, name the pictures in each column to check whether they are in the right category and to emphasize the alliteration of the beginning sound or the sense of rhyme. Talk once more about how all the things in the category are alike.

• Re-sort. Leave up the headers and distribute the pictures to children in the group, or let them take turns selecting a picture to sort. If mistakes are made, let the mistakes stay. After sorting, check by reading down each column of pictures. If one is misplaced, say, *One of these pictures needs to move to a different column. Let's see if we can find it.*

Emergent-Early Letter Name Library
The library is comprised of little books that correspond to each of the sorts in the Emergent-Early Letter Name stage.

• Use these little books as you would any little books: for picture walks, for choral reading, for echo reading, or for independent reading.

• After completing a sort, read the corresponding book with children. Have them look or listen for words in context that have the feature being studied.

Interactive Resources You may use the DVD-ROM and/or the CD-ROM printable manipulatives to model, instruct, and provide practice with sorts.

Use the DVD-ROM for interactive whiteboard activities or independent practice on a computer.

• Introduce, read, and discuss the rhyme from the *Big Book of Rhymes*. Engage children in reading the rhyme, noticing concepts of print, and identifying words that exemplify the focus of the sort.

• Demonstrate how to drag and drop pictures or letters to complete the sort. Have children take turns sorting, using the whiteboard or a computer.

• Use the whiteboard with children to complete the writing sort.

Use the CD-ROM for printable manipulatives.

• Print out and cut apart the cards for the sort. Introduce the pictures, identifying any that may be unfamiliar to children. For Letter Recognition sorts, identify the letters. Demonstrate how to sort. Have children use the cards to practice sorting.

• Print out the game that accompanies the sort. Use the game for additional practice with the sort. Have children play in pairs or small groups.

• Print out the rhyme that accompanies the sort. Have children take it home to read with family members.

Teacher Tips
• The best way to get children started in sorting is to use real physical objects.

• Once children are introduced to a feature and are experienced sorters, they will need less direct teaching and modeling.

Monitor Progress SPELL CHECKS

Spell Checks are provided at the back of the Emergent-Early Letter Name Student Book. Spell Checks may be used as a pretest to determine what children need to study as well as a posttest.

Spell Check 1
Rhyming Words Use after Sort 13. This Spell Check assesses children's ability to identify rhyming sounds.

1. cat, bat
2. hen, ten
3. mop, top
4. bug, rug
5. tag, bag
6. net, jet

If children miss an unusually high number of rhyming words, have them review Sorts 11 and 12.

Spell Check 2
Beginning Consonants Use after Sort 35. This Spell Check assesses children's ability to identify initial consonant sounds.

1. Ll
2. B/b
3. D/d
4. F/f
5. H/h
6. Y/y
7. Z/z
8. J/j
9. S/s
10. T/t
11. V/v
12. W/w
13. K/k
14. C/c
15. M/m
16. N/n
17. P/p
18. R/r
19. G/g
20. S/s

If children miss a beginning consonant, have them review the corresponding sort for that beginning consonant sound. If children miss an unusually high number of beginning consonants, they should not proceed to the next sort until they have reviewed the previous sorts.

Spell Check 3
Letter Recognition Use after Sort 37. This Spell Check assesses children's ability to match and write capital and lowercase letters.

d, B, r, k, L, n, x, Z, a, A, E, e

Watch for these types of errors: if children write *p* with *B*, review Sorts 17 and 23; if children write *b* with *D*, review Sorts 17 and 28.

Spell Check 4
Digraphs Use after Sort 42. This Spell Check assesses children's ability to identify beginning consonant digraphs.

1. shoe
2. cherry
3. ship
4. whistle
5. thorn
6. shell
7. chair
8. whale
9. thumb
10. thirteen
11. check
12. cheese
13. shirt
14. wheel
15. thick
16. wheat
17. sheep
18. thermos
19. whiskers
20. chain

Watch for these types of errors: if children write *sh* for *ch,* review Sort 40; if children write *w* for *wh*, review Sort 41.

- See Chapter 4 of *Words Their Way: Word Study for Phonics, Vocabulary, and Spelling Instruction, 5th ed.*, for a comprehensive description of the Emergent stage of development and additional activities.

Concept Sort *Fruit/Not a Fruit*

Objectives
- To explore the concept of sorting
- To identify and sort fruit and things that are not fruit

Materials for Emergent-Early Letter Name

Big Book of Rhymes, "Grapes," page 5

Whiteboard Activities DVD-ROM, Sort 1

Teacher Resource CD-ROM, Sort 1 and Match! Game

Student Book, pages 1–4

Words Their Way Library, *Something to Munch*

Pictures

fruit	not fruit
apple	hat
banana	rain
orange	mop
strawberry	bat
cherry	
peach	
grapes	
pear	

Introduce/Model   *Small Groups*

- **Read a Rhyme** Read "Grapes" several times until children become familiar with the rhyme. Repeat the rhyme and have children search the illustration for things that are named in the poem.

- **Model** Use the whiteboard DVD or the CD picture cards. Explain that children will sort the cards into two categories: fruit and things that are not fruit. Demonstrate how to sort the cards. Help children sort and explain their sorts.

Practice the Sort   *Independent/Partner*

- Have children use the Student Book or whiteboard DVD to name the pictures and use the grid to sort according to which are fruits and which are not.

- Have children check and explain their sorts.

Apply   *Independent/Partner/Small Groups*

- Read aloud the directions on Student Book p. 4. Have children draw pictures and write the words in the correct columns.

- **Game** Allow time for children to play Match!, which is on the CD.

- **Little Book** Read *Something to Munch* with children. Have them identify the fruits.

Extend the Sort

ELL English Language Learners

Some children may look at the words *pear* and *peach* and think they are pronounced the same. Write *pear* and *peach*. Point to and say each word several times. Then have children say the words three or four times as you track them. Explain that sometimes the middle letters in two different words may be the same but are pronounced differently. Ask children to remember how to say and spell the words *pear* and *peach*.

Vocabulary Building Vocabulary

Hold up the picture of the pear from the sort. Say the name and invite volunteers to describe the pear. Explain to children that there is another word that sounds just like *pear*, but it has a different spelling and meaning. Write *pair*. Explain that *pair* means "a set of two things that go together," like a pair of shoes or socks.

Teacher Tip

Consider establishing a "reading chair," where children will gather when you read to them. As children learn to associate the chair with reading, they will automatically prepare to listen to a story or poem when they gather at that location.

Objectives

- To explore the concept of sorting
- To identify and sort animals and things that are not animals

Materials for Emergent-Early Letter Name

- Big Book of Rhymes, "Come to the Zoo," page 7

- Whiteboard Activities DVD-ROM, Sort 2

- Teacher Resource CD-ROM, Sort 2 and Guess the Category Game

- Student Book, pages 5–8

- Words Their Way Library, *Vultures on Vacation*

Pictures

animal	not animal
horse	tree
bird	rock
turtle	flowers
fish	rope
dog	
butterfly	
cat	
bear	

Introduce/Model *Small Groups*

- **Read a Rhyme** Read "Come to the Zoo" several times until children become familiar with the rhyme. Track the text as you read the rhyme with children. Have children search the rhyme and illustration for words and pictures of animals. As each is identified, point to the word and to the picture to help children associate the animal and its name.

- **Model** Use the whiteboard DVD or the CD picture cards. Explain that children will sort the cards into two categories: animals and things that are not animals. Demonstrate how to sort the cards. Help children sort and explain their sorts.

Practice the Sort *Independent/Partner*

- Have children use the Student Book or whiteboard DVD to name the pictures and use the grid to sort according to which are animals and which not.

- Have children check and explain their sorts.

Apply *Independent/Partner/Small Groups*

- Read aloud the directions on Student Book p. 8. Have children draw pictures and write the words in the correct columns.

- **Game** Allow time for children to play **Guess the Category**, which is on the CD.

- **Little Book** Read *Vultures on Vacation* with children. Have them identify animals and things that are not animals.

Extend the Sort

Alternative Sort: Count the Legs

Display the animal pictures from the sort. Have children re-sort the pictures by identifying the animals that have four legs and sorting those into a group. Have them count the legs of each animal they choose. Then mix the cards and display the animal pictures. Ask children to re-sort the cards by choosing the animals that have fur coats and placing those together.

Vocabulary Building Vocabulary

Explain that adult animals and young animals have different names. Show the picture of the dog and explain that a young dog is called a puppy. Write the words *dog* and *puppy* on the board. Continue with the pictures of the bear and cat. Ask children to say the name of the young animal for each. *(cub, kitten)* Then challenge children to name other baby animals: *hen (chick), duck (duckling), cow (calf), deer (fawn).*

Teacher Tip

Throughout the year, help children take advantage of other opportunities to practice sorting. For example, as part of a science lesson, children can sort leaves or rocks according to size, shape, or color.

Concept Sort *Shapes*

Objectives

- To explore the concept of sorting
- To identify and sort circles, squares, and triangles

Materials for Emergent-Early Letter Name

Big Book of Rhymes, "I See Shapes," page 9

Whiteboard Activities DVD-ROM, Sort 3

Teacher Resource CD-ROM, Sort 3 and Sort Ourselves Game

Student Book, pages 9–12

Words Their Way Library, *Six Go By*

Pictures

circles	squares	triangles
red circle	yellow square	red triangle
yellow circle	blue square	blue triangle
blue circle	red square	yellow triangle
green circle	green square	green triangle

Introduce/Model   *Small Groups*

- **Read a Rhyme** Read "I See Shapes" several times until children become familiar with the rhyme. Track the text of the rhyme together with children. Have children search the rhyme and illustration for the words *circle(s), square(s),* and *triangle(s)* and pictures of each.

- **Model** Use the whiteboard DVD or the CD picture cards. Explain that children will sort by shapes. Demonstrate how to sort the cards according to shape (triangle, circle, square). Help children sort and explain their sorts.

Practice the Sort   *Independent/Partner*

- Have children use the Student Book or whiteboard DVD to name the shapes and use the grid to sort.

- Have children check and explain their sorts.

Apply   *Independent/Partner/Small Groups*

- Read aloud the directions on Student Book p. 12. Have children draw shapes in the correct columns.

- **Game** Allow time for children to play Sort Ourselves, which is on the CD.

- **Little Book** Read *Six Go By* with children. Have them identify the circles, triangles, and squares in the pictures.

Extend the Sort

Alternative Sort: Colors

When children are comfortable sorting by shape, have them work independently or with a partner to re-sort the cards according to color (red, blue, yellow, green). Remind children that the pictures in each group will be different shapes but the same color.

Vocabulary Building Vocabulary

Review the cards with children, naming each picture. Then help children practice saying the plural form of the words by completing sentences such as "I see one circle, and Hema sees two [circles]."

ELL English Language Learners

Ahead of time, gather items to represent the shapes on the cards (for example, a circular roll of tape, a drafting triangle, square sticky notes). Review the picture cards, naming the shapes. Then work with children to name the shapes of the items you have collected.

Teacher Tip

Triangles may confuse children since their appearance can differ depending on the size of the angles. Explain that any shape with three sides and three corners is a triangle.

Concept Sort *Food, Clothes, Toys*

Objectives

- To explore the concept of sorting
- To identify and sort food, clothes, and toys

Materials for Emergent-Early Letter Name

Big Book of Rhymes, "Lunch at the Beach," page 11

Whiteboard Activities DVD-ROM, Sort 4

Teacher Resource CD-ROM, Sort 4 and Guess the Category Game

Student Book, pages 13–16

Words Their Way Library, *The Hat*

Pictures		
food	*clothes*	*toys*
corn	shirt	blocks
celery	coat	ball
apple	cap	jump rope
cheese	sock	stuffed animal

Introduce/Model   *Small Groups*

- **Read a Rhyme** Read "Lunch at the Beach" several times. Track the text as you point to each word and have children identify the word *ball.* Have them point to the ball in the illustration. Then have children search the illustration for other toys the children brought with them to the beach.

- **Model** Use the whiteboard DVD or the CD picture cards. Explain that children will sort the cards into three categories: food, clothes, and toys. Demonstrate how to sort the cards. Help children sort and explain their sorts.

Practice the Sort   *Independent/Partner*

- Have children use the Student Book or whiteboard DVD to name the pictures and use the grid to sort according to food, clothes, and toys.

- Have children check and explain their sorts.

Apply   *Independent/Partner/Small Groups*

- Read aloud the directions on Student Book p. 16. Have children draw pictures and write the words in the correct columns.

- **Game** Allow time for children to play Guess the Category, which is on the CD.

- **Little Book** Read *The Hat* with children. Have them identify the clothes and the animals.

Extend the Sort

Alternative Sort: Does It Grow?

Have children re-sort the cards according to whether the object in the picture grows outside or doesn't grow.

Vocabulary Building Vocabulary

Explain to children that some words have more than one meaning. Show the picture card for *cap.* Tell children that a cap can be something you wear on your head. Encourage them to tell about a time they saw someone wearing a cap. Then explain that a cap can also be the lid on the top of a bottle, like the cap on a bottle of orange juice.

ELL English Language Learners

Review the cards with children, naming each picture. Then use the picture names in a game of Simon Says. For example, touch your sock and say, "Simon says, 'Touch your sock,'" or pretend to bounce a ball as you say, "Bounce a ball." Remind children to copy your action only if you say "Simon says" before the command.

Concept Sort *Clothes*

Objectives
- To explore the concept of sorting
- To identify and sort clothes

Materials for Emergent-Early Letter Name

  Big Book of Rhymes, "Which Hat?," page 13

  Whiteboard Activities DVD-ROM, Sort 5

  Teacher Resource CD-ROM, Sort 5 and Guess the Category Game

  Student Book, pages 17–20

  Words Their Way Library, *For Sale*

Pictures			
head	*feet*	*body*	*hands*
cap	boots	coat	glove
hat	sneakers	raincoat	mittens
firefighter's hat	skate	sweater	baseball mitt

Introduce/Model *Small Groups*

- **Read a Rhyme** Read "Which Hat?" aloud several times. Track the lines with children as you read. Then have children search the poem for the word *hat*. If time allows, have children search for hats in the picture.

- **Model** Use the whiteboard DVD or the CD picture cards. Explain that children will sort the picture cards into four categories: things you can wear on your head, your feet, your body, and your hands. Demonstrate how to sort the cards. Help children sort and explain their sorts.

Practice the Sort *Independent/Partner*

- Have children use the Student Book or whiteboard DVD to name the pictures and use the grid to sort according to where the clothes are worn.

- Have children check and explain their sorts.

Apply *Independent/Partner/Small Groups*

- Read aloud the directions on Student Book p. 20. Have children draw pictures and write the words in the correct boxes.

- **Game** Allow time for children to play **Guess the Category**, which is on the CD.

- **Little Book** Read *For Sale* with children. Have them identify the clothing.

Extend the Sort

Alternative Sort: Warm, Cold, or Both?

Remove the pictures for *skate, baseball mitt*, and *firefighter's hat*. Have children re-sort the remaining pictures according to whether they would wear the article of clothing on a warm day, a cold day, or on both kinds of days.

Vocabulary Building Vocabulary

Show the picture cards for *glove* and *mittens*. Point out that a glove has a "little pocket" for each finger, while mittens have one big pocket for all the fingers. They both keep your hands warm. Show the card for *baseball mitt* and explain that it protects your hand from being hurt when playing baseball.

Teacher Tip

Reinforce learning by having children work in pairs to name as many kinds of things as they can think of that they can wear on their heads. Ask children to explain to each other what purpose each thing would serve.

Concept Sort *Food*

Objectives

- To explore the concept of sorting
- To identify and sort food

Materials for Emergent-Early Letter Name

▭ Big Book of Rhymes, "We Love Pizza!" page 15

▭ Whiteboard Activities DVD-ROM, Sort 6

◉ Teacher Resource CD-ROM, Sort 6 and Foods Game

▭ Student Book, pages 21–24

▭ Words Their Way Library, *School Lunch*

Pictures

bread	beverage	fruit	vegetable
bread	orange juice	apple	carrot
muffin	milk	cherries	zucchini
pizza	apple juice	grapes	potatoes

Introduce/Model *Small Groups*

- **Read a Rhyme** Read "We Love Pizza!" aloud several times. Track the word *pizza* as children follow along. Then have children count the number of times the word *pizza* is used in the poem.

- **Model** Use the whiteboard DVD or the CD picture cards. Explain that children will sort the cards into four categories of food: bread, beverage, fruit, and vegetable. Demonstrate how to sort the cards. Help children sort and explain their sorts.

Practice the Sort *Independent/Partner*

- Have children use the Student Book or whiteboard DVD to name the pictures and use the grid to sort according to the four categories of food.

- Have children check and explain their sorts.

Apply *Independent/Partner/Small Groups*

- Read aloud the directions on Student Book p. 24. Have children draw pictures and write the words in the correct boxes.

- **Game** Allow time for children to play Foods, which is on the CD.

- **Little Book** Read *School Lunch* with children. Have them identify the food.

Extend the Sort

Alternative Sort: Cold or Hot?

Have children re-sort the pictures according to whether you would eat the food cold or hot. Ask children to explain their sorts. Acknowledge that some foods can be eaten hot or cold and therefore will be in both groups.

Vocabulary Building Vocabulary

Show each picture card and ask children to think of words they can use to describe the food. For example, carrot—*long, orange, hard, rough.* Encourage children to use these words in sentences about the food.

ELL English Language Learners

Have pairs of children take turns showing a picture card and saying the word to their partner. Then have them tell their partner whether or not they like to eat that food.

Teacher Tip

When asking children questions, allow ample wait time before calling on a child. This accommodates children who need extra time to consider a question and formulate a response.

Rhyming Sort *Nose, Knees, Hair, Head*

Objectives

- To identify rhyming words for *nose, knees, hair,* and *head*
- To sort pictures of words that rhyme with *nose, knees, hair,* and *head*

Pictures			
nose	*knees*	*hair*	*head*
rose	trees	chair	red
toes	cheese	pear	bed
hose	keys	bear	bread

Materials for Emergent-Early Letter Name

Big Book of Rhymes, "Hide-and-Seek," page 17

Whiteboard Activities DVD-ROM, Sort 7

Teacher Resource CD-ROM, Sort 7 and Rhyming Path Game

Student Book, pages 25–28

Words Their Way Library, *The Farm*

Introduce/Model *Small Groups*

- **Read a Rhyme** Read "Hide-and-Seek" several times, emphasizing the rhyming words. *(nose, toes; hair, everywhere; knees, trees)* Have children search the poem for words that rhyme with *nose, hair,* and *knees.*

- **Model** Use the whiteboard DVD or the CD picture cards. Explain that children will sort the cards into four categories: words that rhyme with *nose, knees, hair,* and *head.* Demonstrate how to sort the cards. Help children sort and explain their sorts.

Practice the Sort *Independent/Partner*

- Have children use the Student Book or whiteboard DVD to name the pictures and use the grid to sort according to which of the words they rhyme with.

- Have children check and explain their sorts.

Apply *Independent/Partner/Small Groups*

- Read aloud the directions on Student Book p. 28. Have children draw pictures and write the words that rhyme with *nose, knees, hair,* and *head.*

- **Game** Allow time for children to play Rhyming Path, which is on the CD.

- **Little Book** Read *The Farm* with children. Have them identify words that rhyme with *house, pail,* and *rake.*

Extend the Sort

Alternative Sort: Inside or Outside?

Remove the picture cards for *red* and *toes.* Then have children re-sort the remaining pictures according to whether the object is more commonly found inside or outside. Acknowledge that some objects can be found both inside and outside.

Vocabulary Building Vocabulary

Show each picture card and encourage children to ask a question about the object that can be answered by looking at the picture. For example, "What color is the chair? The chair is red." Remind children to answer in complete sentences.

ELL English Language Learners

Point to your nose, knees, hair, and head as you read the poem. Have children join you and speak the words aloud as they point.

Teacher Tip

Try pantomiming the poem to capture children's attention as you read the rhyme. For example, pretend to peek around a tree when you read the words *Just peek behind those trees.* Invite children to imitate your movements.

Objectives

- To identify rhyming words for *clock, fly,* and *pan*
- To sort pictures of words that rhyme with *clock, fly,* and *pan*

Materials for Emergent-Early Letter Name

Big Book of Rhymes, "Where Is That Clock?," page 19

Whiteboard Activities DVD-ROM, Sort 8

Teacher Resource CD-ROM, Sort 8 and Rhyme Time Game

Student Book, pages 29–32

Words Their Way Library, *Look at That!*

Pictures		
clock	**fly**	**pan**
lock	eye	fan
block	pie	can
rock	tie	man
sock	cry	van

Introduce/Model
Small Groups

- **Read a Rhyme** Read "Where Is That Clock?" aloud with children while emphasizing the rhyming words. *(tock/clock, stop/top, you/shoe)* Ask children to find the rhyming words in the poem.

- **Model** Use the whiteboard DVD or the CD picture cards. Explain that children will sort the cards into three categories: words that rhyme with *clock, fly,* and *pan*. Demonstrate how to sort the cards. Elicit that the names of the pictures rhyme because they end with the same sound. Help children sort and explain their sorts.

Practice the Sort
Independent/Partner

- Have children use the Student Book or whiteboard DVD to name the pictures and use the grid to sort pictures that rhyme with *clock, fly,* and *pan*.

- Have children check and explain their sorts.

Apply
Independent/Partner/Small Groups

- Read aloud the directions on Student Book p. 32. Have children draw pictures and write rhyming words in the correct boxes.

- **Game** Allow time for children to play Rhyme Time, which is on the CD.

- **Little Book** Read *Look at That!* with children. Have them identify words that rhyme with *pan* and with *cat*.

Extend the Sort

Alternative Sort: Red or Not Red?

Have children re-sort the pictures according to whether or not they contain the color red. Then have children name other colors they see in the pictures.

Vocabulary Building Vocabulary

Show the picture card for *tie*. Explain that a tie is something you can wear around your neck, but it can also mean to make a knot or a bow, as in to tie a shoe or to tie a ribbon. If possible, show children how to tie a shoe or let them practice tying a bow with a piece of string.

Teacher Tip

Reinforce learning by referring back to various pictures and rhyming sounds throughout the day. For example, you might point to the classroom clock and take a minute with children to brainstorm words that rhyme with *clock*. Make a list of the words and encourage children to add to it.

Rhyming Sort *Bug, Mop, Beet*

Objectives

- To identify rhyming words for *bug, mop,* and *beet*
- To sort pictures of words that rhyme with *bug, mop,* and *beet*

Materials for Emergent-Early Letter Name

- Big Book of Rhymes, "Four Little Kittens," page 21

- Whiteboard Activities DVD-ROM, Sort 9

- Teacher Resource CD-ROM, Sort 9 and Spin 'n Rhyme Game

- Student Book, pages 33–36

- Words Their Way Library, *Little Bug*

Pictures

bug	mop	beet
mug	hop	meat
rug	top	wheat
plug	shop	feet
hug	pop	street

Introduce/Model
Small Groups

- **Read a Rhyme** Read "Four Little Kittens." Reread the poem, emphasizing the rhyming words *leap, creep* and *bug, rug.* Help children understand that these words rhyme because they end with the same sounds.

- **Model** Use the whiteboard DVD or the CD picture cards. Explain that children will sort the cards into three categories: words that rhyme with *bug, mop,* and *beet.* Demonstrate how to sort the cards. Elicit that the names of the pictures rhyme because they end with the same sounds. Help children sort and explain their sorts.

Practice the Sort
Independent/Partner

- Have children use the Student Book or whiteboard DVD to name the pictures and use the grid to sort pictures that rhyme with *bug, mop,* and *beet.*

- Have children check and explain their sorts.

Apply
Independent/Partner/Small Groups

- Read aloud the directions on Student Book p. 36. Have children draw pictures and write words that rhyme with *bug, mop,* and *beet.*

- **Game** Allow time for children to play Spin 'n Rhyme, which is on the CD.

- **Little Book** Read *Little Bug* with children. Have them identify words that rhyme with *bug.*

Extend the Sort

Alternative Sort: People or Not People?

Remove the picture card for *pop.* Then have children re-sort the remaining pictures according to whether the picture shows people or does not show people.

Vocabulary Building Vocabulary

Explain that rhyming words can be made by adding different beginning sounds to the same middle and ending sounds. Demonstrate by writing *bug, hug, mug,* and *rug* in a list. Ask volunteers to circle the beginning letter in each word. Continue with the words that rhyme with *mop.*

Teacher Tip

Encourage children to develop their sorting skills by participating in basic sorting exercises that identify common objects in the classroom (pencils, buttons, colors, and so on).

Objectives

- To identify rhyming words for *jar, crate, bell,* and *grape*
- To sort pictures of words that rhyme with *jar, crate, bell,* and *grape*

Materials for Emergent-Early Letter Name

Big Book of Rhymes, "Grapes," page 5

Whiteboard Activities DVD-ROM, Sort 10

Teacher Resource CD-ROM, Sort 10 and Sweet Rhymes Game

Student Book, pages 37–40

Words Their Way Library, *Funny Faces and Funny Places*

Pictures

jar	*crate*	*bell*	*grape*
bar	gate	smell	scrape
car	skate	well	tape
star	eight	shell	cape

Introduce/Model   *Small Groups*

- **Read a Rhyme** Read "Grapes," emphasizing the rhyming words. *(vine/fine, plate/ate)* Reread the poem and track the word *grapes*. Ask children to find the grapes in the illustration.

- **Model** Use the whiteboard DVD or the CD picture cards. Explain that children will sort the cards into four categories: words that rhyme with *jar, crate, bell,* and *grape*. Demonstrate how to sort the cards. Remind children that rhyming words end with the same sounds. Help children sort and explain their sorts.

Practice the Sort   *Independent/Partner*

- Have children use the Student Book or whiteboard DVD to name the pictures and use the grid to sort pictures that rhyme with *jar, crate, bell,* and *grape*.

- Have children check and explain their sorts.

Apply   *Independent/Partner/Small Groups*

- Read aloud the directions on Student Book p. 40. Have children draw pictures and write words that rhyme with *jar, crate, bell,* and *grape*.

- **Game** Allow time for children to play Sweet Rhymes, which is on the CD.

- **Little Book** Read *Funny Faces and Funny Places* with children. Have them identify words that rhyme with *faces, clown,* and *car*.

Extend the Sort

Alternative Sort: Green or Not Green?

Have children re-sort the cards according to whether or not the picture shows the color green. Then ask children to name other colors in the pictures.

Vocabulary Building Vocabulary

Offer children sentences they can complete with one of the rhyming words. For example, say "Someone rang the ____." Include a context clue *(rang)*. After children complete the sentence, ask them how they chose the word.

ELL English Language Learners

Children may have difficulty naming the picture for *scrape*. Explain that the picture shows someone using a tool to remove ice from a car. Say, "The person is scraping ice from the car." Have children repeat and pantomime the sentence.

Teacher Tip

When possible, have children review previous sorts. Have children work with partners to complete the sorts. Circulate around the room to provide help as needed.

Rhyming Sort *Pairs 1*

Objectives

- To identify pairs of words that rhyme
- To sort pictures of words that rhyme

Materials for Emergent-Early Letter Name

Big Book of Rhymes, "Fox in a Box," page 23

Whiteboard Activities DVD-ROM, Sort 11

Teacher Resource CD-ROM, Sort 11 and Rhyming Go Fish Game

Student Book, pages 41–44

Words Their Way Library, *A Fin, a Grin, and a Pin*

Pictures

fox	box
pail	whale
mouse	house
goat	boat
dish	fish
cake	snake

Introduce/Model
Small Groups

- **Read a Rhyme** Read "Fox in a Box" to children. Reread the poem, emphasizing the rhyming words. *(fox/box, too/you, cat/scat)* Read the poem again and track the words *fox* and *box* with children.

- **Model** Use the whiteboard DVD or the CD picture cards. Explain that children will sort the cards into pairs of words that rhyme. Remind children that words that rhyme end with the same sound. Demonstrate how to find pairs of words that rhyme and sort the cards.

Practice the Sort
Independent/Partner

- Have children use the Student Book or whiteboard DVD to name the pictures and use the grid to sort them into pairs that rhyme.

- Have children check and explain their sorts.

Apply
Independent/Partner/Small Groups

- Read aloud the directions on Student Book p. 44. Have children draw pictures of two things that rhyme and write the words that name them.

- **Game** Allow time for children to play Rhyming Go Fish, which is on the CD.

- **Little Book** Read *A Fin, a Grin, and a Pin* with children. Have them identify the words that rhyme with *in*.

Extend the Sort

Alternative Sort: Animal or Not?

Have children re-sort the pictures into two piles: one pile for pictures of animals and one pile for pictures of things other than animals. Ask children what all the animals have in common.

ELL English Language Learners

Name each picture, and have children repeat the name after you. Then use each word in a sentence. Have children repeat the sentence. Then have them use each word in a sentence of their own.

Teacher Tip

When possible, reinforce rhyming sorts with familiar nursery rhymes or rhyming children's books. Choose two rhyming lines from a poem or a book page that reinforce the rhyming sort and write the lines on the board. Track and read the lines aloud with children several times. Ask volunteers to each say a line as you track the words on the board.

Rhyming Sort *Pairs 2*

Objectives
- To identify pairs of words that rhyme
- To sort pictures of words that rhyme

Materials for Emergent-Early Letter Name

Big Book of Rhymes, "Billy's Toy Box," page 25

Whiteboard Activities DVD-ROM, Sort 12

Teacher Resource CD-ROM, Sort 12 and Think of Rhymes Game

Student Book, pages 45–48

Words Their Way Library, *The Toy Box*

Pictures	
sand	hand
cub	tub
bow	toe
pail	whale
truck	duck
bear	chair

Introduce/Model   *Small Groups*

- **Read a Rhyme** Read "Billy's Toy Box" aloud several times, emphasizing the rhyming words *box, blocks* and *bear, everywhere.* Have children repeat the words, and explain that these words rhyme because they end with the same sounds.

- **Model** Use the whiteboard DVD or the CD picture cards. Explain that children will sort the cards into pairs of words that rhyme. Demonstrate how to sort the cards. Help children sort and explain their sorts.

Practice the Sort   *Independent/Partner*

- Have children use the Student Book or whiteboard DVD to name the pictures and use the grid to sort them into pairs that rhyme.

- Have children check and explain their sorts.

Apply   *Independent/Partner/Small Groups*

- Read aloud the directions on Student Book p. 48. Have children draw pictures of two things that rhyme and write the words that name them.

- **Game** Allow time for children to play Think of Rhymes, which is on the CD.

- **Little Book** Read *The Toy Box* with children. Have them identify the words that rhyme with *blocks*.

Extend the Sort

Alternative Sort: Animals or Not Animals?

Remove the picture cards for *hand* and *toe*. Have children re-sort the remaining pictures into two piles: animals and things that are not animals. Ask them to explain their sort.

ELL English Language Learners

Some children may point out that the word *bow* has other meanings, as in a bow and arrow. If this occurs, explain that many English words have more than one meaning. How the word is used can help children understand which meaning is intended.

Teacher Tip

Reinforce the concept that while rhyming words have the same middle and ending sounds, they may not have the same spelling pattern. Write the words *bow* and *toe* on the board and point to them as you hold up the picture cards. Guide children to identify the different spelling patterns. Repeat with *pail/whale* and *chair/bear*.

Rhyming Sort *Colors*

Objectives

- To identify words that rhyme with color words
- To sort pictures of words that rhyme with color words

Materials for Emergent-Early Letter Name

Big Book of Rhymes, "The River Frog," page 27

Whiteboard Activities DVD-ROM, Sort 13

Teacher Resource CD-ROM, Sort 13 and Color Rhymes Game

Student Book, pages 49–52

Words Their Way Library, *A Pig in a Wig*

Pictures

color	rhyming word
tan	man
pink	drink
white	kite
brown	crown
green	bean
blue	shoe

Introduce/Model
Small Groups

- **Read a Rhyme** Read "The River Frog" several times, emphasizing the rhyming words *frog, log* and *gray, day.* Write the rhyming words in two columns and ask children how the words in each column are alike.

- **Model** Use the whiteboard DVD or the CD picture cards. Explain that children will sort the cards into pairs of words that rhyme. Demonstrate how to sort the cards. Help children sort and explain their sorts.

Practice the Sort
Independent/Partner

- Have children use the Student Book or whiteboard DVD to name the pictures and use the grid to sort them into pairs that rhyme.

- Have children check and explain their sorts.

Apply
Independent/Partner/Small Groups

- Read aloud the directions on Student Book p. 52. Have children draw pictures of things that rhyme and write the words that name them.

- **Game** Allow time for children to play Color Rhymes, which is on the CD.

- **Little Book** Read *A Pig in a Wig* with children. Have them identify the colors in the wigs and the words that rhyme with *wig.*

Extend the Sort

Alternative Sort: Color or Not?

Have children re-sort the picture cards into two groups: those that represent colors and those that do not. Ask children to name the color cards and then find those colors either on the other cards or in the classroom.

ELL English Language Learners

Divide the class into pairs. Have one child pick a card and show it to his or her partner, who should say the word slowly. The first child should then repeat the word. Have pairs continue this process with the remaining cards. Listen and provide guidance as necessary.

Teacher Tip

Have children draw pictures of the rhyming words from the sort that they like best. Then have them color the pictures with colors from the sort. Have children label their pictures using both the color and the rhyming word, such as *green kite.*

Monitor Progress **Spell Check 1**

After completing Sort 13, administer Spell Check 1. See page 35 in this Teacher Resource Guide for instructions.

Beginning Sounds b, m

Objectives

- To identify picture names beginning with the sounds of *b* and *m*
- To sort pictures by their beginning sound and associate each sound with the letter it represents

Materials for Emergent-Early Letter Name

Big Book of Rhymes, "Bubbles," page 29

Whiteboard Activities DVD-ROM, Sort 14

Teacher Resource CD-ROM, Sort 14 and Find the Picture Game

Student Book, pages 53–56

Words Their Way Library, *Monster Mop*

Pictures

b	m
barn	man
bone	meat
ball	mop
bat	map
bed	moon
baby	milk

Introduce/Model *Small Groups*

- **Read a Rhyme** Read "Bubbles" aloud several times, emphasizing *b* and *m* at the beginning of words. Have children search the poem to find examples of words that begin with the sound of *b* or *m*.

- **Model** Use the whiteboard DVD or the CD picture cards. Explain that children will sort the pictures by the beginning sounds of their names. Demonstrate how to sort the cards by the beginning sound *b* or *m*. Help children sort and explain their sorts.

Practice the Sort *Independent/Partner*

- Have children use the Student Book or whiteboard DVD to name the pictures and use the grid to sort according to beginning sound *b* or *m*.

- Have children check and explain their sorts.

Apply *Independent/Partner/Small Groups*

- Read aloud the directions on Student Book p. 56. Have children draw pictures of and write the words for things that begin like *bear* and *mouse*.

- **Game** Allow time for children to play Find the Picture, which is on the CD.

- **Little Book** Read *Monster Mop* with children. Have them identify words that begin with /m/ and give a rhyming word for each that begins with /b/.

Extend the Sort

Vocabulary Building Vocabulary

Hold up the picture of the bat from the sort. Say the name and ask volunteers to describe the bat. Explain that *bat* can also be an action word, meaning "to hit a ball with a bat." Have the group pretend to bat a ball. Continue with the picture of the mop from the sort. Have children describe the mop and then use *mop* as an action word in a sentence. Review with children how *bat* and *mop* can be naming words or action words.

ELL English Language Learners

Model using both lips to form the sound of *b*. Using words that start with *b* followed by a vowel, such as *baby,* helps to emphasize the formation and associated strong initial sound. The use of a mirror can help children check their mouth placement.

Teacher Tip

As you work your way through sorts with beginning consonant sounds, you may want to use alphabet books to provide enrichment for children. Distribute the books to children and ask them to work in pairs to find additional words that begin with each sort's sounds.

Beginning Sounds *r, s*

Objectives

- To identify picture names beginning with the sounds of *r* and *s*
- To sort pictures by their beginning sound and associate each sound with the letter it represents

Materials for Emergent-Early Letter Name

Big Book of Rhymes, "The Raincoat," page 31

Whiteboard Activities DVD-ROM, Sort 15

Teacher Resource CD-ROM, Sort 15 and Go Fish Game

Student Book, pages 57–60

Words Their Way Library, *Sandy*

Pictures

r	s
ring	six
road	seal
rope	sink
rug	sock
rain	sun
roof	soap

Introduce/Model *Small Groups*

- **Read a Rhyme** Read "The Raincoat" aloud, emphasizing the rhyming words. *(play, day, anyway)* Reread the rhyme, emphasizing *r* and *s* at the beginning of words. Have children search the rhyme to find words that begin with the sound of *r* or *s*.

- **Model** Use the whiteboard DVD or the CD picture cards. Explain that children will sort the pictures by the beginning sounds of their names. Demonstrate how to sort the cards by the beginning sound *r* or *s*. Help children sort and explain their sorts.

Practice the Sort *Independent/Partner*

- Have children use the Student Book or whiteboard DVD to name the pictures and use the grid to sort according to beginning sound *r* or *s*.

- Have children check and explain their sorts.

Apply *Independent/Partner/Small Groups*

- Read aloud the directions on Student Book p. 60. Have children draw pictures of and write the words for things that begin like *rock* and *saw*.

- **Game** Allow time for children to play Go Fish, which is on the CD.

- **Little Book** Read *Sandy* with children. Have them identify words that begin with /r/ or /s/.

Extend the Sort

Alternative Sort: Inside or Outside?

Remove the picture cards for *ring*, *six,* and *rope*. Then have children re-sort the remaining cards according to whether you would most likely see them inside or outside.

Vocabulary **Building Vocabulary**

Show the picture card for *ring*. Explain that *ring* can mean "a metal circle," and it can also mean "to make a sound," as in *ring a bell*. Have children make up sentences with each meaning of the word. Repeat with *sink* ("a shallow basin with a drain" and "to go down").

ELL **English Language Learners**

If children are having difficulty pronouncing the sound of *r*, pretend to be a lion. Model how to roar, stretching the beginning sound *(rrrrroar)*. Encourage children to do the same.

Teacher Tip

Challenge children to write the letters *r* and *s* on sticky notes and attach them to items in the classroom whose names begin with the corresponding sound. Children may also enjoy brainstorming a list of words that begin with *s* and incorporating them into a tongue twister.

Beginning Sounds *b, m, r, s*

Objectives

- To identify picture names beginning with the sounds of *b, m, r,* and *s*
- To sort pictures by their beginning sound and associate each sound with the letter it represents

Materials for Emergent-Early Letter Name

Big Book of Rhymes, "Lunch at the Beach," page 11

Whiteboard Activities DVD-ROM, Sort 16

Teacher Resource CD-ROM, Sort 16 and Let's Race! Game

Student Book, pages 61–64

Words Their Way Library, *Two Boys*

Pictures

b	m	r	s
bowl	map	rag	sack
beetle	mitt	rake	sun
band	mop	road	seal
boat	mad	rock	sand

Introduce/Model
Small Groups

- **Read a Rhyme** Read "Lunch at the Beach." Have children identify the rhyming words. *(pails/sails, munch/lunch)* Then have children search the poem to find words that begin with the sound of *b, m, r,* or *s*.

- **Model** Use the whiteboard DVD or the CD picture cards. Explain that children will sort the pictures by the beginning sounds of their names. Demonstrate how to sort the cards by the beginning sound *b, m, r,* or *s*. Help children sort and explain their sorts.

Practice the Sort
Independent/Partner

- Have children use the Student Book or whiteboard DVD to name the pictures and use the grid to sort according to beginning sounds *b, m, r,* and *s*.

- Have children check and explain their sorts.

Apply
Independent/Partner/Small Groups

- Read aloud the directions on Student Book p. 64. Have children draw pictures of and write the words for things that begin like *bell, mouse, ring,* and *saw*.

- **Game** Allow time for children to play Let's Race!, which is on the CD.

- **Little Book** Read *Two Boys* with children. Have them identify words that begin with /b/, /m/, /r/, or /s/.

Extend the Sort

Alternative Sort: Living or Nonliving?

Remove the picture card for *mad.* Then have children re-sort the remaining pictures according to whether they show something that is alive or not alive. Ask them to explain their sort.

Vocabulary Building Vocabulary

Explain to children that the word *band* has more than one meaning. A band can be a group of people that play music together. A band can also be a strip that holds things together, like a rubber band. Encourage children to make up sentences using each meaning of *band*.

Teacher Tip

When picture cards show an object whose name can function as a noun or a verb, use the cards to familiarize children with the concept of names of things and names of actions. For example, show the picture for *rake*. Have one child say the picture's name and another tell what action you perform with the object.

Sort 17

Letter Recognition *Bb, Mm, Aa*

Objectives

- To recognize the letters *Bb, Mm,* and *Aa*
- To identify and sort different print styles and cases of *Bb, Mm,* and *Aa*

Materials for Emergent-Early Letter Name

Big Book of Rhymes, "Where's My Cap?," page 33

Whiteboard Activities DVD-ROM, Sort 17

Teacher Resource CD-ROM, Sort 17 and Find the Letter Game

Student Book, pages 65–68

Words Their Way Library, *Two Boys*

Letters	
Bb	**Mm**
4 variations of *B*	4 variations of *M*
4 variations of *b*	4 variations of *m*
Aa	
4 variations of *A*	
4 variations of *a*	

Introduce/Model   *Small Groups*

- **Read a Rhyme** Read "Where's My Cap?" Track the text by pointing to each word as you read. Then have children search the poem to find examples of capital and lowercase *Bb, Mm,* and *Aa*.

- **Model** Use the whiteboard DVD or the letter cards. Explain that children will sort the letters by their names. Select a capital and a lowercase *b* and ask children how the letters are different. Remind children that despite the differences, the letters are all named *b*. Continue with *m* and *a*. Help children sort and explain their sorts.

Practice the Sort   *Independent/Partner*

- Have children use the Student Book or whiteboard DVD to name the letters and use the grid to sort the cards by letter names.

- Have children check and explain their sorts.

Apply   *Independent/Partner/Small Groups*

- Read aloud the directions on Student Book p. 68. Have children say the names of *Bb, Mm,* and *Aa* and write each letter on the lines.

- **Game** Allow time for children to play Find the Letter, which is on the CD.

- **Little Book** Read *Two Boys* with children. Have them look for the letters *Bb, Mm,* and *Aa*.

Extend the Sort

Alternative Sort: Capital or Lowercase?

Have children re-sort the letters according to whether they are capital letters or lowercase letters. When all the letters are sorted, have children check their work by going through each pile and saying the name of each letter.

ELL English Language Learners

Pair English language learners with children who are proficient in the language. Have the English language learner pick a card and show it to his or her partner, who should say the letter slowly. The English language learner should then repeat the letter. Have partners use the same procedure for the remaining cards. Listen and provide guidance as necessary.

Teacher Tip

If children are having difficulty recognizing letters, have them trace letters on paper or on the board. Help children see they are writing the same letters regardless of how thick or curvy the letters appear to be. If possible, cut out capital and lowercase letters from this sort from a newspaper or magazine and demonstrate how to trace them with different writing tools.

52   Emergent-Early Letter Name

Objectives

- To recognize the letters *Rr, Ss,* and *Ee*
- To identify and sort different print styles and cases of *Rr, Ss,* and *Ee*

Letters	
Rr	**Ss**
4 variations of *R*	4 variations of *S*
4 variations of *r*	4 variations of *s*
Ee	
4 variations of *E*	
4 variations of *e*	

Materials for Emergent-Early Letter Name

Big Book of Rhymes, "Raindrop Song," page 35

Whiteboard Activities DVD-ROM, Sort 18

Teacher Resource CD-ROM, Sort 18 and Letter Eggs Game

Student Book, pages 69–72

Words Their Way Library, *My Red Room*

Introduce/Model
Small Groups

- **Read a Rhyme** Read "Raindrop Song" aloud, emphasizing the words that begin with *r, s,* and *e*. Then have children search the poem to find examples of capital and lowercase *Rr, Ss,* and *Ee*.

- **Model** Use the whiteboard DVD or the letter cards. Explain that children will sort the letters by their names. Select a capital and a lowercase *r* and ask children how the letters are different. Remind children that despite the differences, the letters are all named *r*. Continue with *s* and *e*. Help children sort and explain their sorts.

Practice the Sort
Independent/Partner

- Have children use the Student Book or whiteboard DVD to name the letters and use the grid to sort the cards by letter names.

- Have children check and explain their sorts.

Apply
Independent/Partner/Small Groups

- Read aloud the directions on Student Book p. 72. Have children say the names of *Rr, Ss,* and *Ee* and write each letter on the lines.

- **Game** Allow time for children to play Letter Eggs, which is on the CD.

- **Little Book** Read *My Red Room* with children. Have them look for the letters *Rr, Ss,* and *Ee*.

Extend the Sort

Alternative Sort: Capital or Lowercase?

Have children re-sort the letters according to whether they are capital letters or lowercase letters. When all the letters are sorted, have children check their work by going through each pile and saying the name of each letter.

ELL English Language Learners

Some children may have difficulty pronouncing the letters *s* and *r*. Model how to pronounce these letters. Say *r-r-red* and *s-s-see,* emphasizing the beginning sound in each. Exaggerate the movements of your mouth and teeth so children can see how the sounds are formed. Then have children pronounce the sounds by saying words along with you: *red, seal, read, sand, rat, sun.*

Teacher Tip

If children have difficulty distinguishing capital *s* from lowercase *s*, explain that some capital letters look the same as some lowercase letters. Capital letters are just larger. Explain that it is easier to recognize a capital letter when it is used in a sentence. For the sort, encourage them to place the letter cards side by side and compare them to find which ones are capitals.

Beginning Sounds *t, g*

Objectives
- To identify picture names beginning with the sounds of *t* and *g*
- To sort pictures by their beginning sound and associate each sound with the letter it represents

Materials for Emergent-Early Letter Name

📖 Big Book of Rhymes, "Tubby Turtle," page 37

🖥 Whiteboard Activities DVD-ROM, Sort 19

💿 Teacher Resource CD-ROM, Sort 19 and Bingo! Game

📓 Student Book, pages 73–76

📘 Words Their Way Library, *Nanny Goat's Nap*

Pictures

t	*g*
tie	gold
toes	gate
tooth	girl
tire	goose
top	game
toys	goat

Introduce/Model — *Small Groups*

- **Read a Rhyme** Read "Tubby Turtle" several times aloud. Have children identify the rhyming words *back, snack* and *lunch, bunch*. Then have children search the rhyme to find words that begin with the sound of *t* or *g*.

- **Model** Use the whiteboard DVD or the CD picture cards. Explain that children will sort the pictures by the beginning sounds of their names. Demonstrate how to sort the cards by the beginning sound *t* or *g*. Help children sort and explain their sorts.

Practice the Sort — *Independent/Partner*

- Have children use the Student Book or whiteboard DVD to name the pictures and use the grid to sort according to beginning sound *t* or *g*.

- Have children check and explain their sorts.

Apply — *Independent/Partner/Small Groups*

- Read aloud the directions on Student Book p. 76. Have children draw pictures of and write words for things that begin like *tiger* and *gum*.

- **Game** Allow time for children to play Bingo!, which is on the CD.

- **Little Book** Read *Nanny Goat's Nap* with children. Have them identify words that begin with /t/ or /g/.

Extend the Sort

Alternative Sort: Quiet or Not Quiet?

Have children re-sort cards according to whether the objects in the pictures make noise or do not make noise. After children have sorted their pictures, encourage them to describe the sound made by each object in their "make noise" group.

Vocabulary — Building Vocabulary

Children may not recognize the picture for *top*. Explain that the top in the picture is a kind of toy that spins. Remind children that the word *top* has other meanings too. Challenge them to talk about any other meanings they might know. (top of a table, top of a mountain, top athlete, bottle top)

ELL — English Language Learners

After helping children sort the words according to beginning sound, have them pronounce the picture names that begin with *t*. Check to be sure they are saying the sound for *t* rather than for *d*. To help them, have them hold their hands in front of their lips as they pronounce the words. Explain that they should feel a puff of air on their hands as they say the first sound in each word.

Objectives

- To identify picture names beginning with the sounds of *n* and *p*
- To sort pictures by their beginning sound and associate each sound with the letter it represents

Materials for Emergent-Early Letter Name

Big Book of Rhymes, "The Best Homes," page 39

Whiteboard Activities DVD-ROM, Sort 20

Teacher Resource CD-ROM, Sort 20 and Match It! Game

Student Book, pages 77–80

Words Their Way Library, *Where Is It?*

Pictures

n	p
nap	pie
net	pin
nose	peg
nest	pig
nail	pen
nurse	peach

Introduce/Model   *Small Groups*

- **Read a Rhyme** Read "The Best Homes" aloud with the class. Track the words that begin with the sound of *n* or *p* by pointing to them as you read. Then have children search the poem to find words that begin with the sound of *n* or *p*.

- **Model** Use the whiteboard DVD or the CD picture cards. Explain that children will sort the pictures by the beginning sounds of their names. Demonstrate how to sort the cards by the beginning sound *n* or *p*. Help children sort and explain their sorts.

Practice the Sort   *Independent/Partner*

- Have children use the Student Book or whiteboard DVD to name the pictures and use the grid to sort according to beginning sound *n* or *p*.

- Have children check and explain their sorts.

Apply   *Independent/Partner/Small Groups*

- Read aloud the directions on Student Book p. 80. Have children draw pictures of and write the words for things that begin like *nut* and *pot*.

- **Game** Allow time for children to play Match It!, which is on the CD.

- **Little Book** Read *Where Is It?* with children. Have them identify words that begin with /n/ or /p/.

Extend the Sort

Alternative Sort: Living or Nonliving?

Remove the picture card for *nest*. Then have children re-sort the remaining cards according to whether the cards show something that is living or not living.

Vocabulary Building Vocabulary

Write *pen*. Have children say the word with you several times. (Be sure they are not saying *pin*.) Explain that the word *pen* has more than one meaning. A pen is something you write with. It can also be a fenced area in which to keep animals. Ask children to draw a pig and then draw a pen around the pig.

Teacher Tip

Letter formation may be difficult for some children as they complete Student Book p. 80. Consider creating a chant or rhyme to help children remember the proper strokes to form each letter. While you should not expect perfection, you should encourage both proper handwriting techniques and attempts.

Beginning Sounds *t, g, n, p*

Objectives

- To identify picture names beginning with the sounds of *t, g, n,* and *p*
- To sort pictures by their beginning sound and associate each sound with the letter it represents

Materials for Emergent-Early Letter Name

📖 Big Book of Rhymes, "Go Away, Tiger!," page 41

🖥 Whiteboard Activities DVD-ROM, Sort 21

💿 Teacher Resource CD-ROM, Sort 21 and Around the Farm Game

📚 Student Book, pages 81–84

📗 Words Their Way Library, *Nanny Goat's Nap*

Pictures

t	g	n	p
tape	gas	nurse	pear
tire	goose	nail	pail
tan	goat	nest	pot
tub	game	neck	paint

Introduce/Model
Small Groups

- **Read a Rhyme** Read "Go Away, Tiger!" several times aloud. Track the words *tiger, pig, goat, needs,* and *go* by pointing to each word as you read. Have children search the poem to find examples of words that begin with the sound of *t, g, n,* or *p.*

- **Model** Use the whiteboard DVD or the CD picture cards. Explain that children will sort the pictures by the beginning sounds of their names. Demonstrate how to sort the cards by the beginning sound *t, g, n* and *p.* Help children sort and explain their sorts.

Practice the Sort
Independent/Partner

- Have children use the Student Book or whiteboard DVD to name the pictures and use the grid to sort according to beginning sound *t, g, n,* and *p.*

- Have children check and explain their sorts.

Apply
Independent/Partner/Small Groups

- Read aloud the directions on Student Book p. 84. Have children draw pictures of and write the words for things that begin like *tent, gum, net,* and *pig.*

- **Game** Allow time for children to play Around the Farm, which is on the CD.

- **Little Book** Read *Nanny Goat's Nap* with children. Have them identify words that begin with /t/, /g/, /n/, or /p/.

Extend the Sort

Alternative Sort: Living or Not Living?

Set aside the cards for *tan, neck,* and *paint.* Then have children re-sort the remaining cards according to whether the pictures show something that is living or something that is not living. (Students may need help determining which objects are living. Explain that living things breathe, eat, and grow.)

Vocabulary Building Vocabulary

Many children will see the card for *tan* and call it brown. Explain that colors have many different shades, and each color shade has its own name. *Tan* is a light brown. If possible, show pictures from magazines that have shades of brown.

ELL English Language Learners

Divide the class into pairs. Have one child pick a card and show it to his or her partner, who should say the word slowly. The first child should then repeat the word. Have pairs continue this process with the remaining cards. Listen and provide guidance as necessary.

Teacher Tip

If children have difficulty sorting a card by beginning sound, have them say the word with each picture name at the top of the grid: *tent, pear; gum, pear; net, pear; pig, pear.* This will help children match the beginning sounds.

Objectives

- To recognize the letters *Tt, Gg,* and *Ee*
- To identify and sort different print styles and cases of *Tt, Gg,* and *Ee*

Materials for Emergent-Early Letter Name

Big Book of Rhymes, "Eagles Fly," page 43

Whiteboard Activities DVD-ROM, Sort 22

Teacher Resource CD-ROM, Sort 22 and Letter Pair! Game

Student Book, pages 85–88

Words Their Way Library, *The Trip*

Letters	
Tt	**Gg**
4 variations of *T*	4 variations of *G*
4 variations of *t*	4 variations of *g*
Ee	
4 variations of *E*	
4 variations of *e*	

Introduce/Model
Small Groups

- **Read a Rhyme** Read "Eagles Fly," emphasizing the rhyming words *sky, by* and *breeze, trees*. Have children search the poem to find examples of capital and lowercase *Tt, Gg,* and *Ee*.

- **Model** Use the whiteboard DVD or the letter cards. Explain that children will sort the letters by their names. Select a capital and a lowercase *t,* and ask children how the letters are different. Remind children that despite the differences, the letters are all named *t*. Continue with *g* and *e*. Help children sort and explain their sorts.

Practice the Sort
Independent/Partner

- Have children use the Student Book or whiteboard DVD to name the letters and use the grid to sort the cards by letter names.

- Have children check and explain their sorts.

Apply
Independent/Partner/Small Groups

- Read aloud the directions on Student Book p. 88. Have children say the names of *Tt, Gg,* and *Ee* and write each letter on the lines.

- **Game** Allow time for children to play Letter Pair!, which is on the CD.

- **Little Book** Read *The Trip* with children. Have them look for the letters *Tt, Gg,* and *Ee*.

Extend the Sort

Alternative Sort: Capital or Lowercase?

Re-sort the letters into capital and lowercase categories. When you show a card, have children identify the letter by name and tell which category it belongs in. Continue until all the cards have been sorted.

ELL English Language Learners

Review the cards with children, naming each letter. Have children say the letter names after you. Show a T-shirt to children, spreading it out on a table or the floor. Ask children to guess how the shirt got its name. (from its T shape)

Teacher Tip

Assign one capital or lowercase letter to each child *(Tt, Gg, Ee)*. Ask children to look for their assigned letters after school as they ride home, eat dinner, and so on. The next day, let children take turns reporting the places where they saw their letter.

Letter Recognition *Nn, Pp, Ii*

Objectives

- To recognize the letters *Nn, Pp,* and *Ii*
- To identify and sort different print styles and cases of *Nn, Pp,* and *Ii*

Materials for Emergent-Early Letter Name

Big Book of Rhymes, "Greg Packs," page 45

Whiteboard Activities DVD-ROM, Sort 23

Teacher Resource CD-ROM, Sort 23 and Match the Letters Game

Student Book, pages 89–92

Words Their Way Library, *Pin It*

Letters	
Nn	***Pp***
4 variations of *N*	4 variations of *P*
4 variations of *n*	4 variations of *p*
Ii	
4 variations of *I*	
4 variations of *i*	

Introduce/Model   *Small Groups*

- **Read a Rhyme** Read "Greg Packs" several times until children become familiar with the rhyme. Guide children to identify the rhyming words *trip/skip, red/sled,* and *crushes/brushes*. Have children search the poem for examples of capital and lowercase *Nn, Pp,* and *Ii*.

- **Model** Use the whiteboard DVD or the letter cards. Explain that children will sort the letters by their names. Select a capital and lowercase *n*, and ask children how the letters are different. Remind children that despite the differences, the letters are all named *n*. Continue with *p* and *i*. Help children sort and explain their sorts.

Practice the Sort   *Independent/Partner*

- Have children use the Student Book or whiteboard DVD to name the letters and use the grid to sort the cards by letter names.

- Have children check and explain their sorts.

Apply   *Independent/Partner/Small Groups*

- Read aloud the directions on Student Book p. 92. Have children say the names of *Nn, Pp,* and *Ii* and write each letter on the lines.

- **Game** Allow time for children to play Match the Letters, which is on the CD.

- **Little Book** Read *Pin It* with children. Have them look for the letters *Nn, Pp,* and *Ii*.

Extend the Sort

Alternative Sort: Capital or Lowercase?

Have children sit on the floor next to a chair. Have them re-sort their letters into two groups, putting the lowercase letters into a "lower" pile on the floor and the capital, or uppercase, letters into an "upper" pile on the chair.

ELL English Language Learners

Review the cards by having children repeat the letter names after you. Then use "Greg Packs" to practice pronunciation. Say the first line and have children say it after you. Continue through the entire poem. Spend extra time on the words that have the letters *Nn, Pp,* and *Ii*.

Teacher Tip

Periodically review letters from previous weeks. Have children work with a partner. One child writes a letter and the other child says the letter name. Then the partners reverse roles.

Beginning Sounds *c, h*

Sort 24

Objectives

- To identify picture names beginning with the sounds of *c* and *h*
- To sort pictures by their beginning sound and associate each sound with the letter it represents

Materials for Emergent-Early Letter Name

Big Book of Rhymes, "Farm Friends," page 47

Whiteboard Activities DVD-ROM, Sort 24

Teacher Resource CD-ROM, Sort 24 and Find the Picture Game

Student Book, pages 93–96

Words Their Way Library, *A Cat and a Hat*

Pictures

c	h
can	hand
cat	ham
cow	hay
cart	horse
cape	hot
comb	hat

Introduce/Model
Small Groups

- **Read a Rhyme** Read "Farm Friends" several times, emphasizing the rhyming words. *(see/be, too/few, guess/yes)* Then have children search the poem to find words that begin with the sound of either *c* or *h*.

- **Model** Use the whiteboard DVD or the CD picture cards. Explain that children will sort the pictures by the beginning sounds of their names. Demonstrate how to sort *can* and *hand*. Help children sort and explain their sorts.

Practice the Sort
Independent/Partner

- Have children use the Student Book or whiteboard DVD to name the pictures and use the grid to sort the cards by their beginning sound.

- Have children check and explain their sorts.

Apply
Independent/Partner/Small Groups

- Read aloud the directions on Student Book p. 96. Have children work independently or with a partner to write words and draw pictures of things whose names begin like *cup* and *hen*.

- **Game** Allow time for children to play Find the Picture, which is on the CD.

- **Little Book** Read *A Cat and a Hat* with children. Have them identify the words that begin with c/k/ or /h/ and words that rhyme.

Extend the Sort

Alternative Sort: On a Farm

Once they are comfortable completing the week's sort, lead children into another sort. Have children sort the pictures into things they might see on a farm and things they probably would not see on a farm. Encourage children to explain their reasoning.

Vocabulary Building Vocabulary

If children are unfamiliar with the word *cape*, explain that it is a type of coat that doesn't have sleeves and is fastened at the neck. Discuss with children how the picture card for *cape* might help them understand the word's meaning.

ELL English Language Learners

Model how to correctly pronounce the beginning sound of *c* as in *cup*. Teach children how to exhale and squeeze their abdominal muscles in order to emphasize the sound. As children focus on the pronunciation of one sound, such as that for *c,* ignore incorrect pronunciations of other sounds.

Teacher Tip

Listen as children complete the sorting activities. Check their pronunciations and their ability to isolate and discriminate among the beginning sounds in the sort.

Emergent-Early Letter Name 59

Beginning Sounds *f, d*

Objectives

- To identify picture names beginning with the sounds of *f* and *d*
- To sort pictures by their beginning sound and associate each sound with the letter it represents

Materials for Emergent-Early Letter Name

Big Book of Rhymes, "Dancing Clown," page 49

Whiteboard Activities DVD-ROM, Sort 25

Teacher Resource CD-ROM, Sort 25 and Pair It Game

Student Book, pages 97–100

Words Their Way Library, *Funny Faces and Funny Places*

Pictures

f	*d*
fish	deer
fire	desk
fan	duck
fox	doll
foot	dog
feather	dive

Introduce/Model *Small Groups*

- **Read a Rhyme** Read "Dancing Clown" several times until children become familiar with the rhyme. Then have children search the poem for words that begin with the sound of either *f* or *d*.
- **Model** Use the whiteboard DVD or the CD picture cards. Explain that children will sort the pictures by the beginning sounds of their names. Demonstrate how to sort *fish* and *deer*. Help children sort and explain their sorts.

Practice the Sort *Independent/Partner*

- Have children use the Student Book or whiteboard DVD to name the pictures and use the grid to sort the cards by their beginning sound.
- Have children check and explain their sorts.

Apply *Independent/Partner/Small Groups*

- Read aloud the directions on Student Book p. 100. Have children work independently or with a partner to write words and draw pictures of things whose names begin like *fork* and *dime*.
- **Game** Allow time for children to play Pair It, which is on the CD.
- **Little Book** Read *Funny Faces and Funny Places* with children. Have them identify words that begin with /f/ or /d/.

Extend the Sort

Alternative Sort: Animals All Around

Re-sort the cards into pictures of animals and pictures of other things. Then say other words that begin with *f* or *d*, such as *fence, ferret, dolphin,* and *dish,* and ask children to tell which category they belong in.

ELL English Language Learners

When introducing the pictures for this week's sort, use each word in a sentence. Have children repeat the word and your example sentence and then use the word in a sentence of their own.

Vocabulary Building Vocabulary

Some children may think that the *fox* picture card shows a dog. Explain that a fox is similar to a dog, but a fox is a wild animal. Encourage children who have seen foxes at a zoo or in the wild to share their experiences.

Teacher Tip

Encourage children to brainstorm other words that begin with *f* or *d*. Invite them to draw pictures of the words and incorporate them into the sort.

Objectives
- To identify picture names beginning with the sounds of *c, h, f,* and *d*
- To sort pictures by their beginning sound and associate each sound with the letter it represents

Materials for Emergent-Early Letter Name

- Big Book of Rhymes, "The Cook," page 51
- Whiteboard Activities DVD-ROM, Sort 26
- Teacher Resource CD-ROM, Sort 26 and Hop to It! Game
- Student Book, pages 101–104
- Words Their Way Library, *Up They Go*

Pictures

c	h	f	d
corn	hose	five	door
cow	house	four	desk
cake	horn	fan	doll
coat	hill	fish	dog

Introduce/Model *Small Groups*

- **Read a Rhyme** Read "The Cook" several times. Track the text by pointing to each word. Guide children to identify the rhyming words. *(dish/wish, bake/cake)* Then have them search the poem for words that begin with the sound of *c, h, f,* or *d*.

- **Model** Use the whiteboard DVD or the CD picture cards. Explain that children will sort the pictures by the beginning sounds of their names. Demonstrate how to sort *corn, door, five,* and *hose*. Help children sort and explain their sorts.

Practice the Sort *Independent/Partner*

- Have children use the Student Book or whiteboard DVD to name the pictures and use the grid to sort the cards by their beginning sound.

- Have children check and explain their sorts.

Apply *Independent/Partner/Small Groups*

- Read aloud the directions on Student Book p. 104. Have children work independently or with a partner to write words and draw pictures of things whose names begin like *cup, hen, fork,* and *dime*.

- **Game** Allow time for children to play Hop to It!, which is on the CD.

- **Little Book** Read *Up They Go* with children. Have them identify words that begin with c/k/, /h/, /f/, or /d/.

Extend the Sort

Alternative Sort: Eyes or No Eyes?

Ask children to sort the cards into pictures of animals or objects that have eyes and pictures of other things. Then say other words that begin with the sounds of the letters *c, h, f,* and *d,* such as *food, cat, horse,* and *deck,* and ask children to tell which category they belong in.

ELL English Language Learners

When introducing the pictures for this week's sort, use each word in a sentence. Have children repeat the word and your example sentence and then use the word in a sentence of their own.

Vocabulary Building Vocabulary

Use groups of crayons or other small objects to demonstrate the numbers *four* and *five*. Count the objects in each group aloud and have the class repeat after you. Label the groups with the words *four* and *five*. Then encourage children to find groups of four or five objects in the classroom.

Teacher Tip

Encourage children to brainstorm other words that begin with the sounds of the letters *c, h, f,* and *d*. Have them draw pictures for the words and say the words aloud to the class.

Objectives

- To recognize the letters *Cc, Hh,* and *Ii*
- To identify and sort different print styles and cases of *Cc, Hh,* and *Ii*

Materials for Emergent-Early Letter Name

📖 Big Book of Rhymes, "Time Talk," page 53

🖥 Whiteboard Activities DVD-ROM, Sort 27

💿 Teacher Resource CD-ROM, Sort 27 and Home Run! Game

📕 Student Book, pages 105–108

📖 Words Their Way Library, *Cat's Trip*

Letters	
Cc	***Hh***
4 variations of *C*	4 variations of *H*
4 variations of *c*	4 variations of *h*
Ii	
4 variations of *I*	
4 variations of *i*	

Introduce/Model   *Small Groups*

- **Read a Rhyme** Read "Time Talk" emphasizing the rhyming words *too/do, quick/tick,* and *chime/time.* Have children raise their hands when they hear words that rhyme. Then have them search the poem for examples of capital and lowercase *Cc, Hh,* and *Ii.*

- **Model** Use the whiteboard DVD or the letter cards. Explain that children will sort the letters by their names. Select a capital and lowercase *c,* and ask children how the letters are different. Remind children that despite the differences, the letters are all named *c.* Continue with *h* and *i.* Help children sort and explain their sorts.

Practice the Sort   *Independent/Partner*

- Have children use the Student Book or whiteboard DVD to name the letters and use the grid to sort the cards by letter names.

- Have children check and explain their sorts.

Apply   *Independent/Partner/Small Groups*

- Read aloud the directions on Student Book p. 108. Have children say the names of *Cc, Hh,* and *Ii* and write each letter on the lines.

- **Game** Allow time for children to play Home Run!, which is on the CD.

- **Little Book** Read *Cat's Trip* with children. Have them look for the letters *Cc, Hh,* and *Ii.*

Extend the Sort

Alternative Sort: Straight or Curved?

Have children re-sort their letter cards, putting letters with straight lines in one group *(H, h, I, i)* and letters with curved lines *(C, c, h)* in another group. Help children recognize that lowercase *h* goes in both groups. Ask them to explain why.

ELL English Language Learners

Review the cards with children. Show each card and name the letter. Then repeat the process, but have children name the letters. Be sure children have their mouths positioned correctly as they say the letter names.

Teacher Tip

If children are having problems identifying or forming the letters correctly, try providing tactile experiences. For example, let children use their fingers to trace letters cut from sandpaper. Encourage them to describe the shape of each letter as they trace it.

Objectives

- To recognize the letters *Ff, Dd,* and *Aa*
- To identify and sort different print styles and cases of *Ff, Dd,* and *Aa*

Materials for Emergent-Early Letter Name

- Big Book of Rhymes, "The River Frog," page 27
- Whiteboard Activities DVD-ROM, Sort 28
- Teacher Resource CD-ROM, Sort 28 and Letter Spin Game
- Student Book, pages 109–112
- Words Their Way Library, *Cat's Trip*

Letters	
Ff	**Dd**
4 variations of *F*	4 variations of *D*
4 variations of *f*	4 variations of *d*
Aa	
4 variations of *A*	
4 variations of *a*	

Introduce/Model *Small Groups*

- **Read a Rhyme** Read "The River Frog" several times. Track the text by pointing to each word. Ask volunteers to track specific words, such as *frog, log, gray,* and *day*. Then have children search the poem for examples of capital and lowercase *Ff, Dd,* and *Aa*.

- **Model** Use the whiteboard DVD or the letter cards. Explain that children will sort the letters by their names. Select a capital and lowercase *f,* and ask children how the letters are different. Remind children that despite the differences, the letters are all named *f*. Continue with *d* and *a*. Help children sort and explain their sorts.

Practice the Sort *Independent/Partner*

- Have children use the Student Book or whiteboard DVD to name the letters and use the grid to sort the cards by letter names.

- Have children check and explain their sorts.

Apply *Independent/Partner/Small Groups*

- Read aloud the directions on Student Book p. 112. Have children say the names of *Ff, Dd,* and *Aa* and write each letter on the lines.

- **Game** Allow time for children to play Letter Spin, which is on the CD.

- **Little Book** Read *Cat's Trip* with children. Have them look for the letters *Ff, Dd,* and *Aa*.

Extend the Sort

Alternative Sort: The Starting Point

To reinforce the idea that proper names begin with capital letters, suggest that children re-sort their cards into two categories according to whether or not you would find the letter at the beginning of a person's name. Show each letter, ask the question, and have children answer *yes* or *no*.

ELL English Language Learners

Bring several recipes to class, printed on recipe cards. Share the recipes with children. Have them practice conversation by talking about their favorite dishes. Then help children review the letter cards by naming the letters, one by one, and looking for the letters on the recipe cards.

Teacher Tip

Have children search their classmates' names for the letters *Ff, Dd,* and *Aa*. Keep track of which letters are found in which names, and save the results to use later in Sorts 32 and 33.

Beginning Sounds *l, k*

Objectives

- To identify picture names beginning with the sounds of *l* and *k*
- To sort pictures by their beginning sound and associate each sound with the letter it represents

Materials for Emergent-Early Letter Name

- Big Book of Rhymes, "Four Little Kittens," page 21

- Whiteboard Activities DVD-ROM, Sort 29

- Teacher Resource CD-ROM, Sort 29 and Kittens in the Kitchen Game

- Student Book, pages 113–116

- Words Their Way Library, *Little Kittens*

Pictures

l	*k*
lips	kite
lizard	kitten
lamp	kitchen
leaf	kangaroo
lock	key
lion	king

Introduce/Model
Small Groups

- **Read a Rhyme** Read "Four Little Kittens" several times. Ask volunteers to track specific words such as *kitten* and *lazy*. When children have demonstrated they can track accurately, have them search the poem for other words that begin with the sound of *l* or *k*.

- **Model** Use the whiteboard DVD or the CD picture cards. Explain that children will sort the pictures by the beginning sounds of their names. Demonstrate how to sort *lips* and *kite*. Help children sort and explain their sorts.

Practice the Sort
Independent/Partner

- Have children use the Student Book or whiteboard DVD to name the pictures and use the grid to sort the cards by their beginning sound.

- Have children check and explain their sorts.

Apply
Independent/Partner/Small Groups

- Read aloud the directions on Student Book p. 116. Have children work independently or with a partner to write words and draw pictures of things whose names begin like *log* and *kick*.

- **Game** Allow time for children to play Kittens in the Kitchen, which is on the CD.

- **Little Book** Read *Little Kittens* with children. Have them identify words that begin with /l/ or /k/.

Extend the Sort

Alternative Sort: Up So High

Ask children to say each picture name and decide whether it names something they might see up high. If it does, have them put the card in one group. If it does not, have them put the card in another group. Encourage children to explain their reasoning.

ELL English Language Learners

Ask children to say the word *lamp*. Tell them that to pronounce the *l,* they should put the tip of their tongue on the roof of their mouth right behind the top teeth and let air pass around the tongue.

Vocabulary Building Vocabulary

Children may have trouble determining which picture card shows a *lock* and which shows a *key*. Explain that a lock is something that keeps a door, lid, or other object fastened, and a key is something that lets you open a lock.

Teacher Tip

Make a clear distinction between letter names and letter sounds. Point out that sometimes the letter name can give you a clue to the letter sound. For example, the sound of *k* is heard at the beginning of the letter name.

Beginning Sounds *j, w, q*

Objectives

- To identify picture names beginning with the sounds of *j, w,* and *q*
- To sort pictures by their beginning sound and associate each sound with the letter it represents

Materials for Emergent-Early Letter Name

- Big Book of Rhymes, "My Jeans," page 55
- Whiteboard Activities DVD-ROM, Sort 30
- Teacher Resource CD-ROM, Sort 30 and Bingo! Game
- Student Book, pages 117–120
- Words Their Way Library, *For Sale*

Pictures

j	*w*
jar	wing
jacket	web
jeans	wave
jet	wagon
jump	wig

q
quilt
quack
question
quarter
quiet

Introduce/Model   *Small Groups*

- **Read a Rhyme** Read "My Jeans" several times until children become familiar with the rhyme. Have children raise their hands when they hear rhyming words. *(yesterday/way, quick/pick)* Then have them search the poem for words that begin with the sound of *j, w,* or *q*.

- **Model** Use the whiteboard DVD or the CD picture cards. Explain that children will sort the pictures by the beginning sounds of their names. Demonstrate how to sort *jar, wing,* and *quilt*. Help children sort and explain their sorts.

Practice the Sort   *Independent/Partner*

- Have children use the Student Book or whiteboard DVD to name the pictures and use the grid to sort the cards by their beginning sounds.

- Have children check and explain their sorts.

Apply   *Independent/Partner/Small Groups*

- Read aloud the directions on Student Book p. 120. Have children work independently or with a partner to write words and draw pictures of things whose names begin like *jeep, watch,* and *queen*.

- **Game** Allow time for children to play Bingo!, which is on the CD.

- **Little Book** Read *For Sale* with children. Have them identify words that begin with /j/ or /w/.

Extend the Sort

Alternative Sort: Handheld

Ask children to sort the cards into pictures of things that can be held with one or two hands and pictures of things that can't be held.

ELL English Language Learners

English language learners may assume that words such as *queen* and *quack* begin with the letter *k*. Point out that the beginning sound in words beginning with *q* is actually /kw/. Read aloud the names of the picture cards that begin with *q*, drawing out the beginning sound. Have children repeat after you.

Vocabulary Building Vocabulary

Help children understand the meaning of the word *question* by explaining that a question is a sentence that asks something. Display the *question* picture card, and tell children that it shows a question mark—a punctuation mark that is always put at the end of a question.

Teacher Tip

Encourage children to play a form of "I Spy" by looking for the letters *j, w,* and *q* and listening for their sounds as they travel to and from school. Ask children to describe what they saw or heard.

Beginning Sounds *l, k, j, w*

Objectives

- To identify picture names beginning with the sounds of *l, k, j,* and *w*
- To sort pictures by their beginning sound and associate each sound with the letter it represents

Materials for Emergent-Early Letter Name

Big Book of Rhymes, "Peg and Ken," page 57

Whiteboard Activities DVD-ROM, Sort 31

Teacher Resource CD-ROM, Sort 31 and Sound It Out Game

Student Book, pages 121–124

Words Their Way Library, *For Sale*

Pictures

l	*k*
leash	kangaroo
leg	kitten
laugh	kick
lap	kite
j	*w*
jack	well
jump	wag
jog	window
jump rope	wet

Introduce/Model　　　*Small Groups*

- **Read a Rhyme** Read "Peg and Ken" several times until children become familiar with the rhyme. Then reread and call on volunteers to track specific words such as *lake, Ken, jumped,* and *wet*. When children have demonstrated they can track accurately, have them search the poem for words that begin with the sound of *l, k, j,* or *w*.

- **Model** Use the whiteboard DVD or the CD picture cards. Explain that children will sort the pictures by the beginning sounds of their names. Demonstrate how to sort *leash, well, kangaroo,* and *jack*. Help children sort and explain their sorts.

Practice the Sort　　　*Independent/Partner*

- Have children use the Student Book or whiteboard DVD to name the pictures and use the grid to sort the cards by their beginning sounds.

- Have children check and explain their sorts.

Apply　　　*Independent/Partner/Small Groups*

- Read aloud the directions on Student Book p. 124. Have children work independently or with a partner to write words and draw pictures of things whose names begin like *lamp, key, jar,* and *watch*.

- **Game** Allow time for children to play Sound It Out, which is on the CD.

- **Little Book** Read *For Sale* with children. Have them identify words that begin with /l/, /k/, /j/, or /w/.

Extend the Sort

Alternative Sort: People

Remove the cards for *leg* and *kick*. Ask children to sort the remaining cards into pictures that show people and pictures that do not show people.

ELL English Language Learners

Ask children to say the word *king*. Tell children that to pronounce the *k*, they should put the back of their tongue on the roof of their mouth.

Vocabulary Building Vocabulary

Children may mistake the *kitten* picture card for *cat*. Remind them that a kitten is a very young cat whose name begins with a *k* sound. Ask children if they have kittens at home, and if so, to describe them.

Teacher Tip

Remind children that sometimes the letter names can give you a clue to the letter sounds. For example, the sound of *l* is heard at the end of the letter name.

Objectives

- To recognize the letters *Ll, Kk,* and *Oo*
- To identify and sort different print styles and cases of *Ll, Kk,* and *Oo*

Materials for Emergent-Early Letter Name

Big Book of Rhymes, "Things to Do," page 59

Whiteboard Activities DVD-ROM, Sort 32

Tacher Resource CD-ROM, Sort 32 and Letter Soup Game

Student Book, pages 125–128

Words Their Way Library, *Little Kittens*

Letters	
Ll	*Kk*
4 variations of *L*	4 variations of *K*
4 variations of *l*	4 variations of *k*
Oo	
4 variations of *O*	
4 variations of *o*	

Introduce/Model — *Small Groups*

- **Read a Rhyme** Read "Things to Do" several times until children become familiar with the rhyme. Track the text by pointing to each word. Have volunteers track specific words such as *Let, Kids,* and *on*. Then have children search the rhyme for examples of capital and lowercase *Ll, Kk,* and *Oo*.

- **Model** Use the whiteboard DVD or the letter cards. Explain that children will sort the letters by their names. Select a capital and lowercase *l,* and ask children how the letters are different. Remind children that despite the differences, the letters are all named *l*. Continue with *k* and *o*. Help children sort and explain their sorts.

Practice the Sort — *Independent/Partner*

- Have children use the Student Book or whiteboard DVD to name the letters and use the grid to sort the cards by letter names.

- Have children check and explain their sorts.

Apply — *Independent/Partner/Small Groups*

- Read aloud the directions on Student Book p. 128. Have children say the names of *Ll, Kk,* and *Oo* and write each letter on the lines.

- **Game** Allow time for children to play Letter Soup, which is on the CD.

- **Little Book** Read *Little Kittens* with children. Have them look for the letters *Ll, Kk,* and *Oo*.

Extend the Sort

Alternative Sort: Capital and Lowercase

Suggest that children re-sort their cards into two piles. One pile should have only capital letters. The other pile should have only lowercase letters. When all the cards have been sorted, have children check their sort by going through each pile and naming the letters.

ELL English Language Learners

Reread "Things to Do" with children. Help children practice conversation by talking about things they do on their own or with friends. If children use words with initial letters *k, l,* or *o* in conversation, write the words on the board, grouped by initial letter, and have children pronounce the words with you.

Teacher Tip

Review the results from the Teacher Tip activity in Sort 28. Have children search their classmates' names for the letters *Ll, Kk,* and *Oo*. Keep track of which letters are found in which names, add them to the earlier results, and save them for Sort 33.

Objectives
- To recognize the letters *Jj, Ww,* and *Qq*
- To identify and sort different print styles and cases of *Jj, Ww,* and *Qq*

Materials for Emergent-Early Letter Name

Big Book of Rhymes, "Jogging," page 61

Whiteboard Activities DVD-ROM, Sort 33

Teacher Resource CD-ROM, Sort 33 and Alphabet Squares Game

Student Book, pages 129–132

Words Their Way Library, *Quack!*

Letters	
Jj	*Ww*
4 variations of *J*	4 variations of *W*
4 variations of *j*	4 variations of *w*
Qq	
4 variations of *Q*	
4 variations of *q*	

Introduce/Model   *Small Groups*

- **Read a Rhyme** Read "Jogging" several times until children become familiar with the rhyme. Have volunteers track specific words, such as *jog, wanted,* and *Quickly*. When children have shown they can track accurately, have them search the poem for examples of capital and lowercase *Jj, Ww,* and *Qq*.

- **Model** Use the whiteboard DVD or the letter cards. Explain that children will sort the letters by their names. Select a capital and lowercase *j*, and ask children how the letters are different. Remind children that despite the differences, the letters are all named *j*. Continue with *w* and *q*. Help children sort and explain their sorts.

Practice the Sort   *Independent/Partner*

- Have children use the Student Book or whiteboard DVD to name the letters and use the grid to sort the cards by letter names.

- Have children check and explain their sorts.

Apply   *Independent/Partner/Small Groups*

- Read aloud the directions on Student Book p. 132. Have children say the names of *Jj, Ww,* and *Qq* and write each letter on the lines.

- **Game** Allow time for children to play Alphabet Squares, which is on the CD.

- **Little Book** Read *Quack!* with children. Have them look for the letters *Jj, Ww,* and *Qq*. Ask children which page has the most *q*'s.

Extend the Sort

Alternative Sort: At the Beginning

Remind children that proper names begin with capital letters. Ask children to re-sort their letter cards depending on whether they answer *yes* or *no* to the following question about the letter: "Will you find this letter at the beginning of a person's name?" After children have sorted all the letters, have them give examples of names and words that begin with each letter.

ELL English Language Learners

Stack the letter cards face down. Ask children to guess the letter on the top card. Check pronunciation as children make their guesses. Turn over the card to see who guessed correctly. Continue with the other cards.

Teacher Tip

Review the results from the Teacher Tip activities in Sorts 28 and 32. Have children search their classmates' names for the letters *Jj, Ww,* and *Qq*. Keep track of which letters are found in which names, add them to the earlier findings, and then present all the results to children.

Beginning Sounds *y, z, v*

Objectives
- To identify picture names beginning with the sounds of *y, z,* and *v*
- To sort pictures by their beginning sound and associate each sound with the letter it represents

Materials for Emergent-Early Letter Name

Big Book of Rhymes, "Seeing Yellow," page 63

Whiteboard Activities DVD-ROM, Sort 34

Teacher Resource CD-ROM, Sort 34 and Concentration Game

Student Book, pages 133–136

Words Their Way Library, *Zebra's Yellow Van*

Pictures

y	z	v
yell	zoo	vest
yarn	zebra	van
yogurt	zero	vine
yo-yo	zucchini	violin
yard	zigzag	vase

Introduce/Model
Small Groups

- **Read a Rhyme** Read "Seeing Yellow" several times until children become familiar with the rhyme. Call on volunteers to track specific words, such as *yellow, zips,* and *van*. When children have demonstrated they can track accurately, have them search the poem for words that begin with the sound of *y, z,* or *v*.

- **Model** Use the whiteboard DVD or the CD picture cards. Explain that children will sort the pictures by the beginning sounds of their names. Demonstrate how to sort *vest, yell,* and *zoo*. Help children sort and explain their sorts.

Practice the Sort
Independent/Partner

- Have children use the Student Book or whiteboard DVD to name the pictures and use the grid to sort the cards by their beginning sound.

- Have children check and explain their sorts.

Apply
Independent/Partner/Small Groups

- Read aloud the directions on Student Book p. 136. Have children work independently or with a partner to write words and draw pictures of things whose names begin like *yawn, zipper,* and *volcano*.

- **Game** Allow time for children to play Concentration, which is on the CD.

- **Little Book** Read *Zebra's Yellow Van* with children. Have them identify words that begin with /y/, /z/, or /v/.

Extend the Sort

Alternative Sort: Beats in a Word

Have children re-sort the words according to the number of beats—one, two, or three—in each word. Say each picture name with children, clapping each beat as you do so.

ELL English Language Learners

Use a different technique to have children complete the sort. Model how to say *yawn,* the first picture name on the grid. Go through the cards, saying each picture name and having children listen only for words that have the same beginning sound as *yawn*. Continue with *zipper* and *volcano*.

Vocabulary Building Vocabulary

Children may confuse a *zucchini* with a cucumber, or they may not be familiar with zucchini at all. Explain that a zucchini is a kind of vegetable called a squash. Encourage children who have eaten zucchini to describe what it tastes like.

Teacher Tip

Children may benefit from a tactile experience. Provide pencils, toothpicks, or other straight objects. Encourage children to use the objects to create letters whose sounds are represented in the sort. Ask children to identify each letter by its name and sound.

Objectives

- To identify picture names ending with the sounds of *t* and *x*
- To sort pictures by their ending sound and associate each sound with the letter it represents

Materials for Emergent-Early Letter Name

Big Book of Rhymes, "Fox in a Box," page 23

Whiteboard Activities DVD-ROM, Sort 35

Teacher Resource CD-ROM, Sort 35 and Find the Picture Game

Student Book, pages 137–140

Words Their Way Library, *Fix It, Fox*

Pictures

t	*x*
hit	fox
jet	ox
pot	six
cat	wax
sit	box
dot	mix

Introduce/Model
Small Groups

- **Read a Rhyme** Read "Fox in a Box" several times until children become familiar with the rhyme. Call on volunteers to track specific words such as *box* and *cat*. When children have demonstrated they can track accurately, have them search the rhyme for words that end with the sound of either *t* or *x*.

- **Model** Use the whiteboard DVD or the CD picture cards. Explain that children will sort the pictures by the ending sounds of their names. Demonstrate how to sort *hit* and *fox*. Help children sort and explain their sorts.

Practice the Sort
Independent/Partner

- Have children use the Student Book or whiteboard DVD to name the pictures and use the grid to sort the cards by their ending sounds.

- Have children check and explain their sorts.

Apply
Independent/Partner/Small Groups

- Read aloud the directions on Student Book p. 140. Have children work independently or with a partner to write the letters and draw pictures of things whose names end like *bat* and *ax*.

- **Game** Allow time for children to play Find the Picture, which is on the CD.

- **Little Book** Read *Fix It, Fox* with children. Have them identify words that end with /t/ or x/ks/.

Extend the Sort

Alternative Sort: Living or Nonliving

Set aside the cards for *sit, hit,* and *mix*. Then have children re-sort the pictures into groups of living and nonliving things. Sort two or three of the pictures into the categories. When you pick up the next picture, have children tell where it will go. Continue until all the pictures have been sorted.

Vocabulary | Building Vocabulary

Some children may not be familiar with oxen. Explain that an *ox* is a large animal that is often used on farms to pull heavy loads or to do hard work. Tell children that two or more of these animals are called *oxen*.

Teacher Tip

To provide additional practice with ending sounds *t* and *x*, say pairs of words that end with these sounds. Tell children to stand if both words end with the same sound and to stay seated if they do not. Use word pairs such as *fox, six; cut, ax; hot, mat;* and so on.

Monitor Progress Spell Check 2

After completing Sort 35, administer Spell Check 2. See page 35 in this Teacher Resource Guide for instructions.

Letter Recognition *Yy, Zz, Vv*

Objectives
- To recognize the letters *Yy, Zz,* and *Vv*
- To identify and sort different print styles and cases of *Yy, Zz,* and *Vv*

Materials for Emergent-Early Letter Name

📘 Big Book of Rhymes, "Come to the Zoo," page 7

📺 Whiteboard Activities DVD-ROM, Sort 36

💿 Teacher Resource CD-ROM, Sort 36 and Fishing for Letters Game

📓 Student Book, pages 141–144

📖 Words Their Way Library, *Zebra's Yellow Van*

Letters

Yy	*Zz*
4 variations of *Y*	4 variations of *Z*
4 variations of *y*	4 variations of *z*

Vv
4 variations of *V*
4 variations of *v*

Introduce/Model   *Small Groups*

- **Read a Rhyme** Read "Come to the Zoo" several times until children become familiar with the rhyme. Call on volunteers to track specific words, such as *yaks, kangaroo,* and *zebra.* When children have shown they can track accurately, have them search the rhyme for examples of capital and lowercase *Yy, Zz,* and *Vv.*

- **Model** Use the whiteboard DVD or the letter cards. Explain that children will sort the letters by their names. Select a capital and lowercase *y,* and ask children how the letters are different. Remind children that despite the differences, the letters are all named *y.* Continue with *z* and *v.* Help children sort and explain their sorts.

Practice the Sort   *Independent/Partner*

- Have children use the Student Book or whiteboard DVD to name the letters and use the grid to sort the cards by letter names.

- Have children check and explain their sorts.

Apply   *Independent/Partner/Small Groups*

- Read aloud the directions on Student Book p. 144. Have children say the names of *Yy, Zz,* and *Vv* and write each letter on the lines.

- **Game** Allow time for children to play Fishing for Letters, which is on the CD.

- **Little Book** Read *Zebra's Yellow Van* with children. Have them look for the letters *Yy, Zz,* and *Vv.*

Extend the Sort

Alternative Sort: How Many Lines?

Have children re-sort the cards into two groups: letters that are made by drawing two lines (*V, v, y*) and letters that are made by drawing three lines (*Y, Z, z*). Have children practice tracing the letters and counting the lines.

ELL English Language Learners

Write a name that contains both forms of a letter, such as *Adam* or *Susan.* Circle the capital and lowercase letter pair. Point out that though the first letter is a capital letter and the second letter is lowercase, they both have the same letter name.

Teacher Tip

Provide a tray of salt or sand. Encourage children to trace each letter in the salt or sand while saying the letter name several times. Have children use the letter cards as guides.

Sort 37
Letter Recognition *Tt, Xx, Uu*

Objectives
- To recognize the letters *Tt, Xx,* and *Uu*
- To identify and sort different print styles and cases of *Tt, Xx,* and *Uu*

Materials for Emergent-Early Letter Name

Big Book of Rhymes, "Billy's Toy Box," page 25

Whiteboard Activities DVD-ROM, Sort 37

Teacher Resource CD-ROM, Sort 37 and Call the Letter Game

Student Book, pages 145–148

Words Their Way Library, *Cat's Trip*

Letters	
Tt	*Xx*
4 variations of *T*	4 variations of *X*
4 variations of *t*	4 variations of *x*
Uu	
4 variations of *U*	
4 variations of *u*	

Introduce/Model
Small Groups

- **Read a Rhyme** Read "Billy's Toy Box" several times until children become familiar with the rhyme. Call on volunteers to track specific words, such as *takes, toys,* and *teddy.* When children have shown they can track accurately, have them search the rhyme for examples of capital and lowercase *Tt, Xx,* and *Uu.*

- **Model** Use the whiteboard DVD or the letter cards. Explain that children will sort the letters by their names. Select a capital and lowercase *t,* and ask children how the letters are different. Remind children that despite the differences, the letters are all named *t.* Continue with *x* and *u.* Help children sort and explain their sorts.

Practice the Sort
Independent/Partner

- Have children use the Student Book or whiteboard DVD to name the letters and use the grid to sort the cards by letter names.

- Have children check and explain their sorts.

Apply
Independent/Partner/Small Groups

- Read aloud the directions on Student Book p. 148. Have children say the names of *Tt, Xx,* and *Uu* and write each letter on the lines.

- **Game** Allow time for children to play Call the Letter, which is on the CD.

- **Little Book** Read *Cat's Trip* with children. Have them look for the letters *Tt, Xx,* and *Uu.*

Extend the Sort

Alternative Sort: Vowel or Not?
Discuss the concept of vowels. Explain that while only five letters are vowels, they are important because every word contains at least one vowel. Point out that the letter *u* is a vowel. Have children re-sort their cards into two piles according to whether or not the letter is a vowel.

ELL English Language Learners
Review vocabulary from "Billy's Toy Box." Discuss the toys in the rhyme—truck, blocks, teddy bear— with children and ask them to find these toys in the illustration. Encourage children to name other toys that could be added to the toy box.

Teacher Tip
As children sort their cards, circulate around the room asking questions and encouraging children to talk about the letters. For example, ask, "How can you tell whether this letter is a *u* or a *t*?"

Monitor Progress Spell Check 3
After completing Sort 37, administer Spell Check 3. See page 35 in this Teacher Resource Guide for instructions.

s, h, and Digraph sh

Objectives
- To identify picture names beginning with the sounds of *s, h,* and *sh*
- To sort pictures by their beginning sound and associate each sound with the letter or digraph it represents

Materials for Emergent-Early Letter Name

Big Book of Rhymes, "On Our Ship," page 65

Whiteboard Activities DVD-ROM, Sort 38

Teacher Resource CD-ROM, Sort 38 and Find the Pairs Game

Student Book, pages 149–152

Words Their Way Library, *She Said*

Pictures

s	h
saw	horse
sock	house
soap	hose
seal	hat
six	hay

sh
shirt
ship
sheep
shark
shoe

Introduce/Model   *Small Groups*

- **Read a Rhyme** Read "On Our Ship" several times until children become familiar with the rhyme. Call on volunteers to track specific words, such as *sail, ship,* and *Hold.* When children have shown they can track accurately, have them search the rhyme to find words that begin with the sound of *s, h,* or *sh.*

- **Model** Use the whiteboard DVD or the CD picture cards. Explain that children will sort the pictures by the beginning sounds of their names. Demonstrate how to sort *horse, shirt,* and *saw.* Help children sort and explain their sorts.

Practice the Sort   *Independent/Partner*

- Have children use the Student Book or whiteboard DVD to name the pictures and use the grid to sort the cards by their beginning sound.

- Have children check and explain their sorts.

Apply   *Independent/Partner/Small Groups*

- Read aloud the directions on Student Book p. 152. Have children work independently or with a partner to write words and draw pictures of things whose names begin like *sun, hand,* and *shovel.*

- **Game** Allow time for children to play Find the Pairs, which is on the CD.

- **Little Book** Read *She Said* with children. Have them identify words that begin with /s/, /h/, or /sh/.

Extend the Sort

Alternative Sort: Can You Wear It?

Remove the picture card for *six.* Lead children to re-sort the remaining cards into two piles, placing things people can wear in one pile and things people cannot wear in another pile.

ELL English Language Learners

Use a word from this week's sort in a sentence. Show the picture card to children as you use the word. Then have children form sentences using the same word. Repeat with other words from the sort.

Vocabulary Building Vocabulary

Use a group of pencils or other small objects to demonstrate the number *six.* Count the objects aloud and have the class repeat after you. Label the group. Then encourage children to find groups of six objects in the classroom.

Teacher Tip

Encourage children to brainstorm other words that begin with *s, h,* or *sh.* Invite them to draw pictures of the words and incorporate them into the sort.

c, h, and Digraph ch

Objectives

- To identify picture names beginning with the sounds of *c, h,* and *ch*
- To sort pictures by their beginning sound and associate each sound with the letter or digraph it represents

Materials for Emergent-Early Letter Name

Big Book of Rhymes, "Fun in the Sun," page 67

Whiteboard Activities DVD-ROM, Sort 39

Teacher Resource CD-ROM, Sort 39 and Follow the Path Game

Student Book, pages 153–156

Words Their Way Library, *Chocolate Chip Cookies*

Pictures

c	h
comb	heart
coat	hat
can	horn
cup	house
cow	horse

ch
chimney
cherry
chin
chick
cheese

Introduce/Model
Small Groups

- **Read a Rhyme** Read "Fun in the Sun" several times. Call on volunteers to track specific words, such as *cover, cheeks,* and *have.* When children have shown they can track accurately, have them search the rhyme to find words that begin with the sound of *c, h,* or *ch.*

- **Model** Use the whiteboard DVD or the CD picture cards. Explain that children will sort the pictures by the beginning sounds of their names. Demonstrate how to sort *heart, chimney,* and *comb.* Help children sort and explain their sorts.

Practice the Sort
Independent/Partner

- Have children use the Student Book or whiteboard DVD to name the pictures and use the grid to sort the cards by their beginning sound.

- Have children check and explain their sorts.

Apply
Independent/Partner/Small Groups

- Read aloud the directions on Student Book p. 156. Have children work independently or with a partner to write words and draw pictures of things whose names begin like *cat, hand,* and *chair.*

- **Game** Allow time for children to play Follow the Path, which is on the CD.

- **Little Book** Read *Chocolate Chip Cookies* with children. Have them identify words that begin with c/k/, /h/, or /ch/.

Extend the Sort

Alternative Sort: Large or Small?

Remove the picture cards for *heart, coat,* and *chimney.* Have children re-sort the remaining cards into two piles: objects or animals that are smaller than a desk and objects or animals that are larger than a desk.

ELL English Language Learners

Model how to correctly pronounce the beginning sound of *ch* as in *cheese.* Point out the placement of the teeth when forming the sound. Have children practice pronouncing *ch* with words from the sort.

Vocabulary Building Vocabulary

Children may identify a *chimney,* but they may not understand its purpose. Explain that a chimney is needed to carry away smoke from a fireplace or a furnace below.

Teacher Tip

Provide magazines and storybooks. Have children search for words that begin with *c, h,* or *ch.* Children can then copy the words on paper.

h and Digraphs *sh, ch*

Objectives

- To identify picture names beginning with the sounds of *h, sh,* and *ch*
- To sort pictures by their beginning sound and associate each sound with the letter or digraph it represents

Materials for Emergent-Early Letter Name

Big Book of Rhymes, "Watch Out, Sheep!," page 69

Whiteboard Activities DVD-ROM, Sort 40

Teacher Resource CD-ROM, Sort 40 and Chasing Clouds Game

Student Book, pages 157–160

Words Their Way Library, *Stan Packs*

Pictures

h	sh
hose	sheep
horse	shoe
house	shark
hat	shed
hay	shop

ch
cheese
chain
chop
chimney
cherry

Introduce/Model
Small Groups

- **Read a Rhyme** Read "Watch Out, Sheep!" several times with children. Call on volunteers to track specific words, such as *Sheep, chugs,* and *hump*. When children have shown they can track accurately, have them search the rhyme to find words that begin with the sound of *h, sh,* or *ch*.

- **Model** Use the whiteboard DVD or the CD picture cards. Explain that children will sort the pictures by the beginning sounds of their names. Demonstrate how to sort *cheese, hose,* and *shop*. Help children sort and explain their sorts.

Practice the Sort
Independent/Partner

- Have children use the Student Book or whiteboard DVD to name the pictures and use the grid to sort the cards by their beginning sound.

- Have children check and explain their sorts.

Apply
Independent/Partner/Small Groups

- Read aloud the directions on Student Book p. 160. Have children work independently or with a partner to write words and draw pictures of things whose names begin like *hand, shovel,* and *chair*.

- **Game** Allow time for children to play Chasing Clouds, which is on the CD.

- **Little Book** Read *Stan Packs* with children. Have them identify words that begin with /h/, /sh/, or /ch/.

Extend the Sort

Alternative Sort: Animals, Actions, or Objects

Have children re-sort the cards into three groups: pictures that show animals, pictures that show actions, and pictures that show objects.

ELL English Language Learners

Display a picture card and use the word it represents in a question. For example, "Do you have a *hat* at home?" Have children form sentences using the word to answer the question. Repeat with other cards from the sort.

Vocabulary Building Vocabulary

Divide the class into three groups. Assign *h, ch,* or *sh* to each group. Provide old magazines, and ask the groups to look for and circle words that have their assigned letters. Have groups point out the words they find and read them aloud together.

Teacher Tip

Be sure children understand that the sound of *ch* is different from the sound of *c* or *h* and that the sound of *sh* is different from the sound of *s* or *h*. Write and have children read these words with you: *cat, hat, chat, sip, hip, ship*.

Digraphs *th, wh*

Objectives

- To identify picture names beginning with the sounds of *th* and *wh*
- To sort pictures by their beginning sound and associate each sound with the digraph it represents

Materials for Emergent-Early Letter Name

Big Book of Rhymes, "What Do You Think?," page 71

Whiteboard Activities DVD-ROM, Sort 41

Teacher Resource CD-ROM, Sort 41 and Pair Up! Game

Student Book, pages 161–164

Words Their Way Library, *Who Has Whiskers?*

Pictures

th	*wh*
thirteen	white
think	whisker
thick	whale
thorn	wheelbarrow
thermos	whistle
thermometer	wheat

Introduce/Model   *Small Groups*

- **Read a Rhyme** Read "What Do You Think?" several times until children become familiar with the rhyme. Then track specific words, such as *think* and *whale*, as children follow along. Finally, have them find words in the rhyme that begin with the sound of *th* or *wh*.

- **Model** Use the whiteboard DVD or the CD picture cards. Explain that children will sort the pictures by the beginning sounds of their names. Demonstrate how to sort *white* and *think*. Help children sort and explain their sorts.

Practice the Sort   *Independent/Partner*

- Have children use the Student Book or whiteboard DVD to name the pictures and use the grid to sort the cards by their beginning sound.

- Have children check and explain their sorts.

Apply   *Independent/Partner/Small Groups*

- Read aloud the directions on Student Book p. 164. Have children work independently or with a partner to write words and draw pictures of things whose names begin like *thumb* and *wheel*.

- **Game** Allow time for children to play Pair Up!, which is on the CD.

- **Little Book** Read *Who Has Whiskers?* with children. Have them identify words that begin with /hw/.

Extend the Sort

Alternative Sort: Can It Grow?

Remove the cards for *think* and *thorn*. Then have children re-sort the remaining cards into two categories: things that grow *(whisker, whale, wheat)* and things that do not grow.

ELL English Language Learners

Have children hold a hand in front of their mouth and say *wh-wh-whale* and *th-th-think*. Have them repeat the routine with *white* and *thorn*. Point out the placement of the tongue when forming the two different sounds

Vocabulary Building Vocabulary

Clarify the meaning of *thick*. Ask children how they or someone else has used *thick* to tell about things. Children can then take turns asking and answering questions, such as "Would you like to have a thick sandwich or a thin sandwich?"

Teacher Tip

Handmade sets of picture cards on cardstock or posterboard can be easily banded together and kept in children's desks to use for practice.

Digraphs *sh, ch, wh, th*

Objectives

- To identify picture names beginning with the sounds of *sh, ch, wh,* and *th*
- To sort pictures by their beginning sound and associate each sound with the digraph it represents

Materials for Emergent-Early Letter Name

Big Book of Rhymes, "Watch Out, Sheep!," page 69

Whiteboard Activities DVD-ROM, Sort 42

Teacher Resource CD-ROM, Sort 42 and Shooting Star Game

Student Book, pages 165–168

Words Their Way Library, *Three White Sheep*

Pictures

sh	ch	wh	th
shoe	chin	wheelbarrow	thirteen
ship	chick	wheel	thick
shirt	chain	whistle	thermos
shelf	chair	whisker	thermometer
shell	cheese	whale	thorn

Introduce/Model   *Small Groups*

- **Read a Rhyme** Read "Watch Out, Sheep!" several times. Ask children to say the rhyme with you, adding sound effects for *beep, chug, thump,* and *bang* as well as expression for the exclamations. Then have children look for words that begin with the sound of *sh, ch, wh,* or *th.*

- **Model** Use the whiteboard DVD or the CD picture cards. Explain that children will sort the pictures by the beginning sounds of their names. Demonstrate how to sort *shoe, chin, wheelbarrow,* and *thirteen.* Help children sort and explain their sorts.

Practice the Sort   *Independent/Partner*

- Have children use the Student Book or whiteboard DVD to name the pictures and use the grid to sort the cards by their beginning sound.

- Have children check and explain their sorts.

Apply   *Independent/Partner/Small Groups*

- Read aloud the directions on Student Book p. 168. Have children work independently or with a partner to write words and draw pictures of things whose names begin like *sheep, cheese, wheel,* and *thumb.*

- **Game** Allow time for children to play Shooting Star, which is on the CD.

- **Little Book** Read *Three White Sheep* with children. Have them identify words that begin with /sh/, /ch/, /hw/, or /th/.

Extend the Sort

Alternative Sort: What Is Alike?

Remove the pictures for *thirteen* and *thick.* Have children take turns looking at the remaining pictures and finding two or three of things that are alike in some way. Examples: *shoe* and *shirt* are things to wear; *chin* and *whisker* are found on a face; *wheel* and *chain* are found on a bike.

ELL English Language Learners

To help children remember the four digraph sounds and spellings, discuss and draw a whale, a shirt, a chain, and a thorn with labels such as <u>wh</u>ale, and post these outlines in the classroom for reference.

Vocabulary Building Vocabulary

Use *whistle* in a sentence as a noun, but explain that *whistle* can be an object, action, or sound. Model for the class how to use *whistle* in sentences with the other meanings. Invite children to use *whistle* in their own sentences.

Monitor Progress Spell Check 4

After completing Sort 42, administer Spell Check 4. See page 35 in this Teacher Resource Guide for instructions.

Letter Name

The Letter Name stage of literacy development is a period of beginnings. Students begin to read and write in a conventional way. That is, they begin to learn words and their writing becomes readable to themselves and others. However, this stage of literacy development needs careful scaffolding because students know how to read and write only a small number of words.

Types of Sorts in Letter Name
- Beginning Consonants
- Same Vowel Word Families
- Digraphs and Blends
- Mixed Vowel Word Families
- Short Vowels
- Preconsonantal Nasals
- *r*-Influenced Vowels
- Contractions

Characteristics of Letter Name Learners

Letter Name learners are usually in late kindergarten and first grade.

Letter Name Learners

- use letter names as cues for spelling.

- have a rudimentary concept of word initially, which means they are able to point to and track words of a memorized text using their knowledge of consonants, but they get off track with two syllable words, and when they are asked to find words in what they read, they are slow and hesitant. A full concept of word is attained during this stage.

- read slowly, word by word. They point to words as they read and read aloud to themselves.

- write words slowly, sound by sound. They can usually read what they write.

Focus of Instruction

- In this level, students first briefly review initial consonants before being introduced to same vowel word families with picture and word sorts. Word families that share the same vowel are a good way to review consonants and introduce students to short vowel sounds.

- Students then move on to consonant digraphs and blends with picture sorts. Because the sorts use pictures only, students do not have to have an extensive sight vocabulary of words with digraphs and blends.

- Students revisit word families in mixed-vowel contrasts that include words with digraphs and blends. As they did with same vowel word families, students practice blending onsets and rimes to figure out words.

- Next, students focus on the short vowels themselves without the support of word families and continue to review initial and final digraphs and blends. Students also study the preconsonantal nasals -*ng*, -*mp*, -*nt*, -*nd*, and -*nk*.

- Finally, students are briefly introduced to *r*-influenced vowels and contractions.

Teacher Tip
- You may want to prepare additional word sorts for learners who are struggling to contrast letters or sounds.

Pace of Instruction

Set as fast a pace as possible during the Letter Name stage because success in beginning reading depends on learning the basic phonics covered at this stage. However, the same pace will not be suitable for every student, so adjust the pace to meet students' needs. You can use the Spell Checks to help determine the focus and pace of instruction.

For students who seem to be catching on quickly, speed up the pace by spending less time on a sort or skip a sort altogether. Conversely, for those students who are not on track for meeting end-of-year goals, spend more time on instruction and provide more practice by creating additional sorts.

Modifying the pace and using flexible small groups allows you to avoid teaching students what they already know and to spend more time on features that need instruction. Use the Spell Checks as pretests to determine instructional needs.

Word Study Routines

Shared Reading The *Big Book of Rhymes* provides a way to introduce the sorts in a meaningful context and provides poems that focus on the features for word study.

- Point to and read the title of the poem and talk about the illustration.

- Point to the words as you read the poem aloud and then talk about it. Reread it several times, pausing before rhyming words at the end of lines to invite student participation. Draw attention to print features such as capitalization and punctuation.

- Have students read with you and point to words as they recite from memory.

- Draw attention to words that exemplify the feature of study. For example, *This rhyme has several words that begin with blends. Here is the word* special. *It begins with* sp. *Can you find other words that begin with* sp? *Yes,* spill *and* spin *begin with* sp.

Introduce the Sort There are several options for introducing the sort. Here are the basic steps for a teacher-directed sort.

- Name the pictures or read the words. Talk about any that students might not know or that have multiple meanings (*bat, track*).

- Introduce the categories and headers. Model how to place several pictures or words in each column while explaining your thinking.

- Have students help you sort the remaining words or pictures and ask them to explain their sorting.

- Name the pictures or read the words in each column. Talk about how the words in each category are alike. Ask questions that help students make their own generalizations. (*How are* green, grow, *and* grab alike?)

- Re-sort. Leave up the headers and distribute the pictures or words to students in the group or let them take turns selecting a picture or word to sort. If mistakes are made, let them stay. After sorting, check by reading down each column. If a picture or word is misplaced, say *One of these needs to move to a different column. Let's see if we can find it.*

Oddballs As students complete sorts at the Letter Name stage, they will encounter the category *Oddballs*. Oddballs are words that do not fit the targeted spelling pattern. For example, the word *put* is an oddball in a sort on short *u* vowels because even though it is spelled with CVC pattern, it does not have a short *u* vowel sound. As students work through the sorts, make sure they understand why a particular word fits in the oddball category.

Letter Name Library The library is comprised of little books that correspond to each of the sorts in the Letter Name stage.

- Use these little books as you would any little books: for picture walks, for choral reading, for echo reading, or for independent reading.

- After completing a sort, read the book with students. Have them look for words in context that have the feature being studied.

- Record words on a chart or have students write them in their word study notebooks.

Interactive Resources You may use the DVD-ROM and/or the CD-ROM printable manipulatives to model, instruct, and provide practice with sorts.

Use the DVD-ROM for interactive whiteboard activities or independent practice on a computer.

- Introduce, read, and discuss the rhyme from the *Big Book of Rhymes*. Engage students in reading the rhyme, noticing features of print, and identifying words that illustrate the focus of the sort.

- Point out the headers for the columns, which indicate the principle of the sort. Demonstrate how to drag and drop pictures or words to complete the sort. Have students take turns sorting, using the whiteboard or a computer.

- Use the whiteboard with students to introduce and complete the writing sort.

Use the CD-ROM for printable manipulatives.

- Print out and cut apart the cards for the sort. Introduce the pictures or words, identifying any that may be unfamiliar to students. Demonstrate how to sort. Have students use the cards to practice sorting.

- Print out the game that accompanies the sort. Use the game for additional practice with the sort. Have students play in pairs or small groups.

- Print out the rhyme that accompanies the sort. Have students take it home to read with family members.

Teacher Tip
- Beginning readers' vocabulary growth is dependent on the richness and frequency of verbal interactions with peers and adults. Comment on and make observations about words throughout the day. This will help your students become "wordsmiths"—kids who are curious about words, their sounds, their meanings, and their usage.

Monitor Progress SPELL CHECKS

Spell Checks are provided at the back of the Letter Name Student Book to use as pretests and posttests.

Spell Check 1
Beginning Consonants Use after Sort 5. This Spell Check assesses students' ability to identify initial consonant sounds.

1. L/l	8. J/j	15. M/m
2. B/b	9. S/s	16. N/n
3. D/d	10. T/t	17. P/p
4. F/f	11. V/v	18. R/r
5. H/h	12. W/w	19. G/g
6. Y/y	13. K/k	20. S/s
7. Z/z	14. C/c	

If students miss a beginning consonant, have them review the corresponding sort for that letter. If students miss an unusually high number of beginning consonants, they should not proceed to the next sort until they have reviewed the previous sorts.

Spell Check 2
Same Vowel Word Families Use after Sort 14. This Spell Check assesses students' ability to distinguish among short vowel sounds and to recognize short vowel words.

1. fan	6. tag	11. hog
2. hat	7. cut	12. wig
3. dad	8. rip	13. bug
4. mop	9. cot	14. bun
5. jet	10. map	15. hill

If students consistently match a word with the correct vowel family but the incorrect beginning sound, have them review Sorts 1–5. If students consistently choose words from the wrong vowel family, have them review the corresponding sorts for those families.

Spell Check 3
Consonant Blends and Digraphs Use after Sort 24. This Spell Check assesses students' ability to identify consonant blends and digraphs at the beginning of words.

1. st	8. pl	15. sl
2. fl	9. th	16. br
3. sm	10. sw	17. gr
4. dr	11. cl	18. qu
5. fr	12. ch	19. tw
6. sh	13. gl	20. tr
7. sn	14. wh	

Watch for these types of errors: If students write *w* for *wh*, review Sorts 16, 17, and 24; if students write *t* for *tr,* review Sort 23; if students write *f* for *fl*, review Sort 21.

Spell Check 4
Mixed Vowel Word Families Use after Sort 34. This Spell Check assesses students' ability to spell and write words containing short-vowel word families.

1. pot	6. rug	11. mill
2. bat	7. dog	12. duck
3. pin	8. cob	13. bed
4. sun	9. peg	14. tack
5. fan	10. ball	15. cash

Watch for these types of errors: If students have trouble distinguishing between *a, i,* and *u* word families, review Sorts 26, 28, 29, 31, 32, 33, and 34; if students have trouble distinguishing between *a* and *e* word families, review Sorts 26, 27, 29, and 30.

Spell Check 5
Short Vowel Words Use after Sort 44. This Spell Check assesses students' ability to spell and write one-syllable short vowel words.

1. bell	6. crab	11. flag
2. fox	7. clock	12. drum
3. can	8. truck	13. plant
4. chin	9. nest	14. hand
5. frog	10. fish	15. ring

Watch for these types of errors: If students write *a* for *e*, review Sorts 37, 39, and 44; if students write *e* for *i*, review Sorts 36, 37, and 44.

Spell Check 6
Preconsonantal Nasals Use after Sort 46. This Spell Check assesses students' ability to write and spell words with preconsonantal nasals.

1. jump	5. king	9. tank
2. lamp	6. ring	10. skunk
3. tent	7. drink	11. hand
4. swing	8. pink	12. stamp

Watch for these types of errors: If students write *g* for *ng* or *p* for *mp*, review Sort 45; if students write *t* for *nt*, *d* for *nd*, or *k* for *nk*, review Sort 46.

Spell Check 7
r-**Influenced Vowels** Use after Sort 48. This Spell Check assesses students' ability to spell words with *r*-influenced vowel patterns.

1. car	5. cart	9. rock
2. corn	6. yard	10. shark
3. thorn	7. card	11. yarn
4. fork	8. horn	12. crab

If students miss *or* words, have them review Sort 47; if students miss *ar* words, have them review Sort 48.

- See Chapter 5 of *Words Their Way: Word Study for Phonics, Vocabulary, and Spelling Instruction, 5th ed.*, for a comprehensive description of the Letter Name stage of development and additional activities.

Beginning Consonants *b, m, r, s*

Objectives
- To recognize the beginning consonant sounds *b, m, r,* and *s*
- To sort pictures by their beginning sound and associate each sound with the letter it represents

Materials for Letter Name

Big Book of Rhymes, "Go Away, Tiger!," page 5

Whiteboard Activities DVD-ROM, Sort 1

Teacher Resource CD-ROM, Sort 1 and Concentration Game

Student Book, pages 1–4

Words Their Way Library, *When We Are Big*

Pictures

Bb	Mm
barn	monkey
bed	map
bear	milk
baby	meat
band	mouse

Rr	Ss
rocket	scissors
ring	soap
road	seal
roof	sink
rain	six

Introduce/Model
Small Groups

- **Read a Rhyme** Read "Go Away, Tiger!" Emphasize the words that begin with the sounds *b, m, r,* and *s*. Reread the poem and have children raise their hands when they hear words that begin with *b, m, r,* and *s*.

- **Model** Use the whiteboard DVD or the CD picture cards. Explain that children will sort the pictures by the beginning sound of their names. Demonstrate how to sort *mouse, rocket, barn,* and *scissors*. Help children sort and explain their sorts.

Practice the Sort
Independent/Partner

- Have children use the Student Book or whiteboard DVD to name the pictures and use the grid to sort the cards by their beginning sound.

- Have children check and explain their sorts.

Apply
Independent/Partner/Small Groups

- Read aloud the directions on Student Book p. 4. Have children write letters and draw pictures of things whose names begin like *ball, mop, rake,* and *saw*.

- **Game** Allow time for children to play Concentration, which is on the CD.

- **Little Book** Read *When We Are Big* with children. Have them identify words that begin with /b/, /m/, /r/, or /s/.

Extend the Sort

Alternative Sort: Odd One Out

Show sets of three pictures in which two items can be categorized as similar, but one is very different, such as *bear, monkey, scissors* (two things are animals). Have children explain which picture does not belong and why.

ELL English Language Learners

Familiarize children with the pictures by doing a concept sort prior to sorting by beginning sound. Pictures can be sorted according to shapes, colors, living/nonliving things, and so forth.

Teacher Tip

Individual sets of picture cards made from card stock or posterboard can be easily banded together and kept in children's desks to use for practice.

Vocabulary Building Vocabulary

Use paper clips or other small objects to demonstrate the number *six*. Count the small objects aloud and have the class repeat after you. Encourage children to find groups of six objects in the classroom.

Beginning Consonants *t, g, n, p*

Objectives

- To recognize the beginning consonant sounds *t, g, n,* and *p*
- To sort pictures by their beginning sound and associate each sound with the letter it represents

Materials for Letter Name

- Big Book of Rhymes, "Go Away, Tiger!," page 5

- Whiteboard Activities DVD-ROM, Sort 2

- Teacher Resource CD-ROM, Sort 2 and Match! Game

- Student Book, pages 5–8

- Words Their Way Library, *On the Farm*

Pictures

Tt	Gg
tire	goose
toe	game
tooth	gate
tie	gold
tail	girl
Nn	**Pp**
nurse	pig
nail	pen
nut	peach
nose	pan
net	pillow

Introduce/Model
Small Groups

- **Read a Rhyme** Read "Go Away, Tiger!" Emphasize the words that begin with the sounds *t, g, n,* and *p.* Reread the poem and have children raise their hands when they hear words that begin with *t, g, n,* and *p.*

- **Model** Use the whiteboard DVD or the CD picture cards. Explain that children will sort the pictures by the beginning sounds of their names. Demonstrate how to sort *tire, goose, nurse,* and *pig.* Help children sort and explain their sorts.

Practice the Sort
Independent/Partner

- Have children use the Student Book or whiteboard DVD to name the pictures and use the grid to sort the cards by their beginning sound.

- Have children check and explain their sorts.

Apply
Independent/Partner/Small Groups

- Read aloud the directions on Student Book p. 8. Have children write letters and draw pictures of things whose names begin like *top, goat, nest,* and *pin.*

- **Game** Allow time for children to play Match!, which is on the CD.

- **Little Book** Read *On the Farm* with children. Have them identify words that begin with /t/, /g/, /n/, or /p/.

Extend the Sort

Alternative Sort: What Is Alike?

Show sets of ten pictures at a time, and have children take turns finding two or three pictures that show things that are alike in some way without revealing to the class how they are alike. Classmates can guess the similarity.

ELL English Language Learners

If children have difficulty pronouncing words from the sort, model using each word in a sentence. Have children repeat the sentence or use the word in a new sentence of their own.

Teacher Tip

To help children keep picture cards separate from different sorts, have them attach together each sort's cards with a paper clip before storing them.

Vocabulary Building Vocabulary

Show children the *goose* picture card. Ask them what other bird it looks like. Explain that a goose is a swimming bird that is like a duck but it has a larger body and longer neck.

Beginning Consonants *c, h, f, d*

Objectives
- To recognize the beginning consonant sounds *c, h, f,* and *d*
- To sort pictures by their beginning sound and associate each sound with the letter it represents

Materials for Letter Name

Big Book of Rhymes, "Time to Shop for School," page 7

Whiteboard Activities DVD-ROM, Sort 3

Teacher Resource CD-ROM, Sort 3 and Bingo! Game

Student Book, pages 9–12

Words Their Way Library, *When We Are Big*

Pictures

Cc	Hh
carrot	ham
camel	hen
cape	hand
candle	hill
cap	hay

Ff	Dd
fish	desk
feet	dinosaur
feather	deer
fire	doll
fan	duck

Introduce/Model   *Small Groups*

- **Read a Rhyme** Read "Time to Shop for School." Emphasize words that begin with *c, h, f,* and *d*. Reread the poem and have children raise their hands when they hear words that begin with *c, h, f,* and *d*.

- **Model** Use the whiteboard DVD or the CD picture cards. Explain that children will sort the pictures by the beginning sound of their names. Demonstrate how to sort *carrot, ham, fish,* and *desk*. Help children sort and explain their sorts.

Practice the Sort   *Independent/Partner*

- Have children use the Student Book or whiteboard DVD to name the pictures and use the grid to sort the cards by their beginning sound.

- Have children check and explain their sorts.

Apply   *Independent/Partner/Small Groups*

- Read aloud the directions on Student Book p. 12. Have children write letters and draw pictures of things whose names begin like *can, hat, fox,* and *dog*.

- **Game** Allow time for children to play Bingo!, which is on the CD.

- **Little Book** Read *When We Are Big* with children. Have them identify words that begin with c/k/, /h/, /f/, or /d/.

Extend the Sort

Alternative Sort: Animals or Not Animals

Have children first re-sort into groups of animals and not animals. Then they can further sort into animals with four legs and other animals.

ELL English Language Learners

Model how to correctly pronounce the beginning sound of *c* as in *cup*. Teach children how to exhale and squeeze abdominal muscles in order to emphasize the sound.

Teacher Tip

Encourage children whose names begin with *c, h, f,* and *d* to play the Bingo! game.

Vocabulary Building Vocabulary

If children are unfamiliar with the word *cape*, explain that it is a type of coat with no sleeves that is fastened at the neck. Ask children where they have seen capes.

Beginning Consonants *l, k, j, w*

Objectives
- To recognize the beginning consonant sounds *l, k, j,* and *w*
- To sort pictures by their beginning sound and associate each sound with the letter it represents

Materials **for Letter Name**

📖 Big Book of Rhymes, "Time to Shop for School," page 7

🖥 Whiteboard Activities DVD-ROM, Sort 4

💿 Teacher Resource CD-ROM, Sort 4 and Match! Game

📕 Student Book, pages 13–16

📘 Words Their Way Library, *The Wet Pet*

Pictures

Ll	Kk
lamp	kitten
lion	kangaroo
lid	key
lips	king
lizard	kitchen

Jj	Ww
jeans	wagon
jar	wing
jet	watch
jacket	wave
jump	web

Introduce/Model *Small Groups*

- **Read a Rhyme** Read "Time to Shop for School." Emphasize the words that begin with *l, k, j,* and *w.* Reread the poem and have children raise their hands when they hear words that begin with *l, k, j,* and *w.*

- **Model** Use the whiteboard DVD or the CD picture cards. Explain that children will sort the pictures by the beginning sound of their names. Demonstrate how to sort *jeans, wagon, king,* and *lamp.* Help children sort and explain their sorts.

Practice the Sort *Independent/Partner*

- Have children use the Student Book or whiteboard DVD to name the pictures and use the grid to sort the cards by their beginning sound.

- Have children check and explain their sorts.

Apply *Independent/Partner/Small Groups*

- Read aloud the directions on Student Book p. 16. Have children write letters and draw pictures of things whose names begin like *leaf, kite, jeep,* and *wagon.*

- **Game** Allow time for children to play Match!, which is on the CD.

- **Little Book** Read *The Wet Pet* with children. Have them identify words that begin with /j/ or /w/.

Extend the Sort

Alternative Sort: Things We Use
Have children re-sort into groups of things people use and other objects. As children identify objects that people use, have them explain how each object is used.

ELL English Language Learners
The names of some of the pictures may contain sounds that do not exist in a child's native language. Guide children by asking them to repeat the name of each picture after you, as needed.

Teacher Tip
If a child is having trouble pronouncing a particular sound, watch the child's mouth to be sure his or her lips and tongue are positioned correctly.

Vocabulary Building Vocabulary
Tell children that some words have more than one meaning. Explain that a watch is a small clock you wear on your wrist. The word *watch* can also be an action word. *Watch* means "to look at and pay attention to."

Beginning Consonants *y, z, v*

Objectives
- To recognize the beginning consonant sounds *y, z,* and *v*
- To sort pictures by their beginning sound and associate each sound with the letter it represents

Materials for Letter Name

- Big Book of Rhymes, "A Day at the Zoo," page 9

- Whiteboard Activities DVD-ROM, Sort 5

- Teacher Resource CD-ROM, Sort 5 and Bingo! Game

- Student Book, pages 17–20

- Words Their Way Library, *Good-bye, Zoo*

Pictures

Yy	Zz	Vv
yo-yo	zigzag	vase
yell	zebra	vine
yard	zero	violin
yarn	zucchini	volcano
yawn	zoo	vest

Introduce/Model
Small Groups

- **Read a Rhyme** Read "A Day at the Zoo" and emphasize words that begin with *y, z,* and *v*. Have children find the words that begin with *y, z,* and *v* and write them in three columns on the board.

- **Model** Use the whiteboard DVD or the CD picture cards. Explain that children will sort the pictures by the beginning sound of their names. Demonstrate how to sort *yo-yo, zigzag,* and *vase.* Help children sort and explain their sorts.

Practice the Sort
Independent/Partner

- Have children use the Student Book or whiteboard DVD to name the pictures and use the grid to sort the cards by their beginning sound.

- Have children check and explain their sorts.

Apply
Independent/Partner/Small Groups

- Read aloud the directions on Student Book p. 20. Have children write letters and draw pictures of things whose names begin like *yarn, zipper,* and *van.*

- **Game** Allow time for children to play Bingo!, which is on the CD.

- **Little Book** Read *Good-bye, Zoo* with children. Have them identify words that begin with /y/, /z/, or /v/.

Extend the Sort

Alternative Sort: Colors
Have children re-sort the pictures according to colors on them. The categories can include pictures that contain blue, red, green, and black.

ELL English Language Learners
Review picture names that might be unfamiliar to children, such as *violin, zucchini, zigzag,* or *volcano.* Ask children to use each word in a sentence.

Vocabulary Building Vocabulary
Use the zigzag card to help children see that a zigzag has sharp turns, first to one side and then the other. Ask them if they have seen lightning zigzag across the sky. Have them demonstrate zigzag as they walk.

Monitor Progress Spell Check 1
After completing Sort 5, administer Spell Check 1. See pp. 80–81 in this Teacher Resource Guide for instructions.

Word Families -at, -an

Objectives

- To identify short *a* rhyming words
- To identify and sort pictures and words with -*at* and -*an*

Materials for Letter Name

- Big Book of Rhymes, "The Snowman," page 11
- Whiteboard Activities DVD-ROM, Sort 6
- Teacher Resource CD-ROM, Sort 6 and Word Maker Game
- Student Book, pages 21–24
- Words Their Way Library, *Eggs!*

Pictures/Words

-at	-an
mat	can
bat	van
hat	fan
rat	man

Bonus Words

flat	ban
chat	plan
scat	scan
that	tan

Introduce/Model
Small Groups

- **Read a Rhyme** Read "The Snowman." Emphasize the rhyming words *fat, hat* and *snowman, pan*. Write them in two columns and ask how the words in each column are alike. (They end with the same sounds and letters and they rhyme.) Read the poem again, omitting the last word in each line, and have children provide the missing words.

- **Model** Use the whiteboard DVD or the CD word and picture cards. Explain that children will sort by the words that rhyme. Demonstrate how to sort the pictures and words for *mat* and *can*. Help children sort and explain their sorts.

Practice the Sort
Independent/Partner

- Have children use the Student Book or whiteboard DVD to name the pictures and words and use the grid to sort the cards by their ending sound.

- Have children check and explain their sorts.

Apply
Independent/Partner/Small Groups

- Read aloud the directions on Student Book p. 24. Have children write words that rhyme with *bat* and *can*.

- **Game** Allow time for children to play Word Maker, which is on the CD.

- **Little Book** Read *Eggs!* with children. Have them identify any words that end with -*an*.

Extend the Sort

Vocabulary Building Vocabulary

Explain that a mat can be a pad used by a door. Ask how it is different from a rug and what its purpose is. Then have children name and discuss other types of mats, such as place mats and exercise mats.

ELL English Language Learners

Review with children some words or pictures of things that end with -*an* and -*at*. Have them say the words aloud and form all sounds in each word. Have children draw out the last sound in each, to help them better hear the difference between -*an* and -*at*.

Teacher Tip

Make large outlines of a cat and a man for posting in the classroom. Have children write all the rhyming words they can think of inside each figure. Then read the words aloud as a group.

Bonus Words Activity

Ask children to find other words that end with -*an* or -*at* in books and other texts. If children need prompting, suggest words from the Bonus Words list. Then have children make word cards for new words. Have them use each in a sentence and then sort the words into categories.

Objectives

- To identify short *a* rhyming words
- To identify and sort pictures and words with *-ad* and *-an*

Materials for Letter Name

📖 Big Book of Rhymes, "Stan Is Sad," page 13

🖥 Whiteboard Activities DVD-ROM, Sort 7

💿 Teacher Resource CD-ROM, Sort 7 and Word Maker Game

📘 Student Book, pages 25–28

📕 Words Their Way Library, *At the Track*

Pictures/Words

-ad	-an
sad	can
dad	man
pad	van
mad	fan

Bonus Words

lad	pan
glad	bran

Introduce/Model
Small Groups

- **Read a Rhyme** Read "Stan Is Sad," emphasizing the rhyming words. Write *sad* on the board, and have children find two words within the poem that rhyme with *sad*. (*had, bad*) Point to *Stan* and *Sad* in the title. Ask children what letter both words begin with.

- **Model** Use the whiteboard DVD or the CD word and picture cards. Explain that children will sort by the words that rhyme. Demonstrate how to sort the pictures and words for *sad* and *can*. Help children sort and explain how the words in each column are alike.

Practice the Sort
Independent/Partner

- Have children use the Student Book or whiteboard DVD to name the pictures and words and use the grid to sort the cards by ending sound.

- Have children check and explain their sorts.

Apply
Independent/Partner/Small Groups

- Read aloud the directions on Student Book p. 28. Have children write words that rhyme with *fan* and *dad*.

- **Game** Allow time for children to play Word Maker, which is on the CD.

- **Little Book** Read *At the Track* with children. Have them identify words that end with *-ad* or *-an*.

Extend the Sort

Vocabulary **Building Vocabulary**

Children may know of pads that are different from the writing pad shown on the picture card. Have them brainstorm different types of pads, such as sports pads, computer mouse pads, launch pads, furniture pads, lily pads, and stamp or ink pads.

ELL **English Language Learners**

Have children work to match picture and word cards. As each match is made, model using the word in a sentence. Then have children pantomime the sentence to check for understanding.

Teacher Tip

If children have difficulty sorting, focus on only one word family. After children demonstrate an understanding of that family, introduce the second family.

Bonus Words Activity

Have children brainstorm *-an* and *-ad* words and write the words on the cards. They can work in pairs or small groups to use each of the words in a sentence and then sort the words into categories.

Word Families -ap and -ag

Objectives

- To identify short *a* rhyming words
- To identify and sort pictures and words with *-ap* and *-ag*

Materials for Letter Name

📖 Big Book of Rhymes, "The Best Cap," page 15

🖥 Whiteboard Activities DVD-ROM, Sort 8

💿 Teacher Resource CD-ROM, Sort 8 and Word Maker Game

📒 Student Book, pages 29–32

📕 Words Their Way Library, *Caps*

Pictures/Words

-ap	-ag
nap	rag
cap	wag
map	flag
lap	tag

Bonus Words

clap	sag
flap	drag
snap	snag

Introduce/Model   *Small Groups*

- **Read a Rhyme** Read "The Best Cap." Emphasize the words that rhyme and then write the words *bag, cap, flap, glad, had,* and *zag* on the board. Ask children to pair up the rhyming words. Have them say the words aloud and notice how each pair of rhyming words ends with the same sound and letters.

- **Model** Use the whiteboard DVD or the CD word and picture cards. Explain that children will sort by the words that rhyme. Demonstrate how to sort into *-ap* and *-ag* word families. Help children sort and explain their sorts.

Practice the Sort   *Independent/Partner*

- Have children use the Student Book or whiteboard DVD to name the pictures and words and use the grid to sort the cards by ending sound.

- Have children check and explain their sorts.

Apply   *Independent/Partner/Small Groups*

- Read aloud the directions on Student Book p. 32. Have children write words that rhyme with *nap* and *wag*.

- **Game** Allow time for children to play Word Maker, which is on the CD.

- **Little Book** Read *Caps* with children. Have them identify words that end with *-ap* or *-ag*.

Extend the Sort

Vocabulary Building Vocabulary

Children may know and be able to name several kinds of tags that are different from the blank tag shown on the picture card. Have them brainstorm the different kinds of tags, such as price tags, luggage tags, clothing tags, and dog tags.

ELL English Language Learners

Have children repeat the words after you read them, emphasizing the ending sounds. Have them pantomime the action words and draw pictures of the object words to ensure understanding of each.

Teacher Tip

If children have difficulty sorting, focus on only one word family. After children demonstrate an understanding of that family, introduce the second family.

Bonus Words Activity

Write the Bonus Words on the board and read them aloud. Have children brainstorm *-ag* and *-ap* words that rhyme with the Bonus Words and create a rhyming sentence using one of the Bonus Words.

Word Families -ad, -ap, -ag

Objectives

- To identify short *a* rhyming words
- To identify and sort pictures and words with *-ad, -ap,* and *-ag*

Materials for Letter Name

- Big Book of Rhymes, "The Best Cap," page 15

- Whiteboard Activities DVD-ROM, Sort 9

- Teacher Resource CD-ROM, Sort 9 and Find the Cap Game

- Student Book, pages 33–36

- Words Their Way Library, *Haddie's Caps*

Pictures/Words

-ad	-ap	-ag
sad	nap	rag
dad	cap	wag
pad	lap	bag

Bonus Words

lad	clap	sag
glad	flap	drag
	snap	snag

Introduce/Model   *Small Groups*

- **Read a Rhyme** Read "The Best Cap," emphasizing the rhyming words. (*cap/nap, dad/bad, wag/rag*). Reread, having children identify the rhyming words. Write them in three columns and ask how the words in each column are alike. (They end with the same sounds and letters and they rhyme.)

- **Model** Use the whiteboard DVD or the CD word cards. Explain that children will sort by the words that rhyme. Demonstrate how to sort into *-ad, -ap,* and *-ag* word families. Elicit that the names of the pictures are alike because they rhyme and end with the same two letters. Help children sort and explain their sorts.

Practice the Sort   *Independent/Partner*

- Have children use the Student Book or whiteboard DVD to name the pictures, read the words, and use the grid to sort.

- Have children check and explain their sorts.

Apply   *Independent/Partner/Small Groups*

- Read aloud the directions on Student Book p. 36. Have children write words that rhyme with *sad, lap,* or *bag*.

- **Game** Allow time for children to play Find the Cap, which is on the CD.

- **Little Book** Read *Haddie's Caps* with children. Have them identify words that end with *-ad, -ap,* or *-ag*.

Extend the Sort

Alternative Sort: Actions or Things

Re-sort the pictures or words except *sad* and *dad*. Begin sorting the cards into actions (*nap, wag*) and things (*rag, pad, bag, cap, lap*). As you pick up each card, have children identify where it will go. Do this until all cards have been sorted.

ELL English Language Learners

Have children match picture and word cards. As each match is made, model using the word in a sentence. Then have children pantomime the sentence to check for understanding.

Bonus Words Activity

Write a Bonus Word and read it aloud. Then say a rhyming word and have a child show how to change the first word to make the second word. Repeat for the other word families.

Word Families -op, -ot, -og

Objectives
- To identify short *o* rhyming words
- To identify and sort pictures and words with -*op*, -*ot*, and -*og*

Materials for Letter Name

📖 Big Book of Rhymes, "One Hot Day," page 17

🖥 Whiteboard Activities DVD-ROM, Sort 10

💿 Teacher Resource CD-ROM, Sort 10 and Rock Hop Game

📒 Student Book, pages 37–40

📕 Words Their Way Library, *Lost in the Fog*

Pictures/Words

-op	-ot	-og
mop	pot	frog
hop	dot	hog
top	hot	log
pop	cot	jog

Bonus Words

chop	slot	bog
plop	spot	cog
flop	plot	clog
shop	trot	

Introduce/Model　　　*Small Groups*

- **Read a Rhyme** Read "One Hot Day." Emphasize the words that rhyme. (*dog, hog; frog, log; spot, hot; do, too*) Write the rhyming words in three columns on the board. Ask how the words in each column are alike. (They end with the same sound and letters.) Read the poem again, omitting the last word in each line, and have children provide the missing words.

- **Model** Use the whiteboard DVD or the CD word and picture cards. Define any unfamiliar words. Then demonstrate how to sort into -*op*, -*ot*, and -*og* word families. Introduce the word cards, and ask children to match each word card to its picture.

Practice the Sort　　　*Independent/Partner*

- Have children use the Student Book or whiteboard DVD to name the pictures and words and use the grid to sort the cards by ending sound.

- Have children check and explain their sorts.

Apply　　　*Independent/Partner/Small Groups*

- Read aloud the directions on Student Book p. 40. Have children write words that rhyme with *hop, hot,* and *hog*.

- **Game** Allow time for children to play Rock Hop, which is on the CD.

- **Little Book** Read *Lost in the Fog* with children. Have them identify words that end with -*og*.

Extend the Sort

Alternative Sort: Identify My Category

Re-sort the pictures and words into groups of living and nonliving things. Begin by sorting three of the cards into categories. When you pick up the next picture or word card, invite children to identify where it will go. Continue until all the cards have been sorted and children are able to identify the categories.

ELL English Language Learners

Review the pictures and words. Explain that a *hog* is similar to a pig, that a *cot* is a small bed, and that *jog* is the same as run. Have children pronounce each word to be sure they are differentiating among the three endings.

Teacher Tip

During a repeated sort, do not correct children when they place a picture or word in the wrong column. Wait until they have completed the sort, and have them read the words in each column. If they still don't find the misplaced card, tell them which column it is in, and have them find it.

Bonus Words Activity

Have children find other words that end with -*op*, -*ot*, and -*og*. Then have them make word cards for these new words and sort the words into categories.

Word Families *-ip, -ig, -ill*

Objectives

- To identify short *i* rhyming words
- To identify and sort pictures and words with *-ip*, *-ig*, and *-ill*

Materials for Letter Name

Big Book of Rhymes, "Mr. Fig Met a Pig," page 19

Whiteboard Activities DVD-ROM, Sort 11

Teacher Resource CD-ROM, Sort 11 and Zip Up the Hill Game

Student Book, pages 41–44

Words Their Way Library, *Mr. Fin's Trip*

Pictures/Words

-ip	*-ig*	*-ill*
zip	pig	Jill
rip	wig	sill
lip	dig	mill

Bonus Words

chip	rig	chill
slip	twig	drill
flip	jig	still
lip		spill

Introduce/Model — *Small Groups*

- **Read a Rhyme** Read "Mr. Fig Met a Pig." As you read, have children find and say the rhyming words *hill, Jill; pig, big;* and *flip, zip.* Write them in three columns on the board and remind children that these words rhyme because they end with the same sound and letters. Read the poem again, omitting the last word in each line, and have children provide the missing words.

- **Model** Use the whiteboard DVD or the CD word and picture cards. Define any unfamiliar words. Then demonstrate how to sort into *-ip, -ig,* and *-ill* word families. Introduce the word cards, and ask children to match each word card to its picture.

Practice the Sort — *Independent/Partner*

- Have children use the Student Book or whiteboard DVD to name the pictures and words and use the grid to sort the cards by ending sound.

- Have children check and explain their sorts.

Apply — *Independent/Partner/Small Groups*

- Read aloud the directions on Student Book p. 44. Have children write words that rhyme with *lip, dig,* and *mill.*

- **Game** Allow time for children to play Zip Up the Hill, which is on the CD.

- **Little Book** Read *Mr. Fin's Trip* with children. Have them identify words that end with *-ip.* You may also want children to identify words that end with *-in* or *-it.*

Extend the Sort

Alternative Sort: Object or Action

Re-sort the pictures and words into groups of actions and things. First sort two or three cards into categories. When you pick up the next picture or word card, ask children to identify where it goes. Continue until all the cards have been sorted.

Vocabulary Building Vocabulary

Explain that a mill is a building with large machines that grind grain into flour. Also explain that there are small mills that people can have in their homes to grind coffee and pepper. Then show children the mill picture, and discuss which type it is.

Teacher Tip

Post a list of the word families. Have children add words to the word families as they read more texts and study across the curriculum.

Bonus Words Activity

List some or all of the Bonus Words. Guide children as they read the list. Then model how they can take turns using Bonus Words as the answer to a puzzle: "I'm thinking of a word that rhymes with *hill.* It can mean "quiet." What is it?" (*still*)

Word Families *-ug, -ut, -un*

Objectives

- To identify short *u* rhyming words
- To identify and sort pictures and words with *-ug, -ut,* and *-un*

Materials for Letter Name

Big Book of Rhymes, "A Bug and a Nut," page 21

Whiteboard Activities DVD-ROM, Sort 12

Teacher Resource CD-ROM, Sort 12 and Rhyming Go Fish Game

Student Book, pages 45–48

Words Their Way Library, *Good Night, Little Bug*

Pictures/Words

-ug	-ut	-un
bug	cut	run
rug	hut	bun
mug	nut	sun

Bonus Words

plug	strut	fun
slug	rut	spun
snug	shut	stun

Introduce/Model   *Small Groups*

- **Read a Rhyme** Read "A Bug and a Nut." As you read, have children find and say the rhyming words. (*sun, run, fun; tug, rug*) Ask them which word in the title rhymes with *tug* and *rug*. Write all of the words in two columns on the board and remind children that these words rhyme because they end with the same sound and letters.

- **Model** Use the whiteboard DVD or the CD word and picture cards. Define any unfamiliar words and then demonstrate how to sort into *-ug, -ut,* and *-un* word families. Introduce the word cards, and ask children to match each word card to its picture.

Practice the Sort   *Independent/Partner*

- Have children use the Student Book or whiteboard DVD to name the pictures and words and use the grid to sort the cards by ending sound.

- Have children check and explain their sorts.

Apply   *Independent/Partner/Small Groups*

- Read aloud the directions on Student Book p. 48. Have children write words that rhyme with *rug, hut,* and *run*.

- **Game** Allow time for children to play Rhyming Go Fish, which is on the CD.

- **Little Book** Read *Good Night, Little Bug* with children. Have them identify words that end with *-ug* or *-un*.

Extend the Sort

Alternative Sort: In the Rhyme

Display "A Bug and a Nut." Children can sort cards into the categories of words that can be found in the rhyme and words that are not in the rhyme.

ELL English Language Learners

If children confuse medial short vowels *e* and *u*, such as *beg* and *bug*, pair them with proficient English speakers to work with the confused words.

Teacher Tip

Individual sets of letter cards, on card stock or posterboard, can be made for children to keep in their desks and used for word-building practice.

Bonus Words Activity

Help children make seven letter cards: *g, l, n, p, s, t, u.* They can build *sun*, change it to *spun*, and then make another change to build *stun*. As words are built, discuss their meanings and model their usage in sentences. Repeat the process for *plug* to *slug* to *snug*.

Objectives

- To identify short *e* rhyming words
- To identify and sort pictures and words with *-et*, *-eg*, and *-en*

Materials for Letter Name

Big Book of Rhymes, "Ben's Red Hen," page 23

Whiteboard Activities DVD-ROM, Sort 13

Teacher Resource CD-ROM, Sort 13 and Find the Hen Game

Student Book, pages 49–52

Words Their Way Library, *Ben's Pets*

Pictures/Words

-et	-eg	-en
net	leg	pen
pet	peg	hen
jet	beg	men
wet	Meg	ten

Bonus Words

bet	Greg	Ben
let		den
set		when
fret		then

Introduce/Model
Small Groups

- **Read a Rhyme** Read "Ben's Red Hen." Have children identify the words that rhyme at the end of lines. (*hen, ten; leg, Meg; bet, met*) Have them find the two other words that rhyme with *hen*. (*Ben, then*) Write all of the rhyming words on the board. Ask children how the words in each column are alike.

- **Model** Use the whiteboard DVD or the CD word and picture cards. Define any unfamiliar words. Then demonstrate how to sort into *-et*, *-eg*, and *-en* word families. Introduce the word cards, and ask children to match each word card to its picture.

Practice the Sort
Independent/Partner

- Have children use the Student Book or whiteboard DVD to name the pictures and words and use the grid to sort the cards by ending sounds.

- Have children check and explain their sorts.

Apply
Independent/Partner/Small Groups

- Read aloud the directions on Student Book p. 52. Have children write words that rhyme with *net, peg,* and *pen*.

- **Game** Allow time for children to play Find the Hen, which is on the CD.

- **Little Book** Read *Ben's Pets* with children. Have them identify words that end with *-et*, *-eg*, or *-en*.

Extend the Sort

Alternative Sort: One and More Than One

Remove *wet* and *beg*, and then re-sort the cards into "words that name one thing" (*net, pet, jet, leg, peg, pen, hen*) and "words that name more than one thing" (*men, ten*). Have children read the rhyming words in each column.

Vocabulary **Building Vocabulary**

Display the *peg* picture card and discuss how pegs are used. Create a list of places where children have seen pegs being used, such as pegs for hanging clothing or cups or for marking a score in a game.

ELL **English Language Learners**

If any child has difficulty recalling an English word for a picture in this sort, focus on the word at the time of the confusion. Model and have all children in the group repeat several sentences about the picture, using the particular word in each sentence.

Bonus Words Activity

Ask children to find other words that end with *-et*, *-eg*, or *-en*. Have them make word cards for these new words and work in small groups to sort the words into categories.

Word Families -ed, -et, -eg, -ell

Objectives

- To identify short *e* rhyming words
- To identify and sort words with *-ed, -et, -eg,* and *-ell*

Materials for Letter Name

📖 Big Book of Rhymes, "Ben's Red Hen," page 23

🖥 Whiteboard Activities DVD-ROM, Sort 14

💿 Teacher Resource CD-ROM, Sort 14 and Sled Down the Hill Game

📓 Student Book, pages 53–56

📔 Words Their Way Library, *Ted's Red Sled*

Words

-ed	-et	-eg	-ell
bed	get	leg	tell
led	bet	peg	sell
red	set	beg	fell
wed	wet	Meg	shell
sled	met		bell

Bonus Words

bled	fret	Greg	swell
shred	let		spell

Introduce/Model *Small Groups*

- **Read a Rhyme** Read "Ben's Red Hen" and have children identify the words that rhyme at the end of lines. (*hen, ten; leg, Meg; bet, met*) Then have children search the poem to find the word that rhymes with *bed* (*red*) and the word that rhymes with *tell* (*yell*). Write those rhyming pairs on the board.

- **Model** Use the whiteboard DVD or the CD word cards. First define any unfamiliar words, and then demonstrate how to sort into *-ed, -et, -eg,* and *-ell* word families.

Practice the Sort *Independent/Partner*

- Have children use the Student Book or whiteboard DVD to read the words and use the grid to sort the cards by ending sounds.

- Have children check and explain their sorts.

Apply *Independent/Partner/Small Groups*

- Read aloud the directions on Student Book p. 56. Have children write words that rhyme with *bed, met, leg,* and *bell*.

- **Game** Allow time for children to play Sled Down the Hill, which is on the CD.

- **Little Book** Read *Ted's Red Sled* with children. Have them identify words that end with *-ed*.

Extend the Sort

Alternative Sort: More Actions or People/Things

First remove the words for *red* and *wet*, and then re-sort into two groups: actions and people/things. Hold up *shell* and explain that a shell is an object. Hold up *tell* and explain that *tell* is an action. *Sled* and *set* fall into both categories; allow children to explain their choices.

Teacher Tip

Children may also enjoy using words in a word family to create tongue twisters, such as *I fell on a shell and yelled for a spell. I didn't feel well and my foot started to swell.*

Bonus Words Activity

Ask children to find other words that end with *-ed, -et, -eg,* or *-ell*. Then have children make word cards for these new words and work in small groups to sort the words into categories.

Monitor Progress **Spell Check 2**

After completing Sort 14, administer Spell Check 2. See pp. 80–81 in this Teacher Resource Guide for instructions.

Sort 15

Consonant Digraphs *ch, sh*

Objectives

- To identify the digraphs *ch* and *sh*
- To sort pictures by the beginning sounds *ch* and *sh*

Materials for Letter Name

Big Book of Rhymes, "On Our Ship," page 25

Whiteboard Activities DVD-ROM, Sort 15

Teacher Resource CD-ROM, Sort 15 and Bingo! Game

Student Book, pages 57–60

Words Their Way Library, *The Ship*

Pictures

ch	sh
chick	shirt
chair	shell
chimney	shoe
check	ship
chin	shadow
cheese	shelf

Introduce/Model
Small Groups

- **Read a Rhyme** Read "On Our Ship." Reread the first line, and have children listen for the word *ship*. Write *sh* on the board and point out that the beginning sound of *ship* is spelled with two letters. Reread the third line, and repeat the process for *chance*. Read the poem again, omitting the two words, and have children provide those words.

- **Model** Use the whiteboard DVD or the CD picture cards. Then demonstrate how to sort the pictures by their beginning sound. Have children describe how the names for the pictures in each group are alike and which letters make each sound.

Practice the Sort
Independent/Partner

- Have children use the Student Book or whiteboard DVD to name the pictures and use the grid to sort the cards by beginning sounds.

- Have children check and explain their sorts.

Apply
Independent/Partner/Small Groups

- Read aloud the directions on Student Book p. 60. Have children write letters and draw pictures of things whose names begin like *cherry* and *sheep*.

- **Game** Allow time for children to play Bingo!, which is on the CD.

- **Little Book** Read *The Ship* with children. Have them identify words that begin with /ch/ or /sh/.

Extend the Sort

Alternative Sort: Can People Make It?

Children can re-sort into two categories: things that people can make (*chair, chimney, check, cheese, shirt, shelf, shoe, ship, shadow*) and things that people cannot make (*chick, chin, shell*).

Vocabulary **Building Vocabulary**

Children may not understand the purpose of a chimney. Help them understand that a chimney is needed to carry away smoke from a fireplace or furnace below.

ELL **English Language Learners**

To strengthen concepts while practicing pronunciation and usage, display picture cards, and show them at the place they are used in a sentence, such as "I am wearing a *shoe* and a *shirt*." and "I have a *chair* and a *shelf* in my home."

Teacher Tip

Previously learned word families can be used to demonstrate that the sound of *ch* is different from the sound of either *c* or *h*, and the sound of *sh* is different from the sound of *s* or *h*.

96 Letter Name

Objectives

- To identify the digraphs *th* and *wh*
- To sort pictures by the beginning sounds *th* and *wh*

Materials for Letter Name

- Big Book of Rhymes, "What Do You Think?," page 27
- Whiteboard Activities DVD-ROM, Sort 16
- Teacher Resource CD-ROM, Sort 16 and Concentration Game
- Student Book, pages 61–64
- Words Their Way Library, *Humpback Whales*

Pictures

th	*wh*
thirteen	white
think	whisker
thick	whale
thorn	wheelbarrow
thermos	whistle
thumb	wheat

Introduce/Model
Small Groups

- **Read a Rhyme** Read "What Do You Think?" and emphasize the words *think, whale, when,* and *why.* Reread the first line, and have children find the word *think.* Write *think* on the board and underline *th.* Tell children that the beginning sound of *think* is spelled with two letters. Repeat the routine for the words that begin with *wh.*

- **Model** Use the whiteboard DVD or the CD picture cards. Then demonstrate how to sort the picture names by their beginning sound. Have children describe how the names for the pictures in each column are alike and which letters make each sound.

Practice the Sort
Independent/Partner

- Have children use the Student Book or whiteboard DVD to name the pictures and use the grid to sort the cards by beginning sounds.

- Have children check and explain their sorts.

Apply
Independent/Partner/Small Groups

- Read aloud the directions on Student Book p. 64. Have children write letters and draw pictures of things whose names begin like *thumb* and *wheel.*

- **Game** Allow time for children to play Concentration, which is on the CD.

- **Little Book** Read *Humpback Whales* with children. Have them identify words that begin with /th/ or /hw/.

Extend the Sort

Alternative Sort: Does It Grow and Change?

Re-sort the pictures except *think, thirteen, thick,* and *white.* Use the categories "things that grow and change" (*thorn, thumb, whisker, whale, wheat*) and "things that cannot grow" (*thermos, wheelbarrow*).

Vocabulary **Building Vocabulary**

Clarify the meaning of *thick.* Ask children how they or someone else have used *thick* to tell about things. Children can then take turns asking and answering such questions as "Would you like to have a thick sandwich or a thin sandwich?"

ELL **English Language Learners**

Point out the placement of the tongue when forming the two digraphs. Have children hold a hand in front of their mouths and say *wh-wh-whale* and *th-th-think.* Repeat the routine with *white* and *thumb.*

Teacher Tip

If children note that *th* has a different sound in words such as *then, that, this,* and *the,* it is an opportunity to begin comparative lists and compliment children on good thinking about words.

Sort 17

Consonant Digraphs *sh, ch, wh, th*

Objectives

- To identify and review consonant digraphs
- To identify and sort pictures with *sh, ch, wh,* and *th*

Materials for Letter Name

📔 Big Book of Rhymes, "Watch Out, Sheep!," page 29

🖥 Whiteboard Activities DVD-ROM, Sort 17

💿 Teacher Resource CD-ROM, Sort 17 and Shear the Sheep Game

📖 Student Book, pages 65–68

📕 Words Their Way Library, *Chipmunk Chili*

Pictures

sh	ch	wh	th
shoe	chin	wheelbarrow	thirteen
ship	chick	wheel	thick
shirt	chain	whistle	thermos
shelf	chair	whisker	thermometer
shell	cheese	whale	thorn

Introduce/Model
Small Groups

- **Read a Rhyme** Read "Watch Out, Sheep!" Encourage children to listen for words beginning with *sh, ch, wh,* and *th*. (*sheep, chugs, when, thump*) Write each word on the board and underline the consonant digraph. Remind children that two letters stand for one sound. Read the poem again, omitting these words, and have children provide them.

- **Model** Use the whiteboard DVD or the CD picture cards. Then demonstrate how to sort the pictures by their beginning sounds. Have children describe how the names for the pictures in each column are alike and which letters stand for each beginning sound.

Practice the Sort
Independent/Partner

- Have children use the Student Book or whiteboard DVD to name the pictures and use the grid to sort the cards by beginning sounds.

- Have children check and explain their sorts.

Apply
Independent/Partner/Small Groups

- Read aloud the directions on Student Book p. 68. Have children write letters and draw pictures of things whose names begin like *sheep, cheese, wheel,* and *thumb*.

- **Game** Allow time for children to play Shear the Sheep, which is on the CD.

- **Little Book** Read *Chipmunk Chili* with children. Have them identify words that begin with /sh/, /ch/, /hw/, or /th/.

Extend the Sort

Alternative Sort: What Is Alike?

Display twelve pictures. Have children find two or three pictures that are alike in some way without telling how they are alike (such as *shoe* and *shirt* are things to wear; *chin* and *whisker* are found on a face). Other children can guess the category.

Vocabulary **Building Vocabulary**

Use *whistle* in a sentence as a noun, but explain that *whistle* can be an object, action, or sound. Model for the class how to use *whistle* in a sentence with other meanings. Then have children use *whistle* in sentences and tell what it means in each.

ELL **English Language Learners**

To help children remember the four digraph sounds and spellings, draw outlines of a whale, a shirt, a chain, and a thorn with labels *whale, shirt, chain,* and *thorn*. Post the sound/letter reminders in the classroom for reference.

Teacher Tip

Have children hunt for more examples of *sh, ch, wh,* and *th* pictures and words in books and magazines. Make time for sharing their results.

98   Letter Name

Beginning Consonants and Blends *s, t, st*

Objectives

- To identify the sounds of consonants *s, t,* and the *st* blend
- To identify, differentiate, and sort pictures with *s, t,* and *st*

Materials for Letter Name

- Big Book of Rhymes, "Stan Is Sad," page 13
- Whiteboard Activities DVD-ROM, Sort 18
- Teacher Resource CD-ROM, Sort 18 and Match! Game
- Student Book, pages 69–72
- Words Their Way Library, *My Lost Top*

Pictures

s	t	st
sun	tag	steak
soap	tire	stamp
saw	tiger	stairs
sit	tape	star
seal	top	stove

Bonus Words

set	tab	stun
sob		stack
		stub

Introduce/Model   *Small Groups*

- **Read a Rhyme** Read "Stan Is Sad," emphasizing words that begin with *s, t,* and *st.* Read the poem again, and have children raise their hands when they hear words that begin with *s, t,* and *st.* Lead children in saying "*St-St-Stan, s-s-sad, t-t-top*" to compare the beginning sounds.

- **Model** Use the whiteboard DVD or the CD picture cards. Then demonstrate how to sort the picture names by their beginning sound. Have children describe how the names for the pictures in each column are alike and which letter or letters stand for each beginning sound.

Practice the Sort   *Independent/Partner*

- Have children use the Student Book or whiteboard DVD to name the pictures and use the grid to sort the cards by beginning sounds.

- Have children check and explain their sorts.

Apply   *Independent/Partner/Small Groups*

- Read aloud the directions on Student Book p. 72. Have children write letters and draw pictures of things whose names begin like *sink, tooth,* and *stool.*

- **Game** Allow time for children to play Match!, which is on the CD.

- **Little Book** Read *My Lost Top* with children. Have them identify words that begin with /s/, /t/, or /st/.

Extend the Sort

Alternative Sort: Odd One Out

Show sets of three pictures in which two items can be categorized as similar, but one is very different, such as *sun, star, tag* (things in the sky); *tire, steak, stove* (things in the kitchen). Have children explain how two are alike and why the third does not belong.

Vocabulary Building Vocabulary

Show the stove picture, and emphasize that *stove* is one word for the object. Ask children to share other words they have heard or used to name the item in the picture. Invite children to tell about other kinds of stoves they've seen.

ELL English Language Learners

Focus on meaning and speedy recall of the pictures and words for *st.* You may need to discuss that a *steak* is one kind of meat, *steps* can be called *stairs* (which begins with *st*), and *stove* is like an oven.

Bonus Words Activity

Write each Bonus Word on a card. Show each card and invite children to say the word. Then have children sort the cards into words that begin with *s, t,* and *st.*

Consonant Blends *sp, sk, sm*

Objectives

- To identify *s* blends
- To identify, differentiate, and sort pictures with *sp, sk,* and *sm* blends

Materials for Letter Name

Big Book of Rhymes, "My Special Skill," page 31

Whiteboard Activities DVD-ROM, Sort 19

Teacher Resource CD-ROM, Sort 19 and Let's Skateboard Game

Student Book, pages 73–76

Words Their Way Library, *Sally's Spaceship*

Pictures

sp	sk	sm
spill	skis	smoke
spider	skate	smock
spear	skunk	smell
sponge	sky	smile
spout	skirt	small

Bonus Words

spin	skin	smack
spun	skill	
	skull	

Introduce/Model
Small Groups

- **Read a Rhyme** Read "My Special Skill," and emphasize the words that begin with *sp, sk,* and *sm*. Ask children to find the words that begin with *sp, sk,* and *sm*. (*special, skill, spill, spin, spinning, smile*) Write each word on the board and have children identify the four words that begin with *sp*.

- **Model** Use the whiteboard DVD or the CD picture cards. Then demonstrate how to sort the picture names by their beginning sound. Have children describe how the names for the pictures in each column are alike and which letters stand for the beginning sounds.

Practice the Sort
Independent/Partner

- Have children use the Student Book or whiteboard DVD to name the pictures and use the grid to sort the cards by beginning blend.

- Have children check and explain their sorts.

Apply
Independent/Partner/Small Groups

- Read aloud the directions on Student Book p. 76. Have children write letters and draw pictures of things whose names begin like *spoon, skateboard,* and *smile*.

- **Game** Allow time for children to play Let's Skateboard, which is on the CD.

- **Little Book** Read *Sally's Spaceship* with children. Have them identify words that begin with *s* blends.

Extend the Sort

Alternative Sort: Odd One Out

Show sets of three pictures in which two items can be categorized as similar, but one is very different, such as *skis, skate, spider* (things people put on their feet or things used in sports); *sponge, smock, skirt* (clothing). Have children explain how two pictures are alike and why the third does not belong.

Vocabulary Building Vocabulary

Children may not recognize a smock or recall its name. Clarify that a smock is a loose outer shirt worn to protect clothing, and then have children suggest times a smock could be used.

ELL English Language Learners

Use the picture cards to focus on one blend each day. After several blends have been reviewed, show all the picture cards, and have children repeat the picture names after you. Mix the cards, and then have children take turns saying the picture names.

Bonus Words Activity

List the Bonus Words on the board. With the children, decode each word. Then ask children to use the words in sentences.

Consonant Blends *sc, sn, sw*

Objectives
- To identify the sounds of consonant blends with *s*
- To identify, differentiate, and sort pictures with *sc, sn,* and *sw* blends

Materials for Letter Name

Big Book of Rhymes, "I Fly High," page 33

Whiteboard Activities DVD-ROM, Sort 20

Teacher Resource CD-ROM, Sort 20 and Swinging High Game

Student Book, pages 77–80

Words Their Way Library, *Winter's Song*

Pictures

sc	sn	sw
scale	snake	sweater
scooter	snow	swan
scout	snowman	switch
scarf	snail	swing
school	snap	swim

Bonus Words

scat	snap	sweep
scam	snip	
	snug	

Introduce/Model
Small Groups

- **Read a Rhyme** Read "I Fly High" and emphasize the words that begin with *sc, sn,* and *sw*. Have children listen for the words *swing, snag,* and *scare* and raise their hand when they hear them. Call attention to the sounds of *sc, sn,* and *sw*. Read the poem again, omitting the target words, and have children say them.

- **Model** Use the whiteboard DVD or the CD picture cards. Then demonstrate how to sort the picture names by their beginning sounds.

Practice the Sort
Independent/Partner

- Have children use the Student Book or whiteboard DVD to name the pictures and use the grid to sort the cards by beginning blend.

- Have children check and explain their sorts.

Apply
Independent/Partner/Small Groups

- Read aloud the directions on Student Book p. 80. Have children write letters and draw pictures of things whose names begin like *scarecrow, sneakers,* and *swan*.

- **Game** Allow time for children to play Swinging High, which is on the CD.

- **Little Book** Read *Winter's Song* with children. Have them identify words that begin with *s* blends.

Extend the Sort

Alternative Sort: What Is Alike?

Lead children to make connections among the items pictured. Display ten pictures at a time, and have children take turns finding two or three pictures that show things that are alike in some way without revealing to the class how they are alike. Classmates can guess the similarity.

Vocabulary Building Vocabulary

Explain that the boy shown in the picture is a member of a scouting organization and that is why he's wearing a uniform. Invite children who are members of a scouting organization to talk about some activities they participate in.

ELL English Language Learners

If children confuse the names of pictures or have problems with pronunciation, hold up a picture card. First emphasize the blend, drawing out the beginning sound: *sn, sn-sn-snail*. Then take turns with children forming sentences about a snail.

Bonus Words Activity

In random order, list the bonus words on the board, and then write the labels *sc, sn,* and *sw*. Encourage children to say the words and then copy them under the correct label.

Consonant Blends *pl, sl, bl, fl*

Objectives

- To identify the sounds of *l* blends
- To identify, differentiate, and sort pictures with *pl, sl, bl,* and *fl* blends

Materials for Letter Name

Big Book of Rhymes, "Hurry to My Place!," page 35

Whiteboard Activities DVD-ROM, Sort 21

Teacher Resource CD-ROM, Sort 21 and Pool Play Game

Student Book, pages 81–84

Words Their Way Library, *Glenda the Lion*

Pictures

pl	*sl*	*bl*	*fl*
plant	sled	blocks	flag
plow	slices	black	flower
plug	sleep	blue	flute
pliers	slippers	blanket	float
plum	slide	blouse	flashlight

Bonus Words

plan	slip	blot	flip
plot	slug	bland	flap

Introduce/Model   *Small Groups*

- **Read a Rhyme** Read "Hurry to My Place!" Read the poem several times and have children listen for words that begin with *pl, sl, bl,* and *fl*. Make a list of those words on the board. (*place, plan, blue, float, slippery, slide*)

- **Model** Use the whiteboard DVD or the CD picture cards. Then demonstrate how to sort the picture names by their beginning sounds. Have children describe how the picture names in each column are alike and which letter stands for each sound.

Practice the Sort   *Independent/Partner*

- Have children use the Student Book or whiteboard DVD to name the pictures and use the grid to sort the cards by beginning blend.

- Have children check and explain their sorts.

Apply   *Independent/Partner/Small Groups*

- Read aloud the directions on Student Book p. 84. Have children write letters and draw pictures of things whose names begin like *plate, slide, blindfold,* and *fly*.

- **Game** Allow time for children to play Pool Play, which is on the CD.

- **Little Book** Read *Glenda the Lion* with children. Have them identify words that begin with *l* blends.

Extend the Sort

Alternative Sort: Odd One Out

Show sets of three pictures in which two items can be categorized as similar, but one is very different, such as *plum, blanket, zucchini* (things to eat); *plug, blocks, slide* (things to play with). Children explain how two are alike and why the third does not belong. Allow children to take over and build sets.

Vocabulary Building Vocabulary

Display the picture of a plow being pulled by a tractor. Explain how the plow turns up soil before seeds are put into the ground. Discuss how animals can also be used to pull plows.

ELL English Language Learners

Discuss how a *plug* is not the same thing as a cord; *pliers* are one type of tool; something *sliced* usually means cut by a knife; a *blouse* is not a boy's shirt; a *flute* is not the same as a horn.

Bonus Words Activity

Write each Bonus Word on a card, and make copies to distribute to children. Have children say the words, sort them according to their beginning blend, and make sentences using the words.

Objectives

- To identify the sounds of *r* and *l* blends
- To identify, differentiate, and sort pictures with *cr, cl, fr, gl,* and *gr* blends

Materials for Letter Name

- Big Book of Rhymes, "The River Frog," page 37
- Whiteboard Activities DVD-ROM, Sort 22
- Teacher Resource CD-ROM, Sort 22 and Match! Game
- Student Book, pages 85–88
- Words Their Way Library, *The River Grows*

Pictures

cr	cl	fr	gl	gr
crane	cloud	fry	glue	grass
crown	claw	fruit	glasses	grill
crib	clock	frame	glass	grasshopper
crackers	class	freezer	globe	groceries

Bonus Words

cr	cl	fr	gl	gr
crop	clan	frill	glad	grip
	clap	fret		
	clip			

Introduce/Model   *Small Groups*

- **Read a Rhyme** Read "The River Frog." Write the word *frog* on the board and underline *fr*. Say *frog*, emphasizing *fr*. Remind children that *fr* is a consonant blend—two sounds that blend together but each sound is still heard. Have children search for *cr, cl, fr, gl,* and *gr* words in the poem. List them on the board. (*frog, gleams, green, gray, croaks, clamps, flies*)

- **Model** Use the whiteboard DVD or the CD picture cards. Then demonstrate how to sort the picture names by their beginning consonant blend. Have children name the pictures in the columns and identify the consonant blend common to each word.

Practice the Sort   *Independent/Partner*

- Have children use the Student Book or whiteboard DVD to name the pictures and use the grid to sort the cards by beginning consonant blend.

- Have children check and explain their sorts.

Apply   *Independent/Partner/Small Groups*

- Read aloud the directions on Student Book p. 88. Have children write letters and draw pictures of things whose names begin like *crab, clown, frog, glove,* and *grapes*.

- **Game** Allow time for children to play Match!, which is on the CD.

- **Little Book** Read *The River Grows* with children. Have them identify words that begin with consonant blends.

Extend the Sort

Alternative Sort: Inside or Outside

Set aside *fry* and hold up the remaining cards, one by one. Ask children if the item on the card would usually be found outside or inside. Sort the cards into an "outside" pile and an "inside" pile.

ELL English Language Learners

Explain to children that the word *glasses* might refer to either drinking containers or eyewear.

Teacher Tip

When you introduce a new card, you can quickly check children's pronunciation and understanding by asking children to use the word in a sentence.

Bonus Words Activity

Ask children to think of other words that begin with *cr, cl, fr, gl,* and *gr*. Then have children make word cards for these new words, as well as the Bonus Words. Children can work in pairs or small groups to sort the words according to their beginning blend.

Sort 23

Consonant Blends *pr, tr, dr, br*

Objectives

- To identify the sounds of *r*-blends
- To identify, differentiate, and sort pictures with *pr, tr, dr,* and *br* blends

Materials for Letter Name

📖 Big Book of Rhymes, "Sack Race," page 39

🖥 Whiteboard Activities DVD-ROM, Sort 23

💿 Teacher Resource CD-ROM, Sort 23 and Sack Race Game

📕 Student Book, pages 89–92

📘 Words Their Way Library, *At the Track*

Pictures

pr	tr	dr	br
princess	tray	dragon	bread
prize	track	draw	brush
prince	triangle	dream	bridge
pretzel	tree	drill	broom
present	truck	drum	bride

Bonus Words

prance	trap	drag	bran
proud	trip	drip	Brad
prime	trot	drop	brag
		drug	

Introduce/Model
Small Groups

- **Read a Rhyme** Read "Sack Race," emphasizing the words beginning with *pr, tr, dr,* and *br*. Write *pr* on the board and tell children that /p/ and /r/ blend together. Reread the poem, and have children raise their hands when they hear the word that begins with *pr*. (*prizes*) Continue in the same manner with *tr, dr,* and *br*. (*track, dream, Bravo*)

- **Model** Use the whiteboard DVD or the CD picture cards. Demonstrate how to sort the picture names by their beginning consonant blend. Have children name the pictures in the columns and identify the beginning blend common to each word.

Practice the Sort
Independent/Partner

- Have children use the Student Book or whiteboard DVD to name the pictures and use the grid to sort the cards by beginning consonant blend.

- Have children check and explain their sorts.

Apply
Independent/Partner/Small Groups

- Read aloud the directions on Student Book p. 92. Have children write letters and draw pictures of things whose names begin like *present, truck, dress,* and *brick*.

- **Game** Allow time for children to play Sack Race, which is on the CD.

- **Little Book** Read *At the Track* with children. Have them identify words that begin with consonant blends.

Extend the Sort

Alternative Sort: What Is Alike?

Display twelve pictures and have children take turns finding two or three that show things alike in some way without telling how they are alike. Have others guess their similarity.

Vocabulary ▸ Building Vocabulary

Children may recognize a basic triangle, but make sure they know that a triangle has three sides and three angles. Draw different shapes on the board, including triangles of varying side lengths and angles, and have children identify the triangles.

Teacher Tip

To model blending, hold a *d* letter card in one hand and an *r* letter card in the other. Have children say the sounds for each letter. Then move the cards together and have children blend the sounds.

Bonus Words Activity

List the Bonus Words on the board. With children, decode each word. Then ask children to use the words in sentences.

Beginning Sounds *k, wh, qu, tw*

Objectives

- To identify the beginning sounds of *k, wh, qu,* and *tw*
- To identify, differentiate, and sort pictures with beginning sounds *k, wh, qu,* and *tw*

Materials for Letter Name

Big Book of Rhymes, "Whales Can Do Tricks," page 41

Whiteboard Activities DVD-ROM, Sort 24

Teacher Resource CD-ROM, Sort 24 and Concentration Game

Student Book, pages 93–96

Words Their Way Library, *Humpback Whales*

Pictures

k	*wh*	*qu*	*tw*
kangaroo	wheelbarrow	question	twenty
kitten	whistle	quack	twine
key	wheat	quilt	twig
kite	whisker	queen	twelve
kick	whale	quiet	twins

Bonus Words

kin	whip	quit	twin
	when		

Introduce/Model
Small Groups

- **Read a Rhyme** Read "Whales Can Do Tricks." Write *killer whale* on the board, underline *k* and *wh*, pronounce the two words, and explain that killer whales use their sharp teeth to feed on fish and ocean animals. Reread the poem, and have children raise their hands when they hear words that begin with *k, wh, qu,* or *tw*. List those words on the board. (*killer, whale, white, quick, when, twirls, twist*)

- **Model** Use the whiteboard DVD or the CD picture cards. Show children how to say the picture names and then sort them according to their beginning sounds. Have children name the pictures in the columns and identify the beginning sounds common to each word.

Practice the Sort
Independent/Partner

- Have children use the Student Book or whiteboard DVD to name the pictures and use the grid to sort the cards by their beginning sounds.

- Have children check and explain their sorts.

Apply
Independent/Partner/Small Groups

- Read aloud the directions on Student Book p. 96. Have children write letters and draw pictures of things whose names begin like *king, wheel, quarter,* and *twins*.

- **Game** Allow time for children to play Concentration, which is on the CD.

- **Little Book** Read *Humpback Whales* with children. Have them identify words that begin with /k/ or /hw/.

Extend the Sort

Alternative Sort: I Spy

Show objects from the cards around the classroom. Place some keys and a ball of twine on your desk, and write a question with the numbers 12 and 20 on the board. Children can sort cards into two piles: things they see (either in the classroom or out the window) and things they do not see.

Vocabulary Building Vocabulary

Display the question mark picture card and help children understand *question*. Explain that a question is a sentence that asks something and this is a question mark—a kind of punctuation that is always found at the end of a question.

Bonus Words Activity

Help children brainstorm other words that begin with *k, wh, qu,* and *tw*. Then have children make word cards for these new words, as well as the Bonus Words. Children can work in pairs or small groups to sort the words into categories.

Monitor Progress Spell Check 3

After completing Sort 24, administer Spell Check 3. See pp. 80–81 in this Teacher Resource Guide for instructions.

Objectives

- To recognize and read words in word families *-at*, *-ot*, and *-it*
- To identify and sort words with *-at*, *-ot*, and *-it*

Materials for Letter Name

📖 Big Book of Rhymes, "The Cat," page 43

🖥 Whiteboard Activities DVD-ROM, Sort 25

💿 Teacher Resource CD-ROM, Sort 25 and Word Maker Game

📕 Student Book, pages 97–100

📖 Words Their Way Library, *You Can, Too!*

Words

-at	*-ot*	*-it*
that	not	fit
bat	cot	bit
fat	dot	hit
mat	got	kit
flat	slot	lit
rat	spot	pit
chat	trot	quit

Bonus Words

brat	plot	grit
slat	shot	skit
scat	blot	slit

Introduce/Model
Small Groups

- **Read a Rhyme** Read "The Cat," emphasizing rhyming words. (*cat, sat; hot, not; fit, sit*) Have children identify the rhyming pairs and write them in three columns. Ask how the words in each column are alike. (They end with the same sounds and letters and they rhyme.)

- **Model** Use the whiteboard DVD or the CD word cards. Explain that children will sort by words that rhyme. Demonstrate how to sort into *-at*, *-ot*, and *-it* word families. Help children sort and explain their sorts.

Practice the Sort
Independent/Partner

- Have children use the Student Book or whiteboard DVD to read the words and use the grid to sort their cards into *-at*, *-ot*, and *-it* word families.

- Have children check and explain their sorts.

Apply
Independent/Partner/Small Groups

- Read aloud the directions on Student Book p. 100. Have children use the letters or combinations of letters to write words in the *-at*, *-ot*, and *-it* word families.

- **Game** Allow time for children to play Word Maker, which is on the CD.

- **Little Book** Read *You Can, Too!* with children. Have them identify words that end with *-at* or *-ot*.

Extend the Sort

Alternative Sort: Objects or Actions

Set aside cards for *fat, not, that,* and *flat.* Have children sort the words for objects and actions. Point out that some words, such as *fit, bat, dot, hit, pit,* and *chat,* can have more than one meaning.

Vocabulary Building Vocabulary

Write *kit* on the board. Explain that *kit* can mean "a group of items collected for a purpose," such as a first-aid kit. Ask children if they know another meaning for the word *kit*. Point out that a *kit* can also be "a young animal with fur," such as a fox or beaver.

Bonus Words Activity

Give each child three blank word cards. Have children write a word on each card from the *-at*, *-ot*, and *-it* word families. Collect and mix cards. Give one card to each child. Have children sort themselves into word family groups.

Teacher Tip

If children are working with partners to sort cards, remind them that both children should take part in the activity. Suggest that one child can place a card while the other child confirms the placement. Then children can switch roles.

Objectives
- To recognize and read words in word families *-an, -in, -en,* and *-un*
- To identify and sort words with *-an, -in, -en,* and *-un*

Materials for Letter Name

Big Book of Rhymes, "Grand Slam," page 45

Whiteboard Activities DVD-ROM, Sort 26

Teacher Resource CD-ROM, Sort 26 and In the Pocket Game

Student Book, pages 101–104

Words Their Way Library, *The Merry-Go-Round*

Words

-an	*-in*	*-en*	*-un*
fan	thin	then	bun
man	skin	pen	run
plan	win	hen	fun
ran	chin	when	
pan	grin	men	
than	fin		

Bonus Words

bran	bin	den	pun
tan	tin	yen	sun

Introduce/Model
Small Groups

- **Read a Rhyme** Read "Grand Slam," emphasizing rhyming words. (*fun, run*) Write the last word of the second line (*fun*) and the last word of the fourth line (*run*) on the board. Read the words and ask children how they are the same. (They rhyme.)

- **Model** Use the whiteboard DVD or the CD word cards. Explain that children will sort by words that rhyme. Demonstrate how to sort into *-an, -in, -en,* and *-un* word families. Help children sort and explain their sorts.

Practice the Sort
Independent/Partner

- Have children use the Student Book or whiteboard DVD to read the words and use the grid to sort their cards into *-an, -in, -en,* and *-un* word families.

- Have children check and explain their sorts.

Apply
Independent/Partner/Small Groups

- Read aloud the directions on Student Book p. 104. Have children use one of the letters or combinations of letters to write words in the *-an, -in, -en,* and *-un* word families.

- **Game** Allow time for children to play In the Pocket, which is on the CD.

- **Little Book** Read *The Merry-Go-Round* with children. Have them identify words that end with *-an, -in, -en,* or *-un.*

Extend the Sort

Alternative Sort: Letter Count

Have children work independently or with partners to re-sort the word cards into piles according to the number of letters in each word. Children should make two piles, one for three-letter words and one for four-letter words.

ELL English Language Learners

To help children learn to discriminate among short vowel sounds, say two words, such as *pan* and *pen*. Elongate each vowel sound. Have children repeat the words after you in the same way and tell whether the words have the same vowel sound. Repeat with other pairs, making sure to include word pairs from the same word family.

Bonus Words Activity

Write *-an, -in, -en,* and *-un* in large letters in columns on chart paper and on separate cards. Give one card to each child. Children should think of and write words that end with the word family listed on their card. If needed, make suggestions from the Bonus Words list. Have children place their card in the corresponding column.

Teacher Tip

If children have difficulty coming up with words in the same word family, suggest that they go through the alphabet, trying each consonant. Often this method quickly turns up many words.

Mixed Vowel Word Families -ad, -ed, -ab, -ob

Objectives
- To recognize and read words in word families -ad, -ed, -ab, and -ob
- To identify and sort words with -ad, -ed, -ab, and -ob

Materials for Letter Name

Big Book of Rhymes, "Bob's Sled," page 47

Whiteboard Activities DVD-ROM, Sort 27

Teacher Resource CD-ROM, Sort 27 and Word Maker Game

Student Book, pages 105–108

Words Their Way Library, *Ted's Red Sled*

Words

-ad	-ed	-ab	-ob
mad	red	tab	rob
had	fed	lab	blob
bad	led	grab	mob
pad	shed	cab	sob
glad	sled		glob
			job

Bonus Words

fad	wed	dab	knob
lad	fled	nab	throb
sad	sped	scab	gob

Introduce/Model
Small Groups

- **Read a Rhyme** Read "Bob's Sled." Ask children to listen for words that rhyme. After reading, write the word endings -ad, -ed, -ab, and -ob on the board. Ask children to identify words that rhyme with the four word endings on the board. Write the words under their corresponding word ending.

- **Model** Use the whiteboard DVD or the CD word cards. Explain that children will sort by words that rhyme. Demonstrate how to sort into -ad, -ed, -ab, and -ob word families. Help children sort and explain their sorts.

Practice the Sort
Independent/Partner

- Have children use the Student Book or whiteboard DVD to read the words and use the grid to sort their cards into -ad, -ed, -ab, and -ob word families.

- Have children check and explain their sorts.

Apply
Independent/Partner/Small Groups

- Read aloud the directions on Student Book p. 108. Have children use the letters or combinations of letters to write words in the -ad, -ed, -ab, and -ob word families.

- **Game** Allow time for children to play Word Maker, which is on the CD.

- **Little Book** Read *Ted's Red Sled* with children. Have them identify words that end with -ad or -ed.

Extend the Sort

Bonus Words Activity

Ask children to think of other words that end with -ad, -ed, -ab, and -ob. If children need prompting, make suggestions from the Bonus Words list. Help children make word cards for these new words. Encourage them to work in pairs or small groups to sort the words into word families.

Alternative Sort: What I Feel

Have children complete the Bonus Words activity before this alternate sort. Discuss with children words that describe feelings. Following the discussion, have children work with a partner to sort the cards into words that name feelings and those that do not. Once the cards have been sorted, invite the first partner to pantomime one of the feeling cards. After the other partner guesses the word, children can switch roles and repeat the activity.

Teacher Tip

Listen as children complete the sorting activities. Check to make sure they are enunciating correctly in order to avoid making mistakes.

Objectives

- To recognize and read words in word families -ap, -ip, -op, and -up
- To identify and sort words with -ap, -ip, -op, and -up

Materials for Letter Name

📓 Big Book of Rhymes, "Look What We Can Do," page 49

📋 Whiteboard Activities DVD-ROM, Sort 28

💿 Teacher Resource CD-ROM, Sort 28 and Word Maker Game

📘 Student Book, pages 109–112

📖 Words Their Way Library, *Jump Right In*

Words

-ap	-ip	-op	-up
snap	flip	top	cup
clap	whip	hop	up
zap	hip	chop	
tap	dip	crop	
lap	trip	pop	
trap	ship	drop	

Bonus Words

chap	chip	plop	hiccup
flap	slip	flop	sunup
wrap	zip	stop	teacup

Introduce/Model
Small Groups

- **Read a Rhyme** Read "Look What We Can Do." Ask children to listen for words that rhyme. (*run, fun; hop, stop; Do, too, you*) Write them in three columns. Then write the headings -ap, -ip, -op, and -up. Read the poem again and ask children to raise their hands when they hear a word that rhymes with one of these word endings. Write the words under their corresponding heading.

- **Model** Use the whiteboard DVD or the CD word cards. Explain that children will sort by words that rhyme. Demonstrate how to sort into -ap, -ip, -op, and -up word families. Help children sort and explain their sorts.

Practice the Sort
Independent/Partner

- Have children use the Student Book or whiteboard DVD to read the words and use the grid to sort their cards into -ap, -ip, -op, and -up word families.

- Have children check and explain their sorts.

Apply
Independent/Partner/Small Groups

- Read aloud the directions on Student Book p. 112. Have children use letters and blends to write words in the -ap, -ip, -op, and -up word families.

- **Game** Allow time for children to play Word Maker, which is on the CD.

- **Little Book** Read *Jump Right In* with children. Have them identify words that end with -ap, -ip, -op, or -up.

Extend the Sort

Alternative Sort: Shake It!

Ask children to re-sort the word cards into two piles: things that they would do as part of a dance, and things they wouldn't do as part of a dance. Then ask children to explain their dance moves to the group.

Bonus Words Activity

List the Bonus Words on the board or on chart paper. Guide children in reading the list. Ask a child to tell the meaning of a word. Ask another child to use that word in a sentence. Repeat with the remaining words.

Vocabulary Building Vocabulary

Write *tap* on the board. Ask children if they know the meaning of *tap*. They will most likely be familiar with the meaning "to touch lightly." Explain that this meaning is an action and that *tap* is also a thing, meaning "faucet."

Mixed Vowel Word Families -*ag*, -*eg*, -*ig*, -*og*, -*ug*

Objectives

- To recognize and read words in word families -*ag*, -*eg*, -*ig*, -*og*, -*ug*
- To identify and sort words with -*ag*, -*eg*, -*ig*, -*og*, and -*ug*

Materials for Letter Name

📖 Big Book of Rhymes, "Someday," page 51

🖥 Whiteboard Activities DVD-ROM, Sort 29

💿 Teacher Resource CD-ROM, Sort 29 and Park Race Game

📕 Student Book, pages 113–116

🦉 Words Their Way Library, *When We Are Big*

Words

-ag	-eg	-ig	-og	-ug
rag	peg	fig	log	hug
bag	Meg	big	jog	rug
wag	beg	wig	frog	drug
flag		dig	hog	slug
snag		twig	fog	plug
		jig		mug

Bonus Words

nag	leg	gig	bog	tug
brag	egg	rig	clog	snug

Introduce/Model
Small Groups

- **Read a Rhyme** Read "Someday," emphasizing the rhyming words. (*dogs, frogs; snug, hug*) Ask children to name the words that rhyme. Write the words in columns. Ask children how the words in each column are alike. (They end with the same sounds and they rhyme.)

- **Model** Use the whiteboard DVD or the CD word cards. Explain that children will sort by words that rhyme. Demonstrate how to sort into -*ag*, -*eg*, -*ig*, -*og*, and -*ug* word families. Help children sort and explain their sorts.

Practice the Sort
Independent/Partner

- Have children use the Student Book or whiteboard DVD to read the words and use the grid to sort their cards into -*ag*, -*eg*, -*ig*, -*og*, and -*ug* word families.

- Have children check and explain their sorts.

Apply
Independent/Partner/Small Groups

- Read aloud the directions on Student Book p. 116. Have children use letters to write words in the -*ag*, -*eg*, -*ig*, -*og*, and -*ug* word families.

- **Game** Allow time for children to play Park Race, which is on the CD.

- **Little Book** Read *When We Are Big* with children. Have them identify words that end with -*ag*, -*eg*, -*ig*, -*og*, or -*ug*.

Extend the Sort

Alternative Sort: Animals, People, and Things

Ask children to re-sort the word cards into three groups: animals, people, things. After children complete the sort, have them tell who has two legs (*Meg*), what has more than two legs (*frog, hog*), and what has no legs (*rag, hug, bag, log, rug, fig, peg, wig, flag, drug, slug, plug, fog, twig, mug, jig*).

Bonus Words Activity

Write the Bonus Words in random order on one side of the board. Then write the labels -*ag*, -*eg*, -*ig*, -*og*, and -*ug*. Point to each word and have children say the word and tell under which label it belongs.

Vocabulary Building Vocabulary

Write *snag* on the board. Explain that *snag* can mean an action or a thing: "to catch on something" or "any sharp or rough point that sticks out from something, such as a thorn on a rosebush." Demonstrate snagging a sleeve or strap on a doorknob. Say, "I caught my sleeve on that snag." Then use *snag* as an action word: "I snagged my sleeve on the doorknob."

Objectives

- To recognize and read words in word families *-ill, -ell,* and *-all*
- To identify and sort words with *-ill, -ell,* and *-all*

Materials for Letter Name

📔 Big Book of Rhymes, "Play Ball!," page 53

🖥 Whiteboard Activities DVD-ROM, Sort 30

💿 Teacher Resource CD-ROM, Sort 30 and Rhyming Go Fish Game

📗 Student Book, pages 117–120

📖 Words Their Way Library, *A Small Baby Raccoon*

Words		
-ill	*-ell*	*-all*
bill	fell	hall
will	well	mall
fill	shell	call
chill	smell	tall
spill	sell	small
hill	tell	fall

Bonus Words		
grill	swell	stall
skill	spell	squall
still	cell	

Introduce/Model
Small Groups

- **Read a Rhyme** Read "Play Ball!," emphasizing the rhyming words. Ask children to name words they hear in the poem that rhyme. (*ball, call, all; Bill, Jill; Nell, well, yell*) Write the words in columns. Help children understand that the words rhyme because they are in the same word family.

- **Model** Use the whiteboard DVD or the CD word cards. Explain that children will sort by words that rhyme. Demonstrate how to sort into *-ill, -ell,* and *-all* word families. Help children sort and explain their sorts.

Practice the Sort
Independent/Partner

- Have children use the Student Book or whiteboard DVD to read the words and use the grid to sort their cards into *-ill, -ell,* and *-all* word families.

- Have children check and explain their sorts.

Apply
Independent/Partner/Small Groups

- Read aloud the directions on Student Book p. 120. Have children use letters or digraphs to write words in the *-ill, -ell,* and *-all* word families.

- **Game** Allow time for children to play Rhyming Go Fish, which is on the CD.

- **Little Book** Read *A Small Baby Raccoon* with children. Have them identify words that end with *-ill, -ell,* or *-all*.

Extend the Sort

Alternative Sort: Places or Actions

Set aside cards for *will, bill, tall, small,* and *shell*. Then have children sort the words for places (*hill, well, hall, mall*) and actions (*fill, chill, spill, fell, smell, sell, tell, call, fall*). You may want to point out that some words, such as *smell* and *well,* can have more than one meaning.

Vocabulary Building Vocabulary

If children are only familiar with a shopping mall, describe an outdoor mall that is like a small park. Have children compare the two kinds of malls and understand that a mall is usually a large area where it is easy to move about and for everyone to use.

Bonus Words Activity

Help children brainstorm other words that end with *-ill, -ell,* or *-all*. Refer to the Bonus Words list as necessary. Then help children make word cards for these words. Encourage them to work in pairs or small groups to sort the words into word families.

Teacher Tip

Children may also enjoy using words in a word family to create tongue twisters such as *Tell Nell I'll sell the shell.* This will help them discriminate among the short *a, e,* and *i* vowels.

Sort 31 Mixed Vowel Word Families *-ack, -ick, -ock, -uck*

Objectives

- To recognize and read words in word families *-ack, -ick, -ock,* and *-uck*
- To identify and sort words with *-ack, -ick, -ock,* and *-uck*

Materials for Letter Name

- Big Book of Rhymes, "Time Talk," page 55
- Whiteboard Activities DVD-ROM, Sort 31
- Teacher Resource CD-ROM, Sort 31 and Word Maker Game
- Student Book, pages 121–124
- Words Their Way Library, *My Clock Is Sick*

Words

-ack	-ick	-ock	-uck
pack	trick	clock	truck
back	thick	rock	stuck
black	kick	flock	tuck
rack	chick	dock	pluck
tack	lick	block	luck

Bonus Words

crack	wick	shock	buck
sack	flick	knock	shuck

Introduce/Model   *Small Groups*

- **Read a Rhyme** Read "Time Talk," emphasizing the rhyming words (*too, do; quick, tick; chime, time*). Ask children to find the rhyming pair *quick* and *tick*. Write the words in a column. Ask children how the words are alike. Read the poem again, omitting the last word of each line and have children supply the word.

- **Model** Use the whiteboard DVD or the CD word cards. Explain that children will sort by words that rhyme. Demonstrate how to sort into *-ack, -ick, -ock,* and *-uck* word families. Help children sort and explain their sorts.

Practice the Sort   *Independent/Partner*

- Have children use the Student Book or whiteboard DVD to read the words and use the grid to sort their cards into *-ack, -ick, -ock,* and *-uck* word families.

- Have children check and explain their sorts.

Apply   *Independent/Partner/Small Groups*

- Read aloud the directions on Student Book p. 124. Have children use letters or combinations of letters to write words in the *-ack, -ick, -ock,* and *-uck* word families.

- **Game** Allow time for children to play Word Maker, which is on the CD.

- **Little Book** Read *My Clock Is Sick* with children. Have them identify words that end with *-ack, -ick, -ock,* or *-uck.*

Extend the Sort

Alternative Sort: Object and Action

Have children re-sort the word cards into two piles: one pile for words that name both an object and an action and one pile for words that do not. Ask a child to say one of his or her words and tell what it means. Ask another child to use the word in a sentence. Have a classroom dictionary available for children to look up words and their meanings if necessary.

Bonus Words Activity

Help children brainstorm other words that end with *-ack, -ick, -ock,* and *-uck.* Refer to the Bonus Words list as needed. Help children make word cards for these new words. Encourage them to work in pairs or small groups to sort the words into categories.

ELL English Language Learners

The distinction between short *a* and short *i* may be difficult for English language learners. To help them hear the difference, say each word in the sort, emphasizing the vowel sound. Have children repeat words with you to reinforce learning.

Objectives

- To recognize and read words in word families -*ash*, -*ish*, and -*ush*
- To identify and sort words with -*ash*, -*ish*, and -*ush*

Materials for Letter Name

Big Book of Rhymes, "Dinnertime," page 57

Whiteboard Activities DVD-ROM, Sort 32

Teacher Resource CD-ROM, Sort 32 and Pick a Dish Game

Student Book, pages 125–128

Words Their Way Library, *Something to Munch*

Words

-*ash*	-*ish*	-*ush*
dash	wish	rush
flash	swish	crush
crash	fish	mush
smash	dish	blush
rash		flush
trash		hush
mash		plush

Bonus Words

gash	squish	slush
stash		brush
clash		

Introduce/Model   *Small Groups*

- **Read a Rhyme** Read "Dinnertime," emphasizing the rhyming words. Ask children to name words they hear in the poem that rhyme. (*rush, crush; dish, fish; crash, trash*) As children find rhyming words, write them in columns. Then ask children how the words are alike. (They rhyme and end with the same sounds.)

- **Model** Use the whiteboard DVD or the CD word cards. Explain that children will sort by words that rhyme. Demonstrate how to sort into -*ash*, -*ish*, and -*ush* word families. Help children sort and explain their sorts.

Practice the Sort   *Independent/Partner*

- Have children use the Student Book or whiteboard DVD to read the words and use the grid to sort their cards into -*ash*, -*ish*, and -*ush* word families

- Have children check and explain their sorts.

Apply   *Independent/Partner/Small Groups*

- Read aloud the directions on Student Book p. 128. Have children use letters to write words in the -*ash*, -*ish*, and -*ush* word families.

- **Game** Allow time for children to play Pick a Dish, which is on the CD.

- **Little Book** Read *Something to Munch* with children. Have them identify words that end with -*ash*, -*ish*, or -*ush*. Point out that *wash* has the same ending letters as *mash*, but it has a different vowel sound.

Extend the Sort

Alternative Sort: Beginning Sound Sort

Have children sort the cards into words that begin with an initial consonant blend and words that begin with one initial consonant. Ask them to explain why each card belongs into its sorted group.

Vocabulary Building Vocabulary

Write the word *swish* on the board. Use *swish* in a sentence as a noun, but explain that *swish* can be an action or a sound. Model for the class how to use *swish* in a sentence with the other meaning. Then invite children to use *swish* in sentences and tell what it means in each.

Bonus Words Activity

Help children brainstorm other words that end with -*ash*, -*ish*, and -*ush*. Refer to the Bonus Words list as necessary. Then help children make word cards for these words. Encourage them to work in pairs or small groups to sort the words into word families.

ELL English Language Learners

Children benefit from learning new words in context. When introducing the words for this sort, use each word in context. Then engage children in speaking activities. Have them repeat the word and your sample sentence and then use the word in sentences of their own.

Mixed Vowel Word Families -ang, -ing, -ong, -ung

Objectives

- To recognize and read words in word families -ang, -ing, -ong, and -ung
- To identify and sort words with -ang, -ing, -ong, and -ung

Materials for Letter Name

📖 Big Book of Rhymes, "I Fly High," page 33

🖥 Whiteboard Activities DVD-ROM, Sort 33

💿 Teacher Resource CD-ROM, Sort 33 and Word Maker Game

📕 Student Book, pages 129–132

📘 Words Their Way Library, *That Pig Can't Do a Thing*

Words

-ang	-ing	-ong	-ung
sang	ring	strong	sung
gang	bring	gong	stung
rang	king	long	rung
clang	ding	song	lung
hang	sting		
fang	sing		

Bonus Words

slang	swing	prong	wrung
twang	cling	tong	

Introduce/Model   *Small Groups*

- **Read a Rhyme** Read "I Fly High," emphasizing the rhyming words. Ask children to find the rhyming pairs. (*swing, wing; air, scare*) Ask children how each pair of words are alike. (They rhyme.)

- **Model** Use the whiteboard DVD or the CD word cards. Explain that children will sort by words that rhyme. Demonstrate how to sort into -ang, -ing, -ong, and -ung word families. Help children sort and explain their sorts.

Practice the Sort   *Independent/Partner*

- Have children use the Student Book or whiteboard DVD to read the words and use the grid to sort their cards into -ang, -ing, -ong, and -ung word families.

- Have children check and explain their sorts.

Apply   *Independent/Partner/Small Groups*

- Read aloud the directions on Student Book p. 132. Have children use the letters and blends to write words in the -ang, -ing, -ong, and -ung word families.

- **Game** Allow time for children to play Word Maker, which is on the CD.

- **Little Book** Read *That Pig Can't Do a Thing* with children. Have them identify words that end with -ang, -ing, -ong, or -ung.

Extend the Sort

Alternative Sort: Beginning *s* Sort

Ask children to re-sort the word cards into two piles, one pile for words that begin with the letter *s* and one pile for words that do not. When children have finished, ask a child to say one of his or her words and tell what it means. Ask another child to use the word in a sentence.

Bonus Words Activity

List some or all of the Bonus Words. Model how children can take turns using Bonus Words as the answer to a puzzle: "I'm thinking of a word that rhymes with *bring*. It's something I like to do at the playground in the summer. What is it?" (*swing*)

ELL English Language Learners

The distinction between -ong and -ung may be difficult for English language learners. Demonstrate the vowel sound in *gong* and *lung* slowly. Have children listen and repeat with you to help them hear the difference. Have children repeat words several times with you to reinforce learning.

Teacher Tip

Encourage children to develop their sorting prowess by participating in basic sorting exercises that identify common objects in the classroom (pencils, buttons, colors, and so on).

Mixed Vowel Word Families -ank, -ink, -unk

Objectives

- To recognize and read words in word families -ank, -ink, and -unk
- To identify and sort words with -ank, -ink, and -unk

Materials for Letter Name

📓 Big Book of Rhymes, "Five Goats in a Boat," page 59

🖥 Whiteboard Activities DVD-ROM, Sort 34

💿 Teacher Resource CD-ROM, Sort 34 and Word Maker Game

📕 Student Book, pages 133–136

📖 Words Their Way Library, *Mr. Wink*

Words

-ank	-ink	-unk
sank	think	bunk
bank	drink	junk
thank	ink	chunk
plank	link	skunk
prank	blink	hunk
blank	stink	dunk
yank	wink	sunk

Bonus Words

rank	pink	clunk
crank	clink	

Introduce/Model   *Small Groups*

- **Read a Rhyme** Read "Five Goats in a Boat," emphasizing rhyming words at the end of the lines. Ask children to name words they hear in the poem that rhyme. (*play, away; shore, more; sank, bank*) Write the words in columns. Help children understand that the words rhyme because they are in the same word family.

- **Model** Use the whiteboard DVD or the CD word cards. Explain that children will sort by words that rhyme. Demonstrate how to sort into -ank, -ink, and -unk word families. Help children sort and explain their sorts.

Practice the Sort   *Independent/Partner*

- Have children use the Student Book or whiteboard DVD to read the words and use the grid to sort their cards into -ank, -ink, and -unk word families.

- Have children check and explain their sorts.

Apply   *Independent/Partner/Small Groups*

- Read aloud the directions on Student Book p. 136. Have children use the letters, blends, and digraphs to write words in the -ank, -ink, and -unk word families.

- **Game** Allow time for children to play Word Maker, which is on the CD.

- **Little Book** Read *Mr. Wink* with children. Have them identify words that end with -ank, -ink, or -unk.

Extend the Sort

Alternative Sort: Sort Short *i*

Ask children to sort the cards into two piles, one pile for words that have the short *i* vowel sound and one pile for words that do not. Demonstrate short *i* several times by repeating *ink* and *wink*. When they have finished sorting, ask children to work in pairs and take turns holding up a card for their partner, who will say the word.

Bonus Words Activity

Help children brainstorm other words that end with -ank, -ink, and -unk. Refer to the Bonus Words list as necessary. Then help children make word cards for these words. Encourage them to work in pairs or small groups to sort the words into word families.

Teacher Tip

If children are overwhelmed by the number of words in the sort, have them sort two or three word cards from each word family at a time. Have them gradually use more cards until they can complete the sort using all the cards.

Monitor Progress **Spell Check 4**

After completing Sort 34, administer Spell Check 4. See pp. 80–81 in this Teacher Resource Guide for instructions.

Objectives

- To identify short vowels *a* and *o*
- To identify and sort words with short vowels *a* and *o*

Materials for Letter Name

📖 Big Book of Rhymes, "Jogging," page 61

🖥 Whiteboard Activities DVD-ROM, Sort 35

💿 Teacher Resource CD-ROM, Sort 35 and Ant Trek Game

📕 Student Book, pages 137–140

📙 Words Their Way Library, *The Ant*

Words

ă	ŏ	oddball
had	top	was
wag	hop	for
ran	box	
ham	lot	
cab	mop	**Bonus Words**
bag	hot	
map	mom	
sad	fox	
jam	got	
	job	

Bonus Words

dad	cot
sat	log
tax	rod
pat	sob

Introduce/Model   *Small Groups*

- **Read a Rhyme** Read "Jogging," emphasizing words with short *a* and *o*. Ask children to name the words in the poem with the short vowel sounds of *a* and *o*. (*ant, jog, ran, fog, trot, hot, sat, nap, log*) Write the words in two columns. Help children understand that the words in each column contain the same short vowel sound.

- **Model** Use the whiteboard DVD or the CD word cards. Demonstrate how to sort into short vowels *a* and *o*. Point out that *was* and *for* are oddballs because they have the same vowels as *sat* and *log* but different vowel sounds. Help children sort and explain their sorts.

Practice the Sort   *Independent/Partner*

- Have children use the Student Book or whiteboard DVD to read the words and use the grid to sort their cards into words with short vowels *a* and *o* and oddball words.

- Have children check and explain their sorts.

Apply   *Independent/Partner/Small Groups*

- Read aloud the directions on Student Book p. 140. Have children write words with short vowels *a* and *o*.

- **Game** Allow time for children to play Ant Trek, which is on the CD.

- **Little Book** Read *The Ant* with children. Have them identify words with a/a/ or o/o/.

Extend the Sort

Alternative Sort: Will It Fit?

Set aside the word cards *hop, had, wag, ran, lot, was, for, hot, got, sad,* and *job*. Have children re-sort the cards into two categories: things that would usually fit into a backpack (*top, ham, box, bag, map, jam*) and things that would not (*mop, mom, cab, fox*).

Vocabulary Building Vocabulary

Write the word *jam* on the board. Tell children that one meaning of *jam* is "a thick fruit spread." Point out that *jam* can also mean "a difficult situation" or "to crowd into." Demonstrate the different meanings in sentences.

ELL English Language Learners

Review the words with children. Emphasize action words that contain short vowels *a* and *o* (*ran, hop*) by having children act out the motions associated with each word.

Bonus Words Activity

Ask children to find other words that include short vowels *a* and *o*. If children need prompting, make suggestions from the Bonus Words list as necessary. Then help children make word cards for these new words. Encourage them to work in pairs or small groups to sort the words into categories.

Objectives

- To identify short vowels *i* and *u*
- To identify and sort words with short vowels *i* and *u*

Materials for Letter Name

- Big Book of Rhymes, "Having Fun," page 63
- Whiteboard Activities DVD-ROM, Sort 36
- Teacher Resource CD-ROM, Sort 36 and Fishing Fun Game
- Student Book, pages 141–144
- Words Their Way Library, *Just Like Us*

Words

ĭ	*ŭ*	oddball
zip	jug	put
will	rub	
rip	tub	
big	cut	**Bonus Words**
win	run	
him	fun	
did	hum	
six	nut	
bit	gum	
pin	but	

Bonus Words

nip	bus
skip	bud
tip	sun
trip	tug

Introduce/ Model   *Small Groups*

- **Read a Rhyme** Read "Having Fun." As you read, emphasize the words that contain the sounds of short *i* and *u*. Ask children to name the words they hear in the poem with the short vowel sounds of *i* and *u*. (*run, fun, trip, big, ship, wig, jig*) Write the words in two columns. Help children understand that the words in each column contain the same short vowel sound.

- **Model** Use the whiteboard DVD or the CD word cards. Explain that children will sort the word cards by vowel sounds. Demonstrate how to sort into short vowels *i* and *u*. Point out that *put* is an oddball because it has the short *u* spelling pattern but not the short *u* vowel sound. Help children sort and explain their sorts.

Practice the Sort   *Independent/Partner*

- Have children use the Student Book or whiteboard DVD to read the words and use the grid to sort their cards into words with short vowels *i* and *u* and oddball words.

- Have children check and explain their sorts.

Apply   *Independent/Partner/Small Groups*

- Read aloud the directions on Student Book p. 144. Have children write words with short vowels *i* and *u*.

- **Game** Allow time for children to play Fishing Fun, which is on the CD.

- **Little Book** Read *Just Like Us* with children. Have them identify words with u/u/.

Extend the Sort

Vocabulary Building Vocabulary

Write the word *hum* on the board. If children are not familiar with the meaning of *hum*, explain that it means "to sing with closed lips, not saying any words." Demonstrate humming for children and then invite them to think of songs they can hum.

ELL English Language Learners

Pair proficient and nonproficient English speakers. Have the pairs re-sort the words into groups of short *i* and short *u* vowel sounds, saying the words aloud together.

Bonus Words Activity

Ask children to find other words that include short vowels *i* and *u*. If children need prompting, make suggestions from the Bonus Words list. Then have children make word cards for these new words. Encourage them to work in pairs or small groups to sort the words into categories.

Teacher Tip

When children are comfortable with this sort, have them repeat the sort with an emphasis on speed. To this end, have children with similar aptitudes work in pairs to race each other to re-sort the words into short *i* and short *u* vowel sounds.

Objectives

- To identify short vowels *e, i, o,* and *u*
- To identify and sort words with short vowels *e, i, o,* and *u*

Materials for Letter Name

- Big Book of Rhymes, "Nighttime," page 65

- Whiteboard Activities DVD-ROM, Sort 37

- Teacher Resource CD-ROM, Sort 37 and Star Trip Game

- Student Book, pages 145–148

- Words Their Way Library, *Night and Day*

Words

ĕ	ĭ	ŏ	ŭ
wet	six	pop	mud
pet	miss	not	bus
yes	his	hot	cub
let	mix		bug
bell	hid		sun

Bonus Words

men	bib	pod	bun
red	lip	nod	hug
set	fix	dot	bud

Introduce/Model — Small Groups

- **Read a Rhyme** Read "Nighttime." As you read, emphasize the words that contain the short *e, i, o,* or *u* vowel sounds. Ask children to name the words they hear in the poem that have short *e, i, o,* or *u* vowel sounds. (*setting, sun, hen, will, rest, upon, nest, chicks, trot, soft, spot*) Write the words in four columns. Help children understand that the words in each column contain the same short vowel sound.

- **Model** Use the whiteboard DVD or the CD word cards. Explain that children will sort the word cards by vowel sounds. Demonstrate how to sort into short vowels *e, i, o,* and *u*. Help children sort and explain their sorts.

Practice the Sort — Independent/Partner

- Have children use the Student Book or whiteboard DVD to read the words and use the grid to sort their cards into words with short vowels *e, i, o,* and *u*.

- Have children check and explain their sorts.

Apply — Independent/Partner/Small Groups

- Read aloud the directions on Student Book p. 148. Have children write words with short vowels *e, i, o,* and *u*.

- **Game** Allow time for children to play Star Trip, which is on the CD.

- **Little Book** Read *Night and Day* with children. Have them identify words with /e/, /i/, /o/, or /u/.

Extend the Sort

Bonus Words Activity

Ask children to find other words that include short vowels *e, i, o,* and *u*. If children need prompting, make suggestions from the Bonus Words list. Then help children make word cards for these new words. Encourage them to work in pairs or small groups to sort the words into categories.

Alternative Sort: Rhyming Sort

Ask children to re-sort the words to make rhyming pairs. For example, children would sort *hot, not* and *let, pet*. Tell children that not all cards will have a rhyming match. Use the Bonus Words for additional matches.

ELL English Language Learners

Review the words with children. Then pair children with proficient English speakers to help them read and understand the words and their meanings.

Teacher Tip

To help children understand relationships, have them sort objects such as buttons, pencils, or paper clips and tell why they made the sorts they did. Encourage children to think of different ways to sort the objects.

Short *a, i* Words With Beginning Blends

Objectives

- To identify short *a* and *i* vowel sounds in words with beginning blends
- To identify and sort words with beginning blends and short vowels *a* or *i*

Materials for Letter Name

📖 Big Book of Rhymes, "This and That," page 67

🖥 Whiteboard Activities DVD-ROM, Sort 38

💿 Teacher Resource CD-ROM, Sort 38 and Word Maker Game

📕 Student Book, pages 149–152

📘 Words Their Way Library, *A Fun Place to Eat*

Words

ă		ĭ	
flag	grab	slip	flip
glad	cram	drill	slid
brag	trap	clip	grill
flat	drag	grip	skip
plan	slap	drip	spin
clap	brat		
crab			

Bonus Words

tram	span	snip	slim
stab	snap	grin	trim
snag		brim	

Introduce/Model
Small Groups

- **Read a Rhyme** Read "This and That." As you read, emphasize the words with beginning blends and that contain short vowels *a* and *i*. (*skin, glad, grin*) Ask children to describe how the words are alike. Help children understand that these words begin with blends and contain short vowels *a* or *i*.

- **Model** Use the whiteboard DVD or the CD word cards. Explain that children will sort the word cards by vowel sounds. Demonstrate how to sort words with beginning blends and short vowels *a* or *i*. Help children sort and explain their sorts.

Practice the Sort
Independent/Partner

- Have children use the Student Book or whiteboard DVD to read the words and use the grid to sort their cards into words with beginning blends and short vowels *a* or *i*.

- Have children check and explain their sorts.

Apply
Independent/Partner/Small Groups

- Read aloud the directions on Student Book p. 152. Have children write words with beginning blends and short vowels *a* and *i*.

- **Game** Allow time for children to play Word Maker, which is on the CD.

- **Little Book** Read *A Fun Place to Eat* with children. Have them identify words that begin with a consonant blend followed by /a/ or /i/.

Extend the Sort

Alternative Sort: Beginning Sounds

Ask children to re-sort the words according to their beginning sounds and place them in columns. When they are done with their sorts, have them make a card as a heading for each column that gives the letter names for the beginning sounds.

ELL English Language Learners

Help children pronounce and distinguish between the beginning sound of *gr* in *grin* and *gl* in *glad*. Have them repeat each word after you. Listen to make sure they pronounce the words correctly.

Bonus Words Activity

Ask children to find other words with beginning blends and short vowels *a* or *i*. If children need prompting, make suggestions from the Bonus Words list. Then help children make word cards for these new words. Encourage them to work in pairs or small groups to sort the words into categories.

Teacher Tip

Extend practice of the sort by having children go on a word hunt to find words in books with beginning blends and short vowels *a* or *i*. Ask children to copy the words they find on cards. Then have children pool and sort their words by beginning blends and short vowels *a* or *i*.

Objectives

- To identify short *e, o,* and *u* vowel sounds in words with beginning blends
- To identify and sort words with short *e, o,* or *u* and beginning blends

Materials for Letter Name

- Big Book of Rhymes, "Greg Packs," page 69

- Whiteboard Activities DVD-ROM, Sort 39

- Teacher Resource CD-ROM, Sort 39 and Let's Shop Game

- Student Book, pages 153–156

- Words Their Way Library, *Stan Packs*

Words

ĕ	ŏ	ŭ
sled	trot	club
fret	plot	slug
bled	drop	plum
dress	cross	drum
	frog	plug
	slob	drug
	slot	truck

Bonus Words

sped	clog	snub
press	prod	cluck

Introduce/Model   *Small Groups*

- **Read a Rhyme** Read "Greg Packs." As you read, emphasize words with short *e, o,* or *u* with beginning blends. (*Greg, dress, trunk, sled, stuff, crushes, spot, brushes*) Ask children to describe how the words are alike. Help children understand that these words begin with blends and contain short vowels *e, o,* or *u*.

- **Model** Use the whiteboard DVD or the CD word cards. Explain that children will sort the word cards by vowel sounds. Demonstrate how to sort words with short vowels *e, o,* or *u*. Help children sort and explain their sorts.

Practice the Sort   *Independent/Partner*

- Have children use the Student Book or whiteboard DVD to read the words and use the grid to sort their cards into words with short vowels *e, o,* or *u*.

- Have children check and explain their sorts.

Apply   *Independent/Partner/Small Groups*

- Read aloud the directions on Student Book p. 156. Have children draw pictures and write words with short vowels *e, o,* or *u* with beginning blends.

- **Game** Allow time for children to play Let's Shop, which is on the CD.

- **Little Book** Read *Stan Packs* with children. Have them identify words that begin with a consonant blend followed by /e/, /o/, or /u/.

Extend the Sort

Alternative Sort: More Beginning Sounds

Ask children to re-sort the words according to their beginning sounds and place them in columns. Then have them make a card for each column that gives the letter names for the beginning sounds.

ELL English Language Learners

Help children pronounce and distinguish between the beginning sounds of *tr* and *dr* in *truck* and *drop*. Have them repeat each word after you. Listen to make sure they pronounce the words correctly.

Bonus Words Activity

Ask children to find other words with short vowels *e, o,* or *u* and beginning blends. If children need prompting, make suggestions from the Bonus Words list. Then have children make word cards for these new words. Encourage them to work in pairs or small groups to sort the words into categories.

Teacher Tip

Have children make three sets of cards, one with a card for each beginning blend (*tr, cl, sl, fr, pl, dr, bl, cr*), one with a card for each short vowel (*e, o, u*), and one with ending letters (*t, b, d, p, g, m, ss, ck*) used in this sort. Have children practice with partners, combining beginning blends with short vowels and final letters to make words.

Objectives

- To identify short *a*, *e*, and *i* vowel sounds in words with beginning digraphs
- To identify and sort words with short *a*, *e*, or *i* and beginning digraphs

Materials for Letter Name

📓 Big Book of Rhymes, "Treasure Chest," page 71

🖥 Whiteboard Activities DVD-ROM, Sort 40

💿 Teacher Resource CD-ROM, Sort 40 and Word Maker Game

📔 Student Book, pages 157–160

📙 Words Their Way Library, *How the Chick Tricked the Fox*

Words

ă	*ĕ*	*ĭ*
that	them	thick
chat	shed	thin
than	then	whip
chap	chest	chill
shack	shell	ship
wham	check	chick
shall	when	whiz

Bonus Words

whack	chess	chip
sham	shelf	which

Introduce/Model *Small Groups*

- **Read a Rhyme** Read "Treasure Chest." As you read, emphasize words with short *a*, *e*, or *i* with beginning digraphs. (*Chen, chest, ship, then, shell, thinks, this*) Ask children to describe how the words are alike. Help children understand that these words begin with digraphs and contain short vowels *a*, *e*, or *i*.

- **Model** Use the whiteboard DVD or the CD word cards. Explain that children will sort the word cards by vowel sounds. Demonstrate how to sort words with short vowel *a*, *e*, or *i* and beginning digraphs. Help children sort and explain their sorts.

Practice the Sort *Independent/Partner*

- Have children use the Student Book or whiteboard DVD to read the words and use the grid to sort their cards into words with short vowels *a*, *e*, or *i*.

- Have children check and explain their sorts.

Apply *Independent/Partner/Small Groups*

- Read aloud the directions on Student Book p. 160. Have children write words with short vowels *a*, *e*, or *i* and beginning digraphs.

- **Game** Allow time for children to play Word Maker, which is on the CD.

- **Little Book** Read *How the Chick Tricked the Fox* with children. Have them identify words that begin with a consonant digraph followed by a short vowel sound.

Extend the Sort

Alternative Sort: Letter Count

Ask children to re-sort the cards according to the number of letters in each word. Have children make two piles, one for four-letter words and one for five-letter words.

ELL English Language Learners

Help children pronounce and distinguish between the beginning sounds of *th* in *thick* and *them*. Ask them to repeat each word after you. Listen to make sure they are pronouncing the words correctly.

Bonus Words Activity

Ask children to find other words with short vowels *a*, *e*, or *i* and beginning digraphs. If children need prompting, make suggestions from the Bonus Words list. Then have children make word cards for these new words. Encourage them to work in pairs or small groups to sort the words into categories.

Teacher Tip

During a subsequent sort, do not correct children when they place a word card in the wrong column. Wait until they have completed the sort and have them read the words in each column to check them. If children still do not find the misplaced word, tell them which column it is in and have them find it.

Short Vowel Words With Beginning Blends

Objectives
- To identify words with short vowels and beginning blends
- To identify and sort words with short vowels and beginning blends

Materials for Letter Name

Big Book of Rhymes, "Greg Packs," page 69

Whiteboard Activities DVD-ROM, Sort 41

Teacher Resource CD-ROM, Sort 41 and Word Maker Game

Student Book, pages 161–164

Words Their Way Library, *Roll Out the Red Rug*

Words

ă	ĕ	ĭ	ŏ	ŭ
flag	bled	slid	slob	fluff
glad	fret	drip	flop	gruff
slap	dress	clip	trot	plug
flat	sled	drill	gloss	truck
crab	fled	spin	plot	slug

Bonus Words

plan	shed	slip	crop	snug
scab	press	still	smog	club
flap	glen	brim	cross	drug
brag	spell	grin	slop	

Introduce/Model — *Small Groups*

- **Read a Rhyme** Read "Greg Packs." As you read, emphasize words with short vowels and beginning blends. (*Greg, plans, trip, skip, dress, trunk, sled, stuff, crushes, spot, brushes*) Write the words in five columns. Help children understand that these words begin with a blend and contain short vowel sounds.

- **Model** Use the whiteboard DVD or the CD word cards. Explain that children will sort the word cards by short vowels *a, e, i, o,* and *u*. Demonstrate how to sort words with short vowels. Help children sort and explain their sorts.

Practice the Sort — *Independent/Partner*

- Have children use the Student Book or whiteboard DVD to read the words and use the grid to sort their cards by short vowels *a, e, i, o,* and *u*.

- Have children check and explain their sorts.

Apply — *Independent/Partner/Small Groups*

- Read aloud the directions on Student Book p. 164. Have children write words with beginning blends and short vowels *a, e, i, o,* and *u*.

- **Game** Allow time for children to play Word Maker, which is on the CD.

- **Little Book** Read *Roll Out the Red Rug* with children. Have them identify words that begin with a consonant blend followed by a short vowel sound.

Extend the Sort

Alternative Sort: Beginning Blends

Have children work in pairs to sort the words according to *l* blends (*slob, flop, bled, flag, fluff, gloss, glad, slid, clip, slap, plot, sled, flat, plug, slug fled*), *r* blends (*trot, fret, gruff, dress, drip, drill, crab, truck*), and *p* blend (*spin*). Then have them sort the *l* blend words into *sl, fl, bl, gl, cl,* and *pl* groups, and the *r* blend words into *tr, fr, gr, dr,* and *cr* groups.

ELL English Language Learners

Review the word cards with children. You may need to place special emphasis on the pronunciation of beginning blends. Try to set aside time to work individually with children to help them pronounce words that contain difficult or unfamiliar sounds.

Bonus Words Activity

Ask children to find other words with short vowels and beginning blends. If children need prompting, make suggestions from the Bonus Words list. Then have children make word cards for these new words. Encourage them to work in pairs or small groups to sort the words into categories.

Short Vowel Words With Final Blends

Objectives
- To identify words with short vowels and final blends
- To identify and sort words with short vowels and final blends

Materials for Letter Name

📓 Big Book of Rhymes, "My Cow," page 73

⬜ Whiteboard Activities DVD-ROM, Sort 42

💿 Teacher Resource CD-ROM, Sort 42 and Bingo! Game

📑 Student Book, pages 165–168

📖 Words Their Way Library, *My Lost Top*

Words

ă	ĕ	ĭ	ŏ	ŭ
mask	melt	list	lost	just
fast	desk	fist	soft	must
raft	best	gift	cost	tusk
past	nest	milk		dust
half	left	lift		husk

Bonus Words

daft	pest	sift	loft	tuft
last	felt	risk	oft	dusk
task	belt	mist	golf	sulk
cast	self	tilt	frost	rust
craft	deft	silk		gulf

Introduce/Model
Small Groups

- **Read a Rhyme** Read "My Cow." As you read, emphasize words with short vowels and final blends. (*best, stands, rest, soft, rump, jump, pink, milk*) Write the words in five columns. Help children understand that these words contain short vowel sounds and a final blend.

- **Model** Use the whiteboard DVD or the CD word cards. Explain that children will sort the word cards by short vowels *a, e, i, o,* and *u.* Demonstrate how to sort words with short vowels. Help children sort and explain their sorts.

Practice the Sort
Independent/Partner

- Have children use the Student Book or whiteboard DVD to read the words and use the grid to sort their cards by short vowels *a, e, i, o,* and *u.*

- Have children check and explain their sorts.

Apply
Independent/Partner/Small Groups

- Read aloud the directions on Student Book p. 168. Have children write words with short vowels *a, e, i, o,* and *u* and final blends.

- **Game** Allow time for children to play Bingo!, which is on the CD.

- **Little Book** Read *My Lost Top* with children. Have them identify words that end with a consonant blend and have a short vowel sound.

Extend the Sort

Alternative Sort: What Can You Give Me?

Have children re-sort the words into two categories, words that describe something you could give to another person and words that don't fit that category. After they complete their sorts, ask children to read the sorts and give reasons for their choices.

Vocabulary Building Vocabulary

Model using *best* versus *good* and *better* by showing one of three books and saying, "I think this story is good." Continue showing and saying which is better and the best of all. Have children use three books or other objects to explain their opinions with *good, better,* and *best.*

ELL English Language Learners

Review the word cards with children. Have children pronounce each word as you listen to be sure they are pronouncing difficult final blends correctly.

Bonus Words Activity

Ask children to find other words with short vowels and final blends. If children need prompting, make suggestions from the Bonus Words list. Then help children make word cards for these new words. Encourage them to work in pairs or small groups to sort the words into categories.

Short Vowel Words With Final Digraphs

Objectives
- To identify words with short vowels and final digraphs
- To identify and sort words with short vowels and final digraphs

Materials for Letter Name

📓 Big Book of Rhymes, "Dinnertime," page 57

🖥 Whiteboard Activities DVD-ROM, Sort 43

💿 Teacher Resource CD-ROM, Sort 43 and Word Maker Game

📕 Student Book, pages 169–172

📘 Words Their Way Library, *Rush, Rush, Rush*

Words

ă	ĕ	ĭ	ŏ	ŭ
class	guess	rich	moth	much
math	fresh	kiss	boss	such
bath		with	toss	rush
pass		which	cloth	brush
grass		miss		

Bonus Words

mass	mess	hiss	moss	muss
path	flesh	swish	slosh	shush
cash	fetch	inch	broth	hutch

Introduce/Model　　*Small Groups*

- **Read a Rhyme** Read "Dinnertime." As you read, emphasize words with short vowels and final digraphs. (*rush, crush, dish, which, fish, crash, toss, trash*) Write the words in four columns. Help children understand that these words contain short vowel sounds and a final digraph.

- **Model** Use the whiteboard DVD or the CD word cards. Explain that children will sort the word cards by short vowels *a, e, i, o,* and *u*. Demonstrate how to sort words with short vowels. Help children sort and explain their sorts.

Practice the Sort　　*Independent/Partner*

- Have children use the Student Book or whiteboard DVD to read the words and use the grid to sort their cards by short vowels *a, e, i, o,* and *u* with final digraphs.

- Have children check and explain their sorts.

Apply　　*Independent/Partner/Small Groups*

- Read aloud the directions on Student Book p. 172. Have children draw pictures and write words with short vowels *a, e, i, o,* and *u.*

- **Game** Allow time for children to play Word Maker, which is on the CD.

- **Little Book** Read *Rush, Rush, Rush* with children. Have them identify words that end with a consonant digraph and have a short vowel sound.

Extend the Sort

Alternative Sort: Final Sounds

Have children re-sort the words into four columns according to their final sounds: /ch/, /th/, /s/, /sh/. When they have completed the sort, have them make a card for each column that gives the letter names for the ending sounds.

Bonus Words Activity

Ask children to find other words with short vowels and final digraphs. If children need prompting, make suggestions from the Bonus Words list. Then have children make word cards for these new words. Encourage them to work in pairs or small groups to sort the words into categories.

ELL English Language Learners

Children having difficulty with the sort may benefit from concentrating on one short vowel sound and/or one final digraph at a time. For example, have children read through all the cards and listen for words that end with *-th* before moving to another final digraph.

Objectives

- To identify short vowels *a, e, i, o,* and *u*
- To identify and sort words with short vowels *a, e, i, o,* and *u*

Materials for Letter Name

- Big Book of Rhymes, "The Trip," page 75
- Whiteboard Activities DVD-ROM, Sort 44
- Teacher Resource CD-ROM, Sort 44 and Let's Shop Game
- Student Book, pages 173–176
- Words Their Way Library, *Fix It, Fox*

Words

ă	ĕ	ĭ	ŏ	ŭ
mask	shed	quick	cloth	gruff
jack	check	chick	fox	truck
cat	desk	grill	moth	drum
shack	nest	pig	toss	bus
flag	sled	ship	cross	club

Bonus Words

clash	blend	blink	loss	stunt
champ	fresh	drink	gloss	slump
crash	spent	sling	slot	brush

Introduce/Model
Small Groups

- **Read a Rhyme** Read "The Trip." As you read, emphasize the words that contain the short vowel sounds. (*Meg, and, Dan, on, trip, shop, skip, gets, cat, Scat, big, red, hat, then, stop, bun, lots, fun*) Ask children to name the words they hear that have short vowel sounds. Write them in five columns.

- **Model** Use the whiteboard DVD or the CD word cards. Explain that children will sort the word cards by vowel sounds. Demonstrate how to sort the words by short vowels. Help children sort and explain their sorts.

Practice the Sort
Independent/Partner

- Have children use the Student Book or whiteboard DVD to read the words and use the grid to sort their cards by short vowels.

- Have children check and explain their sorts.

Apply
Independent/Partner/Small Groups

- Read aloud the directions on Student Book p. 176. Have children write words with short vowels.

- **Game** Allow time for children to play Let's Shop, which is on the CD.

- **Little Book** Read *Fix It, Fox* with children. Have them identify words that have short vowel sounds.

Extend the Sort

Alternative Sort: Animal or Not?

Have children re-sort the words into two groups, one that names animals and one that does not. Sort two or three of the cards into the two categories. Show the next card and ask children to identify where it will go. Continue with the rest of the cards.

Bonus Words Activity

Ask children to find other words that include short vowels. If children need prompting, make suggestions from the Bonus Words list. Then help children make word cards for these new words. Encourage them to work in pairs or small groups to sort the words into categories.

Teacher Tip

Ask children to identify who in the class has a first name that contains a short vowel sound. If no name fits this category, help children think of names that do, such as *Chan, Ella, Kim, Bob,* and *Gus.* Write the names and point out the letter that makes the short vowel sound.

Monitor Progress ✓ **Spell Check 5**

After completing Sort 44, administer Spell Check 5. See pp. 80–81 in this Teacher Resource Guide for instructions.

Preconsonantal Nasals -ng, -mp

Objectives

- To identify preconsonantal nasals -ng and -mp
- To identify and sort words with preconsonantal nasals -ng and -mp

Materials for Letter Name

Big Book of Rhymes, "Watch Out, Sheep!," page 29

Whiteboard Activities DVD-ROM, Sort 45

Teacher Resource CD-ROM, Sort 45 and Match! Game

Student Book, pages 177–180

Words Their Way Library, *That Pig Can't Do a Thing*

Words

-ng		-mp	
rang	ring	jump	ramp
king	bring	camp	stamp
sung	wing	bump	stump
sing	swing	lamp	lump
rung	hung	limp	plump
sang	thing	pump	

Introduce/Model   *Small Groups*

- **Read a Rhyme** Read "Watch Out, Sheep!" As you read, emphasize words with endings -ng and -mp. (along, Ming, thump, bang, hump, bump) Ask children to name words they hear with endings -ng and -mp. Write the words in two columns. Help children understand that the words in each column contain the same ending sounds.

- **Model** Use the whiteboard DVD or the CD word cards. Explain that children will sort the word cards by their ending sounds. Demonstrate how to sort into word endings -ng and -mp. Help children sort and explain their sorts.

Practice the Sort   *Independent/Partner*

- Have children use the Student Book or whiteboard DVD to read the words and use the grid to sort their cards into words with endings -ng and -mp.

- Have children check and explain their sorts.

Apply   *Independent/Partner/Small Groups*

- Read aloud the directions on Student Book p. 180. Have children draw pictures and write words with endings -ng and -mp.

- **Game** Allow time for children to play Match!, which is on the CD.

- **Little Book** Read *That Pig Can't Do a Thing* with children. Have them identify words that end with -ng or -mp.

Extend the Sort

Alternative Sort: Mind Your *A*'s, *I*'s, and *U*'s

Have children re-sort the words by their vowel sound. Tell them they will sort the words into one column each for words with vowel sounds a, i, and u. Have children work in pairs and take turns, with one partner selecting a card and saying the word and the other placing the word in the correct column.

Vocabulary   Building Vocabulary

Point out that *limp* can have more than one meaning. Children may already be familiar with the meaning "to walk slowly or with difficulty." Explain that *limp* can also mean "not stiff." Demonstrate this meaning of *limp* by standing up very straight and then relaxing in a drooping manner with shoulders slumped and arms hanging down. Have children use *limp* in a sentence.

ELL   English Language Learners

Children having difficulty with the sort may benefit from concentrating on one word ending at a time. Have children read through all the cards and listen for words that end with -ng before moving to words that end with -mp.

Preconsonantal Nasals *-nt, -nd, -nk*

Objectives
- To identify preconsonantal nasals *-nt, -nd,* and *-nk*
- To identify and sort words with preconsonantal nasals *-nt, -nd,* and *-nk*

Materials for Letter Name

Big Book of Rhymes, "Five Goats in a Boat," page 59

Whiteboard Activities DVD-ROM, Sort 46

Teacher Resource CD-ROM, Sort 46 and Park Race Game

Student Book, pages 181–184

Words Their Way Library, *That Pig Can't Do a Thing*

Words

-nt	-nd	-nk
went	sand	pink
hunt	send	wink
pant	land	bunk
print	wind	bank
plant	blend	junk
spent	stand	stink
want		drink

Introduce/Model
Small Groups

- **Read a Rhyme** Read "Five Goats in a Boat." Ask children to listen to the endings of words. As you read, emphasize words with endings *-nt* and *-nk.* (*went, sank, bank*) Write the word endings *-nt, -nd,* and *-nk* as column headings. Then write *mint, bond,* and *clank* under the correct heading. Help children understand that the words' endings match the column heads.

- **Model** Use the whiteboard DVD or the CD word cards. Explain that children will sort the word cards by their ending sounds. Demonstrate how to sort into word endings *-nt, -nd,* and *-nk*. Help children sort and explain their sorts.

Practice the Sort
Independent/Partner

- Have children use the Student Book or whiteboard DVD to read the words and use the grid to sort their cards into words with endings *-nt, -nd,* and *-nk*.

- Have children check and explain their sorts.

Apply
Independent/Partner/Small Groups

- Read aloud the directions on Student Book p. 184. Have children write words with endings *-nt, -nd,* and *-nk*.

- **Game** Allow time for children to play Park Race, which is on the CD.

- **Little Book** Read *That Pig Can't Do a Thing* with children. Have them identify words that end with *-nt, -nd,* or *-nk.*

Extend the Sort

Alternative Sort: Is It U in the Middle?

Have children re-sort the words by their vowel sound. Tell them they will sort the words into one column each for words with vowel sounds *a, e, i,* and *u.* Have children work in pairs and take turns, with one partner selecting a card and saying the word and the other placing the word in the correct column.

Vocabulary Building Vocabulary

Write the word *bank* on the board. Children may already be familiar with the meaning "a place to store money." Ask children if they know another meaning for *bank.* Explain that *bank* can also mean "ground at the edge of a body of water."

Teacher Tip

Review the word cards with children. Have children pronounce each word as you listen to be sure they are pronouncing difficult word endings correctly.

Monitor Progress Spell Check 6

After completing Sort 46, administer Spell Check 6. See pp. 80–81 in this Teacher Resource Guide for instructions.

Objectives
- To identify words with short o and or
- To identify and sort words with short o and or

Materials for Letter Name

Big Book of Rhymes, "More Popcorn, Please," page 77

Whiteboard Activities DVD-ROM, Sort 47

Teacher Resource CD-ROM, Sort 47 and Word Maker Game

Student Book, pages 185–188

Words Their Way Library, *Pop Goes the Popcorn*

Words

o	or	oddball
fox	for	your
drop	corn	work
rot	fort	word
spot	born	
trot	sort	
shop	torn	**Bonus Words**
pond	short	sod ford
	sport	snob port
	storm	
	horn	

Introduce/Model — *Small Groups*

- **Read a Rhyme** Read "More Popcorn, Please," emphasizing the words with short o and or. Ask children to name the words they hear with short o and or. Write the words in two columns. Help children understand that the words in each column contain either the short o or or sound.

- **Model** Use the whiteboard DVD or the CD word cards. Demonstrate how to sort words by short o and or. Explain that *your* has the or vowel sound but not the or spelling pattern, and that *word* and *work* have the or spelling pattern but not the or vowel sound. Help children sort and explain their sorts.

Practice the Sort — *Independent/Partner*

- Have children use the Student Book or whiteboard DVD to read the words and use the grid to sort their cards into short o, or, and oddball words.
- Have children check and explain their sorts.

Apply — *Independent/Partner/Small Groups*

- Read aloud the directions on Student Book p. 188. Have children write short o and or words.
- **Game** Allow time for children to play Word Maker, which is on the CD.
- **Little Book** Read *Pop Goes the Popcorn* with children. Have them identify words with /o/ or r-influenced o.

Extend the Sort

Alternative Sort: Beginning Letters

Have children re-sort the cards into two categories: words that begin with two consonants and words that begin with one consonant. After sorting, have children work in pairs, taking turns holding up a card with the other child saying the word.

Vocabulary — Building Vocabulary

Develop children's understanding of *rot*. Remind them that they have probably seen a rotten apple or banana, and ask how these fruits changed as they rotted. The group might experiment by leaving identical fruits in hot sunlight, in a darker location, and in water to observe which begins to rot first.

ELL — English Language Learners

If English language learners become frustrated with distinguishing oddball words, you might set *work, word,* and *your* aside and have them concentrate on the short o and or words.

Bonus Words Activity

Ask children to find other words that include short o and or. If children need prompting, make suggestions from the Bonus Words list as necessary. Then help children make word cards for these new words. Encourage them to work in pairs or small groups to sort the words into categories.

Short *a* and *ar*

Objectives

- To identify words with short *a* and *ar*
- To identify and sort words with short *a* and *ar*

Materials for Letter Name

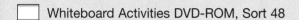

- Big Book of Rhymes, "Grand Slam," page 45

- Whiteboard Activities DVD-ROM, Sort 48

- Teacher Resource CD-ROM, Sort 48 and Word Maker Game

- Student Book, pages 189–192

- Words Their Way Library, *A Sea Star*

Words

a	*ar*	oddball
drag	car	war
crab	far	
rag	farm	
snap	bark	
crash	art	
trap	card	
flag	yard	
brag	dark	
grand	shark	
	jar	

Bonus Words

stand	barn
flap	hard
mash	mark
nag	smart

Introduce/Model
Small Groups

- **Read a Rhyme** Read "Grand Slam," emphasizing the words that contain short *a* and *ar*. Read the poem again and ask children to raise their hands when they hear a short *a* or *ar* word. Write the words in two columns. Help children understand that the words in each column contain either the short *a* or *ar* sound.

- **Model** Use the whiteboard DVD or the CD word cards. Explain that children will sort the word cards by vowel sounds. Demonstrate how to sort words by short *a* and *ar*. Point out that *war* is an oddball. Explain that *war* has the ar spelling pattern, but not the *ar* vowel sound. Help children sort and explain their sorts.

Practice the Sort
Independent/Partner

- Have children use the Student Book or whiteboard DVD to read the words and use the grid to sort their cards into words with short *a* and *ar* and oddball words.

- Have children check and explain their sorts.

Apply
Independent/Partner/Small Groups

- Read aloud the directions on Student Book p. 192. Have children write short *a* and *ar* words.

- **Game** Allow time for children to play Word Maker, which is on the CD.

- **Little Book** Read *A Sea Star* with children. Have them identify words with /a/ or *r*-influenced *a*.

Extend the Sort

Alternative Sort: Ending Letters

Have children re-sort the cards into two categories: words that end with two consonants and words that end with one consonant. After sorting, have children work in pairs, taking turns holding up a card with the other child saying the word.

Vocabulary Building Vocabulary

Write the word *bark* on the board. Ask children if they know the meaning of *bark*. Children will probably be familiar with the meaning "loud sound that a dog makes." Explain that *bark* can also mean "thick covering of a stem or tree."

Bonus Words Activity

Ask children to find other words that include short *a* and *ar*. If children need prompting, make suggestions from the Bonus Words list as necessary. Then help children make word cards for these new words. Encourage them to work in pairs or small groups to sort the words into categories.

Monitor Progress Spell Check 7

After completing Sort 48, administer Spell Check 7. See pp. 80–81 in this Teacher Resource Guide for instructions.

Objectives

- To identify spelling patterns for contractions
- To identify and sort contractions

Materials for Letter Name

📖 Big Book of Rhymes, "Wet Dog," page 79

🖥 Whiteboard Activities DVD-ROM, Sort 49

💿 Teacher Resource CD-ROM, Sort 49 and Bingo! Game

📕 Student Book, pages 193–196

📘 Words Their Way Library, *Flip's Trick*

Words

it is	it's	is not	isn't
he is	he's	was not	wasn't
that is	that's	do not	don't
who is	who's	can not	can't
what is	what's	does not	doesn't
here is	here's	did not	didn't

Bonus Words

where is	where's	has not	hasn't
she is	she's	have not	haven't

Introduce/Model   *Small Groups*

- **Read a Rhyme** Read "Wet Dog," emphasizing the contractions. Write *wasn't* and *didn't* with *was not* and *did not* below them. Say and track each pair of words several times followed by its contraction. Have children repeat with you. Do the same with *it is* and *is not*. Help children understand how to make a contraction. Cover the *i* in *is* and the *o* in *not* and explain that an apostrophe is used to mark the place where the letter has been removed.

- **Model** Use the whiteboard DVD or the CD word cards. Explain that children will sort the word cards into four groups, words with and without contractions using *is* and *not*. Demonstrate how to sort the words. Help children sort and explain their sorts.

Practice the Sort   *Independent/Partner*

- Have children use the Student Book or whiteboard DVD to read the words and use the grid to sort their cards into words with and without contractions using *is* and *not*.

- Have children check and explain their sorts.

Apply   *Independent/Partner/Small Groups*

- Read aloud the directions on Student Book p. 196. Have children write contractions using *is* and *not*.

- **Game** Allow time for children to play Bingo!, which is on the CD.

- **Little Book** Read *Flip's Trick* with children. Have them identify the contractions.

Extend the Sort

Alternative Sort: One Word or Two?

Have children re-sort the cards into two categories: cards that show contractions and those that show two words. After sorting, have children work in pairs taking turns holding up a card from one of the piles. If the card has two words, the partner will say them and then say the contraction. If the card has a contraction, the partner will say it and then the two words that make it.

ELL English Language Learners

Listen to children as they pronounce contractions, particularly with contractions using *not*. Make sure they are pronouncing the *s* to sound like *z* in such words as *doesn't* and *wasn't*.

Bonus Words Activity

Ask children to find other words with and without contractions using is and not. If children need prompting, make suggestions from the Bonus Words list as necessary. Then have children make word cards for these new words.

Teacher Tip

A common error when writing contractions is to place the apostrophe in the wrong place (*is'nt* for example). Remind children often that the apostrophe takes the place of the missing letter (*o* in this case) and should be placed in that spot.

Teacher Notes

Within Word Pattern

The Within Word Pattern stage of literacy development is a transitional period—a time between the beginning stage, when students' reading and writing are quite labored, and the intermediate stage, when students can read nearly all texts they encounter. During the Within Word Pattern stage, students begin to decode and store words more readily, and their sight word vocabulary grows quickly. This enables them to read and write with increasing fluency and expression. Students in this stage become wordsmiths, collecting hundreds of words.

Types of Sorts in Within Word Pattern
- Short and Long Vowels
- Other Long Vowel Patterns
- *r*-Influenced Vowels
- Diphthongs and Other Ambiguous Vowels
- Complex Consonant Clusters
- Homophones

Characteristics of Within Word Pattern Learners

Within Word Pattern learners are mostly in late first, second, third, and early fourth grade.

Within Word Pattern Learners

- spell most single-syllable, short vowel words correctly.

- spell most beginning consonant digraphs and two-letter consonant blends.

- read silently and with more fluency and expression.

- can identify most one-syllable words in context but may still struggle to spell words correctly when they write.

- write more fluently and express their idea with greater sophistication.

- can revise and edit.

Focus of Instruction

- To begin this level, students review short vowels and compare them to long vowel sounds first in pictures and then in common and less common patterns.

- Students then focus on *r*-influenced vowels, vowel diphthongs, vowel digraph *oo*, and other ambiguous vowel patterns that reflect a range of vowel sounds that are neither short nor long.

- Next, students examine complex consonant clusters, including silent consonants and other consonant patterns that are influenced by vowel sounds.

- Students expand their knowledge of consonant clusters to include more difficult three-letter digraphs and blends.

- Finally, students review long *a* and long *i* vowel patterns through the study of homophones, which also provides opportunities to focus on the meanings of words.

Teacher Tips

- For lessons with different vowel sounds and patterns, you might have students sort by sound first. Then they can sort by patterns.

- Help students use dictionaries to look up the meanings of homophones. Then encourage them to show their understanding of the meanings through pictures or context sentences.

Pace of Instruction

Not all students learn and work at the same pace. Therefore, to meet students' needs, make adjustments to the pace of instruction. Through careful observation and assessment, you can decide when and where you can go faster or may need to go slower. The Spell Checks can help you determine the focus and pace of instruction.

For students who catch on quickly, increase the pace by spending less time on some sorts or by skipping some sorts entirely. Conversely, for those students who are not on track for meeting end-of-year goals, spend more time on instruction and provide more practice by creating additional sorts.

If students are in the early part of this stage, there is a greater sense of urgency to catch them up with their peers. Modifying the pace and using flexible small groups allows you to avoid teaching students what they already know and to spend more time on features that need instruction. Use the Spell Checks as pretests to determine instructional needs.

Word Study Routines

Shared Reading The *Big Book of Rhymes* provides a way to introduce the sort in a meaningful context and provides poems that focus on the features for word study. Here are steps for sharing the rhymes.

- Read the title and discuss the illustration with students.

- Read the poem to students, inviting them to read along with you.

- Discuss the feature being studied that week.

- Read the poem again. Ask students to identify words with the targeted feature. For example, *This rhyme has several words with the short o sound. Here is the word* clock. *Can you find other words with the short o sound?*

Introduce the Sort There are several options for introducing the sort. Here are the basic steps for a teacher-directed sort.

- Say *Let's read over these words (name these pictures) to be sure everyone knows how to read them (name them) and what they mean.* Take time to discuss the meaning of any pictures or words that may be unfamiliar.

- Introduce the target sounds and/or patterns that serve as category headers for the sorting columns. Identify the key picture and/or word for each feature.

- Explicitly identify the features that students will look for as they sort. *We are going to sort by short and long a sounds. We will sort the words into categories of words with short* a, *words with long* a *spelled* ai *as in* rain, *and words with long* a *spelled* a *plus* e *as in* face.

- Model how to sort. *This is the word* dash. *It has a short* a *sound. I will put it in this column under the word* cat.

- Continue demonstrating how to sort one or two words for each feature, describing why each word goes in the specific category. Help students complete the sort.

- At this point, you may want to discuss oddballs. **Oddballs** are words that do not fit the targeted spelling pattern. Help students identify an oddball and explain why it is an oddball. *This word is* said. *It has* ai *in its spelling, but it does not make the long* a *vowel sound.* Said *is an oddball because it doesn't fit the pattern*.

- Model how to check the sort by reading down each column to listen for the sound or to look for the pattern. Discuss how all the words in each category are alike.

- Re-sort. Have students sort the words individually or with partners. Encourage them to explain their sorting categories. Help students check by reading down columns for consistency of sounds or patterns. Help students identify a misplaced word and place it in the correct category.

Within Word Pattern Library The library is comprised of little books that correspond to each of the sorts in the Within Word Pattern stage.

- Use these little books as you would any little books: for picture walks, for choral reading, for echo reading, or for independent reading.

- After completing a sort, read the book with students. Have them look for words in context that have the features being studied.

- Record words on a chart or have students write them in their word study notebooks.

Teacher Tip

Students do not automatically see the relationship between spelling words and reading words. In word hunts, students hunt through their reading and writing for words that are additional examples of the sound, pattern, or meaning unit they are studying. Some patterns are found in virtually every text again and again, whereas others are harder to find; thus, word hunts are more appropriate for some features than others.

Interactive Resources You may use the DVD-ROM and/or the CD-ROM printable manipulatives to model, instruct, and provide practice with sorts.

Use the DVD-ROM for interactive whiteboard activities or independent practice on a computer.

- Introduce, read, and discuss the rhyme from the *Big Book of Rhymes*. Engage students in reading the rhyme, noticing concepts of print, and identifying words that exemplify the focus of the sort.

- Point out the headers for the columns, which indicate the principle of the sort. Demonstrate how to drag and drop pictures or words to complete the sort. Have students take turns sorting, using the whiteboard or a computer.

- Use the whiteboard with students to introduce the writing sort. Have students complete it.

Use the CD-ROM for printable manipulatives.

- Print out and cut apart the cards for the sort. Introduce the pictures or words, identifying any that may be unfamiliar to students. Demonstrate how to sort. Have students use the cards to practice sorting.

- Print out the game that accompanies the sort. Use the game for additional practice with the sort. Have students play in pairs or small groups.

- Print out the rhyme that accompanies the sort. Have students take it home to read with family members.

- **See Chapter 6 of *Words Their Way: Word Study for Phonics, Vocabulary, and Spelling Instruction*, 5th ed., for a comprehensive description of the Within Word Pattern stage of development and additional activities.**

Monitor Progress SPELL CHECKS

Spell checks for Within Word Pattern are provided here. Administer the Spell Checks as you would any spelling test, reading the words and having students write them. Spell Checks may be used as pretests and posttests.

Spell Check 1
Short (CVC) and Long (CVCe) Vowels Use after Sort 10. This Spell Check assesses students' ability to identify short and long vowel sounds.

1. hose	8. kick	15. smoke
2. tube	9. sock	16. stove
3. duck	10. mule	17. rake
4. cute	11. bike	18. kite
5. bus	12. flute	19. lock
6. sack	13. five	20. cape
7. bone	14. rock	

Watch for these types of errors: if students write *rak* for *rake*, review Sorts 1 and 2; if students write *bos* for *bus*, review Sorts 5 and 7.

Spell Check 2
Other Common Long Vowel Patterns Use after Sort 22. This Spell Check assesses students' ability to identify and write one-syllable long vowel words.

1. leaf	8. peach	15. fruit
2. suit	9. road	16. fry
3. beach	10. feet	17. snake
4. rain	11. mail	18. soap
5. broke	12. chew	19. spoon
6. teeth	13. peas	20. low
7. chain	14. play	

If students have difficulty spelling words with a specific long vowel pattern, review the corresponding sort.

Spell Check 3
r-Influenced Vowels Use after Sort 29. This Spell Check assesses students' ability to spell words with *r*-influenced vowel patterns.

1. bird	8. deer	15. fern
2. thorn	9. horn	16. fear
3. shirt	10. work	17. corn
4. jar	11. for	18. curb
5. tire	12. chair	19. hare
6. fire	13. first	20. fork
7. sure	14. yarn	

If students miss words with a specific *r*-influenced vowel, review the appropriate sort.

Spell Check 4
Ambiguous Vowels Use after Sort 34. This Spell Check assesses students' ability to spell words with the diphthongs *oi, oy, ou,* and *ow* and the vowel patterns *aw, au, al,* and *ou.*

1. crawl	8. taught	15. yawn
2. chalk	9. dawn	16. salt
3. growl	10. couch	17. haul
4. joy	11. stalk	18. noise
5. spoil	12. drown	19. thought
6. mouth	13. brought	20. fault
7. point	14. cloud	

Watch for these types of errors: If students write *oy* for *oi* (for example, *noyse* for *noise*), review Sort 30; if students write *aw* for *au* (for example, *tawght* for *taught*), review Sort 33.

Spell Check 5
Complex Consonant Clusters Use after Sort 42. This Spell Check assesses students' ability to write words with three-letter blends.

1. squeeze	8. spray	15. shred
2. straight	9. squirt	16. string
3. threw	10. scrape	17. spruce
4. spring	11. through	18. thrill
5. shrink	12. shrank	19. stripe
6. screen	13. scream	20. scrap
7. strong	14. three	

Watch for these types of errors: if students write *trew* for *threw*, review Sort 37; if students write *scream* for *scream*, review Sort 38.

Short and Long *a* (Pictures)

Objectives
- To identify short and long *a* vowel sounds
- To identify and sort pictures and words that contain a short or long *a* vowel sound

Materials for Within Word Pattern

📓 Big Book of Rhymes, "Twin Mix-Up," page 5

🖥 Whiteboard Activities DVD-ROM, Sort 1

💿 Teacher Resource CD-ROM, Sort 1 and Around the Playground Game

📖 Student Book, pages 1–4

📘 Words Their Way Library, *Who Has a Tail?*

Pictures

short *a*	long *a*	Oddball
bag	skate	foot
jack	plate	
crab	rain	
grass	rake	
hat	frame	
man	grapes	
map	game	
bat	snake	

Introduce/Model *Small Groups*

- **Read a Rhyme** Read "Twin Mix-Up." Review the sound of short *a* and long *a*. Point to various words in the poem, or write the words one at a time. Ask students if the word has a short *a*, long *a*, or neither.

- **Model** Use the whiteboard DVD or the CD picture cards. Show the cards as you name each picture. Show students how to sort the cards by picture names that have short *a* or long *a*. Place *toe* in the oddball column and explain this word has neither a short *a* nor long *a* sound. Name each picture in the short *a* column and tell how the picture names are alike and different. Continue with the long *a* column. Help children sort and explain their sorts.

Practice the Sort *Independent/Partner*

- Have students use the Student Book or whiteboard DVD to name the pictures and use the grid to sort.

- Have students check and explain their sorts.

Apply *Independent/Partner/Small Groups*

- Read aloud the directions on Student Book p. 4. Have students write two short *a* words and two long *a* words and draw pictures to match the words.

- **Game** Allow time for students to play Around the Playground, which is on the CD.

- **Little Book** Read *Who Has a Tail?* with students. Then point out pictures of *tail, face, flag, fan, hand,* and *branch;* have students identify the short or long *a* sound in each word.

Extend the Sort

Alternative Sort: Things Around the House

Have students re-sort the cards so that one pile of cards shows pictures of items they could find at home. The remaining cards should go into a second pile. Let a student show the cards with household items on them and describe where they are found or how they are used around the house.

ELL English Language Learners

Review the picture cards. Have students pronounce the words after you. Then, using cards from two card sets, hold up two of the same picture. Help students practice pronouncing the plural of the word. Continue with other card pairs.

Vocabulary Building Vocabulary

Tell students that some words are spelled the same but have more than one meaning. Show the card of a bat and explain that this bat is a stick used to hit a ball in baseball. Then ask students if they know of another meaning of the word *bat*. Explain that another type of bat is an animal with a body like a mouse and wings like a bird. Bats most often come out at night to eat insects.

Short *a* (CVC) and Long *a* (CVCe)

Objectives
- To identify short and long *a* vowel sounds and spelling patterns
- To read, sort, and write words with a short *a* CVC or long *a* CVCe spelling pattern

Materials for Within Word Pattern

Big Book of Rhymes, "Twin Mix-Up," page 5

Whiteboard Activities DVD-ROM, Sort 2

Teacher Resource CD-ROM, Sort 2 and Pancake Chase Game

Student Book, pages 5–8

Words Their Way Library, *The Name Is the Same*

Words

ă CVC	ā CVCe	Oddball
glass	whale	what
bat	gate	
fast	make	
hand	page	
mad	came	**Bonus Words**
snap	face	
last	base	
grass	rake	
ask	same	
sack	made	

Bonus Words

pancake	place
camp	bake
snack	trace
dash	name

Introduce/Model　　　*Small Groups*

- **Read a Rhyme** Read "Twin Mix-Up." Write the name *Jan*. Point out that *a* between two consonants (CVC) is often short. Now write the name *Jane*. Explain that the *a* in this word is long because of the silent *e* at the end (CVCe). Help students identify other short *a* and long *a* words in the poem with these spelling patterns. *(plan; same, name, shame)*

- **Model** Use the whiteboard DVD or the CD word cards. Demonstrate how to sort the words by the short *a* CVC and the long *a* CVCe patterns. Place *what* in the oddball column and explain that it has neither a short *a* nor long *a* sound. Help students sort and explain their sorts.

Practice the Sort　　　*Independent/Partner*

- Have students use the Student Book or whiteboard DVD to read the words and use the grid to sort according to a short or long *a* spelling pattern.

- Have students check and explain their sorts.

Apply　　　*Independent/Partner/Small Groups*

- Read aloud the directions on Student Book p. 8. Have students read each word and write it in the short *a* or long *a* column.

- **Game** Allow time for students to play Pancake Chase, which is on the CD.

- **Little Book** Read *The Name Is the Same* with students. Have them identify short *a* and long *a* words.

Extend the Sort

Alternative Sort: /k/ Endings

Ask students to re-sort the cards into groups of words that end with /k/ *(ask, sack, make, rake)* and words that do not. Then review the words that end in /k/ and have students identify the -*sk*, -*ck*, and -*ke* spellings.

ELL English Language Learners

Review the word cards. Have students repeat each word after you. Give each student a word card to illustrate on a sheet of paper. Show the illustrations one at a time and ask students to guess the words.

Bonus Words Activity

Write the word *pancake*. Point out the CVC pattern in the component *pan* and the CVCe pattern in the component *cake*. Provide tan construction paper and invite students to cut out "pancakes." Have students write a word with short or long *a* on each pancake. Use the Bonus Word list to help students get started. Work together to stack the pancakes in two piles: short *a* and long *a*.

Short and Long *i* (Pictures)

Objectives
- To identify short and long *i* vowel sounds
- To identify and sort pictures and words that contain a short or long *i* vowel sound

Materials for Within Word Pattern

Big Book of Rhymes, "Things to Do," page 7

Whiteboard Activities DVD-ROM, Sort 3

Teacher Resource CD-ROM, Sort 3 and Swim Time Game

Student Book, pages 9–12

Words Their Way Library, *The Kite That Flew Away*

Pictures		
short *i*	**long *i***	**Oddball**
fish	pie	net
lid	slide	
lips	hive	
hill	nine	
twins	smile	
swim	dive	
	fire	
	five	
	prize	
	bride	

Introduce/Model — *Small Groups*

- **Read a Rhyme** Read "Things to Do" to introduce short *i* and long *i*. Make two columns, one for short *i* and one for long *i*. Have students locate words that contain short or long *i* in the poem, pronounce them, and write them in the correct columns.

- **Model** Use the whiteboard DVD or the CD picture cards. Name the pictures as you show the cards. Demonstrate how to sort the cards into columns short *i* and long *i*. Place *net* in the oddball column. Ask a student to name each picture in the short *i* column, tell how the words are alike, and think of another word that belongs in the column. Continue with the long *i* column.

Practice the Sort — *Independent/Partner*

- Have students use the Student Book or whiteboard DVD to name the pictures and use the grid to sort.

- Have students check and explain their sorts.

Apply — *Independent/Partner/Small Groups*

- Read aloud the directions on Student Book p. 12. Have students write two short *i* words and two long *i* words and draw pictures to match the words.

- **Game** Allow time for students to play Swim Time, which is on the CD.

- **Little Book** Read *The Kite That Flew Away* with students. Then point out pictures of *kite, string, lines, sticks,* and *wind;* have students identify the short or long *i* sound in each word.

Extend the Sort

Alternative Sort: Numbers, Things, and Actions Explain to students that these picture cards show numbers, things (nouns), and actions (verbs). Have students re-sort the picture cards into those three categories.

ELL **English Language Learners**
Review the picture cards. Have students pronounce the words after you. Let students practice pronunciation and sentence construction by asking each other yes/no questions, such as: "Did you ever dive into a pool (fly a kite, eat pie, sled down a hill, swim in the ocean)?"

Vocabulary **Building Vocabulary**
Display the picture of a hill. Explain to students that a hill is a high piece of land. Be sure that students do not confuse a hill with a mountain, which is much bigger. Also explain that *hill* can refer to a little heap or pile. Ask students if they have ever seen an anthill, which is the earth that ants pile up around the entrance to their tunnels.

Teacher Tip
If a student is having trouble pronouncing a particular sound, watch the student's mouth to be sure his or her lips and tongue are positioned correctly.

Short *i* (CVC) and Long *i* (CVCe)

Objectives
- To identify short and long *i* vowel sounds and spelling patterns
- To read, sort, and write words with a short *i* CVC or long *i* CVCe spelling pattern

Materials for Within Word Pattern

Big Book of Rhymes, "Things to Do," page 7

Whiteboard Activities DVD-ROM, Sort 4

Teacher Resource CD-ROM, Sort 4 and "I" Sort Game

Student Book, pages 13–16

Words Their Way Library, *Dive In*

Words

ĭ CVC	ī CVCe	Oddball
stick	dice	give
kick	prize	
pin	five	
gift	hike	
flip	life	**Bonus Words**
dish	nice	
rich	drive	
thin	nine	
swim	mice	
spill		

Bonus Words

ditch	rise
twist	size
pitch	dime
mist	chime

Introduce/Model   *Small Groups*

- **Read a Rhyme** Read "Things to Do." Write the word *will* and point out that *i* between two consonants (CVC) is often short. Now write the word *ride* and explain that the *i* in this word is long because of the silent *e* at the end (CVCe). Have students identify other short *i* and long *i* words in the poem. *(swim, in, with, if; bike)*

- **Model** Use the whiteboard DVD or the CD word cards. Demonstrate how you identify the vowel sound and spelling pattern and sort words according to the short *i* CVC and long *i* CVCe patterns. *Give* is an oddball. Ask students to describe how words in the other columns are alike and different. Help students sort and explain their sorts.

Practice the Sort   *Independent/Partner*

- Have students use the Student Book or whiteboard DVD to read the words and use the grid to sort according to a short or long *i* spelling pattern.

- Have students check and explain their sorts.

Apply   *Independent/Partner/Small Groups*

- Read aloud the directions on Student Book p. 16. Have students read each word and write it in the short *i* or long *i* column.

- **Game** Allow time for students to play "I" Sort, which is on the CD.

- **Little Book** Read *Dive In* with students. Have them identify short *i* and long *i* words.

Extend the Sort

Alternative Sort: Rhyme Time

Ask students to say the words in each column and listen for rhyming words. Encourage them to sort the words according to words that end with /n/, /s/, and all other endings. Have students identify the words that rhyme in the /n/ group *(pin, thin)* and the /s/ group *(dice, nice, mice)*. Invite students to think of other words that rhyme with these sets of words.

ELL English Language Learners

To help students with letter-sound association, focus on one column of the sort at a time. Point to each word, read it, and have students repeat it after you. Then say a word at random. Have students locate the word, point to it, read the word, and identify the spelling pattern. Repeat with several words from the sort.

Bonus Words Activity

Write the Bonus Words and read them aloud. Have students match the rhyming words, tell whether each pair has a short *i* vowel sound or long *i* vowel sound, and identify the spelling pattern.

Short and Long *o* (Pictures)

Objectives
- To identify short and long *o* vowel sounds
- To identify and sort pictures and words that contain a short or long *o* vowel sound

Materials for Within Word Pattern

Big Book of Rhymes, "Where Is That Clock?," page 9

Whiteboard Activities DVD-ROM, Sort 5

Teacher Resource CD-ROM, Sort 5 and Alarm Clock Race Game

Student Book, pages 17–20

Words Their Way Library, *When Bob Woke Up Late*

Pictures

short *o*	long *o*	Oddball
rock	toe	vase
mop	road	
dot	nose	
lock	goat	
fox	coat	
top	soap	
clock	hose	
box	boat	

Introduce/Model   *Small Groups*

- **Read a Rhyme** Read "Where Is That Clock?" As you read, emphasize words that contain short and long *o*. (*tock, clock, woke, not, stop, phone, on, top, oh*) Review short and long sounds. Reread the poem and have students point out short and long *o* words. Write the words in columns.

- **Model** Use the whiteboard DVD or the CD picture cards. Show the cards and name each picture. Demonstrate how to sort the pictures by short *o* and long *o* sounds. *Vase* is an oddball. Ask students to name each picture in the short *o* column and identify the short *o* sound. Continue with the long *o* column. Help students sort and explain their sorts.

Practice the Sort   *Independent/Partner*

- Have students use the Student Book or whiteboard DVD to name the pictures and use the grid to sort.

- Have students check and explain their sorts.

Apply   *Independent/Partner/Small Groups*

- Read aloud the directions on Student Book p. 20. Have students write two short *o* words and two long *o* words and draw pictures to match the words.

- **Game** Allow time for students to play Alarm Clock Race, which is on the CD.

- **Little Book** Read *When Bob Woke Up Late* with students. Then point out pictures of *clock, Bob, Mom,* and *note;* have students identify the short or long *o* sound in each word.

Extend the Sort

Alternative Sort: In the House or Not? Have students re-sort the cards into two piles according to whether or not the card shows a picture of something one might find in a house.

ELL **English Language Learners**

Place the picture cards face up on a table and review their names. Then create short and long vowel *o* riddles, such as: "Say the picture name that has the long *o* sound and names something on your face." *(nose)*

Vocabulary **Building Vocabulary**

Write the word *fox*. Ask students to describe a fox. Explain that a fox is a member of the dog family. It has perky ears, a slender snout, a bushy tail, and reddish-brown or gray fur. Point out that in many stories and tales, such as "The Gingerbread Man," the fox is often a sly character.

Teacher Tip

Remind students that they may come across *o* words that do not have the typical short *o* or long *o* sound. For example, the *o* in the word *shoe* combines with *e* to make a brand-new sound.

Objectives

- To identify short and long *o* vowel sounds and spelling patterns
- To read, sort, and write words with a short *o* CVC or long *o* CVCe spelling

Materials for Within Word Pattern

- Big Book of Rhymes, "Where Is That Clock?," page 9
- Whiteboard Activities DVD-ROM, Sort 6
- Teacher Resource CD-ROM, Sort 6 and Going to Gram's Game
- Student Book, pages 21–24
- Words Their Way Library, *Summer at Cove Lake*

Words

ŏ CVC	ō CVCe	Oddball
clock	rope	come
pot	hope	some
job	those	
hot	rode	
rock	hose	
spot	joke	
chop	home	
	hole	
	stove	
	broke	

Bonus Words

crop	note
stop	chose
knock	whole
hop	code

Introduce/Model   *Small Groups*

- **Read a Rhyme** Read "Where Is That Clock?." Review the sound of short *o* and long *o*. Ask students to listen for words with short and long *o* as you reread the poem. List the words in columns and have students identify the short *o* CVC and long *o* CVCe spelling patterns.

- **Model** Use the whiteboard DVD or the CD word cards. Demonstrate how to sort the words by the short *o* CVC and long *o* CVCe patterns. *Come* and *some* are oddballs. Have students read the words in the other columns and discuss how the words are alike. Help students sort and explain their sorts.

Practice the Sort   *Independent/Partner*

- Have students use the Student Book or whiteboard DVD to read the words and use the grid to sort according to a short or long *o* spelling pattern.

- Have students check and explain their sorts.

Apply   *Independent/Partner/Small Groups*

- Read aloud the directions on Student Book p. 24. Have students read each word and write it in the short *o* or long *o* column.

- **Game** Allow time for students to play Going to Gram's, which is on the CD.

- **Little Book** Read *Summer at Cove Lake* with students. Have them identify short *o* and long *o* words.

Extend the Sort

Alternative Sort: Consonant Count

Have students re-sort the cards according to the number of consonants in the words. They will need to make piles for words with two, three, and four consonants.

ELL English Language Learners

Invite students to use a voice recorder to record themselves reading the words in each group. Have them replay the recording, listening to the pronunciations of the vowel sound in each sorted group of words.

Bonus Words Activity

Provide strips of colored paper, approximately 1 inch wide and 7 inches long. Have students write an *o* word with the CVC or CVCe spelling pattern on each strip. Use the Bonus Word list to help students get started. Then link the strips together to make two paper chains, one for each spelling pattern.

Teacher Tip

Encourage students to continue to add to the paper chains (Bonus Words Activity) as they come across words with short *o* and long *o*.

Short and Long *u* (Pictures)

Objectives
- To identify short and long *u* vowel sounds
- To identify and sort pictures and words that contain a short or long *u* vowel sound

Materials for Within Word Pattern

📓 Big Book of Rhymes, "I Like Bugs!," page 11

🖥 Whiteboard Activities DVD-ROM, Sort 7

💿 Teacher Resource CD-ROM, Sort 7 and Sound Match Game

📒 Student Book, pages 25–28

📕 Words Their Way Library, *Cubby's Gum*

Pictures

long *u*	short *u*	Oddball
glue	rug	cake
suit	nut	
spoon	tub	
mule	bug	
moon	truck	
shoe	plug	
fruit	sun	
flute	drum	
	trunk	

Introduce/Model
Small Groups

- **Read a Rhyme** Read "I Like Bugs!" Explain that you will read the poem again, and students who like bugs should raise their hands when they hear a short *u* word. *(bugs, but, up)* The other students should raise their hands for long *u* words. *(true, cute, blue)* Read the poem again and have students point out short and long *u* words.

- **Model** Use the whiteboard DVD or the CD picture cards. Name each picture as you introduce the cards. Show students how to sort the cards into categories: short *u* and long *u*. Place *cake* in the oddball column. Help students sort and explain their sorts.

Practice the Sort
Independent/Partner

- Have students use the Student Book or whiteboard DVD to name the pictures and use the grid to sort according to a short or long vowel *u* sound.

- Have students check and explain their sorts.

Apply
Independent/Partner/Small Groups

- Read aloud the directions on Student Book p. 28. Have students write two short *u* words and two long *u* words and draw pictures to match the words.

- **Game** Allow time for students to play Sound Match, which is on the CD.

- **Little Book** Read *Cubby's Gum* with students. Then point out pictures of *gum, blue, truck,* and *flute;* have students. identify the short or long *u* sound in each word.

Extend the Sort

Alternative Sort: Rhyming Words
Encourage students to further sort each column into words that rhyme. *(glue, shoe; suit, fruit, flute; spoon, moon; rug, bug, plug)* Help students understand that the words rhyme because they end with the same sounds. Encourage students to name other words that rhyme with the picture names from the sort.

ELL English Language Learners
Review the picture cards. Have students pronounce the words after you. Students can practice vocabulary by naming words associated with each picture. Words associated with the fruit picture, for example, would be the names of the different fruits.

Vocabulary Building Vocabulary
Tell students that some words have more than one meaning. Display the picture card for *trunk*. Explain that the picture shows the long flexible nose of an elephant. Ask students if they know other meanings of the word *trunk*. Guide them to state that a trunk is also a large lidded box, the storage area in the rear of a car, the woody main stem of a tree, or the main part of the human body.

Short *u* (CVC) and Long *u* (CVCe)

Objectives
- To identify short and long *u* vowel sounds and spelling patterns
- To read, sort, and write words with a short *u* CVC or long *u* CVCe spelling pattern

Materials for Within Word Pattern

Big Book of Rhymes, "I Like Bugs!," page 11

Whiteboard Activities DVD-ROM, Sort 8

Teacher Resource CD-ROM, Sort 8 and U Name It! Game

Student Book, pages 29–32

Words Their Way Library, *Cubby's Gum*

Words

ŭ CVC	ū CVCe	Oddball
bus	cube	put
cut	mule	
plus	huge	
just	cute	
drum	tune	**Bonus Words**
jump	June	bump prune
hunt	rude	skunk crude
shut	flute	trust rule
such	use	run
club		

Introduce/Model
Small Groups

- **Read a Rhyme** Read "I Like Bugs!" Review the sounds of short and long *u*. Reread the poem and have students listen for words with short *u* and long *u* vowel sounds. List the words in separate columns. Point out a word with a short *u* CVC pattern *(bugs)* and a word with a long *u* CVCe pattern *(cute).*

- **Model** Use the whiteboard DVD or the CD word cards. Demonstrate how to sort words by short and long *u* sounds. Help students identify the spelling pattern for the vowel sounds in each group. *Put* is an oddball. Help students sort and explain their sorts.

Practice the Sort
Independent/Partner

- Have students use the Student Book or whiteboard DVD to read the words and use the grid to sort according to a short or long *u* spelling pattern.

- Have students check and explain their sorts.

Apply
Independent/Partner/Small Groups

- Read aloud the directions on Student Book p. 32. Have students read each word and write it in the short *u* or long *u* column.

- **Game** Allow time for students to play U Name It!, which is on the CD.

- **Little Book** Read *Cubby's Gum* with students. Have them identify short *u* and long *u* words.

Extend the Sort

Alternative Sort: How Many Letters?

Have students re-sort the cards according to how many letters in the word. Students will need three stacks: one for three-letter words, one for four-letter words, and one for five-letter words.

ELL English Language Learners

Review the word cards with students by having them repeat each word after you. You may need to explain the meanings of some words. Point out the word *June* and the capital letter at the beginning. Explain that the names of months always begin with a capital letter.

Bonus Words Activity

Write the Bonus Words and read them aloud. Have students choose two or more of the words and use them to make up a silly sentence.

Teacher Tip

If some students are having difficulty sorting words with short *u* and long *u*, pair them with students who are more proficient.

Sort 9

Short and Long e (Pictures)

Objectives

- To identify short and long *e* vowel sounds
- To identify and sort pictures and words that contain a short or long *e* vowel sound

Materials for Within Word Pattern

Big Book of Rhymes, "Jean's Dream," page 13

Whiteboard Activities DVD-ROM, Sort 9

Teacher Resource CD-ROM, Sort 9 and Vowel Spin Game

Student Book, pages 33–36

Words Their Way Library, *Steve's Room*

Pictures		
short *e*	**long *e***	**Oddball**
sled	cheese	fork
vest	seal	
pen	leaf	
bell	sheep	
dress	tree	
desk	jeep	
leg	queen	
nest	sleep	

Introduce/Model   *Small Groups*

- **Read a Rhyme** Read "Jean's Dream." Review the sounds of short and long e. Help students use sticky notes of one color to mark the short e words in the poem. *(ten, red, kept, them, bed, when, went, head, special, necklace, best, ever)* Then use sticky notes of a different color to mark the long e words. *(Jean, beads, she, sleep, seen, dream)*

- **Model** Use the whiteboard DVD or the CD picture cards. Show the cards and name each picture. Sort the cards into short e and long e. *Fork* is an oddball. Have the class name each picture in each column and tell how the words are alike. Help students explain their sorts.

Practice the Sort   *Independent/Partner*

- Have students use the Student Book or whiteboard DVD to name the pictures and use the grid to sort.

- Have students check and explain their sorts.

Apply   *Independent/Partner/Small Groups*

- Read aloud the directions on Student Book p. 36. Have students write two short e words and two long e words and draw pictures to match the words.

- **Game** Allow time for students to play Vowel Spin, which is on the CD.

- **Little Book** Read *Steve's Room* with students. Then point out pictures of *Steve, shells, desk, nests, shelf, jets, chest,* and *nets;* have students identify the short or long e sound in each word.

Extend the Sort

Alternative Sort: /t/, /p/, or /n/ Endings

Have students re-sort the picture cards according to their ending sounds. Cards with picture names that end in /t/ should go in one pile, cards with picture names that end in /p/ should go in a second pile, and those that end in /n/ should go in a third pile. All other cards should go in a fourth pile.

ELL English Language Learners

Review the picture cards. Give one card to each child. Let students take turns describing their pictures without showing them to the other students. Have the other students guess what is on the card.

Vocabulary Building Vocabulary

Display the picture card for vest and explain that a vest is a sleeveless garment, usually worn over a shirt. Ask students if any of them own a vest or can describe a time they have seen someone who was wearing a vest.

Teacher Tip

With the past few sorts, students have worked with the vowels *a, e, i, o,* and *u.* You may want to check to see if each student knows the short and long vowel sounds. Review these sounds if needed.

144   Within Word Pattern

Review Short Vowel (CVC) and Long Vowel (CVCe) Patterns

Objectives

- To review short and long vowel sounds and spelling patterns
- To read, sort, and write words with a short vowel CVC spelling pattern or long vowel CVCe spelling pattern

Materials for Within Word Pattern

📖 Big Book of Rhymes, "My Summer Vacation," page 15

🖥 Whiteboard Activities DVD-ROM, Sort 10

💿 Teacher Resource CD-ROM, Sort 10 and Spin and Say Game

📖 Student Book, pages 37–40

📙 Words Their Way Library, *When Bob Work Up Late*

Words

CVC-short	CVCe-long	Oddball
wax	mule	done
skin	rule	have
crab	safe	
lots	wife	
gum	cape	
drip	tide	
which	vote	
	wipe	

Introduce/Model   *Small Groups*

- **Read a Rhyme** Read "My Summer Vacation." Write the word *dad*. Point out that *a* and other vowels, when they come between two consonants (CVC), are often short. Now write the word *June*. Explain that the *u* in this word is long because of the silent *e* at the end (CVCe).

- **Model** Use the whiteboard DVD or the CD word cards. Demonstrate how to sort the words by the short vowel CVC and long vowel CVCe patterns. Put the oddball words *(done, have)* in a separate pile. Help students sort and explain their sorts.

Practice the Sort   *Independent/Partner*

- Have students use the Student Book or whiteboard DVD to read the words and use the grid to sort.

- Have students check and explain their sorts.

Apply   *Independent/Partner/Small Groups*

- Read aloud the directions on Student Book p. 40. Have students read each word and write it in the short or long vowel column.

- **Game** Allow time for students to play Spin and Say, which is on the CD.

- **Little Book** Read *When Bob Woke Up Late* with students. Have them identify short vowel CVC and long vowel CVCe words.

Extend the Sort

Alternative Sort: /p/ and /f/ Endings
Ask students to re-sort the cards into three groups: words that end with the /p/ sound *(drip, cape, wipe)*, words that end with the /f/ sound *(safe, wife)*, and words that end with other sounds.

ELL English Language Learners
Review the word cards with students by having them repeat each word after you. To reinforce vocabulary, give each student a word card to illustrate on a separate sheet of paper. Show the illustrations one at a time and ask students to guess the words.

Teacher Tip
Offer advanced students additional challenges. After sorting the words, invite them to alphabetize the words in each group and then take turns using the words in sentences.

Monitor Progress **Spell Check 1**

After completing Sort 10, administer Spell Check 1. See p. 135 in this Teacher Resource Guide for instructions.

Sort 11

Short *a* (CVC) and Long *a* (CVCe and CVVC-*ai*)

Objectives

- To identify short and long *a* vowel sounds and spelling patterns
- To read, sort, and write words with the short *a* CVC spelling pattern and the long *a* CVCe and CVVC-*ai* spelling patterns

Materials for Within Word Pattern

Big Book of Rhymes, "Pancakes for Breakfast," page 17

Whiteboard Activities DVD-ROM, Sort 11

Teacher Resource CD-ROM, Sort 11 and Vowel *a* Patterns Game

Student Book, pages 41–44

Words Their Way Library, *Pancakes!*

Words

ă CVC	ā CVVC-*ai*	ā CVCe	Oddball
black	brain	bake	said
camp	faint	blame	want
dash	main	crane	
flash	paint	mane	
snack	snail	place	
stamp	train	snake	

Introduce/Model   *Small Groups*

- **Read a Rhyme** Read "Pancakes for Breakfast." Write the word *pancakes* and draw a line between *pan* and *cakes*. Call attention to the short *a* in *pan* and the long *a* in *cakes*. Read the poem again and ask students to listen for and name more short *a* words (*pan, as, can, can't, stacks, dad, am, glad*) and long *a* words (*makes, wait, plate, ate, made*).

- **Model** Use the whiteboard DVD or the CD word cards. Demonstrate how to sort words by the short *a* CVC, long *a* CVCe, and CVVC-*ai* patterns. *Said* and *want* are oddballs. Help students sort and explain their sorts.

Practice the Sort   *Independent/Partner*

- Have students use the Student Book or whiteboard DVD to read the words and use the grid to sort according to a short or long *a* spelling pattern.

- Have students check and explain their sorts.

Apply   *Independent/Partner/Small Groups*

- Read aloud the directions on Student Book p. 44. Have students read each word and write it in the appropriate column according to spelling pattern.

- **Game** Allow time for students to play Vowel *a* Patterns, which is on the CD.

- **Little Book** Read *Pancakes!* with students. Have them identify words with short *a* CVC, long *a* CVCe, and long *a* spelled *ai*.

Extend the Sort

Alternative Sort: How Many Letters?

Have students re-sort the cards according to how many letters in each word. Students will need two stacks: one for four-letter words and one for five-letter words.

ELL English Language Learners

Model the pronunciation of oddball words *said* and *want* so that students can hear the difference and see that your mouth forms the vowel sounds in these words differently than in short *a* or long *a* words. Have students repeat the words after you, carefully using proper pronunciation.

Vocabulary Building Vocabulary

Point out the word *camp*. Explain that *camp* can be an action—going out into nature to sleep and do other leisure activities—as well as a place where you go to do these things.

Teacher Tip

When students complete a sort, remind them to read each word in a column and note its spelling pattern to check their work. Some students may find it helpful to trace each short *a* and long *a* spelling pattern with a different color crayon or marker.

Short *a* (CVC) and Long *a* (CVCe, CVVC-*ai* and Open Syllable-*ay*)

Objectives

- To identify short and long *a* vowel sounds and spelling patterns
- To read, sort, and write words with the short *a* CVC and long *a* CVCe, CVVC-*ai*, and open syllable-*ay* spelling patterns

Materials for Within Word Pattern

Big Book of Rhymes, "The Cat Chaser," page 19

Whiteboard Activities DVD-ROM, Sort 12

Teacher Resource CD-ROM, Sort 12 and Animal Race Game

Student Book, pages 45–48

Words Their Way Library, *Who Has a Tail?*

Words

ă CVC	ā CVCe	aī CVVC	āy CVV
class	blame	brain	clay
grass	brave	drain	gray
past	shade	gain	play
smash	shape	grain	stay
stand	taste	nail	stray
trash	wade	raise	tray

Bonus Words

grand	grave	faith	jay
brass	graze	stain	sway
task	slate	fail	ray
tramp	stale	praise	slay

Introduce/Model
Small Groups

- **Read a Rhyme** Read "The Cat Chaser." Write the title and point out short *a* in *Cat* and long *a* in *Chaser*. Reread the poem and ask students to listen for and name more short *a* words (*have, as, fast, can, at, and*) and long *a* words (*named, Ray, chases, Nate, way, space, waits, chase*).

- **Model** Use the whiteboard DVD or the CD word cards. Demonstrate how to sort the words by the spelling patterns short *a* CVC, long *a* CVCe, long *a* CVVC-*ai*, and long *a* CVV-*ay*. Explain that a syllable or a one-syllable word ending in *a* long vowel sound, such as *stray*, is called an open syllable. An open-syllable pattern can be labeled CV or CVV, since the *y* acts as a vowel in these long *a* words. Help students sort and explain their sorts.

Practice the Sort
Independent/Partner

- Have students use the Student Book or whiteboard DVD to read the words and use the grid to sort.

- Have students check and explain their sorts.

Apply
Independent/Partner/Small Groups

- Read aloud the directions on Student Book p. 48. Have students read each word and write it in the appropriate column according to spelling pattern.

- **Game** Allow time for students to play Animal Race, which is on the CD.

- **Little Book** Read *Who Has a Tail?* with students. Have them identify words with short *a* CVC, long *a* CVCe, and long *a* spelled *ai* or *ay*.

Extend the Sort

Alternative Sort: One Sound or Two?

Tell students that some of this sort's words, such as *smash* and *brave*, begin with a consonant blend. Have students sort words into two piles: words that begin with a consonant blend and words that do not.

ELL English Language Learners

Check students' pronunciation and understanding of the words. Ensure they can discriminate between short *a* and long *a* vowel sounds. Explain that, although there are different spelling patterns for the long *a* words, all have the same vowel sound.

Bonus Words Activity

Ask students to think of other words with short *a* and long *a* spelling patterns. If needed, make suggestions from the Bonus Words list. Then have students play Spelling Pattern Tic Tac Toe. Each player chooses a colored pencil or marker and a spelling pattern. Player 1 begins by writing a word with his or her chosen spelling pattern on the Tic Tac Toe board. Player 2 then writes a word from his or her chosen spelling pattern. Play continues until one player writes three words in a row across, down, or diagonally or until all nine spaces have been filled in.

Short *o* (CVC) and Long *o* (CVCe and CVVC-*oa*)

Objectives

- To identify short and long *o* spelling patterns
- To read, sort, and write words with the short *o* CVC and the long *o* CVCe and CVVC-*oa* spelling patterns

Materials for Within Word Pattern

📖 Big Book of Rhymes, "Let's Go to Grandma's!," page 21

💻 Whiteboard Activities DVD-ROM, Sort 13

💿 Teacher Resource CD-ROM, Sort 13 and Pair of Long *o*'s Game

📕 Student Book, pages 49–52

📖 Words Their Way Library, *Tiger's Tummy Ache*

Words

ŏ CVC	ō CVCe	ō CVVC	Oddball
clock	chose	boat	love
crop	joke	coat	none
cross	note	float	
knock	slope	soap	
lock	stone	toad	
shop	whole	toast	

Introduce/Model   *Small Groups*

- **Read a Rhyme** Read "Let's Go to Grandma's!" Review the sounds of short and long *o*. Reread the poem and have students listen for words with the short *o* vowel sound and the long *o* vowel sound. List the words in separate columns. Point out an example of the CVCe and CVVC-*oa* patterns in the long *o* words.

- **Model** Use the whiteboard DVD or the CD word cards. Demonstrate how to sort the words by the short *o* CVC and the long *o* CVCe and CVVC-*oa* patterns. Place the words *love* and *none* in the oddball column. Help students sort and explain their sorts.

Practice the Sort   *Independent/Partner*

- Have students use the Student Book or whiteboard DVD to read the words and use the grid to sort according to a short or long *o* spelling pattern.

- Have students check and explain their sorts.

Apply   *Independent/Partner/Small Groups*

- Read aloud the directions on Student Book p. 52. Have students read each word and write it in the short *o* or long *o* column according to spelling pattern.

- **Game** Allow time for students to play Pair of Long *o*'s, which is on the CD.

- **Little Book** Read *Tiger's Tummy Ache* with students. Have them identify words with short *o* CVC, long *o* CVCe, and long *o* spelled *oa*.

Extend the Sort

Alternative Sort: /t/ or /p/ Endings

Ask students to re-sort the word cards according to their ending sounds. Cards with words that end in /t/ should go in one pile (*note, boat, float, coat, toast*) and cards with words that end in /p/ should go in a second pile (*crop, shop, slope, soap*). All other cards should go in a third pile.

ELL English Language Learners

To reinforce vocabulary, give each student a word card to illustrate on a separate sheet of paper. Show the illustrations one at a time and ask students to guess the words.

Vocabulary Building Vocabulary

Tell students that some words can be both nouns and verbs. Point out the word *note*. Explain that as a noun, the word *note* can be a musical symbol or a short written message. When *note* is used as a verb it means "to see and notice" or "to state." Use *note* in one sentence as a noun and in another sentence as a verb. Have students identify the meaning and part of speech each time.

Teacher Tip

Some students may benefit from completing the sort in two steps. First, encourage students to sort the word cards according to short *o* or long *o*. Then have them examine the spelling patterns in the sorted long *o* words and complete the sort.

Short *o* (CVC) and Long *o* (CVCe, CVVC-*oa*, and CVV-*ow*)

Objectives
- To identify short and long *o* spelling patterns
- To read, sort, and write words with short *o* CVC and long *o* CVCe, CVVC-*oa*, and CVV-*ow* spelling patterns

Materials for Within Word Pattern

Big Book of Rhymes, "Follow the Wind," page 23

Whiteboard Activities DVD-ROM, Sort 14

Teacher Resource CD-ROM, Sort 14 and Snow Ride Game

Student Book, pages 53–56

Words Their Way Library, *Grandpa, Grandma, and the Tractor*

Words

ŏ CVC	ō CVCe	ōa CVVC	ōw CVV	Oddball
chop	close	boat	blow	lose
drop	dome	coach	grow	
gloss	globe	loaf	know	
long	note	roam	slow	
shop	wrote	roast	throw	

Bonus Words

dock	sole	cloak	flow
prompt	pose	boast	glow
stomp	quote	coax	show
blond	zone	loan	stow

Introduce/Model   *Small Groups*

- **Read a Rhyme** Read "Follow the Wind," emphasizing the end rhymes. Write *ow* and *oa* as column heads, and write words from the poem in the appropriate column. Tell students they will learn more words with these spelling patterns and other long *o* patterns in this week's sort.

- **Model** Use the whiteboard DVD or the CD word cards. Work with students to sort the words by the target spelling patterns. Explain that a one-syllable word that ends with a long vowel sound, such as *slow*, is called an open syllable. Place *lose* in the oddball category. Help students sort and explain their sorts.

Practice the Sort   *Independent/Partner*

- Have students use the Student Book or whiteboard DVD to read the words and use the grid to sort.

- Have students check and explain their sorts.

Apply   *Independent/Partner/Small Groups*

- Read aloud the directions on Student Book p. 56. Have students read each word and write it in the short *o* or long *o* column according to spelling pattern.

- **Game** Allow time for students to play Snow Ride, which is on the CD.

- **Little Book** Read *Grandpa, Grandma, and the Tractor* with students. Have them identify words with short *o* CVC, long *o* CVCe, and long *o* spelled *ow*.

Extend the Sort

Alternative Sort: Rhyming Words

Encourage students to further sort each column into words that rhyme and words that do not rhyme. Help students understand that all of the -*ow* words rhyme because the -*ow* spelling pattern comes at the end of the word.

Vocabulary Building Vocabulary

Explain to students that a dome is a shape found on the top of some buildings. Show children a globe. Tell students to imagine cutting the globe in half. The result would be a dome.

Bonus Words Activity

Have students sort the Bonus Words according to spelling patterns. Allow students to play a game in small groups. Using a small cube-shaped box, write a spelling pattern on each side. You can use a pattern more than once. Invite Player 1 to roll the "pattern cube" and identify the spelling pattern. The student should then say and spell a Bonus Word with the corresponding spelling pattern. Another player then takes a turn.

Sort 15

Long *o* (CVCe, CVVC-*oa*, CVV-*ow*, VCC)

Objectives

- To identify long *o* spelling patterns
- To read, sort, and write words with the long *o* CVCe, CVVC-*oa*, CVV-*ow*, and VCC spelling patterns

Materials for Within Word Pattern

Big Book of Rhymes, "The Snow Ride," page 25

Whiteboard Activities DVD-ROM, Sort 15

Teacher Resource CD-ROM, Sort 15 and Vowel Pattern Match Game

Student Book, pages 57–60

Words Their Way Library, *Wilbert Took a Walk*

Words

ō CVCe	ōa CVVC	ōw CVV	ō VCC	Oddball
cone	coast	blown	both	toe
owe	groan	glow	cold	
rode	loan	know	ghost	
those	road	slow	poll	
throne		throw	told	

Introduce/Model · Small Groups

- **Read a Rhyme** Read "The Snow Ride." Review the sounds of long *o* and the various spelling patterns. Reread the poem, having students draw a letter *o* in the air when they hear a long *o* word. Write the words students identify in the appropriate column.

- **Model** Use the whiteboard DVD or the CD word cards. Demonstrate how to sort the words by the long *o* CVCe, CVVC-*oa*, CVV-*ow*, and VCC spelling patterns. Help students sort and explain their sorts.

Practice the Sort · Independent/Partner

- Have students use the Student Book or whiteboard DVD to read the words and use the grid to sort according to long *o* spelling patterns.

- Have students check and explain their sorts.

Apply · Independent/Partner/Small Groups

- Read aloud the directions on Student Book p. 60. Have students read each word and write it in the appropriate column according to spelling pattern.

- **Game** Allow time for students to play Vowel Pattern Match, which is on the CD.

- **Little Book** Read *Wilbert Took a Walk* with students. Have them identify words with short *o* CVC, long *o* CVCe, and long *o* spelled *oa* or *ow*.

Extend the Sort

Alternative Sort: /k/ or /g/ Beginnings

Ask students to re-sort the word cards according to the first sound of the words. Cards with words that begin with /k/ should go in one pile and cards with words that begin with /g/ should go in a second pile. All other cards should go in a third pile.

Vocabulary · Building Vocabulary

If students are unfamiliar with the word *coast*, explain that a coast is the land along an ocean or sea. On a map, show students where the East and West coasts of the United States and the Gulf Coast along the Gulf of Mexico are.

Teacher Tip

When students work together in pairs or small groups, suggest that they take turns being the "teacher." It is the teacher's responsibility to check the work of the other student or students and help them understand how to correctly sort the cards.

Objectives
- To identify short and long *u* CVCe and CVVC spelling patterns
- To read, sort, and write words with the short *u* CVC spelling pattern and the long *u* CVCe and CVVC spelling patterns

Materials for Within Word Pattern

📖 Big Book of Rhymes, "Goodbye, Flu!," page 27

🖥 Whiteboard Activities DVD-ROM, Sort 16

💿 Teacher Resource CD-ROM, Sort 16 and One Card! Game

📓 Student Book, pages 61–64

📗 Words Their Way Library, *The Doctor Has the Flu*

Words

ŭ CVC	*ū* CVCe	*ū* CVVC		Oddball
		oo	*ui*	
bump	crude	bloom	bruise	build
grunt	cute	moon	cruise	built
plus	flute	smooth	juice	
skunk	mule	spoon	suit	
trust	prune	tooth		

Bonus Words

rust	mute	loop
fuss	fume	scoop
blush	fuse	loom
gust	muse	booth

Introduce/Model   *Small Groups*

- **Read a Rhyme** Read "Goodbye, Flu!" Review the sounds of short and long *u*. Reread the poem and have students listen for words with short and long *u*. List the words in separate columns. Point out the different spellings of the long *u* sound. Help students identify an example of each spelling pattern.

- **Model** Use the whiteboard DVD or the CD word cards. Demonstrate how to sort the words by short and long *u* vowel sounds. Then model how to sort the words according to the following patterns: short *u* CVC and long *u* CVCe, CVVC-*ui*, CVVC-*oo*. Put the oddball words (*build, built*) in a separate pile. Help students sort and explain their sorts.

Practice the Sort   *Independent/Partner*

- Have students use the Student Book or whiteboard DVD to read the words and use the grid to sort according to a short or long *u* spelling pattern.

- Have students check and explain their sorts.

Apply   *Independent/Partner/Small Groups*

- Read aloud the directions on Student Book p. 64. Have students read each word and write it in the short *u* or long *u* column according to spelling pattern.

- **Game** Allow time for students to play One Card!, which is on the CD.

- **Little Book** Read *The Doctor Has the Flu* with students. Have them identify words with short *u* CVC, long *u* CVCe, and long *u* spelled *ui* or *oo*.

Extend the Sort

Alternative Sort: Perfect Fit

Draw five small boxes. Instruct students to make two piles, one pile for five-letter words (the words that would fit one letter perfectly into each of the five boxes) and one pile for the other words.

Bonus Words Activity

Draw a four-leaf clover as a model. Have each student draw and cut apart a large four-leaf clover from green construction paper. Instruct them to write *Lucky U* on the stem and words on each of the four leaves, using a different spelling pattern on each leaf (short *u* CVC, long *u* CVCe, long *u* CVVC-*ui,* and long *u* CVVC-*oo*). If students need prompting to help them think of words, make suggestions from the Bonus Words list.

Vocabulary Building Vocabulary

Discuss the word *trust*. Explain that if you can count on someone to do what is right, you can trust that person. Name something you trust the students to do. For example, tell students you trust them to do their best on the word sorts.

Short *u* (CVC) and Long *u* (Open Syllable-*ew* and -*ue*)

Objectives

- To identify short and long *u* vowel sounds and spelling patterns
- To read, sort, and write words with the short *u* and long *u* spelling patterns

Materials for Within Word Pattern

🗂 Big Book of Rhymes, "Big Baby Sue," page 29

🖥 Whiteboard Activities DVD-ROM, Sort 17

💿 Teacher Resource CD-ROM, Sort 17 and Match the Pattern Game

📘 Student Book, pages 65–68

🦉 Words Their Way Library, *The World's Biggest Baby*

Words

ŭ CVC	*ēw* CVV	*ūe* CVV		Oddball
brush	chew	blue	glue	do
dump	drew	clue	sue	sew
junk	few	flue	true	truth
plump	grew			
truck	knew			
trunk	stew			

Bonus Words

crumb	shrew	hue
tusk	whew	cue
husk	brew	rue
slump	dew	argue

Introduce/Model   *Small Groups*

- **Read a Rhyme** Read "Big Baby Sue" and ask students to name words that rhyme with *Sue*. *(knew, grew, true, to, do)* Write the words and point out the spelling patterns. Then ask students to identify the vowel sound they hear in *much*. (long *u*)

- **Model** Use the whiteboard DVD or the CD word cards. Demonstrate how to sort the words according to spelling patterns short *u* CVC, long *u* CVV-*ew*, and long *u* CVV-*ue*. Tell students that the *w* in *ew* acts like a vowel and makes an open-syllable pattern. Place *do, truth,* and *sew* in the oddball column. Help students sort and explain their sorts.

Practice the Sort   *Independent/Partner*

- Have students use the Student Book or whiteboard DVD to read the words and use the grid to sort.

- Have students check and explain their sorts.

Apply   *Independent/Partner/Small Groups*

- Read aloud the directions on Student Book p. 68. Have students write the words in the short *u* or long *u* column according to spelling pattern.

- **Game** Allow time for students to play Match the Pattern, which is on the CD.

- **Little Book** Read *The World's Biggest Baby* with students. Have them identify words with short *u* CVC, long *u* CVCe, and long *u* spelled *ue* or *ew*.

Extend the Sort

Alternative Sort: Many Meanings

Have students sort the words according to those that have one meaning *(knew)* and those that have more than one meaning *(brush)*. Then have them read each word and identify its meaning or meanings.

(ELL) English Language Learners

Have English language learners work with more proficient English speakers as they complete the sort. Encourage the English language learner to say each word with the more proficient speaker.

Bonus Words Activity

Ask students to name other words with the short and long *u* spelling patterns from this sort. If students need prompting, make suggestions from the Bonus Words list. Then help students use a blank grid to make word cards for these new words. Have students work independently or with a partner to sort the words into categories.

Objectives

- To identify short and long *e* vowel sounds and spelling patterns
- To read, sort, and write words with the short *e* CVC and long *e* CVVC spelling patterns

Materials for Within Word Pattern

Big Book of Rhymes, "Shopping," page 31

Whiteboard Activities DVD-ROM, Sort 18

Teacher Resource CD-ROM, Sort 18 and Shopping Spree Game

Student Book, pages 69–72

Words Their Way Library, *Something Everyone Needs*

Words

ĕ CVC	ēe CVVC	ēa CVVC	Oddball
dress	jeep	clean	been
next	keep	heat	
vest	sleep	leaf	
web	sweep	team	
west	teeth	weak	
when	week	wheat	

Bonus Words

stem	speech	least
pest	speed	deal
went	greed	meal
them	creep	treat

Introduce/Model
Small Groups

- **Read a Rhyme** Read "Shopping." Review the sounds of short and long *e*. Reread the poem and instruct students to raise their hands when they hear a long *e* and to lower their hands when they hear a short *e*. Ask students to find examples of spelling patterns for short and long *e*: short *e* CVC *(spent)*, long *e* CVVC-*ee* *(need, succeed)*, and long *e* CVVC-*ea* *(beat)*.

- **Model** Use the whiteboard DVD or the CD word cards. Read each word. Demonstrate how to sort the words by short and long *e*. Then show students how to sort by spelling patterns short *e* CVC, long *e* CVVC-*ee*, and long *e* CVVC-*ea*. Explain that *been* does not fit the spelling/pronunciation pattern, so it is an oddball. Help students sort and explain their sorts.

Practice the Sort
Independent/Partner

- Have students use the Student Book or whiteboard DVD to read the words and use the grid to sort.

- Have students check and explain their sorts.

Apply
Independent/Partner/Small Groups

- Read aloud the directions on Student Book p. 72. Have students read each word and write it in the short *e* or long *e* column according to spelling pattern.

- **Game** Allow time for students to play Shopping Spree, which is on the CD.

- **Little Book** Read *Something Everyone Needs* with students. Have them identify words with short *e* CVC and long *e* spelled *ee* or *ea*.

Extend the Sort

Alternative Sort: Twin Letters

Have students re-sort the cards by words with "twin" (double) consonants or vowels and words without twin consonants or vowels.

Bonus Words Activity

On index cards, have students write and illustrate words that show the different spelling patterns from this sort: short *e* CVC, long *e* CVVC-*ee,* and long *e* CVVC-*ea*. If students need prompting to help them think of words, make suggestions from the Bonus Words list. Display the cards on a bulletin board or mount them in a photo album. Have students help you group them according to the various spelling patterns.

Vocabulary Building Vocabulary

Write the words *week* and *weak*, and ask students to read the two words. Explain that some words, called homophones, sound alike but have different spellings and different meanings. Review the definitions of *week* (seven days) and *weak* (not strong). Help students think of another pair of long *e* words that sound alike but have different spellings and meanings *(meet/meat)*.

More Short *e* (CVC and CVVC) and Long *e* (CVVC)

Objectives

- To identify short and long *e* vowel sounds and spelling patterns
- To read, sort, and write words with short *e* CVC, short *e* CVVC, and long *e* CVVC spelling patterns

Materials for Within Word Pattern

- Big Book of Rhymes, "Eagles Fly," page 33
- Whiteboard Activities DVD-ROM, Sort 19
- Teacher Resource CD-ROM, Sort 19 and Eagle Race Game
- Student Book, pages 73–76
- Words Their Way Library, *An Eagle Flies High*

Words

ĕ CVC	*eă* CVVC	*eā* CVVC	*ēe* CVVC	Oddball
best	bread	beach	greed	great
desk	breath	bead	queen	
next	head	dream	sleep	
sled	thread	reach	street	
web	threat	steam	sweet	

Bonus Words

swept	health	flea	beef
shelf	read	peak	geese
help	dread	leak	breeze
left	tread	leash	greet

Introduce/Model *Small Groups*

- **Read a Rhyme** Read "Eagles Fly." Ask students to identify words from the poem with short *e* between two consonants. *(head, when)* Point out the different spellings of short *e* in these words. Then have children name words with the long *e* sound. *(see, eagle, breeze, trees)* Point out the *ee* and *ea* spellings for the long *e* vowel sound.

- **Model** Use the whiteboard DVD or the CD word cards. Read each word. Demonstrate how to sort the words by spelling patterns: short *e* CVC, short *e* CVVC-*ea*, long *e* CVVC-*ea*, and long *e* CVVC-*ee*. Explain that *great* is an oddball because it has neither a short nor long *e* vowel sound. Help students sort and explain their sorts.

Practice the Sort *Independent/Partner*

- Have students use the Student Book or whiteboard DVD to read the words and use the grid to sort.

- Have students check and explain their sorts.

Apply *Independent/Partner/Small Groups*

- Read aloud the directions on Student Book p. 76. Have students read each word and write it in the short *e* or long *e* column according to spelling pattern.

- **Game** Allow time for students to play Eagle Race, which is on the CD.

- **Little Book** Read *An Eagle Flies High* with students. Have them identify words with short *e* CVC, short *e* CVVC, and long *e* spelled *ee* or *ea*.

Extend the Sort

Alternative Sort: Beginning Blends

Have students re-sort the cards by words that begin with consonant blends and words that do not.

ELL English Language Learners

Review the word cards with students, having them repeat each word after you. As students say the words, watch students' mouths to make sure they are pronouncing the words clearly and correctly.

Bonus Words Activity

Have each student fold a paper in half vertically and then horizontally. Instruct students to cut along the folds to make four squares. Tell students to write a word on each of the four squares, using a different spelling pattern from this sort on each square. Make suggestions from the Bonus Words list if needed. Have students work together to arrange their squares into groups that contain four words with the same spelling pattern for short or long *e*.

Teacher Tip

When decoding, students may not know how to pronounce an *ea* word. They may wonder if the vowel sound should be short *e* or long *e*. Suggest that students try both ways and then select the pronunciation that produces a real word.

Review CVVC Patterns *ai, oa, ee, ea*

Objectives
- To review the long vowel spelling patterns *ai, oa, ee,* and *ea*
- To read, sort, and write words with the long vowel spelling patterns *ai, oa, ee,* and *ea*

Materials for **Within Word Pattern**

📖 Big Book of Rhymes, "A Bad Day," page 35

⬜ Whiteboard Activities DVD-ROM, Sort 20

💿 Teacher Resource CD-ROM, Sort 20 and Match the Category Game

📕 Student Book, pages 77–80

📖 Words Their Way Library, *Pete's Bad Day*

Words

ai	*oa*	*ee*	*ea*
bait	coast	beet	beach
grain	coat	cheek	beast
pail	goat	need	cheat
tail	road	sheep	cream
train	throat	three	neat
wait	toast	wheel	seat

Bonus Words

rail	moan	sleep	pea
chain	load	teeth	feast
claim	croak	green	least
plain	coach	meet	reach

Introduce/Model
Small Groups

- **Read a Rhyme** Read "A Bad Day" and then write "___ai___." Ask students to look through the poem and identify a word with the long *a* sound spelled *ai. (pain)* Have a student fill in the blanks to write *pain*. Continue with long *o* spelled *oa (groaned)*, long *e* spelled *ee (feet)*, and long *e* spelled *ea (eat, screamed)*.

- **Model** Use the whiteboard DVD or the CD word cards. Read each word, and define in context any that may be unfamiliar to students. Demonstrate how to sort the words into four columns: *ai, oa, ee,* and *ea.* Starting with the first column, have students read the words with you. Ask volunteers to explain how all the words in the column are alike and how they are different. Continue with the other columns. Help students sort and explain their sorts.

Practice the Sort
Independent/Partner

- Have students use the Student Book or whiteboard DVD to read the words and use the grid to sort.

Apply
Independent/Partner/Small Groups

- Read aloud the directions on Student Book p. 80. Have students write two words that follow each long vowel pattern and draw pictures to match.

- **Game** Allow time for students to play Match the Category, which is on the CD.

- **Little Book** Read *Pete's Bad Day* with students. Have them identify words with long vowels spelled *oa, ee,* or *ea.* You may also want students to identify long *a* words spelled *ay*.

Extend the Sort

Alternative Sort: Alphabet Sort

Have students sort their cards alphabetically into two piles, one for words that begin with letters A to N and one for words that begin with letters O to Z.

ELL English Language Learners

Review the word cards with students, having them repeat each word after you. To practice language skills, give each student one or two cards, and have him or her create sentences using those words.

Bonus Words Activity

Provide old magazines and help students find words with the long vowel sounds spelled *ai, oa, ee,* and *ea.* If students cannot find words, they can cut out and combine letters to create their own words. If students need prompting, make suggestions from the Bonus Words list. Then they can sort the words into four piles, one for each spelling pattern.

Teacher Tip

Encourage students to continue to add words to their sort piles (Bonus Words activity) as they come across words with long vowel CVVC spelling patterns.

Short *i* (CVC) and Long *i* (CVCe, VCC-*igh*, and CV Open Syllable-*y*)

Objectives

- To identify the spelling patterns of short *i* and long *i*
- To read, sort, and write words with short *i* and long *i* spelling patterns

Materials for Within Word Pattern

- Big Book of Rhymes, "Don't Cry," page 37
- Whiteboard Activities DVD-ROM, Sort 21
- Teacher Resource CD-ROM, Sort 21 and Fly Away Game
- Student Book, pages 81–84
- Words Their Way Library, *The Princess and the Wise Woman*

Words

ĭ CVC	*ī* CVCe	*īgh* VCC	*y* = *ī* CV
bliss	grime	bright	cry
grill	quite	fight	dry
grim	rise	high	shy
quit	twice	night	sky
whisk	white	sigh	try

Bonus Words

filth	chime	fright	fly
risk	crime	light	sly
swift	prime	slight	spry
twist	spice	thigh	why

Introduce/Model
Small Groups

- **Read a Rhyme** Read "Don't Cry," emphasizing the end rhymes. Write the rhyming words *cry, sky* and *mile, while*. Have students identify the vowel sound and note the spelling in each pair. Read the poem again and ask students to identify and name other long *i* words. *(my, kite, flying, high, smile, lights)* Repeat with short *i* words. *(little, in, it, will, string)*

- **Model** Use the whiteboard DVD or the CD word cards. Model how to sort the words by the following spelling patterns: short *i* CVC and long *i* CVCe, VCC-*igh*, and CV open syllable-*y*. Ask students to describe how the words in each column are alike and how they are different. Help students sort and explain their sorts.

Practice the Sort
Independent/Partner

- Have students use the Student Book or whiteboard DVD to read the words and use the grid to sort.

- Have students check and explain their sorts.

Apply
Independent/Partner/Small Groups

- Read aloud the directions on Student Book p. 84. Have students read each word and write it in the appropriate column according to spelling pattern.

- **Game** Allow time for students to play Fly Away, which is on the CD.

- **Little Book** Read *The Princess and the Wise Woman* with students. Have them identify words with short *i* CVC, long *i* CVCe, and long *i* spelled *igh* or *y*.

Extend the Sort

Alternative Sort: Rhyme Time

Students can re-sort the words according to whether they rhyme with *might* or whether they do not rhyme with *might*. Remind them that rhyming words will have the same vowel sound and end sound but are not always spelled the same way.

ELL English Language Learners

To help students with letter-sound association, focus on one column at a time. Point to each word, read it, and have students repeat it. Then say a word at random. Have students locate the word, point to it, read the word, and identify the spelling pattern. Repeat with several words from the sort.

Bonus Words Activity

Ask students to name other words with a long or short *i* spelling pattern. If students need prompting, make suggestions from the Bonus Words list. Have students use a blank grid to make word cards for these new words and use the cards to play charades. One player draws a card and acts out the word; other students guess the word.

Teacher Tip

Give advanced students consonant letter cards, vowel letter cards, and cards with some of the spelling patterns learned so far *(oa, ow, ew, ue, igh)*. Invite students to use the cards to create words. Have them make a list of the words and see how many different words they can create.

Objectives

- To identify long *i* spelling patterns
- To read, sort, and write words with long *i* spelling patterns

Materials for Within Word Pattern

Big Book of Rhymes, "Once Upon a Time," page 39

Whiteboard Activities DVD-ROM, Sort 22

Teacher Resource CD-ROM, Sort 22 and Spelling Match Game

Student Book, pages 85–88

Words Their Way Library, *All About Bats*

Words

ī CVCe	*īgh* VCC	*y = ī* CV	*ī* iCC	Oddball
mice	flight	fly	blind	guy
nice	might	fry	child	
spice	right	my	kind	
stripe	sight	spy	mind	
write		why	sign	

Introduce/Model
Small Groups

- **Read a Rhyme** Read "Once Upon a Time" and have students listen for words with the long *i* sound. List the words in separate columns. Point out the different spellings of the long *i* sound: CVCe *(nice, time)*, VCC-*igh* *(fight)*, and VCC *(kind, wild)*.

- **Model** Use the whiteboard DVD or the CD word cards. Introduce the words and define in context any that may be unfamiliar to students. Model how to sort the words according to the long *i* spelling patterns CVCe, VCC-*igh*, CV open syllable-*y*, and iCC. Put the oddball word *(guy)* in a separate pile. Help students sort and explain their sorts.

Practice the Sort
Independent/Partner

- Have students use the Student Book or whiteboard DVD to read the words and use the grid to sort according to long *i* spelling patterns.

- Have students check and explain their sorts.

Apply
Independent/Partner/Small Groups

- Read aloud the directions on Student Book p. 88. Have students read each word and write it in the appropriate column according to spelling pattern.

- **Game** Allow time for students to play Spelling Match, which is on the CD.

- **Little Book** Read *All About Bats* with students. Have them identify words with long *i* CVCe and long *i* spelled *igh* or *y*.

Extend the Sort

Alternative Sort: Person, Place, or Thing

Instruct students to re-sort the cards into two piles: one pile for words that name a person, place, or thing (nouns) and one pile for the other words.

ELL English Language Learners

Review the word cards by having students repeat each word after you. To reinforce vocabulary, give each student a word card to illustrate on a separate sheet of paper. Show the illustrations one at a time and ask students to guess the words.

Vocabulary Building Vocabulary

Discuss the word *mind*. Explain that *mind* can be both a noun (a naming word) and a verb (an action word). The noun *mind* refers to the part of a person that thinks, feels, and makes decisions. The verb *to mind* means "to pay attention to" (as in "Mind your manners!") or "to have a concern about" (as in "I don't mind getting wet").

Monitor Progress Spell Check 2

After completing Sort 22, administer Spell Check 2. See p. 135 in this Teacher Resource Guide for instructions.

Sort 23

r-Influenced Vowel Patterns *ar, ir, or, ur*

Objectives

- To identify *r*-influenced vowel spelling patterns
- To read, sort, and write words with *r*-influenced vowel spelling patterns *ar, ir, or,* and *ur*

Materials for Within Word Pattern

Big Book of Rhymes, "Third Base," page 41

Whiteboard Activities DVD-ROM, Sort 23

Teacher Resource CD-ROM, Sort 23 and Find the Spider Game

Student Book, pages 89–92

Words Their Way Library, *A Fox Lives Here*

Words

ar	ir	or	ur
dark	birth	corn	burn
harm	dirt	fork	burst
harp	first	horn	curb
shark	girl	north	curl
sharp	stir	porch	hurt
start	swirl	storm	surf

Bonus Words

arch	firm	fort	blurt
lark	sir	pork	burr
scar	thirst	scorn	lurch
smart	whirl	sworn	spurt

Introduce/Model
Small Groups

- **Read a Rhyme** Read "Third Base" and then review the sounds of short and long vowels *a, i, o,* and *u*. Write *Barb, third, sport,* and *burst,* underlining the *r* in each. Have students listen as you pronounce each word. Point out that they do not hear a short or a long vowel sound. Explain that when a vowel is followed by *r*, the *r* influences the vowel to create a different sound.

- **Model** Use the whiteboard DVD or the CD word cards. Ask students what they notice about all the words. Demonstrate how to sort the words according to their *r*-influenced vowel pattern. Have students read the words in each column and tell how they are alike. Point out that *ir* and *ur* are pronounced the same. Then help students sort and explain their sorts.

Practice the Sort
Independent/Partner

- Have students use the Student Book or whiteboard DVD to read the words and use the grid to sort.

- Have students check and explain their sorts.

Apply
Independent/Partner/Small Groups

- Read aloud the directions on Student Book p. 92. Have students write sort words in the appropriate columns, according to *r*-influenced vowel patterns.

- **Game** Allow time for students to play Find the Spider, which is on the CD.

- **Little Book** Read *A Fox Lives Here* with students. Have them identify words with *ar* or *ur*.

Extend the Sort

Alternative Sort: Sound Sort

Write *part, bird, form,* and *turn,* underlining the *r*-influenced vowel patterns. Ask students which two sets of underlined letters have the same sound. *(ir, ur)* Then have students re-sort their cards according to whether or not the word has that sound.

Bonus Words Activity

Let students work in pairs to make lists of other words with *ar, ir, or,* or *ur.* If students need prompting, make suggestions from the Bonus Words list. Have students include a blank where each vowel belongs (for example, *b_rn*). Then have students exchange papers and fill in the missing vowels. Note that there may be several possible answers, such as *born, barn,* or *burn.*

Vocabulary Building Vocabulary

Explain that *surf* refers to waves breaking on the ocean shore. In the sport of surfing, people ride surfboards on the top of ocean waves. Sometimes people talk about surfing (browsing) television channels or the Internet.

r-Influenced Vowel Patterns *ar, are, air*

Objectives
- To identify *r*-influenced vowel spelling patterns
- To read, sort, and write words with *r*-influenced vowel patterns *ar, are,* and *air*

Materials for **Within Word Pattern**

📓 Big Book of Rhymes, "Scarecrow in the Garden," page 43

🖥 Whiteboard Activities DVD-ROM, Sort 24

💿 Teacher Resource CD-ROM, Sort 24 and Find the Scarecrow Game

📖 Student Book, pages 93–96

📕 Words Their Way Library, *The Not-So Scary Scarecrow*

Words

ar	are	air	Oddball
dark	bare	chair	bear
harm	fare	fair	heart
shark	hare	lair	pear
sharp	square	pair	wear
start	stare	stair	where

Introduce/Model
Small Groups

- **Read a Rhyme** Read "Scarecrow in the Garden." Reread the poem, omitting the last word from each line. Have students supply each end word, and write the poem's rhyming words *(air, hair, stare, scare)* Underline *air* in *air* and *hair* and *are* in *stare* and *scare*.

- **Model** Use the whiteboard DVD or the CD word cards. Demonstrate for students how to sort the words by *ar, are,* and *air* spelling patterns. Point out that five words are oddballs, because they have the same sounds as *ar, are,* and *air* but are spelled differently. Help students sort and explain their sorts.

Practice the Sort
Independent/Partner

- Have students use the Student Book or whiteboard DVD to read the words and use the grid to sort according to the *r*-influenced vowel pattern.

- Have students check and explain their sorts.

Apply
Independent/Partner/Small Groups

- Read aloud the directions on Student Book p. 96. Have students write a homophone for each word in the grid and draw a picture to match it.

- **Game** Allow time for students to play Find the Scarecrow, which is on the CD.

- **Little Book** Read *The Not-So Scary Scarecrow* with students. Have them identify words with *ar, are,* or *air*.

Extend the Sort

Alternative Sort: Same Sound, Different Meaning

Have students sort the words into homophone pairs—words that sound the same but have different spellings and different meanings *(bear, bare; fare, fair; stare, stair; pair, pear; where, wear)* and words that are not homophones.

ELL English Language Learners

Show each pair of homophones, and have students say them after you. Make sure students understand that the words sound the same. Point out that the words are spelled differently and have different meanings. Use each word in a sentence. As you read, pick up the word card that goes with the sentence.

Vocabulary Building Vocabulary

Explain that a fare is the fee you pay for transportation. Brainstorm with students a list of modes of transportation that usually require passengers to pay a fare.

Teacher Tip

Check students' pronunciations and their ability to isolate and discriminate among the *r*-influenced vowel sounds. Regional dialects often show up in *r*-influenced vowels in words. Provide guidance and reinforcement when necessary.

r-Influenced Vowel Patterns *er, ear, eer*

Objectives

- To identify *r*-influenced vowel spelling patterns
- To read, sort, and write words with *r*-influenced vowel patterns *er, ear,* and *eer*

Materials for Within Word Pattern

- Big Book of Rhymes, "Arctic Fox," page 45
- Whiteboard Activities DVD-ROM, Sort 25
- Teacher Resource CD-ROM, Sort 25 and Word Create Game
- Student Book, pages 97–100
- Words Their Way Library, *A Fox Lives Here*

Words

er	ear	eer	ear = ur
clerk	clear	cheer	earth
fern	dear	peer	heard
germ	fear	steer	learn
herd	near		
perch	year		

Bonus Words

herb	hear	deer	yearn
perk	sear	leer	
stern	shear	sneer	

Introduce/Model   *Small Groups*

- **Read a Rhyme** Read "Arctic Fox." Write *clear, near,* and *eerie*. Read the words aloud, emphasizing the *r*-influenced vowel sound in each. Then circle the *r*-influenced vowel patterns in the words *(ear* in *clear* and *near* and *eer* in *eerie)*. Repeat with *perch* and *summer*.

- **Model** Use the whiteboard DVD or the CD word cards. Model how to sort the words by *er, eer,* and *ear* spelling patterns. Read down each list. Explain that three *ear* words—*earth, heard,* and *learn*—go in a separate column, because they sound like words with the *r*-influenced *er* vowel pattern but are spelled with *ear*. Help students sort and explain their sorts.

Practice the Sort   *Independent/Partner*

- Have students use the Student Book or whiteboard DVD to read the words and use the grid to sort according to the *r*-influenced vowel pattern.

- Have students check and explain their sorts.

Apply   *Independent/Partner/Small Groups*

- Read aloud the directions on Student Book p. 100. Have students write words from the sort in columns according to their vowel sound and spelling pattern.

- **Game** Allow time for students to play Word Create, which is on the CD.

- **Little Book** Read *A Fox Lives Here* with students. Have them identify words with *er* or *ear*.

Extend the Sort

Alternative Sort: Noun or Verb

Students can re-sort the words into nouns and verbs. Remind them that nouns are words that name a person, place, or thing, and verbs are action words. Point out that some of the words, such as *perch, steer,* and *herd,* can be both a noun and a verb.

ELL English Language Learners

Make sure students understand the difference between the sound of *er* as in *clerk* and the sound of *ear* and *eer* as in *dear* and *deer*. Help them with pronunciation by pointing out the differences in mouth position. Suggest students use a handheld mirror to help them with their enunciation.

Bonus Words Activity

Have students make a flower for each spelling pattern of the sort and write one vowel pattern in the center of each flower. They can then write a Bonus Word that corresponds to that flower's spelling pattern on the petals.

Teacher Tip

Have students create ten fill-in-the-blank sentences. Each sentence's missing word should be a word from the sort. Students can exchange sentences with a partner and complete the sentences with the missing words.

r-Influenced Vowel Patterns *ir, ire, ier*

Objectives

- To identify *r*-influenced vowel spelling patterns
- To read, sort, and write words with *r*-influenced vowel patterns *ir, ire,* and *ier*

Materials for Within Word Pattern

- Big Book of Rhymes, "Third Base," page 41
- Whiteboard Activities DVD-ROM, Sort 26
- Teacher Resource CD-ROM, Sort 26 and Around the Bases Game
- Student Book, pages 101–104
- Words Their Way Library, *Miss Muffet and the Spider*

Words

ir	ire	ier	Oddball
birth	hire	crier	fur
fir	tire	flier	their
girl	wire	frier	
shirt		pliers	
third			

Bonus Words

firm	mire
first	sire
sir	spire
stir	

Introduce/Model
Small Groups

- **Read a Rhyme** Read "Third Base." Write rhyming words *umpire, wire* and *higher, flier,* underlining the *r*-influenced vowel pattern in each. Then reread the poem, omitting the rhyming words, and have students supply them. Guide students to find another word in the poem that contains an *ir*. Write *third* and underline *ir*.

- **Model** Use the whiteboard DVD or the CD word cards. Model how to sort words by *ir, ire,* and *ier* spelling patterns. Read the word lists. Explain that *their* and *fur* belong in the oddball category because they do not follow the pronunciation/spelling patterns in the sort. Help students sort and explain their sorts.

Practice the Sort
Independent/Partner

- Have students use the Student Book or whiteboard DVD to read the words and use the grid to sort according to the *r*-influenced vowel pattern.

- Have students check and explain their sorts.

Apply
Independent/Partner/Small Groups

- Read aloud the directions on Student Book p. 104. Have students write words from the sort in columns according to the vowel sound and spelling pattern.

- **Game** Allow time for students to play Around the Bases, which is on the CD.

- **Little Book** Read *Miss Muffet and the Spider* with students. Have them identify words with *ir* or *ire*.

Extend the Sort

Alternative Sort: Syllables

Review the meaning of *syllables* with students. Then students can re-sort the words by number of syllables. Read a word on a card and clap the syllables as you do so. Continue sorting by one-syllable words and two-syllable words.

ELL English Language Learners

Be sure students understand the difference between the sound of *ir* in *birth* and the sound of *ire* and *ier* in *hire* and *crier*. To help them with the oral discrimination and pronunciation of the different sounds, point out differences in mouth position.

Bonus Words Activity

Ask students to name other words with *r*-influenced vowel patterns *ir, ire,* and *ier,* making suggestions from the Bonus Words if needed. Have students write each word on two cards. Then pairs can play Concentration with the word cards.

Teacher Tip

Write words with *ir, ire,* and *ier* on index cards, with a blank line in place of the *r*-influenced vowel pattern. Encourage students to analyze each word and fill in the correct *r*-influenced vowel pattern.

r-Influenced Vowel Patterns *or, ore, oar*

Objectives
- To identify *r*-influenced vowel spelling patterns
- To read, sort, and write words with *r*-influenced vowel patterns *or, ore,* and *oar*

Materials for Within Word Pattern

Big Book of Rhymes, "The Snoring Horse," page 47

Whiteboard Activities DVD-ROM, Sort 27

Teacher Resource CD-ROM, Sort 27 and Guess the Picture Game

Student Book, pages 105–108

Words Their Way Library, *Friends Forever*

Words

or	*ore*	*oar*	*w + or*	Oddball
corn	more	boar	work	floor
for	sore	hoarse	world	four
fork	store	oar	worm	poor
horse	tore	roar	worse	
storm	wore	soar		

Bonus Words

chord	core	coarse
ford	lore	hoard
sworn	swore	worry

Introduce/Model
Small Groups

- **Read a Rhyme** Read "The Snoring Horse." Write the rhyming words *roar, store, door, more,* and *anymore.* Reread the poem, omitting each rhyming word, and have students supply them. Circle *oar* in *roar* and *ore* in *anymore, store,* and *more.* Point out that *door* has the same vowel sound but a different spelling pattern.

- **Model** Use the whiteboard DVD or the CD word cards. Model how to sort the words into *or, ore, oar,* and *w + or* spelling patterns. Explain that *floor, four,* and *poor* do not fit these patterns and therefore belong in the oddball category. Help students sort and explain their sorts.

Practice the Sort
Independent/Partner

- Have students use the Student Book or whiteboard DVD to read the words and use the grid to sort.

- Have students check and explain their sorts.

Apply
Independent/Partner/Small Groups

- Read aloud the directions on Student Book p. 108. Have students write words from the sort in columns according to the vowel sound and spelling pattern.

- **Game** Allow time for students to play Guess the Picture, which is on the CD.

- **Little Book** Read *Friends Forever* with students. Have them identify words with *or, ore,* or *oar.*

Extend the Sort

Alternative Sort: Three-Way Sort

First set aside the card *for.* Then students can re-sort by naming words (nouns), action words (verbs), and describing words (adjectives). Point out that some words, such as *work,* can be both a noun and a verb. Students should choose a meaning and then sort the card accordingly.

ELL English Language Learners

Model strategies to help students read and spell words with *r*-influenced vowel patterns. By "thinking aloud," you can give students the opportunity to hear how a proficient English speaker reaches a conclusion regarding pronunciation and spelling.

Bonus Words Activity

Ask students to name other words with *r*-influenced vowel patterns *or, ore, oar,* and *w + or,* making suggestions from the Bonus Words list if needed. Have them draw a picture of a store with shelves; label the shelves *or, ore, oar,* and *w + or;* and write the words on the appropriate shelves.

Vocabulary Building Vocabulary

Point out homophones *horse* and *hoarse.* Explain that *hoarse* means "having a rough voice." Describe scenarios that might make someone hoarse, such as yelling at a ball game.

Objectives

- To identify *r*-influenced vowel spelling patterns
- To read, sort, and write words with *r*-influenced vowel patterns *ur, ure,* and *ur-e*

Materials for Within Word Pattern

Big Book of Rhymes, "Watching for Sea Turtles," page 49

Whiteboard Activities DVD-ROM, Sort 28

Teacher Resource CD-ROM, Sort 28 and Sure Pairs Game

Student Book, pages 109–112

Words Their Way Library, *Sea Turtle Night*

Words

ur		ure	ur-e
blur	curb	cure	curse
burn	curl	lure	nurse
burst	hurl	pure	purse
church	hurt		
churn	surf		

Bonus Words

blurt	insure	purge
burr		splurge
lurch		surge
purple		urge

Introduce/Model
Small Groups

- **Read a Rhyme** Read "Watching for Sea Turtles," emphasizing *turtles, curved, hurry,* and *surely.* Ask students to locate those words in the poem. Write the words, and circle *ur* in *turtles, curved,* and *hurry* and *ure* in *surely.* Read the poem again, omitting those words, and have students supply the missing words.

- **Model** Use the whiteboard DVD or the CD word cards. Demonstrate how to sort the words into *ur, ure,* and *ur-e* spelling patterns. Read down each list. Ask students how the words in each group are alike. Then help students sort and explain their sorts.

Practice the Sort
Independent/Partner

- Have students use the Student Book or whiteboard DVD to read the words and use the grid to sort according to the *r*-influenced vowel pattern.

- Have students check and explain their sorts.

Apply
Independent/Partner/Small Groups

- Read aloud the directions on Student Book p. 112. Have students write words from the sort in columns according to their vowel sound and spelling pattern.

- **Game** Allow time for students to play Sure Pairs, which is on the CD.

- **Little Book** Read *Sea Turtle Night* with students. Have them identify words with *ur* or *ure.*

Extend the Sort

Alternative Sort: Guess My Category

Re-sort the words into groups that name things and words that do not name things. Begin by sorting two or three cards into categories. When you pick the next word card, have students tell where it will go. Continue until all cards have been sorted and students can guess the categories.

ELL English Language Learners

Give each child one or two cards, and have students create sentences using the words on their cards. Watch and listen to pronunciations of the *ur, ure,* and *ur-e* words to ensure students are forming the sounds properly.

Bonus Words Activity

Ask students to name other words with *r*-influenced vowel patterns *ur, ure,* and *ur-e.* Make suggestions from the Bonus Words list if needed. Then have students draw the outline of a purse and write the Bonus Words on it. Suggest that students circle each *r*-influenced vowel pattern.

Teacher Tip

During a repeated sort, do not correct students when they place a word in the wrong column. Wait until they are done and have them read the words in each column. If they don't find the misplaced word, tell them what column it is in and have them find it.

Review of *ar*, Schwa Plus *r*, and *or*

Objectives

- To identify *r*-influenced vowel spelling patterns
- To read, sort, and write words with the *r*-influenced vowel patterns *ar*, schwa + *r*, and *or*

Materials for Within Word Pattern

Big Book of Rhymes, "Fern's Monsters," page 51

Whiteboard Activities DVD-ROM, Sort 29

Teacher Resource CD-ROM, Sort 29 and "R" Spin Game

Student Book, pages 113–116

Words Their Way Library, *The Monster Under the Bed*

Words		
ar	**ər**	**or**
bar	earn	bore
card	nerve	chore
hard	pearl	horse
jar	search	score
march	spur	snore
sharp	worst	snort
yard	worth	torn

Introduce/Model
Small Groups

- **Read a Rhyme** Read "Fern's Monsters," emphasizing the words with *r*-influenced vowel sounds. *(monsters, orchard, park, Fern, dark, under, her, large, store, forgets, more)* Write the words, and ask students how they are alike. Have students locate these words in the poem. Help them understand that they all have *r*-influenced vowel sounds.

- **Model** Use the whiteboard DVD or the CD word cards. Model how to sort the words by sound pattern: *ar*, schwa + *r*, and *or*. Ask students to tell how the words in each group are alike. Then help students sort and explain their sorts.

Practice the Sort
Independent/Partner

- Have students use the Student Book or whiteboard DVD to read the words and use the grid to sort according to *r*-influenced vowel patterns.

- Have students check and explain their sorts.

Apply
Independent/Partner/Small Groups

- Read aloud the directions on Student Book p. 116. Have students read each word and write it in the appropriate column according to spelling pattern.

- **Game** Allow time for students to play "R" Spin, which is on the CD.

- **Little Book** Read *The Monster Under the Bed* with students. Have them identify words with *ar*, *or*, or schwa + *r*.

Extend the Sort

Alternative Sort: Act It Out

Students can re-sort the cards into two groups: words that can tell an action and words that cannot. When the sort is complete, have students take turns acting out each action word.

ELL English Language Learners

You may need to explain that *spur* can be used as a noun (meaning "a sharp wheel attached to a boot heel that a rider uses to urge on a horse") or a verb (meaning "to move to action").

Teacher Tip

Encourage students to develop their own criteria for completing the sort. This exercise should be used to encourage students to find new and unexpected meanings and rules underlying their organization of the words.

Monitor Progress **Spell Check 3**

After completing Sort 29, administer Spell Check 3. See p. 135 in this Teacher Resource Guide for instructions.

Diphthongs *oi*, *oy*

Objectives
- To identify spelling patterns of diphthongs *oi* and *oy*
- To read, sort, and write words with diphthongs *oi* and *oy*

Materials for Within Word Pattern

Big Book of Rhymes, "Digging for Treasure," page 53

Whiteboard Activities DVD-ROM, Sort 30

Teacher Resource CD-ROM, Sort 30 and Treasure Hunt Game

Student Book, pages 117–120

Words Their Way Library, *What Joy Found*

Words

oi		oy
boil	joint	joy
broil	moist	soy
coil	oil	toy
coin	soil	
join	spoil	

Bonus Words

choice	annoy
foil	coy
noise	enjoy
voice	ploy

Introduce/Model   *Small Groups*

- **Read a Rhyme** Read "Digging for Treasure," emphasizing words that contain diphthongs *oi* or *oy* (*coins, soil, enjoy*) and have students locate these words in the poem. Write them in a single column and ask students why one of the words belongs in a second column. (The word *enjoy* has a different spelling for the sound.)

- **Model** Use the whiteboard DVD or the CD word cards. Demonstrate how to sort the words by diphthongs *oi* and *oy*. Read each list with students, emphasizing the sound of the diphthongs. Then help students sort and explain their sorts.

Practice the Sort   *Independent/Partner*

- Have students use the Student Book or whiteboard DVD to read the words and use the grid to sort according to the diphthongs *oi* and *oy*.

- Have students check and explain their sorts.

Apply   *Independent/Partner/Small Groups*

- Read aloud the directions on Student Book p. 120. Have students make words by using the provided letters before and after diphthongs *oi* and *oy*.

- **Game** Allow time for students to play Treasure Hunt, which is on the CD.

- **Little Book** Read *What Joy Found* with students. Have them identify words with *oi* or *oy*.

Extend the Sort

Alternative Sort: Student-Centered Sorts

Allow students to work in pairs to devise their own categories for re-sorting the words. When they have re-sorted, give them time to share their sort categories with other students.

ELL English Language Learners

Review the word cards with students by having them repeat each word after you. Make sure students understand that the vowel sounds in words with *oi* or *oy* are pronounced identically.

Vocabulary Building Vocabulary

Ask students to name other words with *oi* or *oy*. If students need prompting, make suggestions from the Bonus Words list. Have students write each word on two cards. Then have pairs of students play Concentration with the Bonus Words.

Bonus Words Activity

Explain that *moist* means "slightly wet." Wet a paper towel and wring it out well, or supply moist towelettes, and let students feel them to get an idea of how *moist* is different from *wet*. Ask students to think of things that could be moist, such as sweaty hands, sponges, bathing suits, and laundry.

Vowel Digraph *oo*

Objectives

- To identify spelling patterns of vowel digraph *oo*
- To read, sort, and write words with vowel digraph *oo*

Materials for Within Word Pattern

📖 Big Book of Rhymes, "The Puppet Show," page 55

🖥 Whiteboard Activities DVD-ROM, Sort 31

💿 Teacher Resource CD-ROM, Sort 31 and Follow the Dragon Game

📓 Student Book, pages 121–124

📔 Words Their Way Library, *The House That Stood on Booker Hill*

Words

ŏŏ		ōō = ū		Oddball
brook	nook	fool	spool	could
crook	soot	groom	spoon	should
foot	stood	hoop	stool	would
hood	wood	noon	tool	
hook	wool	root	troop	

Introduce/Model
Small Groups

- **Read a Rhyme** Read "The Puppet Show," and emphasize words with the vowel digraph *oo*. *(wood, book, took; soon, noon)* Ask students to locate these words, and help them write the words in two columns, according to vowel sound. Help students hear the different pronunciations of the vowel digraph *oo*.

- **Model** Use the whiteboard DVD or the CD word cards. Define in context any that may be unfamiliar to students. Demonstrate how to sort the words according to the sound of the digraph *oo*. Point out that *would, could,* and *should* do not contain the digraph *oo*, so they belong in the oddball category. Help students sort and explain their sorts.

Practice the Sort
Independent/Partner

- Have students use the Student Book or whiteboard DVD to read the words and use the grid to sort.

- Have students check and explain their sorts.

Apply
Independent/Partner/Small Groups

- Read aloud the directions on Student Book p. 124. Have students make words by using the provided letters before and after *oo* and write them in the correct column, according to vowel sound.

- **Game** Allow time for students to play Follow the Dragon, which is on the CD.

- **Little Book** Read *The House That Stood on Booker Hill* with students. Have them identify words with the vowels *oo*.

Extend the Sort

Alternative Sort: Brainstorming

Ask students to think of other words that contain *oo*. Write their responses on index cards. When students have completed brainstorming, ask them to identify and sort all the words they named according to the vowel sound of *oo*.

ELL English Language Learners

Explain that a *nook* is "a hidden place," and that *groom* can have several meanings, including "a person who takes care of horses" and "the man who marries a bride." Have students repeat each word to be sure they are differentiating between the two vowel sounds of *oo*.

Vocabulary Building Vocabulary

Explain that *crook* has several meanings, and all are related to the idea of "not straight." A person who steals things might be called a *crook*. A *crook* is also the name of the curved staff once carried by shepherds, or it can name a curved or bent part of something, as in "the crook of one's arm."

Teacher Tip

Provide extra practice with identifying *ŏŏ* and *ōō* sounds by showing four word cards, three of which have the same vowel sound and one that has a different vowel sound. Challenge students to identify the word card that doesn't belong, and repeat with other cards.

Diphthongs *ou, ow*

Objectives
- To identify spelling patterns of diphthongs *ou* and *ow*
- To read, sort, and write words with diphthongs *ou* and *ow*

Materials for **Within Word Pattern**

Big Book of Rhymes, "New Jeans Now," page 57

Whiteboard Activities DVD-ROM, Sort 32

Teacher Resource CD-ROM, Sort 32 and One Card! Game

Student Book, pages 125–128

Words Their Way Library, *Squirrels*

Words

ou		ow		Oddball
cloud	mouth	clown	growl	grown
couch	pound	crown	howl	rough
count	scout	drown	owl	tough
found	shout	frown	plow	
ground	south	gown	town	

Bonus Words

drought	brow
foul	fowl
loud	prowl
stout	scowl

Introduce/Model
Small Groups

- **Read a Rhyme** Read "New Jeans Now!" Write *brown* as a column header, and have students name other words in the poem that have the same vowel sound. *(how, now, out)* Write these words in the column. Ask students why you should move one of the words into a second column. (The word *out* has a different spelling for the sound.)

- **Model** Use the whiteboard DVD or the CD word cards. Demonstrate how to sort the words into three categories: words with *ou* as in *sound,* words with *ow* as in *brown*, and words with different sounds spelled with *ou* or *ow*. Then help students sort and explain their sorts.

Practice the Sort
Independent/Partner

- Have students use the Student Book or whiteboard DVD to read the words and use the grid to sort according to diphthong *ou* or *ow*.

- Have students check and explain their sorts.

Apply
Independent/Partner/Small Groups

- Read aloud the directions on Student Book p. 128. Have students make words by using the provided letters before and after diphthongs *ou* and *ow*.

- **Game** Allow time for students to play One Card!, which is on the CD.

- **Little Book** Read *Squirrels* with students. Have them identify words with *ou* or *ow/ou/*.

Extend the Sort

Alternative Sort: Noun, Verb, or Both?

Use each word in a sentence. Point out the words that can be both a noun or a verb. *(pound, ground, frown, howl, count, growl, crown, plow, cloud, scout, mouth, clown)* Let students take over the sort and categorize words as nouns, verbs, or both.

ELL English Language Learners

To practice pronouncing troublesome words, have students study them within rhyming sets, such as *pound, ground,* and *found.* Study one set at a time, calling attention to the spelling pattern.

Bonus Words Activity

Encourage pairs of students to brainstorm or look for additional *ou* and *ow* words, making suggestions from the Bonus Words list if needed. Have students write the new words on blank cards to share with the group. Combine all of the cards and re-sort them by *ou* and *ow* patterns.

Teacher Tip

Encourage partners to take turns flashing the cards for a specified number of seconds. Have each reader count the cards that were read correctly and record the final number. See if students can read the cards faster another day.

Within Word Pattern 167

Sort 33

Ambiguous Vowels *aw, au*

Objectives

- To identify ambiguous vowel spelling patterns *aw* and *au*
- To read, sort, and write words with *aw* and *au*

Materials for **Within Word Pattern**

Big Book of Rhymes, "The Lobster Boat," page 59

Whiteboard Activities DVD-ROM, Sort 33

Teacher Resource CD-ROM, Sort 33 and Word Maker Game

Student Book, pages 129–133

Words Their Way Library, *Lobster Fishing at Dawn*

Words

aw	au	Oddball
claw	cause	laugh
crawl	fault	
dawn	haul	
draw	haunt	
hawk	launch	
law	pause	
lawn	sauce	
paw	taught	
straw	vault	
yawn		

Bonus Words

bawl	haunch
shawl	staunch
thaw	caught

Introduce/Model
Small Groups

- **Read a Rhyme** Read "The Lobster Boat" and write *claws* as a column header. Have students name other words in the poem with the same vowel sound. *(dawn, haul, awesome)* Write them in the column. Ask students to identify the two spelling patterns for the vowel sound.

- **Model** Use the whiteboard DVD or the CD word cards. Emphasize the vowel sound in each word and explain that it is not short, long, or a diphthong. Have students assist as you sort into three categories: words with the vowel sound spelled *au*, words with the vowel sound spelled *aw,* and the oddball *laugh*. Help students sort and explain their sorts.

Practice the Sort
Independent/Partner

- Have students use the Student Book or whiteboard DVD to read the words and use the grid to sort.

- Have students check and explain their sorts.

Apply
Independent/Partner/Small Groups

- Read aloud the directions on Student Book p. 132. Have students make words by using the provided letters before and after *aw* and *au*.

- **Game** Allow time for students to play Word Maker, which is on the CD.

- **Little Book** Read *Lobster Fishing at Dawn* with students. Have them identify words with *aw* or *au*.

Extend the Sort

Alternative Sort: Beat the Clock

Have students try a speed sort. They can time themselves with a stopwatch as they sort the words into categories. After obtaining a baseline speed, have students repeat the sort several times and attempt to beat their own time.

ELL English Language Learners

Read the words and have students repeat them after you. Then distribute the cards. Let students work in pairs to read the words on their cards and use them in sentences. Encourage students to help each other with pronunciation, vocabulary, and sentence structure.

Bonus Words Activity

Write the Bonus Words and help students understand their meanings. Show students how to create word search puzzles using sort words and Bonus Words. On graph paper, make a block of 20 squares by 20 squares. Write the words above the block. Write the words in the block, one letter per square (horizontal, vertical, or diagonal) and then fill in the remaining squares in the block with random letters.

Teacher Tip

You may wish to have students use a free Internet-based puzzle generator to make word search puzzles for the Bonus Words activity.

Objectives

- To identify ambiguous vowel spelling patterns
- To read, sort, and write words with ambiguous vowel patterns *wa, al,* and *ou*

Materials for Within Word Pattern

Big Book of Rhymes, "Arctic Fox," page 45

Whiteboard Activities DVD-ROM, Sort 34

Teacher Resource CD-ROM, Sort 34 and Vowel Treasures Game

Student Book, pages 133–136

Words Their Way Library, *Lobster Fishing at Dawn*

Words

wa	al	ou
swap	almost	bought
swat	also	brought
walk	chalk	cough
wand	salt	fought
wash	tall	ought
wasp		

Bonus Words

wa	al	ou
wad	bald	sought
waddle	halt	trough
watt	stalk	
	stall	

Introduce/Model   *Small Groups*

- **Read a Rhyme** Read "Arctic Fox," emphasizing words with the target spelling patterns and vowel sound. *(watch, small, call, fall, ought)* Ask students to locate these words and write them in three columns, according to spelling pattern. Read the words to help students hear that the vowel sound is the same.

- **Model** Use the whiteboard DVD or the CD word cards. Emphasize the vowel sound in the words and explain that the sound is neither short nor long. Demonstrate how to sort the words into three categories: words with the *wa* pattern, words with the *al* pattern, and words with the *ou* pattern. Then help students sort and explain their sorts.

Practice the Sort   *Independent/Partner*

- Have students use the Student Book or whiteboard DVD to read the words and use the grid to sort.

- Have students check and explain their sorts.

Apply   *Independent/Partner/Small Groups*

- Read aloud the directions on Student Book p. 136. Have students read each word and write it in the appropriate column according to spelling pattern.

- **Game** Allow time for students to play Vowel Treasures, which is on the CD.

- **Little Book** Read *Lobster Fishing at Dawn* with students. Have them identify words beginning with *wa*.

Extend the Sort

Alternative Sort: Action Words

When students are comfortable with this sort, have them re-sort the word cards according to whether the word describes an action or not.

ELL English Language Learners

Review the word cards with students by having them repeat each word after you. To reinforce vocabulary, give each student a word card to illustrate on a separate sheet of paper. Show the illustrations, one at a time, and ask students to guess the words.

Bonus Words Activity

Have students brainstorm rhyming words for the words in the sort. If students need prompting, make suggestions from the Bonus Words list. When students have several sets of rhyming words, have them write a short poem, using as many words from the sort and from their brainstorming as they can.

Monitor Progress **Spell Check 4**

After completing Sort 34, administer Spell Check 4. See p. 135 in this Teacher Resource Guide for instructions.

Sort 35

Final /k/ Sound Spelled -ck, -ke, -k

Objectives

- To identify spelling patterns of final /k/ sound
- To read, sort, and write words with final /k/ sound spelled -ck, -ke, and -k

Materials for Within Word Pattern

Big Book of Rhymes, "Jake Bakes," page 61

Whiteboard Activities DVD-ROM, Sort 35

Teacher Resource CD-ROM, Sort 35 and Final /k/ Spin Game

Student Book, pages 137–140

Words Their Way Library, *Pick Up Nick!*

Words

-ck short	-ke long	-k other
duck	bike	book
lick	duke	cook
lock	like	look
pack	shake	shook
sick	smoke	
sock	spoke	
truck	strike	

Bonus Words

brick	brake	brook
pluck	flake	crook
quack	quake	hook
stack	spike	nook

Introduce/Model *Small Groups*

- **Read a Rhyme** Read "Jake Bakes" and have students listen for words that end with final /k/. (*chick, Jake, snack, cake, book, cook*) List the words and explain that the final /k/ sound can have different spellings. Ask students to identify and count the different spellings in the word list.

- **Model** Use the whiteboard DVD or the CD word cards. Demonstrate how to sort the word cards into three categories according to the spelling of the final /k/ sound. Help students sort and explain their sorts.

Practice the Sort *Independent/Partner*

- Have students use the Student Book or whiteboard DVD to read the words and use the grid to sort according to the spelling of the final /k/ sound.

- Have students check and explain their sorts.

Apply *Independent/Partner/Small Groups*

- Read aloud the directions on Student Book p. 140. Have students write words from the sort on the lines according to the spelling of their final /k/ sound.

- **Game** Allow time for students to play Final /k/ Spin, which is on the CD.

- **Little Book** Read *Pick Up Nick!* with students. Have them identify words with final /k/ spelled *ck, ke,* or *k.*

Extend the Sort

Alternative Sort: Consonant Count

Ask students to re-sort according to the number of consonants in each word. Students will make piles of words with two, three, and four consonants.

ELL English Language Learners

Review the word cards with students, having them repeat each word after you. Many of the words in this week's sort can be used either as nouns or as verbs. Have students use some of these words (*lock, pack, duck, bike, cook, shake, spoke*) in sentences.

Bonus Words Activity

Label three containers *-ck, -ke,* and *-k.* Challenge the class to fill each container with words ending in these /k/ sound spellings. Each student should think of and contribute one or more words per spelling, writing each word on an index card. Make suggestions from the Bonus Words if needed.

Teacher Tip

Offer advanced students additional challenges. After sorting the words, invite them to alphabetize the words in each group.

170 Within Word Pattern

Silent Beginning Consonants *kn-, wr-, gn-*

Objectives
- To identify spelling patterns of silent beginning consonants
- To read, sort, and write words with the silent beginning consonant patterns *kn-, wr-,* and *gn-*

Materials for Within Word Pattern

Big Book of Rhymes, "My Puppy Gus," page 63

Whiteboard Activities DVD-ROM, Sort 36

Teacher Resource CD-ROM, Sort 36 and Use Those Clues Game

Student Book, pages 141–144

Words Their Way Library, *A Lot Happened Today*

Words

kn-	wr-	gn-	Oddball
knack	wrap	gnaw	night
knight	wreath		not
knit	wreck		rap
knob	wren		ring
knoll	wring		
knot	wrist		
known	write		

Bonus Words

knead	wreak	gnarl
knee	wrinkle	gnash
knelt		gnome
knew		gnu
knock		

Introduce/Model
Small Groups

- **Read a Rhyme** Read "My Puppy Gus." Point out the word *wriggle*, and ask students what they notice about this word's beginning sound and spelling. Repeat with *gnats, gnaws,* and *know*. Write these words, and underline their beginning consonants. Help students understand that the first consonant in each of these letter patterns is silent.

- **Model** Use the whiteboard DVD or the CD word cards. Model sorting by silent beginning consonants. Point out that *rap, ring, night,* and *not* are oddballs because their beginning consonants aren't silent. Help students sort and explain their sorts.

Practice the Sort
Independent/Partner

- Have students use the Student Book or whiteboard DVD to read the words and use the grid to sort according to silent beginning consonants.

- Have students check and explain their sorts.

Apply
Independent/Partner/Small Groups

- Read aloud the directions on Student Book p. 144. Have students write words from the sort on the lines according to silent beginning consonants.

- **Game** Allow time for students to play Use Those Clues, which is on the CD.

- **Little Book** Read *A Lot Happened Today* with students. Have them identify words beginning with *wr*.

Extend the Sort

Alternative Sort: Homophone Challenge

Call attention to the homophones *wrap* and *rap*. Have students find the other homophones. (*ring, wring; night, knight; not, knot*) Then challenge students to make a homophone card for another word in the sort. (*write, right*)

ELL English Language Learners

Review homophones students have learned in this sort. (*wrap, rap; wring, ring; knight, night; knot, not*) Help students make sentences, such as *The knight rides into the night,* to familiarize them with the words' meanings, usage, and spelling.

Bonus Words Activity

Ask students to name other words that begin with *kn-, wr-,* or *gn-*. Suggest Bonus Words, if needed. Have students make word cards for the new words and sort them by silent beginning consonant.

Teacher Tip

During repeated sorts, do not immediately correct students' mispronunciations. Instead, have them reread columns to correct their own mistakes. If further help is needed, draw their attention to the same initial spelling in a word they have pronounced correctly.

Consonant Digraphs Plus *r*-Blends and *squ-*

Objectives

- To identify spelling patterns of consonant blends
- To read, sort, and write words with the consonant blends *thr-*, *shr-*, and *squ-*

Materials for Within Word Pattern

📖 Big Book of Rhymes, "Running Squirrels," page 65

🖥 Whiteboard Activities DVD-ROM, Sort 37

💿 Teacher Resource CD-ROM, Sort 37 and Clues and Categories Game

📕 Student Book, pages 145–148

📘 Words Their Way Library, *Squirrels*

Words

thr-	shr-	squ-
threat	shrewd	squash
threw	shriek	squawk
thrifty	shrimp	squeak
thrill	shrink	squeeze
throne	shrub	squint
through	shrug	squirm
throw	shrunk	squish

Bonus Words

thrash	shred	squall
thread	shrivel	squirt

Introduce/Model   *Small Groups*

- **Read a Rhyme** Read "Running Squirrels," emphasizing *shrubs* and *through*. Call attention to *sh* and *th* followed by *r* and how these sounds are pronounced as blended sounds. Remind students that *u* always follows *q*, even though it is not heard in the beginning blend of *squirrels*.

- **Model** Use the whiteboard DVD or the CD word cards. Demonstrate how to sort the words by beginning blend. Help students sort and explain their sorts.

Practice the Sort   *Independent/Partner*

- Have students use the Student Book or whiteboard DVD to read the words and use the grid to sort according to beginning blend.

- Have students check and explain their sorts.

Apply   *Independent/Partner/Small Groups*

- Read aloud the directions on Student Book p. 148. Have students write words from the sort in columns according to beginning consonant blend.

- **Game** Allow time for students to play Clues and Categories, which is on the CD.

- **Little Book** Read *Squirrels* with students. Have them identify words beginning with *squ-*.

Extend the Sort

Alternative Sort: Nouns and Actions

First remove *through*, and then re-sort into categories of things, actions happening now, and actions that have already happened. If students notice that words that can be a thing or an action, encourage them to make duplicate cards and place the words in both categories.

ELL English Language Learners

Clarify differences in meaning among *squirm/ shrug/squint* and *shriek/squeak/squawk* through pantomime and discussion.

Bonus Words Activity

Help students brainstorm other words that begin with *thr-*, *shr-*, or *squ-*. Suggest Bonus Words, if needed. Have students make word cards for these new words. Invite students to play charades with the new words and those from the sort.

Vocabulary Building Vocabulary

Write *thrifty* on the board, cover *y*, and ask students what *thrift* means. Define it if necessary, uncover *y*, and explain that *y* makes the noun *thrift* into a describing word. Encourage students to complete this sentence: *We can be thrifty by ___.*

Triple *r*-Blends *scr-*, *str-*, *spr-*

Objectives
- To identify spelling patterns of triple *r*-blends
- To read, sort, and write words with triple *r*-blends *scr-*, *str-*, and *spr-*

Materials for Within Word Pattern

📖 Big Book of Rhymes, "The Journey," page 67

🖥 Whiteboard Activities DVD-ROM, Sort 38

💿 Teacher Resource CD-ROM, Sort 38 and Island Hop Game

📓 Student Book, pages 149–152

📙 Words Their Way Library, *Winter's Song*

Words

scr-	str-	spr-
scram	straight	spray
scrap	strange	spread
scrape	stress	sprout
scratch	stretch	spruce
scream	strict	
scribe	string	
script	stripe	

Bonus Words

scr-	str-	spr-
scramble	stream	sprawl
screech	strewn	sprinkle
screw	stride	sprung
scroll	stroll	spry

Introduce/Model   *Small Groups*

- **Read a Rhyme** Read "The Journey" and emphasize *stroke, strange, spray,* and *scraps.* Then write the words, underline the first three letters in each, and call attention to how these letters are pronounced as blended sounds. Ask students to tell other words they know that begin with these blends.

- **Model** Use the whiteboard DVD or the CD word cards. Introduce the words and define in context any that may be unfamiliar to students, such as *scribe, strict,* and *spruce.* Demonstrate how to sort the words according to beginning blend. Help students sort and explain their sorts.

Practice the Sort   *Independent/Partner*

- Have students use the Student Book or whiteboard DVD to read the words and use the grid to sort according to beginning blend.

- Have students check and explain their sorts.

Apply   *Independent/Partner/Small Groups*

- Read aloud the directions on Student Book p. 152. Have students write words from the sort in columns according to beginning blend.

- **Game** Allow time for students to play Island Hop, which is on the CD.

- **Little Book** Read *Winter's Song* with students. Have them identify words beginning with triple *r*-blends.

Extend the Sort

Alternative Sort: Vowel Sounds

Have students re-sort the words by vowel sound. Suggest they make three columns: short vowel sounds, long vowel sounds, and other vowel sounds.

ELL English Language Learners

Help students become more aware of how the blends are produced differently in the mouth by practicing sets of words such as *ring/spring/string, rap/scrap/strap,* and *rain/strain/sprain.*

Bonus Words Activity

Help students brainstorm other words that begin with *scr-, str-,* or *spr-.* If needed, suggest Bonus Words. Then have students make word cards for these new words, sort them by beginning blend, and reread the columns aloud.

Teacher Tip

For practice or informal assessment, give students *scr-, str-,* and *spr-* cards. Have students hold up the blend they hear as you say different words.

Hard and Soft *c* and *g*

Objectives
- To identify hard and soft *c* and *g*
- To read, sort, and write words with hard and soft *c* and *g*

Materials for **Within Word Pattern**

- Big Book of Rhymes, "Goose Goes to the City," page 69

- Whiteboard Activities DVD-ROM, Sort 39

- Teacher Resource CD-ROM, Sort 39 and Category Challenge Game

- Student Book, pages 153–156

- Words Their Way Library, *The City Cat and the Country Cat*

Words

hard *c*	soft *c*	hard *g*	soft *g*
calf	cease	game	gem
cart	cell	golf	germ
coat	cent	goose	gist
code		guess	gym
corn		guest	
cub		guide	

Bonus Words

carrot	center	garden	gel
case	ceiling	guard	gentle
comb	circle	gulp	giant

Introduce/Model
Small Groups

- **Read a Rhyme** Read "Goose Goes to the City." Explain that the letters *c* and *g* each have a hard and a soft sound. Have students identify words in the poem that begin with *c* or *g*. Write *country, giraffe, goose, city,* and *cars.* Point out the two words with a hard *c* sound. *(country, cars)* Guide students to identify whether the other words have a soft *c*, hard *g*, or soft *g* sound.

- **Model** Use the whiteboard DVD or the CD word cards. Then demonstrate how to sort the words by beginning hard and soft *c* and *g* sounds. Help students sort and explain their sorts.

Practice the Sort
Independent/Partner

- Have students use the Student Book or whiteboard DVD to read the words and use the grid to sort.

- Have students check and explain their sorts.

Apply
Independent/Partner/Small Groups

- Read aloud the directions on Student Book p. 156. Have students read each word and write it in the appropriate column according to beginning hard and soft *c* and *g* sounds.

- **Game** Allow time for students to play Category Challenge, which is on the CD.

- **Little Book** Read *The City Cat and the Country Cat* with students. Have them identify words with hard and soft *c*.

Extend the Sort

Alternative Sort: First Vowels

Students can re-sort the cards by the first vowel in each word: words with a first vowel of *a, o,* or *u* in one pile and words with *e, i,* or *y* in another. Discuss the new sorts. Help students see that the vowel that follows *c* or *g* determines whether the *c* or *g* has a hard or soft sound.

ELL English Language Learners

Model using a word in a sentence, and then have students repeat the sentence after you. Ask students questions, such as "Did you wear a *coat* to school today?" and have each student respond, using the word in his or her answer.

Bonus Words Activity

Have students work in pairs to name other words that begin with hard or soft *c* or *g*. If students need prompting, suggest Bonus Words. Have pairs make two sets of word cards for these new words and use them to play Concentration.

Vocabulary Building Vocabulary

Use stories and articles that students have read recently to make statements using the word *gist*. When they figure out that *gist* means "the main idea," have them make statements about the gist of other texts.

Word Endings *-dge*, *-ge*

Objectives
- To identify *-dge* and *-ge* spelling patterns
- To read, sort, and write words that end in *-dge* or *-ge*

Materials for Within Word Pattern

Big Book of Rhymes, "Big Baby Sue," page 29

Whiteboard Activities DVD-ROM, Sort 40

Teacher Resource CD-ROM, Sort 40 and Island Hopping Game

Student Book, pages 157–160

Words Their Way Library, *Friends Forever*

Words

-dge	-ge	r, l, n + -ge
badge	cage	bulge
bridge	huge	change
dodge	page	charge
fudge	rage	range
judge	stage	sponge
ridge		surge

Bonus Words

hedge	sage	hinge
ledge	stooge	plunge
lodge	village	splurge
pledge		urge

Introduce/Model *Small Groups*

- **Read a Rhyme** Read "Big Baby Sue," emphasizing *huge, budge,* and *judge.* Ask students to locate these words in the poem and identify the end sound in each. Write them in a single column, and ask students why you should move one of the words into a different column. (The word *huge* has a different spelling for the end sound.)

- **Model** Use the whiteboard DVD or the CD word cards. Have students assist as you demonstrate how to sort the words into three categories according to their ending: *-dge, -ge,* or *r, l, n + -ge.* Help students sort and explain their sorts.

Practice the Sort *Independent/Partner*

- Have students use the Student Book or whiteboard DVD to read the words and use the grid to sort according to word endings *-dge, -ge,* or *r, l, n + -ge.*

- Have students check and explain their sorts.

Apply *Independent/Partner/Small Groups*

- Read aloud the directions on Student Book p. 160. Have students write words from the sort in the columns according to *-dge* or *-ge* word endings.

- **Game** Allow time for students to play Island Hopping, which is on the CD.

- **Little Book** Read *Friends Forever* with students. Have them identify words ending with *-ge.*

Extend the Sort

Alternative Sort: Short or Long?

Have students re-sort the words into three categories: short vowel sound, long vowel sound, and *r*-influenced or other vowel sound. When the re-sort is completed, bring to students' attention that *-dge* always follows a short vowel.

Bonus Words Activity

Ask students to think of other words that end in *-dge* or *-ge.* If students need prompting, make suggestions from the Bonus Words list. Then have students write a short poem containing at least four of the new words.

Vocabulary Building Vocabulary

Students may have heard *surge* used in connection with surge protectors that protect electronic equipment from surges, or sharp increases in electrical power. Ask them to guess what "a surge of enthusiasm" would be. ("a sharp increase in enthusiasm") Similarly, "a surge in the sea" is an increase in the number or size of waves.

Sort 41 Word Endings -ce, -ve, -se

Objectives

- To identify words ending in -ce, -ve, and -se
- To read, sort, and write words ending in -ce, -ve, and -se

Materials for Within Word Pattern

Big Book of Rhymes, "Once Upon a Time," page 39

Whiteboard Activities DVD-ROM, Sort 41

Teacher Resource CD-ROM, Sort 41 and Castle Maze Game

Student Book, pages 161–164

Words Their Way Library, *The Princess and the Wise Woman*

Words

-ce	-ve	-se
bounce	glove	cheese
dance	leave	choose
fence	prove	raise
glance	shove	tease
peace	solve	wise
piece	twelve	
prince		

Bonus Words

price	above	hose
since	brave	rise
twice	drive	those
voice	serve	phase

Introduce/Model   *Small Groups*

- **Read a Rhyme** Read "Once Upon a Time." Point out the word *once* and ask students what they notice about its final sound and spelling. Do the same for *cave* and *chose*. Then have students find other words in the poem that end like *once* and *cave*. (*nice, prince, brave*)

- **Model** Use the whiteboard DVD or the CD word cards. Introduce the words and define in context any that may be unfamiliar to students, such as *glance, shove,* and *prove.* Then demonstrate sorting the words by final -ce, -ve, and -se. Help students sort and explain their sorts.

Practice the Sort   *Independent/Partner*

- Have students use the Student Book or whiteboard DVD to read the words and use the grid to sort.

- Have students check and explain their sorts.

Apply   *Independent/Partner/Small Groups*

- Read aloud the directions on Student Book p. 164. Have students choose beginning and middle letters to form words ending in -ce, -ve, and -se and then write them in the appropriate column according to word ending.

- **Game** Allow time for students to play Castle Maze, which is on the CD.

- **Little Book** Read *The Princess and the Wise Woman* with students. Have them identify words ending with -ce, -ve, or -se.

Extend the Sort

Alternative Sort: Guess My Category

Begin sorting words into the following categories: a beginning single consonant, a beginning digraph, a beginning blend. When students recognize the categories, let them complete the sort.

ELL English Language Learners

Check that students are saying the final sound of each word correctly, especially those spelled -se. Help them practice one set of words that share the same final sound and spelling at a time.

Bonus Words Activity

Have students name other words that end in -ce, -ve, or -se. If students need prompting, make suggestions from the Bonus Words list. Then help students make word cards for these new words. They can work with a partner to sort the words first into the categories of the sort and then into categories of their choosing.

Vocabulary Building Vocabulary

Explain that a *glance* is a quick look, but the word has other meanings. Ask "Did you glance at yourself in the mirror this morning?" and "Have you ever seen a basketball glance off a backboard?" Tell students that *glance* in the second question means "to hit something and go off on a slant."

176   Within Word Pattern

Objectives

- To identify *-tch* and *-ch* spelling patterns
- To read, sort, and write words that end in *-tch* and *-ch*

Materials for Within Word Pattern

Big Book of Rhymes, "Goodbye, Flu!" page 27

Whiteboard Activities DVD-ROM, Sort 42

Teacher Resource CD-ROM, Sort 42 and Which Ending? Game

Student Book, pages 165–168

Words Their Way Library, Title *All About Bats*

Words

-tch	*-ch*	*r, l, n + -ch*	Oddball
fetch	beach	bench	rich
hutch	coach	branch	much
match	peach	crunch	which
pitch	screech	gulch	
sketch	speech	munch	
witch	teach	torch	

Bonus Words

batch	preach	arch
switch	reach	brunch
watch	touch	mulch

Introduce/Model
Small Groups

- **Read a Rhyme** Read "Goodbye, Flu!" Write the words *such, batch,* and *lunch.* Circle the *ch* ending in each. Underline *t* in *batch* and *n* in *lunch.* Have students look for other words in the poem that end in *-tch, -ch,* or *r, l, n + -ch.*

- **Model** Use the whiteboard DVD or the CD word cards. Demonstrate how to sort the cards into three columns according to the word endings: *-tch, -ch,* or *r, l, n + -ch.* Note that since words ending with *-ch* usually have a long vowel sound, the words *which, rich,* and *much* are the oddballs because they have a short vowel sound. Help students sort and explain their sorts.

Practice the Sort
Independent/Partner

- Have students use the Student Book or whiteboard DVD to read the words and use the grid to sort.

- Have students check and explain their sorts.

Apply
Independent/Partner/Small Groups

- Read aloud the directions on Student Book p. 168. Have students write each word in the appropriate column according to the word ending.

- **Game** Allow time for students to play Which Ending? which is on the CD.

- **Little Book** Read *All About Bats* with students. Have them identify words ending with *-tch.*

Extend the Sort

Alternative Sort: Rhyme Time

Have students re-sort the words into piles of words that rhyme. Words that do not have a rhyming match can go into a separate oddball pile.

ELL English Language Learners

Review the word cards by showing and reading each word. Have students repeat each word after you. Distribute the cards and ask students to use the words on their cards in sentences. Listen carefully to be sure students are correctly pronouncing the words.

Bonus Words Activity

Let students work in pairs to list other words in the three categories *-tch, -ch,* and *r, l, n + -ch.* Make suggestions from the Bonus Words list if needed. Suggest that pairs create silly sentences using all their *-tch* words (or as many as possible), for example: I started to *twitch* and *stretch* and *scratch* so I couldn't *snatch the patch.* Continue with the other two categories.

Monitor Progress Spell Check 5

After completing Sort 42, administer Spell Check 5. See pp. 135 in this Teacher Resource Guide for instructions.

Long *a* Homophones #1

Objectives

- To identify homophones with a long *a* or *r*-influenced *a* vowel sound
- To read, sort, and write homophones with a long *a* or *r*-influenced *a* vowel sound

Materials for Within Word Pattern

Big Book of Rhymes, "Pancakes for Breakfast," page 17

Whiteboard Activities DVD-ROM, Sort 43

Teacher Resource CD-ROM, Sort 43 and Find a Match Game

Student Book, pages 169–172

Words			
stake	steak	bear	bare
fair	fare	whale	wail
wait	weight	tale	tail
bail	bale	mane	main
made	maid	stair	stare
plane	plain	hair	hare

Introduce/Model *Small Groups*

- **Read a Rhyme** Read "Pancakes for Breakfast." Write *wait* and have students locate it in the poem. Explain that *wait* sounds just like another word and write *weight*. Use both words in sentences to help students understand the meanings. Explain that *wait* and *weight* are homophones, or words that sound the same but have different spellings and different meanings.

- **Model** Use the whiteboard DVD or the CD word cards. Then model how to sort the words by finding homophone pairs. Help students sort and explain their sorts.

Practice the Sort *Independent/Partner*

- Have students use the Student Book or whiteboard DVD to read the words and use the grid to sort the words into pairs of homophones.

- Have students check and explain their sorts.

Apply *Independent/Partner/Small Groups*

- Read aloud the directions on Student Book p. 172. Have students read each word, write a homophone for the word, and then write a sentence using the homophone.

- **Game** Allow time for students to play Find a Match, which is on the CD.

Extend the Sort

Alternative Sort: Vowel Sound Sort

Remind students that all the words in this sort have either a long *a* sound or an *r*-influenced *a* sound. Have students re-sort the words into two categories according to vowel sound.

ELL English Language Learners

Review the word cards. To check that students understand and can distinguish between the different meanings of homophones, give them word cards for two or three sets of homophones. Use words one at a time in context-rich sentences, and have students raise the word card that matches each sentence.

Vocabulary Building Vocabulary

Ask students to tell you what it means if you say you like *plain* yogurt. (not flavored, not fancy) Then explain that *plain* is also a geographical word for a flat area of land. On a map of the United States, point out the Great Plains region and tell students this part of our country is mostly flat land.

Teacher Tip

Homophones are the basis for many puns and jokes. You may want to help students look in books or on the Internet (using keywords such as "puns for kids") to find a homophone-based pun to share with classmates.

Long *a* Homophones #2

Objectives

- To identify homophones with a long *a* or *r*-influenced *a* vowel sound
- To read, sort, and write homophones with a long *a* or *r*-influenced *a* vowel sound

Materials for Within Word Pattern

Big Book of Rhymes, "Pancakes for Breakfast," page 17

Whiteboard Activities DVD-ROM, Sort 44

Teacher Resource CD-ROM, Sort 44 and Tricky Sentences Game

Student Book, pages 173–176

Words

rein	rain	
waist	waste	
pale	pail	
pain	pane	
eight	ate	
raise	rays	
brake	break	
sale	sail	
weigh	way	
pear	pair	pare
vein	vain	vane

Introduce/Model
Small Groups

- **Read a Rhyme** Reread "Pancakes for Breakfast." Remind students that homophones are words that sound the same but have different spellings and different meanings. Have students take turns locating words in the poem that are homophones and write them on the board.

- **Model** Use the whiteboard DVD or the CD word cards. Model how to sort the words by finding homophone sets. Point out that two of the sets have three words in them. Help students sort and explain their sorts.

Practice the Sort
Independent/Partner

- Have students use the Student Book or whiteboard DVD to read the words and use the grid to sort the words into pairs or trios of homophones.

- Have students check and explain their sorts.

Apply
Independent/Partner/Small Groups

- Read aloud the directions on Student Book p. 176. Have students read each word, write a homophone for the word, and then write a sentence using the homophone.

- **Game** Allow time for students to play Tricky Sentences, which is on the CD.

Extend the Sort

Alternative Sort: Naming, Describing, Doing

Have students re-sort the words into three categories: words that name a thing (nouns), words that describe a person or thing (adjectives), and words that tell an action (verbs).

ELL English Language Learners

Review the word cards with students by having them repeat each word after you. Because of the different spellings, students may try to say the words differently. Help them understand that these pairs are pronounced identically by modeling pronunciation word pair by word pair.

Vocabulary Building Vocabulary

Write *vain* on the board. Explain that a vain person is someone who thinks a lot about how he or she looks. *Vain* can also be used to describe something that is unsuccessful, as in "His preparations for the camping trip were in vain because the trip was cancelled."

Teacher Tip

Encourage each student to select a set of homophones to use together in a sentence (for example, "I found a sail on sale"). Have students write and illustrate their sentences. Display the pictures in the classroom to reinforce the lesson.

Short and Long *i* Homophones

Objectives

- To identify homophones with a long or short *i* vowel sound
- To read, sort, and write homophones with a long or short *i* vowel sound

Materials for Within Word Pattern

- Big Book of Rhymes, "I Like Bugs!," page 11

- Whiteboard Activities DVD-ROM, Sort 45

- Teacher Resource CD-ROM, Sort 45 and Spin and Match Game

- Student Book, pages 177–180

Words			
short *i*		**long *i***	
mist	missed	dye	die
its	it's	night	knight
build	billed	fined	find
in	inn	write	right
him	hymn	side	sighed
		high	hi
		I	eye

Introduce/Model
Small Groups

- **Read a Rhyme** Read "I Like Bugs!" Review that homophones are words that sound the same but have different spellings and different meanings. Write *I* on the board. Explain that *I* sounds just like another word students know. *(eye)* Have students locate other homophones in the poem and write homophone pairs on the board.

- **Model** Use the whiteboard DVD or the CD word cards. Introduce the words and define in context any that may be unfamiliar to students, such as *fined, sighed, inn,* and *hymn.* Then model how to sort the words by finding homophone pairs. Help students sort and explain their sorts.

Practice the Sort
Independent/Partner

- Have students use the Student Book or whiteboard DVD to read the words and use the grid to sort the words into pairs of homophones.

- Have students check and explain their sorts.

Apply
Independent/Partner/Small Groups

- Read aloud the directions on Student Book p. 180. Have students read each word, write a homophone for the word, and then write a sentence using the homophone.

- **Game** Allow time for students to play Spin and Match, which is on the CD.

Extend the Sort

Alternative Sort: Past or Present

Have students re-sort the words in two steps. First, have them sort into categories of action words and other words. Then tell students to sort the action words into two categories: words that tell an action that has already happened and words that tell an action that is happening now.

ELL English Language Learners

Review the word cards. Then use the past-tense verbs in the sort to check pronunciation of the past-tense ending *-ed*. Remind students who may be adding an extra syllable to their pronunciation that *ed* becomes a new syllable only when the base word ends in a /d/ or /t/ sound.

Teacher Tip

Give advanced students an opportunity to extend the sort by brainstorming additional homophones. Suggest that they consider another vowel family, such as long and short *o* sounds.

Teacher Notes

Syllables and Affixes

The Syllables and Affixes stage of literacy development is a time of expanding reading interests and fine-tuning reading strategies. Students will be expected to read more informational text as classroom instruction shifts to a greater emphasis on content area subjects. It is also a time for students to make new and richer connections among the words they already know and the words they will learn. The Syllable and Affixes stage represents a new point in word analysis because students will learn to look at words in a new way, not as single-syllable units, but as two or more syllabic or meaning units. Developing word knowledge allows students to read more fluently, which in turn allows them to exercise and expand their increasing level of cognitive and language sophistication.

Types of Sorts in Syllables and Affixes
• Compound Words
• Inflected Endings
• Open and Closed Syllables
• Accented Syllables
• Unaccented Syllables
• Consonants
• Prefixes and Suffixes
• Homophones and Homographs

Characteristics of Syllables and Affixes Learners

Students in the Syllables and Affixes stage of development are usually in the upper elementary grades and middle school (grades 3 through 8).

Syllables and Affixes Learners

- are able to spell most one-syllable words correctly and therefore have the foundational knowledge needed to spell base words to which affixes (both prefixes and suffixes) are added.

- are ready to look for familiar vowel patterns in two-syllable words.

- make errors at syllable juncture (where syllables meet in words) and in unaccented syllables.

- read with good fluency and expression.

- read faster silently than orally.

- write responses that are becoming more sophisticated and critical.

Focus of Instruction

- Students are introduced to two-syllable words first through compound words. Then they explore plural endings (-s, -es) and how to add other inflected endings (-ed, -ing) to words using the "double, drop, or no change" rules.

- Next, students study the patterns of vowels and consonants at places where syllables meet, called syllable juncture patterns. These include open and closed syllables and their variations.

- Following syllable juncture, the long-vowel patterns students studied at the Within Word Pattern stage are reviewed in the stressed or accented syllables of two-syllable words. Similarly, r-influenced and ambiguous vowels (oy, oi, ow, ou, au, aw, al) are reexamined in two-syllable words.

- Students then look at the unstressed syllables that occur most commonly at the end of two-syllable words, such as -le, -el, -er, and -en, and study some unusual consonant sounds and spellings, such as hard and soft c and g, k, qu, and silent consonants.

- Finally, students are introduced to base words and affixes, focusing on common prefixes, such as re-, un-, dis-, and mis-, and common suffixes, such as -y, -ly, -ness, and -ful, that change the meanings and usage of words in generally straightforward ways. This level ends with a look at homophones and homographs.

Teacher Tip

An important responsibility for word study instruction at this stage is to engage students in examining how word elements—prefixes, suffixes, and base words—combine. Use the following to model how to examine a word for meaningful parts.

- If there are prefixes and/or suffixes, remove them so you can find the base.

- Look at the base to see if you know it or if you can think of a related word (a word that has the same base).

- Reassemble the word, explaining the meanings of the base, the suffix, and then the prefix.

- Try out the meaning in the sentence; check if it makes sense in the context of the sentence and the larger context of the text that is being read.

Pace of Instruction

At this stage, word study should take place in two ways: (1) it should be systematic as you identify stages of development and features students need to study, and (2) it should take place whenever you see an opportunity to draw students' attention to words that arise in reading, writing, and content areas. However, the pace of instruction should be adjusted to meet students' needs. The Spell Checks can help you determine the focus and pace of instruction.

For students who catch on quickly, spend less time on a series of sorts or skip some sorts altogether. For those students who are not on track for meeting end-of-year goals, spend more time on instruction and provide more practice by creating additional sorts.

Modifying the pace and using flexible small groups allows you to avoid teaching students what they already know and to spend more time on features that need instruction.

Word Study Routines

Introduce the Sort There are several options for introducing the sort. Here are the basic steps for a teacher-directed sort.

- Read all the words with students and talk about any that may be unfamiliar (*timid, rodent*) or that have multiple meanings (*leaves, ruler*). Say the words, define them, and use them in sentences.

- Introduce the categories. Say or point out the headers explicitly so that students know what features they are to look for.

- Model how to sort two or three words in each category and explain why each word goes in that category.

- At this point, you may want to discuss oddballs. **Oddballs** are words that do not fit the targeted spelling pattern. If necessary, help students identify an oddball word and explain why it is an oddball. *This word is uncle. It begins with un-, like the other words in this sort, such as* unable *and* unkind. *But the un- in* uncle *is not a prefix, which makes it an oddball in this sort.* Uncle *doesn't fit the pattern.*

- Have students help you complete the sort and ask them to explain their word placements.

- Model how to check the words in each column. Have students create a generalization about each set of words. Ask *What do you notice about the words in this column? How are they alike?* If necessary, prompt with more specific questions: *What ending do the words have? What vowel sound do the words have in the first syllable?*

- Re-sort. Have students sort the words individually or with a partner. Remind them to check their sort by reading the words in each column and to move a word to another column if they decide it is misplaced.

Interactive Resources You may use the DVD-ROM and/or the CD-ROM printable manipulatives to model, instruct, and provide practice with sorts.

Use the DVD-ROM for interactive whiteboard activities or independent practice on a computer.

- Point out the headers for the columns, which indicate the principle of the sort. Demonstrate how to drag and drop words to complete the sort. Have students take turns sorting, using the whiteboard or a computer.

- Use the whiteboard to introduce the writing sort. Have students complete it.

Use the CD-ROM for printable manipulatives.

- Print out and cut apart the cards for the sort. Introduce the words, identifying any that may be unfamiliar to students. Demonstrate how to sort. Have students use the cards to practice sorting.

- Print out the game that accompanies the sort. Use the game for additional practice with the sort. Have students play in pairs or small groups.

···

Teacher Tip
Keep dictionaries handy and encourage their use when questions about syllable division, accented syllables, or word meanings arise.

···

- **See Chapter 7 of *Words Their Way: Word Study for Phonics, Vocabulary, and Spelling Instruction*, 5th ed., for a comprehensive description of the Syllables and Affixes stage of development and additional activities.**

Monitor Progress SPELL CHECKS

Spell Checks for Syllables and Affixes are provided here. Administer the Spell Checks as you would any spelling test, reading the words and having students write them. Spell Checks may be used as pretests and postests.

Spell Check 1
Compound Words Use after Sort 2. This Spell Check assesses students' ability to spell and write compound words. Use these words:

1. cookbook	8. sideways	15. sunlight
2. downtown	9. outfield	16. snowstorm
3. something	10. headlight	17. myself
4. daytime	11. snowplow	18. lighthouse
5. yourself	12. anyone	19. bookcase
6. bookmark	13. outside	20. inside
7. flashlight	14. countdown	

If students misspell an unusually high number of compound words, review Sorts 1 and 2.

Spell Check 2
Inflected Endings Use after Sort 11. This Spell Check assesses students' ability to add *-s* or *-es, ing,* and *-ed* to base words. Use these words:

1. tripped	8. swimming	15. moving
2. chased	9. peaches	16. liked
3. wishes	10. smiled	17. grinning
4. racing	11. horses	18. snowed
5. taxes	12. grabbed	19. pushing
6. needed	13. dreaming	20. standing
7. jogging	14. dressed	

If students have difficulty adding *-s* or *-es*, review Sort 3. If students have difficulty adding *-ing*, review Sorts 5–7. If students have difficulty adding *-ed*, review Sorts 8–10.

Spell Check 3

Open and Closed Syllables Use after Sort 19. This Spell Check assesses students' ability to recognize syllables when spelling words. Use these words:

1. lazy	9. number	17. pilot
2. finish	10. humor	18. complete
3. lion	11. hundred	19. tulip
4. summer	12. easy	20. kingdom
5. English	13. sister	21. student
6. penny	14. leader	22. planet
7. river	15. poet	23. pillow
8. video	16. habit	24. inspect

If students have difficulty identifying open and closed syllables, review Sorts 14 and 17. If students have difficulty discriminating syllable juncture in VCV or VCCV words, review Sorts 12–15.

Spell Check 4
Accented Syllables Use after Sort 32. This Spell Check assesses students' ability to spell and write words with long vowel patterns, ambiguous vowels, and r-influenced vowel patterns in accented syllables. Use these words:

1. explode	8. pleasant	15. normal
2. partner	9. advice	16. annoy
3. powder	10. freedom	17. perfect
4. faucet	11. poster	18. amount
5. fifteen	12. lightning	19. learner
6. complain	13. appear	20. amuse
7. noodle	14. bracelet	

If students have difficulty spelling words with a specific long vowel pattern, ambiguous vowels, or r-influenced vowel patterns, review the corresponding sort.

Spell Check 5
Unaccented Syllables Use after Sort 39. This Spell Check assesses students' ability to spell and write words with unaccented initial and final syllables. Use these words:

1. paddle	8. chosen	15. creator
2. total	9. degree	16. bargain
3. after	10. jungle	17. ribbon
4. doctor	11. dreamer	18. novel
5. dollar	12. stronger	19. measure
6. afraid	13. stencil	20. began
7. fountain	14. picture	

If students miss words with unaccented initial syllables, review Sort 39. If they miss words with a specific unaccented final syllable, review the corresponding sort.

Spell Check 6
Consonants Use after Sort 46. This Spell Check assesses students' ability to spell and write words with hard and soft c and g, final -s, ck, -ic, -x, qu, gh, ph, and silent consonants. Use these words:

1. center	8. village	15. golden
2. liquid	9. collect	16. picnic
3. index	10. guide	17. arrange
4. sentence	11. listen	18. nephew
5. laughter	12. express	19. brought
6. giraffe	13. wrestle	20. league
7. rocket	14. rhythm	

If students have difficulty spelling words with hard and soft c and g, review Sorts 40–42. If they have difficulty spelling words with silent consonants, review Sort 45.

Spell Check 7
Prefixes and Suffixes Use after Sort 53. This Spell Check assesses students' ability to add prefixes, suffixes, and comparatives to base words. Use these words:

1. refill	8. stormy	15. universe
2. unselfish	9. weakly	16. cooler
3. dislike	10. angrily	17. prettiest
4. misjudge	11. expand	18. kindness
5. precaution	12. nonfiction	19. truthful
6. bisect	13. insight	20. harmless
7. triangle	14. foremost	

If students miss words with a specific prefix or suffix, review the corresponding sort. If students have difficulty adding suffixes or -er and -est to words that end in y, review Sorts 51 and 52.

Compound Words

Objectives
- To identify words that make up compound words
- To sort and spell compound words

Materials *Syllables and Affixes*

Whiteboard Activities DVD-ROM, Sort 1

Teacher Resource CD-ROM, Sort 1 and Compound Word Search Game

Student Book, pages 1–4

Words

bookcase	*lighthouse*	*downhill*	*headline*	*snowman*
bookmark	lightweight	downstairs	headfirst	snowflake
bookworm	daylight	downtown	headlight	snowstorm
cookbook	flashlight	downpour	headphones	snowplow
scrapbook	sunlight	countdown	headstrong	snowball
	(headlight)			

Introduce/Model *Small Groups*

- Use the whiteboard DVD or the CD word cards to introduce the words. Ask students what they notice about each of the words.

- Discuss how the meaning of the compound word often relates to the two words that make it up. For example, a *bookmark* marks your place in a book.

- Have students assist you as you demonstrate how to sort the words into groups that share common word parts. Point out that *headlight* fits in two different columns.

- Have students read aloud the words and describe how the words in each group are alike and how they are different.

Practice the Sort *Independent/Partner*

- Have students use the Student Book or whiteboard DVD to say each word and use the grid to sort the words several times according to common word parts.

- Have students check and explain their sorts.

Apply *Independent/Partner/Small Groups*

- Read aloud the directions on Student Book p. 4. Have students write the words that make up each compound word and the word itself. Then have them illustrate each compound word.

- **Game** Allow time for students to play Compound Word Search, which is on the CD.

Extend the Sort

Vocabulary **Word Of the Week:**
headstrong Tell students that some compound words cannot be interpreted literally. Explain that *headstrong* does not literally mean "strong in the head" but rather "strong-willed."

Alternative Sort: Will It Fit?

Have students sort the words according to words that name things and words that do not. Then they can sort the words that name things into those that would fit in a drawer and those that would not.

ELL English Language Learners

Help students understand the meanings of compound words by explaining the meaning of each individual word part. For example, explain the meaning of *cook* and of *book*, and then tell students what a cookbook is.

Teacher Tip

Ask students to identify the parts of words that might be hard to spell, such as *weight* in *lightweight*. Have students underline the word part that is shared by all the words in each column.

More Compound Words

Objectives

- To identify words that make up compound words
- To sort and spell compound words

Materials for Syllables and Affixes

☐ Whiteboard Activities DVD-ROM, Sort 2

◉ Teacher Resource CD-ROM, Sort 2 and Compound Word Spin Game

▱ Student Book, pages 5–8

Words

somebody	_himself_	_everything_	_without_	_inside_
something	themselves	anything	outside	beside
sometime	yourself	nothing	throughout	sideways
somewhere	herself	(something)	checkout	(outside)
somehow	myself		outfit	
someone	itself		outfield	

Introduce/Model   *Small Groups*

- Use the whiteboard DVD or the CD word cards to introduce the words. Explain to students that some of the compound words in this sort are difficult to define because they do not name specific things or actions.

- Define in context unfamiliar words, such as *beside, checkout, themselves,* and *throughout.*

- Have students assist you as you demonstrate how to sort the words into groups that share common word parts.

- Guide students to realize that *something* and *outside* can fit into two different columns.

Practice the Sort   *Independent/Partner*

- Have students use the Student Book or whiteboard DVD to say each word and use the grid to sort the words several times according to common word parts.

- Have students check and explain their sorts.

Apply   *Independent/Partner/Small Groups*

- Read aloud the directions on Student Book p. 8. Have students write the two words that make up each compound word and the compound word itself.

- **Game** Allow time for students to play Compound Word Spin, which is on the CD.

Extend the Sort

Vocabulary **Word Of the Week:**

checkout Tell students that *checkout* can be the act, time, or place of checking out, as at a hotel, a supermarket, or a library. Model using the word in sentences.

Alternative Sort: People or Things?

Help students sort as many words as possible into groups that refer to people and words that refer to things.

ELL **English Language Learners**

Review the words with students. Write the words *herself* and *themselves*. Then have students identify the word parts *her, them, self,* and *selves*. Explain that pronouns such as *herself* and *themselves* are formed with the singular and plural forms of the word *self*.

Monitor Progress ✔ **Spell Check 1**

After completing Sorts 1 and 2, administer Spell Check 1. See pp. 184–185 in this Teacher Resource Guide for instructions.

Plural Endings -es, -s

Objectives

- To identify spelling patterns of plurals whose base words end with final -ch, -sh, -x, and -s
- To sort plurals whose base words end with final -ch, -sh, -x, and -s

Materials for Syllables and Affixes

Whiteboard Activities DVD-ROM, Sort 3

Teacher Resource CD-ROM, Sort 3 and Spell It Game

Student Book, pages 9–12

Words

+ -es				+ -s
branches	leashes	taxes	buses	voices
churches	wishes	mixes	kisses	horses
speeches	ashes			changes
scratches	crashes			places
peaches	splashes			
lunches	eyelashes			

Introduce/Model   *Small Groups*

- Use the whiteboard DVD or the CD word cards to introduce the words. Lead students to notice that all of these words end with -s but the endings of the base words in each column are different.

- Have students assist you in identifying the base words that end in -ch, -sh, -x, and -s.

- Have students identify the base words in the column where only -s has been added.

- Have students read aloud the words and describe how the words in each group are alike and how they are different.

Practice the Sort   *Independent/Partner*

- Have students use the Student Book or whiteboard DVD to say each word and use the grid to sort the words.

- Have students check and explain their sorts.

Apply   *Independent/Partner/Small Groups*

- Read aloud the directions on Student Book p. 12. Have students change the singular words to plurals by adding -s or -es.

- **Game** Allow time for students to play Spell It, which is on the CD.

Extend the Sort

Vocabulary **W**ord **O**f the **W**eek:

eyelashes Tell students that *eyelashes* is a compound word that can be interpreted literally. The two smaller words—*eye* and *lashes*—create the compound that means "the hairs on the edge of the eyelid."

Alternative Sort: Noun or Verb

The words in this sort are all nouns, but some of the base words can also be used as verbs. Have students work in pairs to find the base word of each word in the sort and determine if the base word can also be a verb. Then have students sort according to the part of speech of the base word: only noun or noun/verb.

ELL English Language Learners

Explain to students how all of the words in this sort are plurals and remind them that *plural* means "more than one." Have students identify and then underline each base word. Challenge them to use each plural and its singular base word in sentences, such as: *I ride a bus to school. Sometimes the buses are late.*

Teacher Tip

Remind students that most singular nouns are made plural by adding -es or -s. However, they should always look at and think about the ending of a base word before choosing -es or -s.

Unusual Plurals

Objectives

- To identify spelling patterns of words with unusual plural forms
- To sort and spell words and their unusual plurals

Materials for Syllables and Affixes

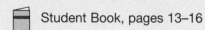 Whiteboard Activities DVD-ROM, Sort 4

Teacher Resource CD-ROM, Sort 4 and Swamp Adventure Game

Student Book, pages 13–16

Words

-f or -fe to -ves		vowel change		no change
leaf	leaves	woman	women	deer
loaf	loaves	mouse	mice	sheep
life	lives	tooth	teeth	
wolf	wolves	goose	geese	
knife	knives			

Introduce/Model *Small Groups*

- Use the whiteboard DVD or the CD word cards to introduce the words. Ask students what they notice about these words.
- Explain that these are unusual plurals because they do not follow specific rules. However, certain groups of irregular plurals follow certain patterns.
- Display the headers *(-f or -fe to -ves, vowel change, no change)*. Have students assist you as you sort the words. Explain to students that they will need to memorize the irregular plural forms.
- Have students read aloud the words and describe how the words in each group are alike and how they are different.

Practice the Sort *Independent/Partner*

- Have students use the Student Book or whiteboard DVD to say each word and use the grid to sort the words with unusual plural forms.
- Have students check and explain their sorts.

Apply *Independent/Partner/Small Groups*

- Read aloud the directions on Student Book p. 16. Have students underline the plural word in each sentence. Then have them write the singular form of the word.
- **Game** Allow time for students to play Swamp Adventure, which is on the CD.

Extend the Sort

Vocabulary Word Of the Week:

loaf Discuss the meaning of the word *loaf* and its irregular plural, *loaves*. Explain that a loaf is a quantity of bread that is shaped and baked as a whole. Have students form sentences that contain the words *loaf* and *loaves*.

Alternative Sort: One or More Than One

Have students sort the words into two categories: words that are singular and words that are plural. Remind students that *sheep* and *deer* can be either singular or plural.

ELL English Language Learners

Find pictures of one deer and many deer, and one sheep and many sheep. Demonstrate the singular and plural forms of the words by using the words in sentences and pointing to the pictures.

Teacher Tip

During a second sort, do not correct students when they place a word in the wrong column. When finished, have them read the words in each column to check them. If students still don't find the misplaced word, tell them what column it is in and have them find it.

Adding *-ing* to Words With VC and VCC Patterns

Objectives

- To recognize how *-ing* is added to words with VC or VCC spelling patterns
- To sort and spell VC and VCC base words and their *-ing* forms

Materials for Syllables and Affixes

 Whiteboard Activities DVD-ROM, Sort 5

Teacher Resource CD-ROM, Sort 5 and Finding Bats Game

Student Book, pages 17–20

Words

VC base word	double + -ing	VCC base word	+ -ing
swim	swimming	yell	yelling
run	running	rest	resting
sit	sitting	pass	passing
put	putting	stand	standing
		pick	picking
		jump	jumping

Introduce/Model
Small Groups

- Use the whiteboard DVD or the CD word cards to introduce the words. Have students identify the words *base word* in the headers.

- Have students sort the words into base words and *-ing* words. Then discuss the headers *VC base word* and *VCC base word.*

- Have students sort the base words according to whether they contain a VC or VCC spelling pattern. Have students describe what happens to a VC base word before *-ing* is added. (final consonant is doubled)

- Have students read aloud the words and describe how the words in each group are alike and how they are different.

Practice the Sort
Independent/Partner

- Have students use the Student Book or whiteboard DVD to say each word and use the grid to sort the base words and words with *-ing*.

- Have students check and explain their sorts.

Apply
Independent/Partner/Small Groups

- Read aloud the directions on Student Book p. 20. Have students add *-ing* to the word in parentheses and write it on the line to complete each sentence.

- **Game** Allow time for students to play Finding Bats, which is on the CD.

Extend the Sort

Vocabulary **W**ord **O**f the **W**eek:

putting Write *putting* and underline the base word, *put*. Use both words in sentences. Then underline *putt* in *putting*. Explain that the base word *putt* means "to hit the ball in the game of golf." Point out that the *-ing* forms of both *put* and *putt* is *putting*, but the base words follow different spelling patterns.

Alternative Sort: Double Consonant

Have students sort the words according to whether or not the word contains a double consonant. When they are finished, note that the double consonants in *yelling* and *passing* are also in the base words (*yell, pass*); they were not added when *-ing* was added.

ELL English Language Learners

To practice pronunciation and usage, show a word pair such as *swim* and *swimming*, and have students repeat this sentence pattern: "I [*swim*]. I was [*swimming*]." Continue similarly with the other word pairs.

Teacher Tip

Lead students to understand that *-ing* verbs are often accompanied by helping verbs, such as *am, has been*, and *were*.

Objectives

- To recognize how *-ing* is added to words with VCe or VVC spelling patterns
- To sort and spell VCe and VVC base words and their *-ing* forms

Materials for Syllables and Affixes

Whiteboard Activities DVD-ROM, Sort 6

Teacher Resource CD-ROM, Sort 6 and Hungry Puppy Game

Student Book, pages 21–24

Words

VCe base word	e-drop + -ing	VVC base word	+ -ing
blame	blaming	eat	eating
use	using	rain	raining
score	scoring	read	reading
tune	tuning	load	loading
ride	riding	clean	cleaning
drive	driving		

Introduce/Model   *Small Groups*

- Use the whiteboard DVD or the CD word cards to introduce the words. Explain that this week's sort includes base words and their *-ing* forms. The base words end in VCe and VVC.

- Have students assist as you sort all of the base words into a pile. Then sort the base words into columns according to their endings. Have students assist as you place the *-ing* words next to the corresponding base words.

- Have students discuss what happens to VCe words before *-ing* is added (the *e* is dropped) and what happens to the VVC words (no change).

- Have students read aloud the words and describe how the words in each group are alike and how they are different.

Practice the Sort   *Independent/Partner*

- Have students use the Student Book or whiteboard DVD to say each word and use the grid to sort the base words and words with *-ing*.

- Have students check and explain their sorts.

Apply   *Independent/Partner/Small Groups*

- Read aloud the directions on Student Book p. 24. Have students make new words by adding *-ing* to each base word. Then have students write a sentence that contains each new word.

- **Game** Allow time for students to play Hungry Puppy, which is on the CD.

Extend the Sort

Vocabulary **W**ord **O**f the **W**eek:

write Tell students that *write* and *right* are homophones (words with the same pronunciation but different spellings). Discuss both words. Help students find other words that have homophones.

Alternative Sort: Double Duty

These words are all verbs, but some of them can also be used as nouns or adjectives. Have students sort words according to part of speech: verb only, verb/noun, verb/adjective, or verb/noun/adjective.

ELL English Language Learners

Read the words and have students repeat them. Arrange the cards face up. Let students take turns finding a pair of words and using them in sentences. Encourage students to help each other with pronunciation and usage.

Teacher Tip

If students forget to drop the final *e* before adding *-ing*, write each letter of a VCe word (*w-a-v-e*) and *-ing* on separate cards. Use the cards to spell the VCe word and then remove the final *e*. Add *-ing* to make a new word. Continue with various words.

Review Inflected Ending -*ing*

Objectives
- To review methods of adding -*ing*
- To sort and spell words ending in -*ing*

Materials for Syllables and Affixes

Whiteboard Activities DVD-ROM, Sort 7

Teacher Resource CD-ROM, Sort 7 and Flying Home Game

Student Book, pages 25–28

Words		
double + -*ing*	**e-drop + -*ing***	**+ -*ing***
cutting	moving	adding talking
stopping	living	spelling snowing
humming	coming	floating working
begging	taking	chewing pushing
grinning	having	
jogging	smiling	

Introduce/Model
Small Groups

- Use the whiteboard DVD or the CD word cards to introduce the words. Explain to students that they will be reviewing adding -*ing* endings.

- Review that with VC base words, the final consonant is doubled before adding -*ing*. Review that with VCe base words, *e* is dropped before adding -*ing*.

- Review that with VVC base words and VCC base words, there is no change before adding -*ing*.

- Have students read aloud the words and describe how the words in each group are alike and how they are different.

Practice the Sort
Independent/Partner

- Have students use the Student Book or whiteboard DVD to say each word. Use the grid to sort the words according to the method of adding -*ing*.

- Have students check and explain their sorts.

Apply
Independent/Partner/Small Groups

- Read aloud the directions on Student Book p. 28. Have students make new words by adding -*ing* to each base word and write the new words.

- **Game** Allow time for students to play Flying Home, which is on the CD.

Extend the Sort

Vocabulary **Word Of the Week:**

having Explain that the verb *having* is used in a number of popular phrases. Discuss what it means when two people are "*having* it out." (The people are fighting or arguing to settle an issue.) Ask what it means to say someone is "*having* a ball." (The person is enjoying himself or herself.)

Alternative Sort: No Change Sort

Explain that the "+ -*ing*" category has three different patterns (VVC, VCC, oddball). Have students use those patterns to sort the cards from the "+ -*ing*" category.

ELL English Language Learners

Review the words in this week's sort. Have students say both the -*ing* form and the base word. For extra practice with pronunciation and vocabulary, let students take turns secretly choosing a word and then acting it out. Have other students guess the word.

Teacher Tip

The base words for <u>chew</u>ing and <u>snow</u>ing may appear to be VC words (requiring doubling). However, in both cases, the final *w* in the base word acts as part of a vowel pattern (*ew*, *ow*), not as a consonant. Therefore, there is no change before adding -*ing*.

Adding -ed (Double/No Change)

Objectives

- To identify spelling patterns of words with the -ed ending
- To sort and spell words with the -ed ending

Materials for Syllables and Affixes

Whiteboard Activities DVD-ROM, Sort 8

Teacher Resource CD-ROM, Sort 8 and Say and Spell Game

Student Book, pages 29–32

Words

double + -ed		+ -ed	
tripped	tugged	spoiled	asked
slipped	stirred	shouted	chained
snapped	sobbed	mailed	guarded
dipped	chopped	cheered	washed
dripped	shipped	pointed	loaned
dropped	zipped	punted	jumped
		pouted	hissed

Introduce/Model   *Small Groups*

- Use the whiteboard DVD or the CD word cards to introduce the words. Ask students what they notice about these words.

- Display the header *double + -ed*. Have students identify the doubled letter in each word. Guide students to identify the VC spelling pattern and base word of each verb.

- Display the header *+ -ed*. Guide students to identify the VVC or VCC spelling patterns and each base word.

- Have students read aloud the words and describe how the words in each group are alike and how they are different.

Practice the Sort   *Independent/Partner*

- Have students use the Student Book or whiteboard DVD to say each word and use the grid to sort the words with the -ed ending.

- Have students check and explain their sorts.

Apply   *Independent/Partner/Small Groups*

- Read aloud the directions on Student Book p. 32. Have students write words that end in -ed that match the spelling patterns.

- **Game** Allow time for students to play Say and Spell, which is on the CD.

Extend the Sort

Vocabulary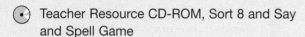

hissed Have students listen carefully as you say *hissed*. Explain that the sound of *ss* in the word *hissed* makes the sound of a hiss ("to make a sound like *ss*").

Alternative Sort: What Do You Hear?

Challenge students to sort words by the sound of the -ed ending. Say words that are examples of each sound: /t/, /d/, /ed/. Guide students to see letter patterns in the base words in each column.

ELL English Language Learners

Explain to students that verbs with the ending -ed signal that something has already happened and are in the "past tense." Demonstrate by saying the following and having students repeat after you: *I will mail my letter today. Miriam mailed her letter yesterday.* Allow time for students to continue the routine using other verbs.

Teacher Tip

Point out to students that even when a word sounds like it should be spelled with a *t* at the end (as in *walked* and *asked*), the past tense must be spelled with -ed.

Adding -ed (Double/e-Drop/No Change)

Objectives

- To identify spelling patterns of words with the -ed ending
- To sort and spell words with the -ed ending

Materials for Syllables and Affixes

Whiteboard Activities DVD-ROM, Sort 9

Teacher Resource CD-ROM, Sort 9 and Spin and Spell Game

Student Book, pages 33–36

Words

double + -ed	e-drop + -ed		+ -ed
wagged	baked	wasted	handed
clipped	tasted	waved	marked
rubbed	scored	stared	started
knitted	skated	traded	bailed
knotted	graded		stamped
scarred			roared
whizzed			farmed
			rocked

Introduce/Model
Small Groups

- Use the whiteboard DVD or the CD word cards to introduce the words. Ask students what they notice about these words.

- Display the header *double + -ed*. Have students identify the doubled letter in each word. Guide students to identify the VC spelling pattern and base word of each verb.

- Display the header *e-drop + -ed*. Help students identify each base word and the VCe pattern.

- Display the header *+ -ed*. Guide students to notice that these base words have two different patterns: VCC and VVC.

Practice the Sort
Independent/Partner

- Have students use the Student Book or whiteboard DVD to say each word and use the grid to sort the words according to the way -ed was added.

- Have students check and explain their sorts.

Apply
Independent/Partner/Small Groups

- Read aloud the directions on Student Book p. 36. Have students add -ed to each base word, write the new word, and then write a sentence with the new word.

- **Game** Allow time for students to play Spin and Spell, which is on the CD.

Extend the Sort

Vocabulary **W**ord **O**f the **W**eek:

whizzed Provide the definition of *whizzed*: "moved or rushed with a hissing sound." Guide students to notice that when the word is spoken, the *zz* makes a hissing sound.

Alternative Sort: One or Two Syllables

Read aloud the words with students, guiding them to notice that some words contain one syllable and others have two. Have students sort the words into two categories: words with one syllable and words with two syllables.

ELL **English Language Learners**

Remind students that words with -ed endings are in the past tense. Review the words in this sort and have students name the base word (present tense) and the -ed form (past tense). Give students the opportunity to say each past tense verb, clearly pronouncing one or two syllables.

Teacher Tip

During class discussion, point out some verbs that students use frequently. Write those verbs and challenge students to add the ending -ed.

Adding *-ed* to Words With VC, VCe, VVC, and VCC Patterns

Objectives

- To identify how *-ed* is added to words with VC, VCe, VVC, or VCC spelling patterns
- To sort and spell *-ed* forms of VC, VCe, VVC, or VCC base words

Materials for Syllables and Affixes

- Whiteboard Activities DVD-ROM, Sort 10
- Teacher Resource CD-ROM, Sort 10 and Moon Madness Game
- Student Book, pages 37–40

Words

VC	VCe	VVC	VCC	Oddball
planned	saved	waited	wanted	mixed
grabbed	closed	seemed	helped	
nodded	liked	shouted	started	
stepped	lived		passed	
dropped	named		called	
			hunted	

Introduce/Model   *Small Groups*

- Use the whiteboard DVD or the CD word cards to introduce the words. Ask students what they notice about the words.
- Have students assist you as you demonstrate how to sort the word cards into five columns, according to the type of base word (VC, VCe, VVC, VCC, oddball).
- Discuss with students that the final consonant was doubled before *-ed* was added to certain base words, and that *e* was dropped in others. Continue with the other categories.
- Have students read aloud the words and describe how the words in each group are alike and how they are different.

Practice the Sort   *Independent/Partner*

- Have students use the Student Book or whiteboard DVD to say each word and use the grid to sort the words according to patterns of the base words.
- Have students check and explain their sorts.

Apply   *Independent/Partner/Small Groups*

- Read aloud the directions on Student Book p. 40. Have students add *-ed* to the end of each base word and write the new words.
- **Game** Allow time for students to play Moon Madness, which is on the CD.

Extend the Sort

Vocabulary Word Of the Week:

waited Invite students to explain different meanings of the word *waited*. They can look in a dictionary to learn that *waited* means: "stayed in readiness" (*waited* until he arrived); "served" (*waited* on customers in a restaurant); "remained inactive" (*waited* out the storm); "put off going to bed" (*waited* up for her).

Alternative Sort: Last Sound

Students can sort the cards according to the sound of the *-ed* ending. Students should make three piles for the sounds: /t/, /d/, and /ed/.

ELL English Language Learners

Explain that words with *-ed* endings are in the past tense. This means something has already happened. Review the words in this sort and have students name the base word (present tense) and the *-ed* form (past tense).

Teacher Tip

The base word of *mixed* has a VC pattern, but unlike most VC words, the final consonant is not doubled before adding *-ed*. One explanation for this is that a double *x* does not occur in the English language.

Unusual Past-Tense Words

Objectives

- To recognize unusual past-tense words
- To sort and spell irregular verbs and their past-tense forms

Materials for Syllables and Affixes

- Whiteboard Activities DVD-ROM, Sort 11
- Teacher Resource CD-ROM, Sort 11 and Dinosaur Trail Game
- Student Book, pages 41–44

Words

present	past
draw	drew
keep	kept
shine	shone
sweep	swept
throw	threw
know	knew
freeze	froze
drive	drove
slide	slid
bleed	bled

Introduce/Model
Small Groups

- Use the whiteboard DVD or the CD word cards to introduce the words. Ask students what they notice about the words.

- Explain to students that the past tense of an irregular verb is not formed by adding -ed. Have students assist you in matching the present and past tense of each verb.

- Read the words together, using this pattern: *Today I [draw]. Yesterday, I [drew].*

- Have students read aloud the words and describe how the words in each group are alike and how they are different.

Practice the Sort
Independent/Partner

- Have students use the Student Book or whiteboard DVD to say each word and use the grid to sort the words according to present tense and past tense.

- Have students check and explain their sorts.

Apply
Independent/Partner/Small Groups

- Read aloud the directions on Student Book p. 44. Have students write the past-tense form of each verb and then a sentence containing that past-tense verb.

- **Game** Allow time for students to play Dinosaur Trail, which is on the CD.

Extend the Sort

Vocabulary **Word Of the Week:**

freeze Show students the word cards *freeze* and *froze*. Have students point out which verb is present tense and which is past tense. Discuss how to *freeze* water. Ask what it means when someone says, "I *froze* in my tracks." (The person did not move.)

Alternative Sort: Irregular Sort

Have students work in pairs to come up with categories that reflect the kind of changes made to form the past tense of the words. In some cases the vowel is changed to *e* (*know/knew, throw/threw, draw/drew*).

ELL **English Language Learners**

Irregular verbs are difficult for students whose native language is not English. Review the words from this sort. Then play a game of concentration with students matching the present and past tense of each verb.

Monitor Progress **Spell Check 2**

After completing Sort 11, administer Spell Check 2. See pp. 184–185 in this Teacher Resource Guide for instructions.

Syllable Juncture in VCV and VCCV Patterns

Objectives

- To recognize VCV and VCCV syllable-juncture patterns in words
- To sort and spell words with VCV and VCCV syllable-juncture patterns

Materials for Syllables and Affixes

- Whiteboard Activities DVD-ROM, Sort 12
- Teacher Resource CD-ROM, Sort 12 and Unlikely Friends Game
- Student Book, pages 45–48

Words

-VCV-		-VCCV-		Oddball
crazy	over	dinner	penny	busy
diner	paper	happy	pretty	
even	ruler	hello	puppy	
later	tiger	kitten	rabbit	
open	tiny	lesson	summer	

Introduce/Model
Small Groups

- Use the whiteboard DVD or the CD word cards to introduce the words. Call attention to headers -*VCV*- and -*VCCV*-. Explain that the hyphens on either side mean there may be another letter or letters on each side.

- Read each word. Have students identify the VCV or VCCV pattern and note if the first syllable is long or short.

- Guide students to notice that: words with the VCV pattern have a long vowel in the first syllable; words with the VCCV pattern have a short vowel in the first syllable; the word *busy* is an oddball, because it has the VCV pattern but does not contain a long *u* sound in the first syllable.

- Have students read aloud the words and describe how the words in each group are alike and how they are different.

Practice the Sort
Independent/Partner

- Have students use the Student Book or whiteboard DVD to say each word and use the grid to sort the words according to syllable-juncture patterns.

- Have students check and explain their sorts.

Apply
Independent/Partner/Small Groups

- Read aloud the directions on Student Book p. 48. Have students write the words in the correct column and draw a line between the syllables in each word.

- **Game** Allow time for students to play Unlikely Friends, which is on the CD.

Extend the Sort

Vocabulary **Word Of the Week:**

diner Point out how the words *diner* and *dinner* are alike and how they are different. Explain that doubling the *n* in *dinner* closes the first syllable and changes the vowel in the first syllable from long to short. Have students tell what *dinner* they would like to eat at the *diner*.

Alternative Sort: What's the Vowel Sound?

Have students sort the words according to the vowel sound in the first syllable of each word. Before students begin, review the long and short sounds of *a, e, i, o,* and *u*. Guide students to notice that *busy* does not contain either the long or short *u* sound.

ELL English Language Learners

As students complete the sort, listen for their vowel pronunciations. Provide help as needed for switching between long and short vowels.

Teacher Tip

When students look for more VCV juncture words, they will encounter many in which the first vowel is short. These types of words will be featured in Sort 15. For now, just consider these oddballs.

Objectives

- To recognize VCV and VCCV syllable-juncture patterns in words
- To sort and spell words with VCV and VCCV syllable-juncture patterns

Materials for Syllables and Affixes

Whiteboard Activities DVD-ROM, Sort 13

Teacher Resource CD-ROM, Sort 13 and Who Has a Pair? Game

Student Book, pages 49–52

Words

-VCV-	-VCCV- doublet	-VCCV- different	Oddball
female	bottom	blanket	water
fever	butter	chapter	
moment	follow	finger	
final	matter	member	
	pattern	number	
	pillow	problem	
	yellow	sister	
		winter	

Introduce/Model
Small Groups

- Use the whiteboard DVD or the CD word cards to introduce the words. Call attention to the first two headers. Lead students to notice that these are the same patterns and syllable junctures from the previous sort.

- Display the third header, calling attention to the word *different*. Ask students how the words *pattern* and *blanket* are similar and different. Discuss that both words follow the -VCCV- pattern, but the consonants in the pattern are different.

- Have students assist you as you demonstrate the sort. When a word is said aloud, ask students to divide the word into syllables and note if the first syllable is long or short.

- Have students read aloud the words and describe how words in each group are alike and different.

Practice the Sort
Independent/Partner

- Have students use the Student Book or whiteboard DVD to say each word and use the grid to sort.

- Have students check and explain their sorts.

Apply
Independent/Partner/Small Groups

- Read aloud the directions on Student Book p. 52. Have students write the words in the correct column and draw a line between the syllables in each word.

- **Game** Allow time for students to play Who Has a Pair?, which is on the CD.

Extend the Sort

Vocabulary **Word Of the Week:**
moment To help students understand the meaning of the word *moment*, ask them how long they think a moment is. Use a clock with a second hand to demonstrate the length of 1 second, 30 seconds, and 1 minute. Invite them to brainstorm activities that last only a moment.

Alternative Sort: Final Sound

Have students say each word and listen for the last sound. Then they can sort the words according to those that end with -*er* and those that do not.

ELL **English Language Learners**

Write *a, e, i, o, u* on an index card for each student. Encourage them to refer to the card when distinguishing between vowels and consonants.

Teacher Tip

To help students recognize consonant and vowel patterns, have them write the words using different colors. For example, when writing the word *silent*, students can use black for the letters not in the pattern (*s, n, t,*), blue for the vowels *i* and *e*, and red for the consonant *l*.

Open and Closed Syllables VCV and VCCV Patterns

Objectives
- To recognize vowel sounds in open and closed syllables
- To sort and spell open and closed syllable words

Materials for Syllables and Affixes

- Whiteboard Activities DVD-ROM, Sort 14

- Teacher Resource CD-ROM, Sort 14 and Take a Card Game

- Student Book, pages 53–56

Words

VCV Closed		VCV Open	
wagon	shiver	robot	siren
frigid	chili	humid	climate
comic	timid	tiger	bison
rapid	cabin	rodent	primate
edit	atom	ripen	china
palace	habit	sofa	tulip

Introduce/Model
Small Groups

- Use the whiteboard DVD or the CD word cards to introduce the words. Ask students what they notice about these words.

- Read several words below *VCV Closed*. Show students how to find the syllable break in each word and have them listen for the vowel sound in the first syllable. Guide students to notice that each of those vowel sounds is short and that the syllable ends with a consonant. These syllables are "closed."

- Read several words below *VCV Open*. Guide students to notice the long vowel sound in the first syllable of each word. These syllables end with a vowel and are "open."

- Have students read aloud the words and describe how the words in each group are alike and how they are different.

Practice the Sort
Independent/Partner

- Have students use the Student Book or whiteboard DVD to say each word and use the grid to sort the words according to open and closed VCV syllable patterns.

- Have students check and explain their sorts.

Apply
Independent/Partner/Small Groups

- Read aloud the directions on Student Book p. 56. Have students write the words in the correct column and draw a line between the syllables in each word.

- **Game** Allow time for students to play Take a Card, which is on the CD.

Extend the Sort

Vocabulary **Word Of the Week:**

frigid Explain how the adjective *frigid* has two meanings. One meaning is "very cold," as in "the *frigid* Arctic." Another meaning refers to how someone can act in a cold manner, as in "because she was angry, her greeting was *frigid*."

Alternative Sort: Vowel Sounds

Have students sort the words by the specific long or short vowel sound in the first syllable: long *a*, long *e*, long *i*, long *o*, long *u*; short *a*, short *e*, short *i*, short *o*, short *u*. After sorting, students should have three empty categories.

ELL English Language Learners

Have students repeat each word after you. Ask Spanish speakers to identify words that are cognates in English and Spanish. Call their attention to differences in spelling and pronunciation.

Teacher Tip

To help students read an unfamiliar word with the VCV pattern, have them try using both a short vowel and a long vowel when reading the word. They can then check the pronunciation against what makes sense or whether they have heard the word before.

Sort 15

Syllable Juncture in VCV and VVCV Patterns

Objectives

- To recognize VCV and VVCV syllable-juncture patterns in words
- To sort and spell words with VCV and VVCV syllable-juncture patterns

Materials for Syllables and Affixes

☐ Whiteboard Activities DVD-ROM, Sort 15

💿 Teacher Resource CD-ROM, Sort 15 and Slap Jack Game

📓 Student Book, pages 57–60

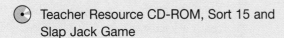
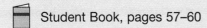

Words

-V/CV- long	-VC/ V- short		-VVCV- long
frozen	finish	present	easy
humor	lemon	river	leader
lazy	minute	second	peanut
music	never	seven	sneaker
pilot	planet		trainer
student			

Introduce/Model   *Small Groups*

- Use the whiteboard DVD or the CD word cards to introduce the words. Ask students what they notice about these words.

- Point out the headers and remind students that they studied V/CV long vowel words and VC/V short vowel words in the previous lesson. The slash marks here indicate the open and closed syllables.

- Introduce the VVCV long pattern. Explain that it is a variation of the open-syllable pattern V/CV. The syllable still ends with a long vowel sound.

- Have students assist you as you sort the words into groups according to their vowel sounds and syllable-juncture patterns.

Practice the Sort   *Independent/Partner*

- Have students use the Student Book or whiteboard DVD to say each word and use the grid to sort the words according to their syllable-juncture patterns.

- Have students check and explain their sorts.

Apply   *Independent/Partner/Small Groups*

- Read aloud the directions on Student Book p. 60. Have students write the words in the correct column and draw a line between the syllables in each word.

- **Game** Allow time for students to play Slap Jack, which is on the CD.

Extend the Sort

Vocabulary **Word Of the Week:**

humor With students, brainstorm a list of things or people that are funny, such as clowns and comic books. Write *humor* at the top of the list. Explain that *humor* is a noun, meaning "the quality of being funny or entertaining."

Alternative Sort: Name It

Invite students to sort the words cards according to words that are nouns and words that are not nouns. Remind them that a noun names a person, place, or thing. Students can further sort according to nouns that name people, nouns that name places, and nouns that name things.

ELL English Language Learners

Encourage students to segment each word into syllables. As they say the first syllable, listen as they identify the vowel sound as long or short. Offer assistance when needed. Repeat the segmentation, this time noting the pattern in the word.

Teacher Tip

Some students may benefit from completing the sort in two steps. First, encourage students to sort the word cards according to whether there is a short or long vowel sound in the first syllable. Then have them examine the vowel and consonant patterns in the sorted long vowel words and complete the sort.

Syllable Juncture in VCCCV and VV Patterns

Sort 16

Objectives

- To recognize VCCCV and VV syllable-juncture patterns in words
- To sort and spell words with VCCCV and VV syllable-juncture patterns

Materials for Syllables and Affixes

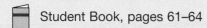 Whiteboard Activities DVD-ROM, Sort 16

Teacher Resource CD-ROM, Sort 16 and Syllable Pattern Spin Game

Student Book, pages 61–64

Words

-VCC/CV-	-VC/CCV-	-VV-
English	children	area
subtract	complete	cruel
kingdom	control	diet
mushroom	hundred	lion
pumpkin	inspect	poet
	kitchen	riot
	monster	trial
		video

Introduce/Model
Small Groups

- Use the whiteboard DVD or the CD word cards to introduce the words. Ask students what they notice about these words.

- Read aloud the words with students and have them divide each word into syllables. Guide them to notice that the VCC/CV words, such as *pump/kin*, are divided after the blend or digraph, and the VC/CCV words, such as *com/plete*, are divided before the blend or digraph.

- Point out that the vowels are closed and short in the first syllable of every VCCCV pattern. Guide students to find the long vowel in the open syllable in each VV pattern.

- Have students read aloud the words and describe how the words in each group are alike and how they are different.

Practice the Sort
Independent/Partner

- Have students use the Student Book or whiteboard DVD to say each word and use the grid to sort the words according to their syllable-juncture patterns.

- Have students check and explain their sorts.

Apply
Independent/Partner/Small Groups

- Read aloud the directions on Student Book p. 64. Have students write the words in the correct column and draw a line between the syllables in each word.

- **Game** Allow time for students to play Syllable Pattern Spin, which is on the CD.

Extend the Sort

Vocabulary **Word Of the Week:**

poet To help students understand the meaning of the word *poet*, teach the rhyme *I'm a poet, and I didn't even know it*. Explain that a poet writes poetry. Brainstorm a list of rhyming words and have students create a rhyming couplet.

Alternative Sort: Noun or Verb

Invite students to sort the cards according to words that are nouns and words that are verbs. Remind them that a verb names an action and a noun names a person, place, or thing. Students can further sort by nouns that name people, nouns that name places, and nouns that name things.

ELL English Language Learners

Place the word cards face up. Point to each word, read it, and have students repeat it after you. Then say a word at random. Have students locate the word card, point to it, read the word, and identify the consonant and vowel pattern.

Teacher Tip

After sorting, invite students to alphabetize the words in each group. They may also enjoy using alliteration to create sentences containing the words. *(In the cruel kingdom, the king has complete control in the kitchen.)*

Syllables and Affixes 201

Open and Closed Syllables and Inflected Endings

Objectives

- To recognize VCV, VCCV, and VVCV syllable-juncture patterns in words
- To sort and spell words with VCV, VCCV, and VVCV syllable-juncture patterns

Materials for Syllables and Affixes

- Whiteboard Activities DVD-ROM, Sort 17

- Teacher Resource CD-ROM, Sort 17 and Crazy Eights Game

- Student Book, pages 65–68

Words		
-VCV-	*-VCCV-*	*-VVCV-*
faded	acted	floated
quoted	getting	leaking
saving	hunted	meeting
skated	nodded	needed
taking	plotting	shouting
using	spelling	waited
writing	standing	
	wanted	

Introduce/Model
Small Groups

- Use the whiteboard DVD or the CD word cards to introduce the words. Ask students what they notice about these words.

- Write the words *hope, hop*, and *clean*. Have students add inflected endings *-ed* and *-ing* to each word. Guide them to summarize the rules for adding word endings (dropping the *e*, doubling the last letter, and leaving the base word as is).

- Have students read aloud each word, divide it into syllables, and note if the first syllable is long or short. Ask them to identify the pattern of vowels and consonants in each word.

- Lead students in making connections between what they have learned about syllable juncture and what they have learned about inflected endings.

Practice the Sort
Independent/Partner

- Have students use the Student Book or whiteboard DVD to say each word and use the grid to sort the words according to VCV, VCCV, or VVCV patterns.

- Have students check and explain their sorts.

Apply
Independent/Partner/Small Groups

- Read aloud the directions on Student Book p. 68. Have students write the words in the correct column and draw a line between the syllables in each word.

- **Game** Allow time for students to play Crazy Eights, which is on the CD.

Extend the Sort

Vocabulary **Word Of the Week:**
quoted Tell students that *quoted* means the words of another person or words in a book are repeated exactly. In print, quotation marks are used to indicate material that has been quoted.

Alternative Sort: *e*-Drop, Double, or No Change

Set aside the word cards *acted, wanted, standing*, and *hunted*. Encourage students to sort the remaining cards according to "e-drop," "double," or "no change."

ELL English Language Learners

Explain that words ending with *-ed* tell about the past and words ending with *-ing* tell about the present. Help students read each word in the sort. When they read a word with the *-ing* ending, students should act it out, indicating that the word shows action that is happening now.

Teacher Tip

At various times during the day, stop and point out a verb you used. Then write the verb, and have students tell how to add the endings *-ed* and *-ing*.

Open and Closed Syllables and Inflected Endings

Objectives
- To recognize VCV, VCCV, and VVCV syllable-juncture patterns in words
- To sort and spell words with VCV, VCCV, and VVCV syllable-juncture patterns

Materials for Syllables and Affixes

Whiteboard Activities DVD-ROM, Sort 18

Teacher Resource CD-ROM, Sort 18 and Catching Fireflies Game

Student Book, pages 69–72

Words

+ -s		-y to i + -es	
monkeys	donkeys	ponies	berries
alleys	boys	babies	families
valleys	trays	ladies	candies
toys	journeys	fireflies	stories
		duties	parties

Introduce/Model
Small Groups

- Use the whiteboard DVD or the CD word cards to introduce the words. Ask students what they notice about these words.

- Lead students to understand that base words that end in -y form plurals in different ways. In some words, an -s is added to the word to make it plural. Words like *play* and *toy* have a vowel before the final -y, so just -s is added. In others, the final -y is changed to *i* and -es is added. Words like *city* and *party* have a consonant before -y, so -y is changed to *i* and -es is added.

- Have students assist you as you demonstrate how to sort the words according to their plural endings.

- Have students read aloud the words in each column and describe how the words are alike and how they are different.

Practice the Sort
Independent/Partner

- Have students use the Student Book or whiteboard DVD to say each word and use the grid to sort the words according to plural endings.

- Have students check and explain their sorts.

Apply
Independent/Partner/Small Groups

- Read aloud the directions on Student Book p. 72. Have students write the plural form of each singular word.

- **Game** Allow time for students to play Catching Fireflies, which is on the CD.

Extend the Sort

Vocabulary **Word Of the Week:**

monkeys *Monkey* is the singular form of *monkeys*. Have students name the other sort words for animals. (*fireflies, donkeys, ponies*) Brainstorm other animal names that end in -y. Help students form the plural of each animal word they name.

Alternative Sort: Student-Centered Sorts

Have students devise their own categories for sorting. You may want to point out that an alternative sort might consist of dividing the words into groups of animals and non-animals.

ELL **English Language Learners**

Review the words with students. Explain that many words can have multiple uses and meanings. Tell students how *babies, toys*, and *journeys* can be used as either nouns or verbs. Explain that *stories* can mean "narratives" or "floors of a building."

Teacher Tip

Encourage students to hone their sorting skills prior to starting the sort. Have them pursue basic sorting exercises that identify common objects (pencils, articles of clothing, colors, shapes) in the classroom.

Adding Inflected Endings -s, -ed, and -ing to Words With Final -y

Objectives

- To identify how -s, -ed, and -ing are added to words with final -y
- To sort and spell -s, -ed, and -ing words whose base words end with final -y

Materials for Syllables and Affixes

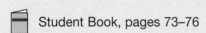 Whiteboard Activities DVD-ROM, Sort 19

Teacher Resource CD-ROM, Sort 19 and One Card! Game

Student Book, pages 73–76

Words

+ -ing	+ -s or -y to i + -es	+ -ed or -y to i + -ed
replying	replies	replied
copying	copies	copied
hurrying	hurries	hurried
studying	studies	studied
carrying	carries	carried
staying	stays	stayed
enjoying	enjoys	enjoyed

Introduce/Model
Small Groups

- Use the whiteboard DVD or the CD word cards to introduce the words. Ask students what they notice about these words.

- Have students identify the base words in the first column. Ask them what they notice about adding -ing to words that end with -y.

- Guide students to notice that when adding -s or -ed to a word that ends with y, the y is only changed to i when it follows a consonant.

- Have students read aloud the words in each column and describe how the words are alike and how they are different.

Practice the Sort
Independent/Partner

- Have students use the Student Book or whiteboard DVD to say each word and use the grid to sort the words according -s, -ed, and -ing endings.

- Have students check and explain their sorts.

Apply
Independent/Partner/Small Groups

- Read aloud the directions on Student Book p. 76. Have students write new words by adding -s, -ed, and -ing to the base words.

- **Game** Allow time for students to play One Card!, which is on the CD.

Extend the Sort

Vocabulary **Word Of the Week:**

stay When -ing or -ed are added to *stay*, the new words are verbs. Explain to students that *stay* can be used as both a verb and a noun. Definitions of the verb *stay* include "remain," "to live for a while," and "to put off." Definitions of the noun *stay* include "a period of time spent" and "a delay."

Alternative Sort: Brainstorming

Have students brainstorm a list of verbs that end in -y, such as *play* or *fly*. Write their responses. Have students spell the -s, -ed, and -ing form of each word and sort them accordingly.

ELL **English Language Learners**

Help students understand that the words ending in -s or -es are present-tense verbs, and the words ending in -ed are past-tense verbs. Say, "Today he *copies* something; yesterday he *copied* something." Show the cards for *copies* and *copied* as you say each word in the sentences.

Monitor Progress ✓ **Spell Check 3**

After completing Sort 19 administer Spell Check 3. See pp. 184–185 in this Teacher Resource Guide for instructions.

Long *a* Patterns in Accented Syllables

Objectives

- To identify long *a* spelling patterns
- To sort and spell words with long *a* in accented syllables

Materials for Syllables and Affixes

Whiteboard Activities DVD-ROM, Sort 20

Teacher Resource CD-ROM, Sort 20 and Chasing Butterflies Game

Student Book, pages 77–80

Words

ā in 1st Syllable		ā in 2nd Syllable		Oddball
basement	painter	amaze	mistake	chocolate
bracelet	pavement	complain	obey	
crayon	payment	decay	parade	
maybe	railroad	escape	remain	
mayor	raisin	explain	today	

Introduce/Model
Small Groups

- Use the whiteboard DVD or the CD word cards to introduce the words. Ask students what they notice about these words. Then review long *a* spelling patterns (*ai, ay, a_e*).

- Read aloud the words in the first column. Explain that the first syllable in each word is accented (spoken with a little more emphasis). Read aloud the words in the third column, stressing the second syllable slightly.

- Have students assist you as you demonstrate how to sort the words. Explain that *chocolate* is an oddball, because it does not have a long *a* sound even though the last syllable has a long *a* pattern.

- Have students read aloud the words in each column and describe how they are alike and different.

Practice the Sort
Independent/Partner

- Have students use the Student Book or whiteboard DVD to say each word and use the grid to sort.

- Have students check and explain their sorts.

Apply
Independent/Partner/Small Groups

- Read aloud the directions on Student Book p. 80. Have students write the words, draw a line between syllables, and underline the accented syllable.

- **Game** Allow time for students to play Chasing Butterflies, which is on the CD.

Extend the Sort

Vocabulary **Word Of the Week:**
basement Depending on where you live, students may not understand what a basement is. Draw a diagram of a house, including a basement, and explain its location and typical function.

Alternative Sort: a's Around

Have students sort the cards according to the long *a* spelling pattern (*ai, ay, a_e*). Note that *obey* will be an oddball since it has the sound of long *a* but not one of the patterns. *Chocolate* has a long *a* pattern, but not the sound.

ELL English Language Learners

Pair English language learners with more proficient English speakers as they complete the sort. Encourage the English language learners to say the word after their partners, and then have students say the word together.

Teacher Tip

To help students recognize the accented syllable in a word, ask them to place a hand under their chin as they say a word from the sort, such as *contain*. Point out that often their chin will hit their hand when saying an accented syllable.

Long *i* Patterns in Accented Syllables

Objectives
- To identify long *i* spelling patterns
- To sort and spell words with long *i* in accented syllables

Materials for Syllables and Affixes

Whiteboard Activities DVD-ROM, Sort 21

Teacher Resource CD-ROM, Sort 21 and Balls Abound Game

Student Book, pages 81–84

Words

ī in 1st Syllable		ī in 2nd Syllable		Oddball
brightly	lightning	advice	describe	favorite
driveway	ninety	arrive	invite	forgive
higher	sidewalk	combine	provide	machine
highway	slightly	decide	surprise	
		delight	survive	

Introduce/Model
Small Groups

- Use the whiteboard DVD or the CD word cards to introduce the words and review long *i* spelling patterns (*igh*, VCe).

- Read aloud the words in the first column. Explain that when these words are spoken, the emphasis is on the first syllable. Read aloud the words in the third column. Guide students to notice that the accent is on the second syllable in these words.

- Demonstrate how to sort the words. Explain that *favorite, forgive,* and *machine* are oddballs, because they do not have a long *i* sound even though the last syllables have a long *i* pattern.

- Have students read aloud the words in each column and describe how they are alike and different.

Practice the Sort
Independent/Partner

- Have students use the Student Book or whiteboard DVD to say each word and use the grid to sort according to which syllable has the long *i* sound.

- Have students check and explain their sorts.

Apply
Independent/Partner/Small Groups

- Read aloud the directions on Student Book p. 84. Have students write the words, draw a line between the syllables, and underline the accented syllable.

- **Game** Allow time for students to play Balls Abound, which is on the CD.

Extend the Sort

Vocabulary **Word Of the Week:**

advice Tell students that advice is an opinion about what should be done. Give examples, such as "Always wash your hands before you eat." Encourage students to share advice. Ask them to begin by saying, "I give you this advice: _____."

Alternative Sort: The *i*'s Have It

Have students sort the cards according to the long *i* spelling pattern (*igh*, *i_e*). Note that *favorite, forgive,* and *machine* are oddballs, because they do not contain the long *i* sound.

ELL English Language Learners

Review the cards by having students repeat each word after you. To practice language skills, give each student one or two cards and have them create sentences using the words on their cards.

Teacher Tip

Encourage students to re-sort the cards according to words that are compound words (*driveway*) and words that contain a base word (*slightly*). Remind students that compound words are made up of two words. Base words have an ending, but the ending cannot stand alone as a word.

Objectives

- To identify long *o* spelling patterns
- To sort and spell words with long *o* in accented syllables

Materials for Syllables and Affixes

Whiteboard Activities DVD-ROM, Sort 22

Teacher Resource CD-ROM, Sort 22 and Post Your Letter Game

Student Book, pages 85–88

Words

ō in 1st Syllable		ō in 2nd Syllable		Oddball
closely	lower	alone	erode	bureau
hostess	owner	approach	explode	Europe
loafer	postage	awoke	remote	
lonely	poster	compose	suppose	
lonesome	soapy	decode		

Introduce/Model   *Small Groups*

- Use the whiteboard DVD or the CD word cards to introduce the words. Ask students what they notice about these word. Then review long *o* spelling patterns (*o, oa, o_e*).

- Read words from both the first column and the third column. Guide students to identify which syllable is accented and contains the long *o* sound.

- Have students assist you as you demonstrate how to sort the words. Explain that *bureau* and *Europe* are oddballs. The long *o* in *bureau* is not in the accented syllable, and *Europe* has a long *o* spelling pattern, but not a long *o* sound. Have students find three words whose base word is *lone*.

- Have students read aloud the words in each column and describe how the words are alike and how they are different.

Practice the Sort   *Independent/Partner*

- Have students use the Student Book or whiteboard DVD to say each word and use the grid to sort.

- Have students check and explain their sorts.

Apply   *Independent/Partner/Small Groups*

- Read aloud the directions on Student Book p. 88. Have students write each word in the column that shows its vowel pattern, draw a line between its syllables, and underline the accented syllable.

- **Game** Allow time for students to play Post Your Letter, which is on the CD.

Extend the Sort

Vocabulary **Word Of the Week:**

erode Explain that *erode* is a verb. *Erode* means "to wear away." If time permits, conduct simple experiments to help convey the meaning of *erode*. For example, you might have students build a "mountain" with sand and then blow through a straw from a few feet away to simulate wind eroding the mountain.

Alternative Sort: Oh, I Know

Have students sort the cards according to the long *o* spelling pattern (*o, oa, o_e*). Note that *bureau* and *Europe* are oddball words.

ELL English Language Learners

Say each word aloud, and demonstrate how to clap the syllables for each word. Clap each accented syllable with more force. Invite students to repeat the words, clapping the syllables for each.

Teacher Tip

When students complete the sort, ask them to divide each word into syllables. Then have them underline the long *o* spelling pattern in each word. This helps learners cement their knowledge of long *o* patterns in accented syllables.

Long *u* Patterns in Accented Syllables

Objectives

- To identify long *u* spelling patterns
- To sort and spell words with long *u* in accented syllables

Materials for Syllables and Affixes

Whiteboard Activities DVD-ROM, Sort 23

Teacher Resource CD-ROM, Sort 23 and Category Match Game

Student Book, pages 89–92

Words

ū in 1st Syllable		*ū in 2nd Syllable*		Oddball
noodle	scooter	amuse	cocoon	beauty
moody	toothache	balloon	pollute	Tuesday
doodle	useful	cartoon	reduce	cougar
		conclude	shampoo	
		confuse	excuse	
		raccoon		
		refuse		

Introduce/Model
Small Groups

- Use the whiteboard DVD or the CD word cards to introduce the words. Ask students what they notice about these word. Then review long *u* spelling patterns (*oo, u_e*).

- Read words from the first two categories. Guide students to identify which syllable is accented and contains the long *u* sound.

- Have students assist you as you demonstrate how to sort the words. Explain that *beauty, Tuesday*, and *cougar* are oddballs, because they have the long *u* sound but not a long *u* spelling pattern.

- Have students read aloud the words in each column and describe how they are alike and different.

Practice the Sort
Independent/Partner

- Have students use the Student Book or whiteboard DVD to say each word and use the grid to sort.

- Have students check and explain their sorts.

Apply
Independent/Partner/Small Groups

- Read aloud the directions on Student Book p. 92. Have students write the words, draw a line between the syllables, and underline the accented syllables.

- **Game** Allow time for students to play Category Match, which is on the CD.

Extend the Sort

Vocabulary **W**ord **O**f the **W**eek:

conclude Explain that *conclude* is a verb. The word can mean "to reach an end" or "to infer." Have students revisit the completed sort and make conclusions, or generalizations, about the words in each column. For example, students can conclude that the stressed syllable usually contains the long *u* sound. Encourage students to use the word *conclude* in their generalizations: "I conclude that _____."

Alternative Sort: Useful *u*'s

Have students sort the cards according to the long *u* spelling pattern (*oo, u_e*). Note that *Tuesday, beauty*, and *cougar* are oddball words.

Teacher Tip

For practice or informal assessment, say the words in the sort aloud. Have students stand up when they hear words in which the first syllable contains the long *u* sound and sit down when they hear words in which the second syllable contains the long *u* sound.

Short and Long e Patterns in Accented Syllables

Objectives

- To identify short and long *e* spelling patterns
- To sort and spell words with short and long *e* in accented syllables

Materials for Syllables and Affixes

Whiteboard Activities DVD-ROM, Sort 24

Teacher Resource CD-ROM, Sort 24 and Ready Answers Game

Student Book, pages 93–96

Words

ē in 1st Syllable	ĕ in 1st Syllable	ē in 2nd Syllable
eastern	healthy	compete
feature	heavy	defeat
freedom	leather	extreme
meaning	pleasant	fifteen
reader	sweater	increase
season	steady	indeed
		repeat
		thirteen

Introduce/Model *Small Groups*

- Use the whiteboard DVD or the CD word cards to introduce the words. Guide students to see that the words have both long and short *e* sounds. Review long *e* spelling patterns (*ee, ea*) and the short *e* spelling pattern *ea*.

- Have students assist you as you demonstrate how to sort the words by long and short *e* sounds in accented syllables.

- As students read aloud the words in each category, help them understand that the vowel sound is clearly heard in the stressed syllable of each word.

- Have students read aloud the words in each column and describe how the words are alike and how they are different.

Practice the Sort *Independent/Partner*

- Have students use the Student Book or whiteboard DVD to say each word and use the grid to sort.

- Have students check and explain their sorts.

Apply *Independent/Partner/Small Groups*

- Read aloud the directions on Student Book p. 96. Have students write each word in the column that shows its vowel pattern and sound, draw a line between its syllables, and underline its accented syllable.

- **Game** Allow time for students to play Ready Answers, which is on the CD.

Extend the Sort

Vocabulary **Word Of the Week:**

compete Use the sports section of a newspaper to help illustrate the word *compete*. Write *compete* and then read a brief article describing the results of a sporting event. Students can describe the people or teams competing.

Alternative Sort: Pattern and Sound

Have students sort the cards according to spelling patterns and sounds. Have students create their own headings and complete the sort independently. Possible headings include: *needle, compete, season, feather*.

ELL English Language Learners

Review the words with students. Have them pronounce each word to be sure they are stressing the correct syllables. Review the sounds of short and long *e*.

Teacher Tip

Some students may benefit from completing the sort in two steps. First, encourage students to sort the word cards according to short *e* or long *e*. Then have them examine the long *e* words and sort them according to the syllable containing the long *e* sound.

Review Long Vowel Patterns in Accented Syllables

Objectives
- To review long vowel patterns in accented syllables
- To sort and spell words with long vowels in accented syllables

Materials for Syllables and Affixes

Whiteboard Activities DVD-ROM, Sort 25

Teacher Resource CD-ROM, Sort 25 and Moon Sliding Game

Student Book, pages 97–100

Words

Long Vowel in 1st Syllable

lightning	useful	flowing
speaker	freezer	frighten
crayon	dainty	brightly

Long Vowel in 2nd Syllable

debate	invade	disease
delete	advice	refrain
remote	enclose	salute
compose	dispute	define
polite	decay	awake

Introduce/Model
Small Groups

- Use the whiteboard DVD or the CD word cards to introduce the words. Ask students what they notice about each of the words.

- Display the headers and start the sort. Point out that in some words, the long vowel sound is heard in the accented syllable. Model how to identify the accented, or stressed, syllable.

- Encourage students to talk about the patterns in each category. Guide them to see that the first category includes words that begin with an open syllable or long vowel, whereas the second category includes words with the long vowel in the second syllable.

- Have students assist you as you complete the sort.

Practice the Sort
Independent/Partner

- Have students use the Student Book or whiteboard DVD to say each word and use the grid to sort the words according to which syllable contains the long vowel.

- Have students check and explain their sorts.

Apply
Independent/Partner/Small Groups

- Read aloud the directions on Student Book p. 100. Have students draw a line between the two syllables, circle the long vowel, and underline the accented syllable of the word in boldface type.

- **Game** Allow time for students to play Moon Sliding, which is on the CD.

Extend the Sort

Vocabulary — Word Of the Week:

remote Write the sentence *There is a remote chance of that happening.* Discuss how, in this case, *remote* means "slight" as in "unlikely." Then have partners work together to think of events with remote chances of happening, such as winning the lottery or vacationing on the moon.

Alternative Sort: Vowel Sort

Encourage students to re-sort the words according to which long vowel sound each one has. Remind students that a long vowel sound may have more than one spelling.

ELL English Language Learners

Have students repeat each word after you. Use pictures, gestures, and examples to help students learn the meanings of the words. Have them choose one word they find difficult and draw a picture and write a sentence using the word.

Teacher Tip

Say the sort words aloud and have students clap once if the first syllable is accented and twice if the second syllable is accented. If students are having difficulty identifying the accented syllable, suggest they rest a hand lightly under their chin. Explain that the chin descends more for the accented syllable.

Objectives

- To identify two-syllable words with the ambiguous vowel patterns *oy, oi, ou,* and *ow*
- To sort and spell two-syllable words with the ambiguous vowel patterns *oy, oi, ou,* and *ow*

Materials for Syllables and Affixes

- Whiteboard Activities DVD-ROM, Sort 26

- Teacher Resource CD-ROM, Sort 26 and Four Down Game

- Student Book, pages 101–104

Words

1st Syllable		2nd Syllable		Oddball
moisture	drowsy	amount	avoid	trouble
poison	coward	allow	annoy	double
noisy	thousand	around	employ	southern
loyal	county	about	appoint	country
pointed	counter	announce	destroy	
voyage				

Introduce/Model *Small Groups*

- Use the whiteboard DVD or the CD word cards to introduce the words. Ask students what they notice about each of the words.

- Start the sort according to the location of the ambiguous vowel pattern. Ask students what they notice about the vowel pattern in the accented syllable in each word.

- Point out that there are four different vowel patterns included under the first header and four under the second.

- Display the headers *oi/oy* and *ou/ow* below *1st Syllable* and *2nd Syllable*. Have students assist you as you complete the sort according to the accented syllable and vowel pattern.

Practice the Sort *Independent/Partner*

- Have students use the Student Book or whiteboard DVD to say each word and use the grid to sort the words according to the vowel patterns and in which syllable it is.

- Have students check and explain their sorts.

Apply *Independent/Partner/Small Groups*

- Read aloud the directions on Student Book p. 104. Have students write words that contain the vowel patterns *oy, oi, ou,* and *ow* in the appropriate columns, circle the vowel pair within each word, and use two words in sentences.

- **Game** Allow time for students to play Four Down, which is on the CD.

Extend the Sort

Vocabulary **Word Of the Week:**

counter Ask students if they know the meaning of the word *counter*. Students will likely suggest that *counter* means "a flat surface used to prepare or serve things" or "someone or something that counts." Provide a sentence that uses a third meaning of *counter*: "to oppose or act against," such as *He countered my idea with one of his own.* Help students figure out the meaning from context.

Alternative Sort: Speed Sort

Have students time themselves as they sort the words by vowel pattern and syllable. Then have students repeat the sort a few times, trying to complete it faster each time.

ELL **English Language Learners**

Point out that the spelling pattern *ou* has three sounds: /aw/, as in *bought, cough,* and *fought,* /u/ as in *rough* and *tough,* and /ou/ as in *house* and *ground.* Explain that students must memorize which sound the spelling pattern has in each word. Write *ou* words in columns according to their sounds.

Sort 27   Ambiguous Vowels *au, aw, al* in Accented Syllables

Objectives

- To identify two-syllable words with the ambiguous vowel patterns *au, aw,* and *al*
- To sort and spell two-syllable words with the ambiguous vowel patterns *au, aw,* and *al*

Materials for Syllables and Affixes

Whiteboard Activities DVD-ROM, Sort 27

Teacher Resource CD-ROM, Sort 27 and Vowel Pattern Match Game

Student Book, pages 105–108

Words

au	*aw*	*al*	*Oddball*
author	awkward	always	laughed
autumn	lawyer	almost	all right
laundry	awesome	already	
caution	gnawed	although	
faucet	gawking		
sausage	flawless		
haunted			
August			
auction			

Introduce/Model   *Small Groups*

- Use the whiteboard DVD or the CD word cards to introduce the words. Ask students what they notice about each of the words.

- Explain to students that the target vowel patterns have different spellings but the same sound. Display the headers and have the students assist you as you complete the sort according to the vowel pattern.

- Encourage discussion about the different ways to spell the same sound. Talk about the oddballs and point out the correct spelling of *all right*.

- Have students read aloud the words and describe how the words in each group are alike.

Practice the Sort   *Independent/Partner*

- Have students use the Student Book or whiteboard DVD to say each word and use the grid to sort the words according to the vowel patterns.

- Have students check and explain their sorts.

Apply   *Independent/Partner/Small Groups*

- Read aloud the directions on Student Book p. 108. Have students write words that contain the listed vowel pattern in the appropriate column, draw a line between the syllables, underline the accented syllables, and use three words in sentences.

- **Game** Allow time for students to play Vowel Pattern Match, which is on the CD.

Extend the Sort

Vocabulary   **Word Of the Week:**

awesome Explain that something that is awesome makes a person feel fear, wonder, or respect. Give students practice associating newly learned words with contexts and activities from their own experiences. Ask students to write a description of something they saw that was awesome, explaining why it made them feel fear, wonder, or respect.

ELL   **English Language Learners**

Spanish speakers may need extra practice to associate the vowel pattern *au* with the English sound /au/. To help them learn English letter-sound correspondences, write the word pairs *couch/caught, pouch/pause, loud/laud, house/haunch, sound/sauce,* and *tout/taut*. Introduce the words and their meanings, and then have students practice reading the pairs aloud.

Teacher Tip

You may wish to explain that the letter pairs *aw* and *al* are considered vowel patterns because the consonants affect the vowel sounds. Use word pairs such as *gnat/gnaw, fan/fawn, pan/pawn, hat/halt, mat/malt,* and *sat/salt* to explore how *w* and *l* change the vowel sound.

r-Influenced *a* in Accented Syllables

Objectives

- To identify the two sounds of *r*-influenced *a* and the patterns associated with them
- To sort and spell words containing *r*-influenced *a*

Materials for Syllables and Affixes

- Whiteboard Activities DVD-ROM, Sort 28
- Teacher Resource CD-ROM, Sort 28 and Spin and Win Game
- Student Book, pages 109–112

Words

ar in 1st Syllable	ā in 1st Syllable	ā in 2nd Syllable	Oddball
market	parents	aware	toward
carpet	haircut	despair	
harvest	dairy	repair	
marble	barefoot	declare	
hardly	careful	beware	
partner	barely		
pardon	fairy		

Introduce/Model *Small Groups*

- Use the whiteboard DVD or the CD word cards to introduce the words. Ask students what they notice about each of the words.
- Sort the words first by vowel sound—either the *ar* sound as in *garden* or long *a* as in *airplane* or *compare*.
- Help students notice that *r*-influenced short *a* is always a CVCC pattern, whereas the *r*-influenced long *a* is either a VVC or CVe pattern.
- Display the headers and have students assist you as you complete the sort according to the vowel sound and syllable in which the *r*-influenced *a* appears.

Practice the Sort *Independent/Partner*

- Have students use the Student Book or whiteboard DVD to say each word and use the grid to sort the words according to whether the *r*-influenced *a* is in the first syllable or the second syllable.
- Have students check and explain their sorts.

Apply *Independent/Partner/Small Groups*

- Read aloud the directions on Student Book p. 112. Have students write words that contain the *r*-influenced *a* in the first or second syllable in the appropriate column and use three words in sentences.
- **Game** Allow time for students to play Spin and Win, which is on the CD.

Extend the Sort

Vocabulary Word Of the Week:

harvest Have students use a dictionary to find out what parts of speech the word *harvest* can be. Challenge students to say or write sentences that use *harvest* as a noun, as a verb, and as an adjective.

Alternative Sort: Compound Words

When students have completed the sort, ask them to identify the compound words from the sort (*haircut, airplane, barefoot*). Then challenge them to brainstorm more compound words for *air, hair,* and *foot*.

ELL English Language Learners

The English pronunciation of *r* differs from that in most other languages. This makes pronunciation of *r*-influenced vowels challenging for English language learners. Have these students listen to English speakers pronounce simple words with *r*-influenced vowels, such as *arm, cart, farm,* and *lark*. Encourage students to echo their classmates.

Teacher Tip

When students do the Alternative Sort, suggest that they use a dictionary both to check the spellings of words they brainstorm and to find additional words.

r-Influenced *o* in Accented Syllables

Objectives

- To identify words with *r*-influenced *o* and the patterns associated with them
- To sort and spell words containing *r*-influenced *o*

Materials for Syllables and Affixes

Whiteboard Activities DVD-ROM, Sort 29

Teacher Resource CD-ROM, Sort 29 and Firefly Chorus Game

Student Book, pages 113–116

Words

or in 1st Syllable	*or* in 2nd Syllable	Oddball
order	record	sorry
forest	perform	reward
normal	ashore	
forty	before	
florist	explore	
northern	ignore	
forward	adore	
corner	inform	
chorus		
corncob		
shorter		
border		

Introduce/Model
Small Groups

- Use the whiteboard DVD or the CD word cards to introduce the words. Ask students what they notice about each of the words.

- Display the headers and have students assist you as you complete the sort according to whether the *r*-influenced *o* is heard in the first or second syllable.

- Guide students to see that regardless of the spelling (*or* or *ore*), the sound is always the same (except with oddballs). Help them see that the oddball *sorry* has the spelling pattern but an unexpected sound, and the oddball *reward* has a different spelling pattern but the same sound as other typical *r*-influenced *o* words.

- Have students read aloud the words in each column and describe how they are alike and different.

Practice the Sort
Independent/Partner

- Have students use the Student Book or whiteboard DVD to say each word and use the grid to sort.

- Have students check and explain their sorts

Apply
Independent/Partner/Small Groups

- Read aloud the directions on Student Book p. 116. Have students write the words with *r*-influenced *o* in the appropriate column. Then have students choose three words to use in sentences.

- **Game** Allow time for students to play Firefly Chorus, which is on the CD.

Extend the Sort

Vocabulary **W**ord **O**f the **W**eek:

reward Have students define *reward* ("something valuable that is given to someone for doing something good"). Then have students make a poster offering a reward for a lost item or pet. Instruct them to choose an item that is valuable to them—either real or imaginary—and to choose a reward that they think is appropriate. Tell students to be sure to include all necessary information on the poster, including how to collect the reward.

ELL English Language Learners

Use pictures and movement to help English language learners learn the meanings of the sort words. Then ask students questions that require them to choose between two sort words. For example, say "Is a person who sells flowers a florist or forest?" Suggest memory aids, such as pointing out that *flower* and *florist* both begin with *fl*.

Teacher Tip

Draw students' attention to the first sound in *chorus*, which has the sound of hard *c* rather than the more familiar /ch/.

Words With *w* or /w/ Before the Vowel

Objectives
- To identify vowels that are influenced by *w* or /w/
- To sort and spell words containing *w* or /w/ before the vowel

Materials for Syllables and Affixes

🖳 Whiteboard Activities DVD-ROM, Sort 30

💿 Teacher Resource CD-ROM, Sort 30 and Four Down Game

📖 Student Book, pages 117–120

Words

/war/	/wor/	/wa/
wardrobe	worse	waffle
warning	world	wander
warden	worry	squat
warrior	worthy	squash
quarter	worship	squabble
quarrel	worthwhile	squad
swarm		
dwarf		
backward		

Introduce/Model *Small Groups*

- Use the whiteboard DVD or the CD word cards to introduce the words. Ask students what they notice about each of the words.

- Explain to students that all the words have the /w/ sound, even those spelled with *qu*, as in *quarter*. Display the headers and have students assist you as you complete the sort according to the vowel and sound pattern.

- Guide students to notice that the *w* exerts influence on the vowel that follows it. For example, in *warmth,* the *ar* sounds like /or/, and in *worker,* the *or* sounds like /ər/. Help students to see that in *watch,* what would normally be a short *a* is instead a broad *a*.

- Have students read aloud the words in each column and describe how the words are alike and how they are different.

Practice the Sort *Independent/Partner*

- Have students use the Student Book or whiteboard DVD to say each word and use the grid to sort.

- Have students check and explain their sorts.

Apply *Independent/Partner/Small Groups*

- Read aloud the directions on Student Book p. 120. Have students write the words that contain *w* or the /w/ sound before the vowel in the appropriate column. Then have students choose three words to use in sentences.

- **Game** Allow time for students to play Four Down, which is on the CD.

Extend the Sort

Vocabulary **Word Of the Week:**

squabble Write *squabble, quarrel, argue, bicker,* and other synonyms for these words. Then have groups work together to fill in graphic organizers that organize the words from lowest to highest (mildest kinds of fights/discussions on the left and most serious fights/disagreements on the right).

ELL **English Language Learners**

The letter *w* is rare in Spanish, occurring only in words borrowed from other languages. In addition, when the letter pair *qu* appears in Spanish, the *u* is silent rather than having the /w/ sound as in English. For these reasons, Spanish speakers may need extra practice to associate *w* and *qu* with the /w/ sound. Write words such as *wade, wag, wall, web, win, quick, quack,* and *quit,* and have students read them aloud after you.

Teacher Tip

Point out to students that some people speak English with different accents and that for this reason, not everyone pronounces words or their vowels in exactly the same way. Have students listen carefully for variations as several volunteers say aloud the same word, such as *warrior.* Point out that a range of pronunciations is considered acceptable.

/ər/ Spelled *er, ir, ur* in First Syllables

Objectives
- To identify spelling patterns for /ər/
- To sort and spell words containing /ər/ spelled *er, ir,* and *ur* in first syllables

Materials for Syllables and Affixes

Whiteboard Activities DVD-ROM, Sort 31

Teacher Resource CD-ROM, Sort 31 and Hurry Along! Game

Student Book, pages 121–124

Words

er	ir	ur	Oddball
person	firmly	purpose	spirit
perfect	dirty	further	merry
certain	birthday	hurry	
mermaid	thirsty	turtle	
perhaps	birdbath	furnish	
service	circle	during	
		Thursday	

Introduce/Model
Small Groups

- Use the whiteboard DVD or the CD word cards to introduce the words. Ask students what they notice about each of the words.

- Display the headers and have the students assist you as you complete the sort according to the spelling patterns.

- Guide students to understand that all the words have the same sound but different spellings: *er, ir,* and *ur.* Encourage students to discuss how the words are alike and different.

- Explain how the oddballs have one of the spelling patterns but different sounds.

Practice the Sort
Independent/Partner

- Have students use the Student Book or whiteboard DVD to say each word and use the grid to sort the words according to the spelling pattern.

- Have students check and explain their sorts.

Apply
Independent/Partner/Small Groups

- Read aloud the directions on Student Book p. 124. Have students write the words that contain *er, ir,* and *ur* in the first syllable in the appropriate column. Then have the students choose three words to use in sentences.

- **Game** Allow time for students to play Hurry Along!, which is on the CD.

Extend the Sort

Vocabulary **Word Of the Week:**

thirsty Ask students how they would act if they were thirsty. Once you have helped students define the word *thirsty*—"feeling a need for a drink"—explain that people also use *thirsty* to describe wanting things other than drinks. For example, a child who isn't allowed to go to school may be "thirsty for knowledge." A dog that isn't being taken care of may be "thirsty for love." Have students work in pairs to write sentences describing people or animals that are thirsty for things other than a drink.

ELL **English Language Learners**

Review the sort words with students. For each word, give students an opportunity to share the pronunciation and meaning if they already know it. Pronounce and define words they do not know, using pictures and movement as appropriate. Have students say the words after you, and provide pronunciation support as needed.

Teacher Tip

Point out to students that since the /ər/ sound has three different spellings, they will need to memorize the correct spelling of each sort word. Have students work as a class or in small groups to come up with memory aids to help them spell the sort words correctly.

Objectives

- To identify /ər/ and r-influenced ē spelling patterns
- To sort and spell words with er, ear, ere, and eer

Materials for Syllables and Affixes

Whiteboard Activities DVD-ROM, Sort 32

Teacher Resource CD-ROM, Sort 32 and Word Search Game

Student Book, pages 125–128

Words

er = /ur/	ear = /ur/	ear/ere/eer
sermon	earthquake	teardrop
serpent	learner	spearmint
hermit	pearly	yearbook
thermos	rehearse	appear
kernel	yearning	dreary
	earnest	sincere
	searching	adhere
		merely
		cheerful

Introduce/Model   *Small Groups*

- Use the whiteboard DVD or the CD word cards to introduce the words. Ask students what they notice about each of the words.

- Separate the /ər/ words into two categories (er and ear), and the r-influenced ē words into three categories (ear, ere, and eer). Display the headers and have students assist you in completing the sort.

- Guide students to hear how the r influences, or affects, the sounds of e in different spellings within accented syllables.

- Have students read aloud the words in each column and describe how the words are alike and how they are different.

Practice the Sort   *Independent/Partner*

- Have students use the Student Book or whiteboard DVD to say each word and use the grid to sort the words according to the r-influenced ē pattern they contain. Encourage students to point out the target spelling patterns and accented syllables.

- Have students check and explain their sorts.

Apply   *Independent/Partner/Small Groups*

- Read aloud the directions on Student Book p. 128. Have students write the words that contain /ər/ and r-influenced ē on the lines and then choose two words to use in sentences.

- **Game** Allow time for students to play Word Search, which is on the CD.

Extend the Sort

Vocabulary **Word Of the Week:**

hermit Ask if students have ever seen a hermit crab and, if so, to describe what it looks like and how it behaves. Discuss how a hermit crab has a shell in which it can hide. Help students to figure out from this that a hermit is someone who hides in some way and only comes out when it is safe. Have students use a dictionary to find out which language the word *hermit* comes from and the word's original meaning (Greek, "uninhabited").

ELL **English Language Learners**

Ensure that students are correctly stressing syllables in addition to pronouncing the sounds correctly. Lead them in asking several questions and answering with sentences to demonstrate usage. (*What can adhere to paper? Tape can adhere to paper*.)

Monitor Progress **Spell Check 4**

After completing Sort 32, administer Spell Check 4. See pp. 184–185 in this Teacher Resource Guide for instructions.

Sort 33 — Unaccented Final Syllable -le

Objectives
- To recognize the final syllable -le sound and spelling
- To sort and spell words with VCle and VCCle spelling patterns

Materials for Syllables and Affixes
- Whiteboard Activities DVD-ROM, Sort 33
- Teacher Resource CD-ROM, Sort 33 and Jungle Walk Game
- Student Book, pages 129–132

Words

VCle	VCCle doublet	VCCle
cradle	middle	tremble
able	settle	single
table	bottle	muscle
rifle	scribble	sample
bridle	paddle	jungle
bugle	rattle	handle
cable	battle	scramble

Introduce/Model *Small Groups*

- Use the whiteboard DVD or the CD word cards to introduce the words. Ask students what they notice about each of the words.
- Have students assist as you sort the words into three columns according to the syllable juncture pattern that precedes the -le ending.
- Guide students to see how the VCle pattern in *title* is divided after the vowel to make an open/long syllable (*ti-tle*), whereas the VCCle pattern in *little* and *simple* is divided between the consonants, resulting in closed/short syllables (*lit-tle* and *sim-ple*).
- Have students read aloud the words and describe how the words in each group are alike.

Practice the Sort *Independent/Partner*

- Have students use the Student Book or whiteboard DVD to say each word and use the grid to sort the words according to the -le pattern they contain.
- Have students check and explain their sorts.

Apply *Independent/Partner/Small Groups*

- Read aloud the directions on Student Book p. 132. Have students fill in the words that best complete each sentence, draw a line between the two syllables, and underline the accented syllables.
- **Game** Allow time for students to play Jungle Walk, which is on the CD.

Extend the Sort

Vocabulary — Word Of the Week:

tremble Have students predict the meaning of the word *tremble* from a sentence such as the following: *The kitten will likely tremble in fear when the big dog barks at it.* Explain that when people or animals tremble, they shake because of some cause such as fear, excitement, or cold. Point out the similarity between the words *tremble* and *tremors* and explain that a tremor is a shaking movement, such as an earthquake.

Alternative Sort: Noun, Verb, or Both?

Have students take turns sorting words according to part of speech: noun, verb, or noun/verb. Have students demonstrate usage in sentences. Words that can be both a noun and verb include *cradle, rifle, muscle, single, paddle, rattle, battle, tremble, sample, handle,* and *scribble*.

ELL English Language Learners

Have students illustrate and label the nouns on index cards. Then say simple sentences, using one word per sentence. Challenge students to hold up the appropriate card and to repeat the sentence. As understanding grows, use two words per sentence.

218 **Syllables and Affixes**

Unaccented Final Syllable /əl/ Spelled -*le*, -*el*, -*il*, -*al*

Objectives
- To recognize the final /əl/sound and its different spelling patterns
- To sort and spell words with a final -*le, -el, -il,* or -*al*

Materials for Syllables and Affixes

Whiteboard Activities DVD-ROM, Sort 34

Teacher Resource CD-ROM, Sort 34 and Race to the Bushel Game

Student Book, pages 133–136

Words

-le	-el	-il	-al	Oddball
saddle	level	April	total	fragile
couple	angel	fossil	metal	special
angle	novel	evil	signal	
needle	cancel	pupil	local	
struggle	jewel	council	journal	
bundle	vowel	stencil	pedal	

Introduce/Model   *Small Groups*

- Use the whiteboard DVD or the CD word cards to introduce the words. Ask students what they notice about the sound of the last syllable in each word.

- Place a word in each of the -*le, -el, -il,* and -*al* columns, and then challenge students to complete the sort.

- Reread the sort. Have students identify where the accent falls in the words.

- Guide students to summarize that final /əl/ can be spelled -*le -el, -il,* and -*al,* and that it appears in the unaccented syllable.

Practice the Sort   *Independent/Partner*

- Have students use the Student Book or whiteboard DVD to say each word and use the grid to sort the words several times according to the final /əl/ spelling patterns.

- Have students check and explain their sorts.

Apply   *Independent/Partner/Small Groups*

- Read aloud the directions on Student Book p. 136. Have students complete the activity.

- **Game** Allow time for students to play Race to the Bushel, which is on the CD.

Extend the Sort

Vocabulary **W**ord **O**f the **W**eek:

signal Point out that the blinkers on a car are called turn signals. Ask students to explain why this might be. (You're telling other drivers which way you're turning.) Have pairs draw labeled pictures of three other examples of signals and write explanations of why each is a signal.

Alternative Sort: Accented Syllables

Have students sort according to the vowel sound in the accented first syllable. (For example: short *a* words: *saddle, angle, cancel*) Remind students that *ou, ow,* and *ew* each make one vowel sound.

ELL **English Language Learners**

Through discussion, drawing, and example sentences, enhance students' understanding of *level* and *slanted; total* and *partial.* Together, compare the meanings of the words.

Unaccented Final Syllable /ər/ Spelled -er, -ar, -or

Objectives

- To recognize the final /ər/ syllable and its different spelling patterns
- To sort and spell words with final -er, -ar, or -or

Materials for Syllables and Affixes

Whiteboard Activities DVD-ROM, Sort 35

Teacher Resource CD-ROM, Sort 35 and Word Building Game

Student Book, pages 137–140

Words

-er	-ar	-or
brother	dollar	doctor
rather	solar	favor
cover	sugar	flavor
silver	grammar	mirror
weather	regular	motor
father	calendar	rumor
flower	popular	tractor
mother	cedar	harbor
after	lunar	error

Introduce/Model　　　　*Small Groups*

- Use the whiteboard DVD or the CD word cards to introduce the words. Ask students what they notice about each of the words.

- Explain to students that the words *cover, doctor,* and *collar* have final syllables that sound alike but are spelled differently. Using the three final /ər/ patterns (*-er, -ar,* and *-or*), have students assist you as you complete the sort. Read the words in the sort.

- Guide students to notice where the accent occurs in the words, to summarize that the final /ər/ can be spelled in different ways, and that it appears in the unaccented syllable.

- Have students read aloud the words and describe how the words in each group are alike.

Practice the Sort　　　*Independent/Partner*

- Have students use the Student Book or whiteboard DVD to say each word and use the grid to sort.

- Have students check and explain their sorts.

Apply　　　*Independent/Partner/Small Groups*

- Read aloud the directions on Student Book p. 140. Have students write words that contain final -er, -ar, or -or in the appropriate columns, draw a line between the two syllables, and underline the accented syllables. Have them choose three words to use in sentences.

- **Game** Allow time for students to play Word Building, which is on the CD.

Extend the Sort

Vocabulary **Word Of the Week:**

harbor Have students define *harbor* as a verb ("to hide or conceal while providing a place of protection") and as a noun ("an area of water that provides shelter for ships"). Explain that not all harbors are for ships and that the word *harbor* can be used to name any safe place. Have students write and share with the class sentences using *harbor* in its noun and verb forms.

ELL English Language Learners

After seems like an easy word, but Americans use it in several verb phrases that can confuse English language learners. The following may be discussed, practiced in sentences, and restated: *look after*—"take care of"; *take after*—"resemble"; *name after*—"name in honor of"; and *clean up after*—"tidy someone's mess" or "fix someone's mistake."

Teacher Tip

Make sure students understand that the final /ər/ sound is not the same as the sounds for *er, ar,* and *or* in the accented part of a word. Clarify with the word *harbor* and other words such as *farther, armor, farmer, herder, tartar,* and *porter.*

Agents and Comparatives

Objectives

- To recognize words for people who do things (agents) and adjectives that compare (comparatives)
- To sort and spell agent and comparative words with the suffixes -e and -or

Materials for Syllables and Affixes

- Whiteboard Activities DVD-ROM, Sort 36

- Teacher Resource CD-ROM, Sort 36 and Word Meaning Game

- Student Book, pages 141–144

Words

People Who Do Things

dreamer	creator	farmer
swimmer	sailor	shopper
voter	visitor	writer
driver	director	editor
jogger	governor	juror

Words to Compare

smaller	older	sooner
fresher	younger	stronger
smoother	later	brighter

Introduce/Model
Small Groups

- Use the whiteboard DVD or the CD word cards to introduce the words. Ask students what they notice about each of the words.

- Explain to students that words such as *bigger* and *older* are alike (they are adjectives with the suffix *-er* and can be used to compare). Explain to students that *dancer* and *farmer* are alike (they refer to people who do things and are called agents).

- Display the headers, start the sort, and have students assist you as you complete the sort.

- Guide students to notice what is alike and different about all the agent, or people, words. (They have the same suffix sound but different spellings.)

Practice the Sort
Independent/Partner

- Have students use the Student Book or whiteboard DVD to say each word and use the grid to sort the words according to meaning and suffix spelling. Point out how the base word changed before the suffix was added (double, *e*-drop, or no change).

- Have students check and explain their sorts.

Apply
Independent/Partner/Small Groups

- Read aloud the directions on Student Book p. 144. Have students make new words by adding the suffix *-er* or *-or*, write the new words, and decide if each word is an agent or comparative.

- **Game** Allow time for students to play Word Meaning, which is on the CD.

Extend the Sort

Vocabulary **Word Of the Week:**

editor Have students define *editor* ("a person who edits or checks something to make sure it is ready to be published"). Discuss different kinds of editors such as newspaper, film, or sound editors and ask students what tasks they think that each kind of editor would perform.

Alternative Sort: Syllable Sort

Have students further sort the words by the spelling of their final unaccented syllable (*-er* or *-or*), or by the number of syllables (two or three).

ELL **English Language Learners**

Have students follow your lead in pantomiming agents and comparatives. Encourage them to use nearby objects or people for actual comparisons. Have students explain their actions using the sort words.

Teacher Tip

Challenge students to name agents and use one or more comparatives in a sentence, such as "Josh the *jogger* ran *faster* than *younger* runners. Sadie the *sailor* sailed *sooner* than Sid. *Farmer* Farley sold *fresher, smoother* vegetables."

Final Syllable /ər/ Spelled -cher, -ture, -sure, -ure

Objectives

- To recognize /ər/ and its spelling patterns at the ends of words
- To sort and spell words with final -cher, -ture, -sure, or -ure

Materials for Syllables and Affixes

Whiteboard Activities DVD-ROM, Sort 37

Teacher Resource CD-ROM, Sort 37 and Word Sort Game

Student Book, pages 145–148

Words

-cher = /chur/	-ture = /chur/	-sure = /zhur/	-ure= /yur/	Oddball
rancher	nature	pleasure	failure	senior
teacher	capture	leisure	obscure	danger
pitcher	future	treasure	secure	pressure
stretcher	mixture			
marcher	posture			
	culture			
	pasture			

Introduce/Model   Small Groups

- Use the whiteboard DVD or the CD word cards to introduce the words. Ask students what they notice about each of the words.

- Display the headers and explain that the slash marks enclose each sound. Say the first word in each column and stress the sound in the final syllable.

- Have students assist as you complete the sort by matching both sounds and spelling patterns. Point out that senior and danger are oddballs because they have similar final sounds but different spellings, and pressure is an oddball because it has one of the spelling patterns, but a different sound.

- Have students read aloud the words. Have them discuss how the words in each column are alike and different.

Practice the Sort   Independent/Partner

- Have students use the Student Book or whiteboard DVD to say each word and use the grid to sort.

Apply   Independent/Partner/Small Groups

- Read aloud the directions on Student Book p. 148. Have students write words with final -cher, -ture, -sure, and -ure in the correct boxes.

- **Game** Allow time for students to play Word Sort, which is on the CD.

Extend the Sort

Vocabulary Word Of the Week:

senior Explain to students that senior comes from the same Latin word that means "old," as do the words senate and senile. Ask students to look up the definitions for these words and discover how their meanings relate to the idea of being old.

Alternative Sort: Vowel Patterns

Remove the torture card. Have students focus on the accented syllables and sort the words into four columns: short vowel sound spelled by one letter, short vowel sound spelled by two letters, long vowel sound spelled by one letter, and long vowel sound spelled by two letters.

ELL English Language Learners

Check that students are correctly saying the target sounds. If any are problematic, show how they are produced using the mouth, tongue, and breath. Practice as in "lei-sure-sure-sure, leisure."

Teacher Tip

As students become comfortable with this week's sort, have each of them make a set of -cher, -ture, -sure, and -ure cards. Call out words and challenge students to hold up the correct spelling pattern for the word.

Unaccented Final Syllable /ən/ Spelled
-en, -on, -an, -ain

Objectives

- To recognize final /ən/ and its different spelling patterns
- To sort and spell words with final -en, -on, -an, or -ain

Materials for Syllables and Affixes

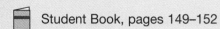 Whiteboard Activities DVD-ROM, Sort 38

Teacher Resource CD-ROM, Sort 38 and Word Building Game

Student Book, pages 149–152

Words

-en	-on	-an	-ain	Oddball
eleven	unison	woman	captain	mission
oxygen	gallon	organ	bargain	
heaven	ribbon	orphan	fountain	
chosen	apron	slogan	curtain	
abdomen	bacon	urban	certain	
children	pardon		villain	

Introduce/Model
Small Groups

- Use the whiteboard DVD or the CD word cards to introduce the words. Ask students what they notice about each of the words.

- Have students brainstorm ways the words in the sort are alike and/or different. Guide them to see that all the words have the same sound in the final syllable but different spellings.

- Point out that *mission* is an oddball because it has the same sound in the unaccented final syllable but a unique spelling.

- Display the headers with a word in each column and have students assist you as you complete the sort by the final spelling pattern. Encourage students to compare spellings of the unaccented syllables.

Practice the Sort
Independent/Partner

- Have students use the Student Book or whiteboard DVD to say each word and use the grid to sort the words according to the spelling of the final sound.

- Have students check and explain their sorts.

Apply
Independent/Partner/Small Groups

- Read aloud the directions on Student Book p. 152. Have students choose -en, -on, -an, or -ain to best complete each word, write the new word, and read it aloud. Students then choose three words and use them in sentences.

- **Game** Allow time for students to play Word Building, which is on the CD.

Extend the Sort

Vocabulary **W**ord **O**f the **W**eek:

mission Ask students to define the word *mission* ("an errand or task that people are sent somewhere to do"). Challenge pairs to come up with a list of different ways the word *mission* can be used, such as *mission to Mars, being on a mission,* and *having a mission in life.*

Alternative Sort: Word Use

Direct students to sort the cards as *Nouns* and *Others*. Ask which words can be used two ways. Have students make duplicate word cards for these words, sort them, and create sentences.

ELL English Language Learners

Review the cards by having students repeat each word after you. Provide blank cards for them to illustrate troublesome words. Honor students' choices of words they need to practice, but add any others that you think are necessary. Challenge students to match the corresponding word and picture cards and to make up sentences with one or two words at a time.

Teacher Tip

Suggest that when students hear the /ən/ sound in a word and they aren't sure how to spell it, they should first try one of the more common spellings (-en or -on).

Unaccented Initial Syllables *a-*, *de-*, *be-*

Objectives

- To recognize unaccented syllable patterns
- To sort and spell words beginning with *a-*, *de-*, and *be-*

Materials for Syllables and Affixes

Whiteboard Activities DVD-ROM, Sort 39

Teacher Resource CD-ROM, Sort 39 and Spin and Win Game

Student Book, pages 153–156

Words

a-	*de-*	*be-*	Oddball
another	degree	believe	divide
awhile	depend	between	direct
among	desire	beneath	upon
aboard	develop	because	
against	defend	begun	
afraid	delete	behavior	
aloud	decision	beforehand	
astonish			
agenda			

Introduce/Model
Small Groups

- Use the whiteboard DVD or the CD word cards to introduce the words. Ask students what they notice about each of the words.

- Guide students to focus on the target initial spelling patterns in the words and discover that initial *a-*, *de-*, and *be-* all appear in the unaccented syllable.

- Have students assist you as you demonstrate how to sort the words by their initial syllables.

- Guide students to notice how the initial syllable may be pronounced with a slightly different vowel sound when the word is said in isolation or when thinking about the spelling.

Practice the Sort
Independent/Partner

- Have students use the Student Book or whiteboard DVD to say each word and use the grid to sort the words according to the initial spelling patterns.

- Have students check and explain their sorts.

Apply
Independent/Partner/Small Groups

- Read aloud the directions on Student Book p. 156. Have students choose the initial syllable *a-*, *de-*, or *be-* that best completes the word. Have them choose two words and use each in a sentence.

- **Game** Allow time for students to play Spin and Win, which is on the CD.

Extend the Sort

Vocabulary **W**ord **O**f the **W**eek:

desire Explain that the word *desire* ("to want something very seriously or to a strong degree") can be used as both a noun and a verb. *A person's greatest desire could be a good education. The countries in conflict might desire peace and sign a treaty.* Ask students to write sentences that use *desire* as both a noun and a verb.

Alternative Sort: Students' Choice

Challenge students to define their own categories for the words. If they have difficulty deciding upon a second sort, suggest categories of words that help tell where, when, why, and how, plus oddball.

ELL **English Language Learners**

Common uses of *against* may confuse English language learners. Explain the word in context by sharing several example sentences, such as these: *The desk is against the wall.* ("touching") *Ali's team will play against Omar's team.* ("in opposition") *A boat can sail against the wind.* ("in the opposite direction of")

Monitor Progress **Spell Check 5**

After completing Sort 39, administer Spell Check 5. See pp. 184–185 in this Teacher Resource Guide for instructions.

Initial Hard and Soft *c* and *g*

Objectives

- To associate sounds of initial *c* and *g* with different vowels
- To sort and spell words with initial *c* and *g*

Materials for Syllables and Affixes

Whiteboard Activities DVD-ROM, Sort 40

Teacher Resource CD-ROM, Sort 40 and Double Crazy Eights Game

Student Book, pages 157–160

Words

Soft *c*	Soft *g*	Hard *c*	Hard *g*
circle	gymnast	common	gossip
central	giraffe	camel	golden
century	genius	college	garage
cyclist	general	custom	gutter
cider	gingerbread	collect	govern
cereal	giant	cavern	gurgle

Introduce/Model *Small Groups*

- Use the whiteboard DVD or the CD word cards to introduce the words. Ask students what they notice about each of the words. Guide students to notice that all the words begin with either *c* or *g*.

- Sort only words that begin with *c*. Help students notice that sometimes initial *c* sounds like /s/ and is "soft," and sometimes it sounds like /k/ and is "hard." Have students assist as you complete the sort.

- Sort only words that begin with *g*. Help students notice that sometimes initial *g* sounds like /j/ and is "soft," and sometimes it sounds like /g/ and is "hard." Have students assist as you complete the sort.

- Guide students to see that *c* and *g* are usually soft when followed by *e, i,* or *y,* and hard when followed by *a, o,* or *u.*

Practice the Sort *Independent/Partner*

- Have students use the Student Book or whiteboard DVD to say each word and use the grid to sort.

- Have students check and explain their sorts.

Apply *Independent/Partner/Small Groups*

- Read aloud the directions on Student Book p. 160. Have students complete each sentence with a word from the box, underline the vowel that follows the *c* or *g,* and circle the word if it has a soft *c* or *g.*

- **Game** Allow time for students to play Double Crazy Eights, which is on the CD.

Extend the Sort

Vocabulary **W**ord **O**f the **W**eek:

gossip Ask students to define *gossip.* They probably will give its definition as a verb: "to reveal personal or sensational facts about others." Provide students with an example that uses *gossip* as a noun, such as *According to the latest gossip, Brad and Sasha were no longer friends.* Ask them to predict the meaning of the noun form from this sentence ("rumor, chatty talk").

Alternative Sort: Second Letter

Combine all the soft *c* and *g* words and all the hard *c* and *g* words and draw attention to the vowel in the first syllable of these words. Suggest that students try sorting the words by the vowel that follows the initial letter.

ELL English Language Learners

Using *common* and *general* can be tricky. Each word can define the other, and the phrases "in common" and "in general" are similar. Help students understand the difference by providing examples: *We have things in common.* ("alike or shared") *In general, we enjoy this magazine.* ("usually")

Sort 41 — Final -s and Soft c and g

Objectives

- To identify *s*, *c*, and *g* spelling patterns in final syllables
- To sort and spell words with final *-ce, -ss, ge,* or *-age*

Materials for Syllables and Affixes

- Whiteboard Activities DVD-ROM, Sort 41
- Teacher Resource CD-ROM, Sort 41 and Challenge! Game
- Student Book, pages 161–164

Words

-ce = /s/	-ss = /s/	ge = /j/	-age = /ij/
police	princess	fidget	garbage
sentence	actress	gadget	manage
distance	address	surgeon	luggage
office	compass	challenge	package
science	possess	arrange	village
practice	express		message
			courage

Introduce/Model *Small Groups*

- Use the whiteboard DVD or the CD word cards to introduce the words. Ask students what they notice about each of the words.
- Have students assist as you sort according to broad final syllable /s/ and /j/ categories.
- Guide students to summarize how words in each column are alike by the sound and different by the spelling pattern for the sound. (Final /s/ can be spelled *-ce* and *-ss,* and the soft sound of *g* is always followed by the letter *e*.)
- Display the headers and have students assist as you complete the sort according to the final /j/ and /s/ spelling pattern.

Practice the Sort *Independent/Partner*

- Have students use the Student Book or whiteboard DVD to say each word and use the grid to sort the words according to the final spelling and sound patterns.
- Have students check and explain their sorts.

Apply *Independent/Partner/Small Groups*

- Read aloud the directions on Student Book p. 164. Have students write words that contain *-ce, -ss, ge,* or *-age* in the final syllable in the correct column.
- **Game** Allow time for students to play Challenge!, which is on the CD.

Extend the Sort

Vocabulary Word Of the Week:

address Ask students to define *address* as a noun ("location of something") and as a verb ("speak or write to someone"). Point out that the stress changes from the first to the second syllable depending on whether the word is used as a noun (**ad**dress) or verb (ad**dress**). Offer sentences using *address* as a noun and as a verb. Have students identify how *address* is used in each case.

Alternative Sort: About People

Invite students to make a sort about people without giving them the categories. They may discover the categories of words for people, what people can do, and what people can have. Encourage them to provide a sentence that proves the category placement as they sort each word.

ELL English Language Learners

As a group, discuss, think of synonyms for, and make contextual sentences for the verb *manage* and nouns *gadget* and *courage*. (*manage/*involves use of some skill; *gadget/*small and handy for one task; *courage/*danger or a great challenge is present) Then practice posing questions and answering. For example, *Is a car a gadget?* (No, a car is too big to be a gadget.)

226 Syllables and Affixes

More Words With *g*

Objectives
- To identify spelling patterns of hard *g*
- To sort and spell words with *gu-*, *-gue*, and *-g*

Materials for Syllables and Affixes

Whiteboard Activities DVD-ROM, Sort 42

Teacher Resource CD-ROM, Sort 42 and Word Search Game

Student Book, pages 165–168

Words

gu-	*-gue*	*-g*	Oddball
guard	vague	zigzag	gauge
guitar	league	shrug	language
guide	fatigue	iceberg	argue
guilty	plague	dialog	strong
guest	intrigue	catalog	penguin
guidance			

Introduce/Model
Small Groups

- Use the whiteboard DVD or the CD word cards to introduce the words. Ask students what they notice about each of the words.

- Leave out the oddballs, and work with students to sort according to broad "beginning hard *g*" and "ending hard *g*" categories. Ask them what they notice about the spelling of hard *g*.

- Display the headers and have students assist as you divide the "ending hard *g*" column into *-gue* and *-g* words. Guide students to generalize that silent *u* is sometimes used to keep the *g* hard before other vowels, such as *a, e,* and *i*.

- Have students read aloud the oddball words and tell why each belongs in that category.

Practice the Sort
Independent/Partner

- Have students use the Student Book or whiteboard DVD to say each word and use the grid to sort the words according to the *g* sound and spelling.

- Have students check and explain their sorts.

Apply
Independent/Partner/Small Groups

- Read aloud the directions on Student Book p. 168. Have students choose and write the word that best completes each sentence.

- **Game** Allow time for students to play Word Search, which is on the CD.

Extend the Sort

Vocabulary **Word Of the Week:**
dialog Make sure students understand that a *dialog* is a conversation between two people. Explain that the prefix *di-* in *dialog* means "two." Have groups look up the meaning of *monologue* ("a long speech by one speaker"). Ask students to explain how the meaning of *monologue* differs from that of *dialog* and how they can tell the two words apart.

ELL **English Language Learners**
Discuss the *-gue* words *league, fatigue, plague,* and *intrigue*. Challenge students to add to their existing sort cards a simple illustration and a description or synonym for each of these words.

Teacher Tip
Ensure that students understand how to sort words in which *u* makes a /w/ sound or a long *u* sound with /g/ instead of being silent (as in the oddball words *language, argue,* and *penguin*). Help students understand that English has many exceptions to patterns.

Objectives

- To identify /k/ spelling patterns in the middle and at the end of words
- To sort and spell words with *ck, -ic,* and *-x*

Materials for Syllables and Affixes

🖥 Whiteboard Activities DVD-ROM, Sort 43

💿 Teacher Resource CD-ROM, Sort 43 and Word Building Game

📕 Student Book, pages 169–172

Words

-ck	ck	-ic	-x	Oddball
quick	pocket	traffic	index	stomach
hammock	nickel	topic	complex	
attack	pickle	picnic	perplex	
unlock	buckle	metric	shoebox	
racetrack	ticket	electric		
struck	jacket	plastic		
	rocket	specific		
		fabric		

Introduce/Model   *Small Groups*

- Use the whiteboard DVD or the CD word cards to introduce the words. Ask students what they notice about each of the words.

- Place a word in each of the *-ck, ck, -ic, -x,* and oddball columns, and then have students assist as you complete the sort.

- Have students read aloud the words. Guide them to notice the /k/ sound in each word (/ks/ in the case of *-x*).

- Help students recognize that the spelling of /k/ and /ks/ varies. Point out how *ck* can spell /k/ in the middle or at the end of a word. Lead students to notice that one-syllable words that end in /k/ are always spelled with *-k* or *-ck* and most two-syllable words end in *-ic* except for compound words.

Practice the Sort   *Independent/Partner*

- Have students use the Student Book or whiteboard DVD to say each word and use the grid to sort.

- Have students check and explain their sorts.

Apply   *Independent/Partner/Small Groups*

- Read aloud the directions on Student Book p. 172. Have students write words that contain the /k/ sound spelled as *ck, -ic,* or *-x* in the appropriate column.

- **Game** Allow time for students to play Word Building, which is on the CD.

Extend the Sort

Vocabulary **Word Of the Week:**

metric Have students brainstorm units of the metric system, such as centimeter, millimeter, and so on. Then ask them to think of other words that end in *meter,* such as *thermometer, barometer,* and *odometer*. Discuss that all of these words have to do with measuring. Then have students create and draw a picture of a meter of their own.

Alternative Sort: Verbs and Adjectives

Challenge students to find the words that can be sorted as verbs (actions) and those that can be sorted as adjectives (describing words). You might provide sentence aids: "Someone can __" for verbs and "Something is __" for adjectives. After the sort, have students replace *someone* and *something* as they use each verb and adjective in a longer sentence.

ELL English Language Learners

Develop understanding of the meanings and uses of *index* and *complex*. Show a book's *index* (noun), *index* cards (adjective), and then how the cards can be put in order to *index* (verb). For *complex*, discuss and then have students sketch a *complex* machine (adjective) and a housing *complex* (noun).

Objectives

- To recognize and compare the /qw/ and /k/ sounds spelled *qu*
- To sort and spell words with *qu*

Materials for Syllables and Affixes

Whiteboard Activities DVD-ROM, Sort 44

Teacher Resource CD-ROM, Sort 44 and Quick Clues Game

Student Book, pages 173–176

Words

1st Syllable	2nd Syllable	qu = /k/
quality	frequent	racquet
squirrel	equipment	mosquito
squirming	equator	conquer
quadrant	banquet	technique
quotation	inquire	critique
quizzes	liquid	
queasy	sequence	
qualify	sequel	
	request	

Introduce/Model *Small Groups*

- Use the whiteboard DVD or the CD word cards to introduce the words. Ask students what they notice about each of the words.

- Lead students to notice how the letters *qu* spell both the /qw/ sound in *quality* and the /k/ sound in *racquet*.

- Have students listen carefully as you read each word and assist as you sort the words into two columns: /qw/ and /k/.

- Say *quality*, emphasizing /kw/ in the first syllable. Then say *frequent*, emphasizing /kw/ in the second syllable. Have students read the /qw/ words aloud and identify which syllable the *qu* appears in.

Practice the Sort *Independent/Partner*

- Have students use the Student Book or whiteboard DVD to say each word and use the grid to sort the words according to the syllable and sound of *qu*.

- Have students check and explain their sorts.

Apply *Independent/Partner/Small Groups*

- Read aloud the directions on Student Book p. 176. Have students choose a word from the box that best completes the sentence, write it on the line, and draw a line between the syllables in each word.

- **Game** Allow time for students to play Quick Clues, which is on the CD.

Extend the Sort

Vocabulary **Word Of the Week:**

inquire Have students define *inquire* ("to try to find out through questions or to search for answers"). Explain that *inquire* is related to *quest*, which means "a search for something." List *query, question,* and *inquest.* Have students explore how these words are related to each other and to the word *inquire.*

Alternative Sort: Accenting

Have students sort the words into two categories: *qu* in an accented syllable and *qu* in an unaccented syllable. Direct them to underline each accented syllable and to check a dictionary for words they are uncertain about.

ELL English Language Learners

Guide discussion to clarify meaning differences of *inquire* and verb usage of *quizzes* and *request.* Model making example questions (to inquire and quiz) and statements (to request). Then give students several opportunities to demonstrate inquiring, quizzing, and requesting.

Teacher Tip

This sort's words offer a good opportunity for students to practice creating alliterative sentences. For example, *Quinn quizzes Quincy about a quotation.*

Words With Silent Consonants

Objectives
- To identify silent consonants in words
- To sort and spell words with a silent *t, g, w, k, h,* or *gh*

Materials for Syllables and Affixes

Whiteboard Activities DVD-ROM, Sort 45

Teacher Resource CD-ROM, Sort 45 and Word Search Game

Student Book, pages 177–180

Words		
Silent *t*	**Silent *g***	**Silent *w***
fasten	resign	wreckage
listen	assignment	wrestle
glisten	campaign	answer
soften	gnarl	sword
Silent *k*	**Silent *h***	**Silent *gh***
knowledge	honor	thought
doorknob	rhyme	brought
kneepad	rhythm	bought
knockout	khaki	though

Introduce/Model
Small Groups

- Use the whiteboard DVD or the CD word cards to introduce the words. Ask students what they notice about each of the words.

- Guide students to notice that each word has a silent consonant and that the focus of the sort is silent consonants, not vowels.

- Place a word in each of the columns headed with a silent letter, and have students assist as you complete the sort.

- Read the sort and discuss the meaning of each word. Have students look up definitions of unfamiliar words.

Practice the Sort
Independent/Partner

- Have students use the Student Book or whiteboard DVD to say each word and use the grid to sort the words according to silent consonants.

- Have students check and explain their sorts.

Apply
Independent/Partner/Small Groups

- Read aloud the directions on Student Book p. 180. Have students choose the silent letter(s) *(t, g, w, k, h, or gh)* that best completes the word, write the new word on the line, and use three words in a sentence.

- **Game** Allow time for students to play Word Search, which is on the CD.

Extend the Sort

Vocabulary **Word Of the Week:**
campaign Explain that the verb *campaign* means "to participate in a series of organized, planned actions for a particular purpose." Have students suggest general categories of things or causes they can campaign for, such as "Animals," "Earth," "School," and "Safety," and list their suggestions.

Alternative Sort: Schwa Review
Remind students that the vowel sound in unaccented syllables of words such as *angle, cover,* and *mitten* is different than short and long vowel sounds. Have them sort words that contain /ə/. Assist as needed while students put the words into new columns: "/ə/ as in *angle*"; "/ər/ as in *cover*"; "/ən/ as in *mitten*."

ELL English Language Learners
Clarify the meanings of *wreckage* and *knowledge* and practice using these nouns. Explain that the words are unusual nouns because they do not have plurals. You may wish to explain what is meant by "common knowledge" and "to the best of my knowledge."

Words With *gh* and *ph*

Objectives

- To identify the sound of /f/ spelled *gh* and *ph* and to review silent *gh*
- To sort and spell words with *gh* and *ph*

Materials for Syllables and Affixes

Whiteboard Activities DVD-ROM, Sort 46

Teacher Resource CD-ROM, Sort 46 and Bright Night Game

Student Book, pages 181–184

Words

ph-	*ph*	*-gh* = /f/	Silent *gh*
physics	elephant	cough	naughty
phantom	nephew	tough	taught
photocopy	dolphin	rough	caught
photograph	trophy	laughter	fought
phonics	telephone		height
	homophone		
	paragraph		

Introduce/Model
Small Groups

- Use the whiteboard DVD or the CD word cards to introduce the words. Ask students what they notice about each of the words.

- Remind students of silent *gh*. Ask them how some of the words with *gh* in this sort are different.

- Have students assist you with a three-column sort, with headers *ph*, *gh* = /f/, and silent *gh* words. Guide students to summarize that *ph* and *gh* represent /f/ and *gh* is often silent in the middle of words.

- Sort the words in the *ph* column into those words with the /f/ sound at the beginning or middle/end of a word.

Practice the Sort
Independent/Partner

- Have students use the Student Book or whiteboard DVD to say each word and use the grid to sort the words several times according to the *ph-*, *ph*, *-gh* = /f/, and silent *gh* categories.

- Have students check and explain their sorts.

Apply
Independent/Partner/Small Groups

- Read aloud the directions on Student Book p. 184. Have students write words on the lines that contain *ph, gh* = /f/, and silent *gh*. Have them choose three words and use each in a sentence.

- **Game** Allow time for students to play Bright Night, which is on the CD.

Extend the Sort

Vocabulary **Word Of the Week:**

photocopy Have students draw a word web. Ask them to write *photo* and its meaning in the center. At the end of a line, students can write the word *photocopy* and its definition. Help students think of other related words to add and discuss, such as *photograph, telephoto,* and *photosynthesis*.

ELL **English Language Learners**

Using verb tenses may be practiced with *cough, taught, caught,* and *fought*. Model sentences using the present and present progressive tenses of the words (i.e., *cough[s], [are/is] coughing*) and stating what already happened with the past and past progressive tenses (*coughed, [were/was] coughing*).

Monitor Progress **Spell Check 6**

After completing Sort 46, administer Spell Check 6. See pp. 184–185 in this Teacher Resource Guide for instructions.

Objectives

- To identify the prefixes *re-* and *un-* and understand how they influence the meanings of words
- To sort and spell words beginning with *re-* and *un-*

Materials for Syllables and Affixes

📋 Whiteboard Activities DVD-ROM, Sort 47

💿 Teacher Resource CD-ROM, Sort 47 and Spin and Spell Game

📚 Student Book, pages 185–188

Words		
re-	***un-***	**Oddball**
recopy	unkind	uncle
recycle	unwrap	reptile
refinish	unselfish	rescue
refill	unbutton	
rewrite	unhappy	
retrace	unpack	
retake	unfair	
return	uneven	
review	unequal	
remodel	unbeaten	

Introduce/Model   *Small Groups*

- Use the whiteboard DVD or the CD word cards to introduce the words. Ask students what they notice about each of the words.

- Place a word in each of the *re-* and *un-* columns, and then have students assist as you complete the sort.

- Read the sort and discuss the meaning of each word. Point out that the meanings of base words, such as *write* and *fill,* are changed by the addition of a prefix such as *re-.*

- Guide students to arrive at some conclusions about what the prefixes mean. (*Re-* means "again" and *un-* means "not" or "the opposite of.") Discuss why the words in the Oddball category don't fit into the prefix categories.

Practice the Sort   *Independent/Partner*

- Have students use the Student Book or whiteboard DVD to say each word and use the grid to sort the words according to their prefixes.

- Have students check and explain their sorts.

Apply   *Independent/Partner/Small Groups*

- Read aloud the directions on Student Book p. 188. Have students write the meanings of the prefixes. Then have them make new words by adding the prefix *re-* or *un-* to the base words.

- **Game** Allow time for students to play Spin and Spell, which is on the CD.

Extend the Sort

Vocabulary **Word Of the Week:**

refinish Help students identify the prefix *re-* and understand that it means "again." If students need help understanding *finish,* provide an example sentence: *The finish on the table was dark brown.* Make sure students understand that *refinish* means "to put another finish on something."

Alternative Sort: Parts of Speech

Have students sort the words according to their parts of speech: verbs, nouns, and adjectives.

ELL English Language Learners

Help students make generalizations about words with *re-* and *un-* prefixes. (*Re-* usually means "again," and *un-* usually means "not" or "the opposite of.") Make sure students understand that not all words beginning with *un-* or *re-* are base words with a prefix (e.g., *uncle, reptile, rescue*).

Teacher Tip

Set up a classroom chart that lists this sort's prefixes and their meanings. Be sure to leave room to include additional prefixes from upcoming sorts and students' suggestions.

Objectives

- To identify prefixes *dis-, mis-,* and *pre-* and understand how they influence the meanings of words
- To sort and spell words beginning with *dis-, mis-,* and *pre-*

Materials for Syllables and Affixes

Whiteboard Activities DVD-ROM, Sort 48

Teacher Resource CD-ROM, Sort 48 and Spin and Spell Game

Student Book, pages 189–192

Words

dis-	*mis-*	*pre-*	Oddball
dislike	mistreat	prefix	precious
disable	mismatch	premature	mister
disobey	misplace	preteen	distant
dishonest	misbehave	preview	
disloyal	misjudge	preheat	
disappear	miscount	pretest	
displace	mistrust	precaution	

Introduce/Model
Small Groups

- Use the whiteboard DVD or the CD word cards to introduce the words. Ask students what they notice about each of the words.

- Place a word in each of the *dis-, mis-,* and *pre-* columns. Have students assist as you complete the sort.

- Read the sort and discuss the meaning of each word. Point out that the meanings of base words, such as *like* and *obey,* are changed by the addition of a prefix such as *dis-.*

- Guide students to arrive at some conclusions about what the prefixes mean. (*Dis-* means "not," *mis-* means "badly," and *pre-* means "before.") Discuss why the words in the Oddball category don't fit into the prefix categories.

Practice the Sort
Independent/Partner

- Have students use the Student Book or whiteboard DVD to say each word and use the grid to sort the words according to their prefixes.

- Have students check and explain their sorts.

Apply
Independent/Partner/Small Groups

- Read aloud the directions on Student Book p. 192. Have students make new words by adding the prefix *dis-, mis-,* or *pre-* to the base words. Then have students choose three derived words and write a definition for each.

- **Game** Allow time for students to play Spin and Spell, which is on the CD.

Extend the Sort

Vocabulary 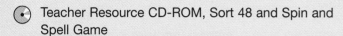 **W**ord **O**f the **W**eek:

precaution Remind students that the prefix *pre-* means "before." Ask them to define the word *precaution* ("something done beforehand to avoid danger or problems"). Have students write descriptions of precautions they might take in preparing for certain situations, such as traveling to a place they have never been before.

Alternative Sort: Base Words

Have students look at the base word in each of the sort words and consider whether some base words could be used with more than one of the prefixes from the sort (for example, *recopy* and *miscopy*).

ELL English Language Learners

Enhance students' understanding of *premature* ("something that happens before the proper time"). *A premature baby is born before the normal nine months of pregnancy.* Provide students with common phrases, such as "a premature decision," "acting prematurely," and "a premature arrival." Have students use these phrases to make their own sentences.

Teacher Tip

Add prefixes *dis-, mis-,* and *pre-* to the class chart and have students add their definitions.

Objectives

- To identify prefixes *ex-, non-, in-,* and *fore-* and understand how they influence the meanings of words
- To sort and spell words beginning with *ex-, non-, in-,* and *fore-*

Materials for Syllables and Affixes

⬜ Whiteboard Activities DVD-ROM, Sort 49

💿 Teacher Resource CD-ROM, Sort 49 and Pick a Card Game

📕 Student Book, pages 193–196

Words

ex-	*non-*	*fore-*	*in-* ("not")	*in-* ("in" or "into")
extend	nonfiction	forearm	incorrect	indoor
explore	nonstop	forehead	indecent	insight
express	nonfat	foresee	inhuman	income
exclude	nonprofit	foreshadow		
explode	nonskid	foremost		
expand				
extra				

Introduce/Model
Small Groups

- Use the whiteboard DVD or the CD word cards to introduce the words. Ask students what they notice about each of the words.

- Place a word in each of the *ex-, non-, in-,* and *fore-* columns, and then have students assist as you complete the sort.

- Read the sort and discuss the meaning of each word. Point out that the meanings of base words, such as *stop* and *fiction*, are changed by the addition of a prefix such as *non-*.

- Guide students to arrive at some conclusions about what the prefixes mean. (*Ex-* means "out"; *non-* means "not"; *in-* means "not," "in," or "into"; *fore-* means "before" or "in front of.")

Practice the Sort
Independent/Partner

- Have students use the Student Book or whiteboard DVD to say each word and use the grid to sort the words according to their prefixes.

- Have students check and explain their sorts.

Apply
Independent/Partner/Small Groups

- Read aloud the directions on Student Book p. 196. Have students write the meanings of the prefixes. Then have students make new words by adding the prefix *ex-, non-, in-,* or *fore-* to the base words.

- **Game** Allow time for students to play Pick a Card, which is on the CD.

Extend the Sort

Vocabulary **Word Of the Week:**

foreshadow Define *foreshadow* as "to indicate beforehand or be a warning of." Provide this example: *The dark clouds in the sky foreshadow a rainstorm.* Explain that authors often foreshadow events by including hints about something that will happen later. Discuss ways that events can be foreshadowed (by describing the setting, character relationships, or character dialogue).

Alternative Sort: Do or Describe?

Have students sort the words according to whether they are words that tell things people can do or words people can use to describe something.

ELL **English Language Learners**

Pair English language learners with more proficient English speakers as they complete the sort. Encourage the English language learners to say the words after their partners. Then have students say the words together.

Teacher Tip

Explain to students that all words in this sort have prefixes, but the rest of the word is not always a base word. For example, students will know that *exit* means "to go out" even though *-it* does not have a related meaning.

Prefixes *uni-*, *bi-*, *tri-*, and Other Numbers

Objectives

- To identify prefixes *uni-*, *bi-*, and *tri-*, and other numbers and understand how they influence the meanings of words
- To sort and spell words beginning with *uni-*, *bi-*, and *tri-*, and other number prefixes

Materials for Syllables and Affixes

Whiteboard Activities DVD-ROM, Sort 50

 Teacher Resource CD-ROM, Sort 50 and Spin and Spell Game

Student Book, pages 197–200

Words

uni-	*bi-*	*tri-*	Other
unity	biweekly	trilogy	pentagon
unicorn	bisect	triangle	octagon
unique	bilingual	triple	octopus
union		triplet	October
unison		tripod	
uniform		trio	
universe			

Introduce/Model
Small Groups

- Use the whiteboard DVD or the CD word cards to introduce the words. Ask students what they notice about each of the words.

- Place a word in each of the *uni-*, *bi-*, *tri-*, and *Other* columns, and then have students assist as you complete the sort.

- Read the sort and discuss the meaning of each word. Point out that the meanings of base words, such as *weekly*, are changed by the addition of a prefix such as *bi-*.

- Guide students to arrive at some conclusions about what the prefixes mean. (*Uni-* means "one"; *bi-* means "two"; *tri-* means "three"; *pent-* means "five"; and *oct-* means "eight.")

Practice the Sort
Independent/Partner

- Have students use the Student Book or whiteboard DVD to say each word and use the grid to sort the words according to their prefixes.

- Have students check and explain their sorts.

Apply
Independent/Partner/Small Groups

- Read aloud the directions on Student Book p. 200. Have students write the meanings of the prefixes. Then have students make new words by adding the prefix *uni-*, *bi-*, *tri-*, or that of some other number to the base words.

- **Game** Allow time for students to play Spin and Spell, which is on the CD.

Extend the Sort

Vocabulary **Word Of the Week:**

unison Explain that when a choir sings in *unison*, everyone sings together. Break the word *unison* into *uni-* and *son*. Ask students what *uni-* means ("one") and explain that *son* here means "sound." Help students understand that to do something in unison means "to do the same thing at the same time," or "to agree." Have students think of and define three more words with the prefix *uni-*.

Alternative Sort: Number Prefix Sort

Have students sort according to whether the prefix means one, two, three, five, or eight.

ELL English Language Learners

Ask students if they know someone who is bilingual ("using or capable of using two languages"), trilingual ("using or capable of using three languages"), or multilingual ("using or capable of using several languages"). Remind students of words they studied earlier, in which *gu* had the sound of /gw/.

Teacher Tip

Ask students to think of other words that begin with these and other number prefixes. Add the new prefixes to your classroom prefix chart.

Suffixes -y, -ly, -ily

Objectives

- To identify the suffixes -y, -ly and -ily and understand how they influence the meanings of words
- To sort and spell words ending with -y, -ly, and -ily

Materials for Syllables and Affixes

Whiteboard Activities DVD-ROM, Sort 51

Teacher Resource CD-ROM, Sort 51 and Wildlife Safari Game

Student Book, pages 201–204

Words

-y	-ly	-ily
rainy	clearly	easily
foggy	quickly	angrily
snowy	loudly	noisily
stormy	quietly	lazily
misty	dimly	daily
windy	roughly	sleepily
cloudy	smoothly	busily
chilly		merrily
breezy		

Introduce/Model
Small Groups

- Use the whiteboard DVD or the CD word cards to introduce the words. Ask students what they notice about each of the words and how the words might be sorted.

- Display the headers (-y, -ly, -ily) and have students assist as you complete the sort. Read the words and guide students to identify the base word in each.

- Discuss that the meanings of base words change by adding -y. Help students conclude that adding -y turns nouns into adjectives that mean "having or like something"; adding -ly and -ily changes adjectives into adverbs that explain how or when something is done.

- Discuss the rules for adding suffixes -y, -ly, and -ily to words (double, e-drop, change -y to i, no change).

Practice the Sort
Independent/Partner

- Have students use the Student Book or whiteboard DVD to say each word and use the grid to sort the words according to suffixes.

- Have students check and explain their sorts.

Apply
Independent/Partner/Small Groups

- Read aloud the directions on Student Book p. 204. Have students choose a base word and add a suffix to it to complete each sentence.

- **Game** Allow time for students to play Wildlife Safari, which is on the CD.

Extend the Sort

Vocabulary **W**ord **O**f the **W**eek:

dimly Ask students to predict what *dimly* might mean. If needed, provide an example sentence, such as *The room was so dimly lit that I could barely see anything.* Elicit that *dimly* means "not brightly" in this context. Further explain that *dimly* can also mean "not clearly," as in the student who *dimly* understands a subject.

Alternative Sort: Adjective or Adverb?

When students have completed this sort, have them re-sort the words according to parts of speech: adjective or adverb. Remind students that adding the suffix -y to words turns nouns into adjectives and adding the suffix -ly or -ily to words turns adjectives into adverbs.

ELL **English Language Learners**

Have students pick out words that describe the weather and review these together. Have students draw pictures to illustrate each weather word.

Objectives

- To identify the comparative suffixes -er and -est and understand how they influence the meanings of words

- To sort and spell words ending with -er, -est, -ier, and -iest

Materials for Syllables and Affixes

- Whiteboard Activities DVD-ROM, Sort 52

- Teacher Resource CD-ROM, Sort 52 and Park Dash Game

- Student Book, pages 205–208

Words

-er	-est	-ier	-iest
calmer	calmest	easier	easiest
closer	closest	prettier	prettiest
fewer	fewest	crazier	craziest
cooler	coolest	dirtier	dirtiest
hotter	hottest	funnier	funniest
weaker	weakest	lazier	laziest

Introduce/Model
Small Groups

- Use the whiteboard DVD or the CD word cards to introduce the words. Ask students what they notice about each of the words.

- Have students assist as you sort according to whether words end in the comparative suffix -er or -est.

- Guide students to arrive at some conclusions about what the comparative suffixes mean. (The suffix -er is used when comparing two things, and -est is used when comparing more than two things.)

- Discuss rules involved in adding the suffixes -er and -est to words (double, e-drop, change -y to i, no change).

Practice the Sort
Independent/Partner

- Have students use the Student Book or whiteboard DVD to say each word and use the grid to sort the words according to their suffixes.

- Have students check and explain their sorts.

Apply
Independent/Partner/Small Groups

- Read aloud the directions on Student Book p. 208. Have students make new words by adding -er or -est to base words and complete the activity.

- **Game** Allow time for students to play Park Dash, which is on the CD.

Extend the Sort

Vocabulary **W**ord **O**f the **W**eek:
cooler/coolest Ask partners to write sentences that use the words *cool, cooler,* and *coolest,* leaving spaces for the places these words go. Remind them to use both the formal ("more cold than hot") and the informal ("excellent or wonderful") meanings of *cool.* Then have partners exchange sentences, fill in the correct form of *cool,* and identify which meaning is being used.

Alternative Sort: Adding Suffixes

Have students sort according to what was done to the base word when the comparative -er or -est was added: double (*hotter*), e-drop (*closer*), change -y to i (*easier*), nothing (*calmer*).

ELL English Language Learners

Review the words and have students repeat them. Then arrange the cards face up. Let students take turns finding a pair of words and using each word in a sentence.

Teacher Tip

Review antonyms by asking students to find opposites among the sort words (*cooler/hotter, calmer/crazier*). Challenge them to look at the remaining sort words and come up with antonyms for as many as they can. Compile a list.

Suffixes *-ness, -ful, -less*

Objectives

- To identify the suffixes *-ness*, *-ful*, and *-less* and understand how they influence the meanings of words
- To sort and spell words ending with *-ness*, *-ful*, and *-less*

Materials for Syllables and Affixes

Whiteboard Activities DVD-ROM, Sort 53

Teacher Resource CD-ROM, Sort 53 and Pick a Card Game

Student Book, pages 209–212

Words

-ness	*-ful*	*-less*	Combination of Suffixes
goodness	colorful	hopeless	thankfulness
weakness	faithful	worthless	helplessness
illness	fearful	restless	thoughtfulness
kindness	painful	harmless	peacefulness
happiness	dreadful	penniless	gratefulness
awareness	plentiful	fearless	truthfulness

Introduce/Model *Small Groups*

- Use the whiteboard DVD or the CD word cards to introduce the words. Ask students what they notice about each of the words.
- Have students assist as you sort according to suffix *-ness*, *-ful*, *-less*, or a combination of suffixes.
- Point out that the meanings of base words are changed by the addition of a suffix. Guide students to determine what the suffixes mean. (*-ness* means "a state of being"; *-ful* means "full of" or "having"; *-less* means "without"; *-ness* can turn an adjective into a noun; adding *-ful* and *-less* can turn a noun into an adjective)
- Lead students to see that for words ending in a consonant or *-e*, you simply add the endings; for those that end in *-y*, you must change *-y* to *i*.

Practice the Sort *Independent/Partner*

- Have students use the Student Book or whiteboard DVD to say each word and use the grid to sort the words according to their suffixes.
- Have students check and explain their sorts.

Apply *Independent/Partner/Small Groups*

- Read aloud the directions on Student Book p. 212. Have students write the meanings of the suffixes and make new words by adding *-ness*, *-ful*, or *-less*, or a combination of these suffixes, to the base words.
- **Game** Allow time for students to play Pick a Card, which is on the CD.

Extend the Sort

Vocabulary **W**ord **O**f the **W**eek:

plentiful Help students define *plenty* as "a supply of all that you need" and have them put this base word together with the suffix to define *plentiful* as "more than enough of what you need." Have students share a story in which something is plentiful.

Alternative Sort: Personal Application

Have students sort the words into two categories: words they would like to apply to themselves and those they would not.

ELL **English Language Learners**

Review the cards with students, breaking each word into its base word and suffix(es). Have students repeat the base word and use it in a sentence. Then use the word with its suffix in a sentence to help them better understand how the suffix changes the meaning of the base word.

Monitor Progress **Spell Check 7**

After completing Sort 53, administer Spell Check 7. See pp. 184–185 in this Teacher Resource Guide for instructions.

Homophones

Objectives

- To identify homophones and their meanings
- To sort and spell homophones by their pronunciation and meanings

Materials for Syllables and Affixes

📺 Whiteboard Activities DVD-ROM, Sort 54

💿 Teacher Resource CD-ROM, Sort 54 and Homophone Solitaire Game

📖 Student Book, pages 213–216

Words

cellar	seller	weather	whether
allowed	aloud	flower	flour
bored	board	vary	very
their	there	hire	higher
desert	dessert	principle	principal
choose	chews	marry	merry

Introduce/Model
Small Groups

- Use the whiteboard DVD or the CD word cards to introduce the words. Ask students what they notice about each of the words.

- Lead students to see that some of these words sound alike but are spelled differently. If they don't know the term *homophone*, explain its meaning: "same sound."

- Display the headers *berry* and *bury*. Have students assist as you pair up words and discuss their meanings.

- Encourage students to identify how some homophone pairs are alike. For example, the pairs *marry/merry* and *vary/very* are alike: both pairs have the same vowel substitutions. The pairs *allowed/aloud* and *flower/flour* are alike because both substitute the letter *u* for the letters *we*.

Practice the Sort
Independent/Partner

- Have students use the Student Book or whiteboard DVD to say each word and use the grid to sort the words so the homophones are paired.

- Have students check and explain their sorts.

Apply
Independent/Partner/Small Groups

- Read aloud the directions on Student Book p. 216. Have students say each word aloud, think of a homophone, write a sentence using that new word, and underline the homophone.

- **Game** Allow time for students to play Homophone Solitaire, which is on the CD.

Extend the Sort

Vocabulary **Word Of the Week:**

vary Have students define *vary* ("to make or become different") and brainstorm different things that could vary. Then have students write instructions that use the word *vary*. For example, *Vary the amount of water you give the flowers each day. Vary the colors of clothes you wear.*

Alternative Sort: Parts of Speech

Have students sort words by parts of speech (including oddball category). When they are done, review how each student sorted the words and discuss how some words could be in more than one pile (e.g., *desert* can be a noun or a verb).

ELL English Language Learners

To review the homophone pairs in this sort, discuss the meanings of the words and help students use them in sentences. For extra practice, let students use the word cards to play matching games.

Teacher Tip

Encourage students to create notebooks in which they write homophones they encounter over time.

Homographs

Objectives

- To identify homographs and their meanings
- To identify and sort homographs by which syllable is accented and by their meanings and parts of speech

Materials for Syllables and Affixes

Whiteboard Activities DVD-ROM, Sort 55

Teacher Resource CD-ROM, Sort 55 and Homograph Concentration Game

Student Book, pages 217–220

Words

Noun		Verb	
desert	**sub**ject	de**sert**	sub**ject**
record	**re**ject	re**cord**	re**ject**
permit	**pro**duce	per**mit**	pro**duce**
rebel	**con**duct	re**bel**	con**duct**
object	**ex**port	ob**ject**	ex**port**
	contract		con**tract**

Introduce/Model
Small Groups

- Use the whiteboard DVD or the CD word cards to introduce the words. Ask students what they notice about each of the words.

- Point out that the boldfaced part of the word indicates which syllable should be accented. Guide students to notice that nouns are accented on the first syllable and verbs on the second.

- Lead students to see that some words are spelled alike but have different pronunciations. Explain the term *homograph*: "same writing or spelling."

- Choose a pair of homograph headers (**pre**sent, pre**sent**) and use each in a sentence. Guide students to see that one is a noun and one is a verb. Have students assist as you continue.

Practice the Sort
Independent/Partner

- Have students use the Student Book or whiteboard DVD to say each word and use the grid to sort.

- Have students check and explain their sorts.

Apply
Independent/Partner/Small Groups

- Read aloud the directions on Student Book p. 220. Have students write a sentence using each word as a noun and a verb.

- **Game** Allow time for students to play Homograph Concentration, which is on the CD.

Extend the Sort

Vocabulary **W**ord **O**f the **W**eek:
de**sert**/**de**sert Explain that both forms of the word *desert* come from the Latin *deserere*, which means "to abandon." Point out that a *desert* is land that has been abandoned because few people live there and that when you *desert* someone, you abandon that person. Have students draw a picture of someone being deserted in a desert and write a caption using both forms of *desert*.

ELL **English Language Learners**

Discuss how using context clues can help students decide which meaning of the word applies. To illustrate this, write sentences such as *I bow down to tie a bow on my shoe. I can't bear to see a bear.* Read the sentences aloud and have students decode the words based on their context clues.

Teacher Tip

Point out how the words *homograph* and *homophone* are related yet different. *Homograph* means "same spelling" or "same writing." *Homophone* means "same sound." Explain that a *homonym* has the same spelling or pronunciation as another word but a different meaning.

Derivational Relations

The term *derivational relations* emphasizes how spelling and vocabulary at this stage grow primarily through *derivation*: from a single base word or word root, a number of related words are *derived* through the addition of prefixes and suffixes. Students at this stage are at a more advanced level of word knowledge, which means word study focuses as much on vocabulary development as it does on spelling development. Analyzing the spelling of words supports vocabulary growth, and vocabulary growth in turn provides helpful support for higher-level spelling development.

Types of Sorts in Derivational Relations
- Prefixes and Suffixes
- Greek and Latin Roots
- Assimilated Prefixes

Characteristics of Derivational Relations Learners

Students in the Derivational Relations stage are mostly found in upper elementary school, middle school, and high school.

Derivational Relations Learners

- are typically advanced readers and writers who are fairly competent spellers.

- have a firm understanding of common syllable juncture patterns, the spelling patterns of stressed and unstressed syllables, and the effects of common prefixes and suffixes on base words.

- have mastered high frequency words.

- read with good fluency and expression.

- read faster silently than orally.

- write responses that often reflect more sophisticated and critical thought.

Focus of Instruction

- Word study at the Derivational Relations stage focuses primarily on the structure and morphology of written words. Students systematically examine how the spelling of words visually represents meaning units, or morphemes.

- To begin, students look at spelling-meaning connections as they study prefixes and suffixes, that include adding *-ion* and *-ian*.

- Students then focus on consonant alternations. A **consonant alternation** is when consonants that are silent in one word are sometimes "sounded " in a related word, as in the words *sign, signal,* and *signature*. A consonant alternation occurs in related words where the spelling of consonants remains the same despite an alternation or change in the sound represented by the spelling.

- Students also study vowel alternations. **Vowel alternations** occur in many related words where the spelling of the vowels remains the same despite an alternation or change in the sound represented by the spelling, as in *nature* to *natural*.

- Next, students move on to Greek and Latin word roots and affixes and their combination with affixes. This knowledge provides a powerful foundation and productive strategy for continuing vocabulary and spelling growth.

- Students study predictable spelling changes in related words and then take another look at suffixes, specifically *-ent/-ence, -ant/-ance, -able,* and *-ible*.

- Finally, students explore the process of prefix assimilation.

Pace of Instruction

Unlike the Letter Name and Within Word Pattern stages, where there is a sense of urgency in moving students along at a steady pace, the Derivational Relations stage is where advanced readers and writers will remain, continuing to elaborate and extend their understandings. The pace of instruction, however, should still be adjusted to meet students' needs. The Spell Checks can help you determine the focus and pace of instruction.

For students who catch on quickly, speed up the pace by spending less time on sorts or skip some sorts altogether. Conversely, for those students who are not on track for meeting end-of-year goals, spend more time on instruction and provide more practice by creating additional sorts.

Modifying the pace and using flexible small groups allows you to avoid teaching students what they already know and to spend more time on features that need instruction.

Teacher Tips

- Vocabulary grows and develops in many ways. It is well established that certain words need to be taught systematically and deeply; that students need to do a lot of reading in order to experience and acquire over time the broad sweep of English vocabulary; and that students need to learn the processes whereby meaningful word elements or morphemes—prefixes, suffixes, base words, and word roots—combine.

- Linguists refer to the knowledge of combining word elements as *generative*. Once students understand the basics according to which these important word parts combine, they can apply this knowledge in *generating* the spellings and meanings of literally thousands of words. This enables them to analyze and learn unfamiliar words they encounter in their reading and their study in specific content areas.

Word Study Routines

Introduce the Sort There are several options for introducing the sort. Here are the basic steps for a teacher-directed sort.

- Introduce the words. Talk about any that may be unfamiliar. Most of the sorts in Derivational Relations include both familiar and unfamiliar words. Knowledge of the meanings for the known words or of the meaningful word parts in the known words will enable student in most instances to infer the meanings of the unfamiliar words.

- Ask students what they notice about the words and how they might be sorted.

- Introduce the categories. Explicitly discuss the headers so that students know what features they are using to sort.

- Model how to sort two or three words and explain why each word goes in that category. Have students complete the sort.

- Discuss the meaning of the words, noting how a prefix or suffix affects the base word.

- Model how to check that the words in each column belong and then have students check the words in each column. Discuss the characteristics of the words in each column, guiding students to develop a generalization.

- Have students re-sort the words individually or with a partner. Have them explain their reasoning for placing words in the categories.

- Remind students to check their sort by reading the words in each column and to move a word to another column if they decide it is misplaced.

Teacher Tip

- Students should be actively involved in the exploration of words; they are then more likely to develop a positive attitude toward word learning and a curiosity about words.

Interactive Resources You may use the DVD-ROM and/or the CD-ROM printable manipulatives to model, instruct, and provide practice with sorts.

Use the DVD-ROM for interactive whiteboard activities or independent practice on a computer.

- Point out the headers for the columns, which indicate the principle of the sort. Demonstrate how to drag and drop words to complete the sort. Have students take turns sorting, using the whiteboard or a computer.

- Use the whiteboard to introduce the writing sort. Have students complete it.

Use the CD-ROM for printable manipulatives.

- Print out and cut apart the cards for the sort. Introduce the words, identifying any that may be unfamiliar to students. Demonstrate how to sort. Have students use the cards to practice sorting.

- Print out the game that accompanies the sort. Use the game for additional practice with the sort. Have students play in pairs or small groups.

Monitor Progress SPELL CHECKS

Spell checks for Derivational Relations are provided here. Administer the spell checks as you would any spelling test, reading the words and having students write them. Spell Checks can be used as pretests and postests.

Spell Check 1
Prefixes and Suffixes Use after Sort 8. This Spell Check assesses students' ability to spell words with prefixes and suffixes that require no spelling changes, e-drop changes, and predictable consonant changes, as well as words with consonant and vowel alternations.

1. exploration	8. careful	15. wordless
2. permission	9. speechless	16. soften
3. grateful	10. instruction	17. persuasion
4. column	11. musician	18. conclusion
5. willful	12. hasten	19. columnist
6. priceless	13. invention	20. electrician
7. fondness	14. invasion	

If students have difficulty adding -ion or -ian review Sorts 3–6. If students have difficulty with consonant alternations, review Sort 7. If students have difficulty with long to short vowel alternations, review Sort 8.

Spell Check 2
Additional Prefixes and Suffixes Use after Sort 17. This Spell Check assesses students' ability to write words with vowel alternations and words with Greek and Latin prefixes.

1. major	8. proclaim	15. revision
2. residence	9. proclamation	16. relative
3. competition	10. multiplication	17. similarity
4. tripod	11. suburban	18. opposition
5. monogram	12. overreact	19. interact
6. combination	13. multiply	20. decathlon
7. metallic	14. consumption	

If students have difficulty adding suffixes to base words with vowel alternations, review Sorts 10–13. If students have difficulty spelling words with Greek and Latin prefixes, review Sorts 15–17.

Spell Check 3
Greek and Latin Roots Use after Sort 35. This Spell Check assesses students' ability to write

words with Latin roots, Greek and Latin elements and roots, prefixes *intra-, inter-,* and *intro-,* and suffixes, *-ent, -ence, able,* and *-ible.*

1. desirable	8. rupture	15. credible
2. dictate	9. portable	16. visible
3. audible	10. breakable	17. abundance
4. rejection	11. motor	18. manicure
5. edible	12. pedestal	19. formulate
6. evidence	13. injection	20. evident
7. inspect	14. introduction	

If students have difficulty with Greek and Latin elements and roots, review the appropriate corresponding sorts. If students have difficulty with words that end in -ent/-ence and words that end in -ant/-ance, review Sorts 32 and 33.

Spell Check 4
Assimilated Prefixes Use after Sort 38. This Spell Check assesses students' ability to write words with assimilated prefixes.

1. irregular	8. irrational	15. illiterate
2. incapable	9. collaborate	16. irresponsible
3. congestion	10. collision	17. company
4. illogical	11. inactive	18. collate
5. committee	12. companion	19. congress
6. concert	13. injustice	20. collapse
7. immature	14. immoral	

Watch for these types of errors: if students write *iresponsible* rather than *irresponsible*, review Sort 36. If they write *conpanion* rather than *companion*, review Sort 37.

- **See Chapter 8 of *Words Their Way: Word Study for Phonics, Vocabulary, and Spelling Instruction,* 5th ed., for a comprehensive description of the Derivational Relations stage of development and additional activities.**

Objectives

- To recognize how the prefixes *pre-, fore-, post-,* and *after-* change the meanings of base words
- To sort and spell words with the prefixes *pre-, fore-, post-,* and *after-*

Materials for Derivational Relations

⬜ Whiteboard Activities DVD-ROM, Sort 1

💿 Teacher Resource CD-ROM, Sort 1 and Spin and Spell Game

📓 Student Book, pages 1–4

Words

pre-	fore-	post-	after-
prejudge	forecourt	postscript	afterword
predetermine	foreknowledge	postseason	afternoon
preseason	foreword	postdate	aftertaste
predate	forewarn		
preposition	foresight		
preoccupied	forearm		
prefix	forego		

Introduce/Model
Small Groups

- Use the whiteboard DVD or the CD word cards to introduce the words. Ask students what they notice about these words. (They all have prefixes.)

- Place a word in each of the *pre-, fore-, post-,* and *after-* columns and then challenge students to complete the sort.

- Read the sort. Discuss how each prefix changes the meaning of the base word. Explain that *pre-* means "earlier, in advance, in front of"; *fore-* means "before, earlier, in front of, front"; *post-* means "after, later, behind"; and *after-* means "behind, later."

- Point out that adding these prefixes requires no change in spelling to the base word.

Practice the Sort
Independent/Partner

- Have students use the Student Book or whiteboard DVD to say each word and use the grid to sort.

- Have students check and explain their sorts.

Apply
Independent/Partner/Small Groups

- Read aloud the directions on Student Book p. 4. Have students complete the activity.

- **Game** Allow time for students to play Spin and Spell, which is on the CD.

Extend the Sort

Vocabulary **Word Of the Week:**

predate Provide a sample sentence using *predate* in context, such as *Dinosaurs predate most of the creatures that live today.* Remind students that thinking about the meaning of the word part can help them define the derived word. Explain that *predate* means "to happen before in time" and also "to mark with a date earlier than the actual one."

Alternative Sort: Syllables

Have students note that these prefixes added one or more syllables to the base word. Have them sort the words into two-, three-, and four-syllable words.

ELL English Language Learners

Through discussion and examples, help students sort the words into those with prefixes that mean "before" or "earlier" and those that mean "following" or "after."

Teacher Tip

Focus early instruction on words whose meanings are clear and literal. For example, *preview* literally means "to view beforehand," whereas *afternoon* literally means "the part of day that is after noon until sunset."

Objectives

- To review how the suffixes -ness, -ful, and -less change the meanings of words
- To sort and spell words with the suffixes -ness, -ful, and -less

Materials for Derivational Relations

- Whiteboard Activities DVD-ROM, Sort 2
- Teacher Resource CD-ROM, Sort 2 and Pick a Card Game
- Student Book, pages 5–8

Words

-ness	-ful	-less	Combination of Suffixes
fondness	beautiful	restless	skillfulness
politeness	graceful	priceless	flawlessness
friendliness	truthful	flawless	thoughtlessness
emptiness	fanciful	tireless	
darkness	careful	speechless	
kindness	respectful	worthless	
	grateful	breathless	
	delightful		

Introduce/Model   *Small Groups*

- Use the whiteboard DVD or the CD word cards to introduce the words. Ask students what they notice about the words. (They all end in suffixes.)

- Place a word in each of the -ness, -ful, and -less columns and then challenge students to complete the sort.

- Read the sort. Have students identify how each suffix changes the meaning of the base word. (-ness creates nouns out of adjectives and suggests a "state of being"; -ful and -less create adjectives meaning "full of" or "without")

- Guide students to see that when a base word ends in *y*, *y* is changed to *i* before adding the suffix (such as beauty/beautiful). Challenge students to identify words in this sort with base words that end in *y*.

Practice the Sort   *Independent/Partner*

- Have students use the Student Book or whiteboard DVD to say each word and use the grid to sort the words several times according to the suffix(es).

- Have students check and explain their sorts.

Apply   *Independent/Partner/Small Groups*

- Read aloud the directions on Student Book p. 8. Have students complete the activity.

- **Game** Allow time for children to play Pick a Card, which is on the CD.

Extend the Sort

Vocabulary **Word Of the Week:**

fanciful Ask students whether they know the meaning of the word *fanciful*. Provide them with an example sentence, such as *Flying from one place to the next with a snap of your fingers is a fanciful idea.* Ask students what they think *fanciful* means now. Then explain that if something is fanciful, it is imaginative rather than ordinary.

ELL English Language Learners

Using their word cards, have students fold each suffix behind its base word so that only the base word is visible. Invite volunteers to read aloud the base word, use it in a sentence, and then unfold each word card one at a time. Have volunteers name the suffix, discuss its meaning, and use the suffixed word in a sentence.

Teacher Tip

Students can create more combination words from the other words in the sort. Provide students with several examples. (*graceful, flawless*) Then have students experiment with the words and suffixes to create additional words.

Sort 3

Adding *-ion* (With No Spelling Change)

Objectives

- To identify how to add *-ion* to base words ending in *-ss* and *-ct*

- To sort and spell base words ending in *-ss* and *-ct* and derivatives ending in *-ion*

Materials for Derivational Relations

Whiteboard Activities DVD-ROM, Sort 3

Teacher Resource CD-ROM, Sort 3 and Butterfly Hunt Game

Student Book, pages 9–12

Words

Base *-ct*	*-ct* + *-ion*	Base *-ss*	*-ss* + *-ion*
correct	correction	confess	confession
collect	collection	discuss	discussion
instruct	instruction	impress	impression
select	selection	process	procession
protect	protection	possess	possession
inspect	inspection	depress	depression
elect	election		

Introduce/Model   *Small Groups*

- Use the whiteboard DVD or the CD word cards to introduce the words. Ask students what they notice about the words. (Base words have the ending *-ion* added to them.)

- Place a word in each of the Base *-ct*, *-ct* + *-ion*, Base *-ss*, and *-ss* + *-ion* columns and then challenge students to complete the sort.

- Read the sort. Help students see that adding *-ion* to a base word results in a word that means "the act or result of."

- Guide students to conclude that when a base word ends in *-ct* or *-ss,* no change in the spelling of the base word is necessary when *-ion* is added.

Practice the Sort   *Independent/Partner*

- Have students use the Student Book or whiteboard DVD to say each word and use the grid to sort the words several times according to the suffix.

- Have students check and explain their sorts.

Apply   *Independent/Partner/Small Groups*

- Read aloud the directions on Student Book p. 12. Have students complete the activity.

- **Game** Allow time for students to play Butterfly Hunt, which is on the CD.

Extend the Sort

Vocabulary **Word Of the Week:**

procession Tell students that a procession of antique cars slowly pass by in a parade. Encourage students to predict what *procession* means. Help students understand that a *procession* is a number of persons or things slowly moving forward in a line.

Alternative Sort: I Spy Sort

Have partners play a game of I Spy. One student sorts the words by spelling patterns and purposefully puts one word in the wrong column. The partner studies the sort to find the incorrect placement and says "I spy *impression* in the *-ct* + *-ion* column; it should be in the *-ss* + *-ion* column." Have students switch roles and play the game again.

ELL **English Language Learners**

Have students repeat the sort words after you. Then say sentences aloud that show the relationship between the base words and their derivatives. (If you predict a winner, you've made a prediction.) Repeat the sentence omitting the derivative and have volunteers supply the word.

Objectives

- To identify how to add *-ion* and *-ian* to base words ending in *-t* and *-ic*
- To sort and spell base words ending in *-t* and *-ic* and derivatives ending in *-ion* and *-ian*

Materials for Derivational Relations

- [ ] Whiteboard Activities DVD-ROM, Sort 4

- ( ) Teacher Resource CD-ROM, Sort 4 and Slap Jack Game

- [ ] Student Book, pages 13–16

Words

Base *-t*	*-t* + *-ion*	Base *-ic*	*-ic* + *-ian*
interrupt	interruption	electric	electrician
exhaust	exhaustion	clinic	clinician
digest	digestion	music	musician
invent	invention	optic	optician
suggest	suggestion		
adopt	adoption		

Introduce/Model
Small Groups

- Use the whiteboard DVD or the CD word cards to introduce the words. Ask students what they notice about the words. (Some base words have the ending *-ion* added and others have the ending *-ian* added.)

- Place a word in each of the Base *-t*, *-t* + *-ion*, Base *-ic*, and *-ic* + *-ian* columns and then challenge students to complete the sort.

- Read the sort. Have students identify how each suffix changes the meaning of the base word. Help them notice how *-ian* is different from *-ion*. (*-ian* usually refers to a specialist or person who does something; adding *-ion* to a base word changes the word to mean "the act or result of" the meaning of the base word.)

- Guide students to conclude that the final /t/ and /ik/ are pronounced /sh/ when *-ion* or *-ian* is added.

Practice the Sort
Independent/Partner

- Have students use the Student Book or whiteboard DVD to say each word and use the grid to sort the words several times according to the suffix.

- Have students check and explain their sorts.

Apply
Independent/Partner/Small Groups

- Read aloud the directions on Student Book p. 16. Have students complete the activity.

- **Game** Allow time for students to play Slap Jack, which is on the CD.

Extend the Sort

Vocabulary **W**ord **O**f the **W**eek:
clinic/clinician Ask students what a clinic is and why people go there ("a place where people go for medical help"). Then ask students what they think a clinician is. Explain that a clinician is a person who works in a clinic and is qualified to practice medicine.

Alternative Sort: Accented Syllable Sort

Have students sort the words by accented syllable—first, second, or third. Then lead them to generalize about the word pairs (in base *-t* and *-t* + *-ion*, the accent occurs in the same syllable; in base *-ic* and *-ic* + *-ian*, the accent in the suffixed word shifts to the next syllable).

ELL English Language Learners

Have students repeat the sort words after you. Have Spanish speakers identify words that are cognates in English and Spanish, and discuss the differences in spelling and pronunciation. Write *digestion* and *digestión* and *adoption* and *adopción*. Point out that words that end in *-tion* in English may end with *-tión* or *-ción* in Spanish.

Sort 5 Adding *-ion* (With e- Drop and Spelling Change)

Objectives

- To identify how to add *-ion* to base words ending in *-te* and *-ce*
- To sort and spell base words ending in *-te* and *-ce* and their derivatives ending in *-ion* and *-tion*

Materials for Derivational Relations

🖥 Whiteboard Activities DVD-ROM, Sort 5

💿 Teacher Resource CD-ROM, Sort 5 and Think Time Game

📕 Student Book, pages 17–20

Words

	e-Drop		e- Drop
Base -te	**+ -ion**	**Base -ce**	**+ -tion**
create	creation	introduce	introduction
calculate	calculation	reduce	reduction
fascinate	fascination	reproduce	reproduction
decorate	decoration		
concentrate	concentration		
generate	generation		
imitate	imitation		
hibernate	hibernation		
coordinate	coordination		

Introduce/Model   *Small Groups*

- Use the whiteboard DVD or the CD word cards to introduce the words.

- First guide students to sort the words into two categories: base words and derived words. Then place a word in each of the Base *-te, e-* Drop + *-ion,* Base *-ce,* and *e-* Drop + *-tion* columns and challenge students to complete the sort.

- Read the sort and have students match base words with derived words.

- Guide students to conclude that the final /t/ becomes /sh/ when *-ion* is added, and the soft *c* becomes a hard *c* when *-tion* is added.

Practice the Sort   *Independent/Partner*

- Have students use the Student Book or whiteboard DVD to say each word and use the grid to sort the words several times according to the suffix.

- Have students check and explain their sorts.

Apply   *Independent/Partner/Small Groups*

- Read aloud the directions on Student Book p. 20. Have students complete the activity.

- **Game** Allow time for students to play Think Time, which is on the CD.

Extend the Sort

Vocabulary **W**ord **O**f the **W**eek:
generate/generation Tell students that you want them to make a list of words that end in *-ion*. Write the word *generate* and ask students what they think this word means. Explain that *generate* means "to produce" or "bring into existence." Tell them that they just generated a list of words. Challenge students to use the words *generate* and *generation* in a sentence.

ELL **English Language Learners**

Have students repeat the sort words after you. Then act out and describe words and have students identify them. For example, pretend to decorate the room for a party and describe what you are doing without using the word *decorate*. Invite volunteers to act out other words.

Teacher Tip

Suggest students write the words they find in sorted lists in their Word Study Notebook and record the rule they learned in their notebook and in a classroom generalizations chart. Tell students that when they find words in which the spelling of the base changes when the suffix is added, they should record these words in a "miscellaneous" category.

Objectives

- To recognize how to add *-ion* to words ending in *-de* and *-it*

- To sort and spell base words ending in *-de* and *-it* and derivatives ending in *-ion*

Materials for Derivational Relations

🖥 Whiteboard Activities DVD-ROM, Sort 6

💿 Teacher Resource CD-ROM, Sort 6 and Think Time Game

📕 Student Book, pages 21–24

Words

Base -de	-de > -sion	Base -it	-it > -ission
persuade	persuasion	emit	emission
intrude	intrusion	omit	omission
invade	invasion	submit	submission
collide	collision	permit	permission
divide	division	transmit	transmission
erode	erosion		
decide	decision		
conclude	conclusion		

Introduce/Model
Small Groups

- Use the whiteboard DVD or the CD word cards to introduce the words. First guide students to sort the words into two categories: base words and derived words.

- Lead students to notice that some base words end in *-de* and others end in *-it.* Then place the base words in each of the Base *-de* and Base *-it* columns. Challenge students to find the matching derivative to complete the sort.

- Read the sort. Have students identify how each suffix changes the base word, which is a verb, to a noun.

- Guide students to notice that the final *-de* is dropped before *-ion* is added, and *-it* is dropped before *-ission* is added.

Practice the Sort
Independent/Partner

- Have students use the Student Book or whiteboard DVD to say each word and use the grid to sort the words several times according to the suffix.

- Have students check and explain their sorts.

Apply
Independent/Partner/Small Groups

- Read aloud the directions on Student Book p. 24. Have students complete the activity.

- **Game** Allow time for students to play Think Time, which is on the CD.

Extend the Sort

Vocabulary 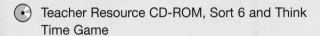 **Word Of the Week:**

erode/erosion Ask whether anyone knows the meaning of *erode* and *erosion*. If necessary, provide example sentences: *Wind and rain can erode the soil. Planting grass will help prevent erosion of the soil.* Ask students what they think *erode* and *erosion* mean now. Explain that *erode* means "to wear or wash away slowly" and *erosion* means "wearing, washing, or eating away."

ELL **English Language Learners**

For each word, give students an opportunity to share the pronunciation and meaning. Then ask questions that require students to choose between two sort words. For example, say, *If you cut an apple in half, do you* divide *it or* decide *it? If you make up your mind about something, have you made a* division *or a* decision? Encourage students to tell why each word is or is not correct.

Alternative Sort: Open Sort

Have students re-sort the words by their similarities in meaning, use, or spelling pattern. This is an open sort where students determine the categories themselves. Have students explain their categories and why they sorted the words the way they did.

Consonant Alternation: Silent and Sounded

Objectives

- To recognize related words that have silent and sounded consonants
- To sort and spell related words with consonant alternation

Materials for Derivational Relations

🖥 Whiteboard Activities DVD-ROM, Sort 7

💿 Teacher Resource CD-ROM, Sort 7 and Quick Clues Game

📙 Student Book, pages 25–28

Words

Silent Consonant	Sounded Consonant
bomb	bombard
hasten	haste
moisten	moist
resign	resignation
crumb	crumble
muscle	muscular
design	designate
soften	soft
column	columnist
limb	limber

Introduce/Model   *Small Groups*

- Use the whiteboard DVD or the CD word cards to introduce the words. Ask students to sort the words into pairs and tell what they see about the pairs of words. (One word can be found in the other word.)

- Read *bomb* and *bombard* aloud. Ask students how the words are pronounced differently. Have students identify which letters are silent and which are sounded.

- Place a word in each of the Silent Consonant and Sounded Consonant columns. Challenge students to complete the sort.

- Guide students to summarize that in some words a consonant is silent but in its related word it is sounded.

Practice the Sort   *Independent/Partner*

- Have students use the Student Book or whiteboard DVD to say each word and use the grid to sort the words according to silent and sounded consonants.

- Have students check and explain their sorts.

Apply   *Independent/Partner/Small Groups*

- Read aloud the directions on Student Book p. 28. Have students complete the activity.

- **Game** Allow time for students to play Quick Clues, which is on the CD.

Extend the Sort

Vocabulary **Word Of the Week:**

haste/hasten Write the words *haste* and *hasten*. Provide example sentences: *Tom did his homework with great haste so he could play soccer. The paramedic hastened to the injured man.* Ask students to tell what the words mean ("speed, quickness in moving"; "to move quickly" or "to hurry").

Alternative Sort: Suffix Sort

Have students sort the words into two categories: words that have a suffix and words that do not. After students finish, discuss the suffixes and how they change each word's meaning.

ELL English Language Learners

Pronounce the words slowly, emphasizing each sound, and have students repeat them. Check that students are correctly saying each word. Emphasize that in related word pairs, the same consonant may be silent in one word and sounded in the other. Make sure students understand *silent* and *sounded*.

Vowel Alternation: Long to Short

Objectives

- To recognize related words in which a vowel sound changes from long to short
- To sort and spell related words with vowel alternation

Materials for Derivational Relations

🖥 Whiteboard Activities DVD-ROM, Sort 8

💿 Teacher Resource CD-ROM, Sort 8 and Slap Jack Game

📓 Student Book, pages 29–32

Words

Long Vowel	Short Vowel
mine	mineral
breathe	breath
revise	revision
nature	natural
nation	national
athlete	athletic
grateful	gratitude
crime	criminal
ignite	ignition
precise	precision

Introduce/Model   *Small Groups*

- Use the whiteboard DVD or the CD word cards to introduce the words. Ask students to sort the words into pairs and tell what they see about the pairs of words. (One word can be found in the other word.)

- Review the sounds of long and short *a, e, i, o,* and *u.* Place a word in each of the Long Vowel and Short Vowel columns. Hold up and read aloud several pairs of words. Challenge students to put those words in the correct columns.

- Complete the sort with students, providing pronunciations when needed. Have students identify which letters change from long to short in each pair of words.

- Guide students to summarize that in some words a consonant is silent but in its related word it is sounded.

Practice the Sort   *Independent/Partner*

- Have students use the Student Book or whiteboard DVD to say each word and use the grid to sort.

- Have students check and explain their sorts.

Apply   *Independent/Partner/Small Groups*

- Read aloud the directions on Student Book p. 32. Have students complete the activity.

- **Game** Allow time for students to play Slap Jack, which is on the CD.

Extend the Sort

Vocabulary **Word Of the Week:**

precise/precision Draw a house. Begin to measure it with a ruler. Say, *If I were going to paint this house, my measurements would need to be precise so that I could figure out how much paint I need. I'd better measure with precision, or I might be in trouble.* Ask what *precise* and *precision* mean ("exact or definite"; "accuracy").

Alternative Sort: Silent *e*

Have students sort the words into those that end in silent *e* and those that do not. Have them read aloud the words, emphasizing the long vowel sounds.

ELL English Language Learners

Have students repeat each word after you. Ask Spanish speakers to identify words that are cognates and identify the differences in spelling and pronunciation. Point out that some cognates have more than one meaning. For example, the Spanish word *agradable* means "grateful" and also "agreeable or pleasant."

Monitor Progress **Spell Check 1**

After completing Sort 8, administer Spell Check 1. See p. 245 in this Teacher Resource Guide for instructions.

Vowel Alternation: Long to Short or /ə/

Objectives

- To recognize related words in which a vowel sound changes from long to short or /ə/ in related words

- To sort and spell related words whose vowel changes from long to short or /ə/

Materials for Derivational Relations

- Whiteboard Activities DVD-ROM, Sort 9

- Teacher Resource CD-ROM, Sort 9 and Vowel Alternation Concentration Game

- Student Book, pages 33–36

Words

Base Word	Derived Word	Base Word	Derived Word
Long Vowel	Short Vowel	Long Vowel	/ə/
reptile	reptilian	compete	competition
mine	mineral	relate	relative
rite	ritual	major	majority
flame	flammable	confide	confidence
nature	natural	define	definition
		reside	residence

Introduce/Model   *Small Groups*

- Use the whiteboard DVD or the CD word cards to introduce the words. Ask students to sort the words into pairs of base words and derivatives.

- Demonstrate the different sounds that can be represented by a vowel when it is long, when it is short, and when it stands for a schwa sound. Place a word in each of the Long Vowel, Short Vowel, and /ə/ columns and then challenge students to complete the sort.

- Take time to talk about the words and how they are related in meaning. Be sure that students understand that *mine* refers to a place where minerals are dug out of the ground and not the pronoun *mine*. Have students identify which vowels changed sounds.

- Guide students to summarize that in some base words a vowel is long and in its related word it is short or a schwa sound.

Practice the Sort   *Independent/Partner*

- Have students use the Student Book or whiteboard DVD to say each word and use the grid to sort.

- Have students check and explain their sorts.

Apply   *Independent/Partner/Small Groups*

- Read aloud the directions on Student Book p. 36. Have students complete the activity.

- **Game** Allow time for students to play Vowel Alternation Concentration, which is on the CD.

Extend the Sort

Vocabulary **Word Of the Week:**

rite/ritual Ask students what the words *rite* and *ritual* mean. Give example sentences: *The wedding rite was performed in the chapel. Most weddings follow a similar ritual.* The word *rite* often refers to religious ceremonies. Rituals are often followed in the ceremony. For example: exchanging rings is a ritual in a wedding.

Alternative Sort: Which Suffix?

Have students sort the words by suffix (*-al, -ian, -able, -tion, -ive, -ity, -ence*).

ELL **English Language Learners**

Focus on the pronunciation of pairs of words. Be sure students understand that the words are related in spelling and meaning, Show how each base word provides a clue for the meaning of the related word. For example, *A flame is the part of a fire that you can see. Flammable refers to things that can be set on fire easily.*

Adding Suffixes: Vowel Alternation (Accented to Unaccented)

Objectives

- To recognize how vowel sounds may change across base words and derived words while the spelling remains constant
- To sort and spell base words and derived words with vowel alternation

Materials for Derivational Relations

📋 Whiteboard Activities DVD-ROM, Sort 10

💿 Teacher Resource CD-ROM, Sort 10 and Flying Home Game

📖 Student Book, pages 37–40

Words

Base Word	Derived Word
familiar	familiarity
combine	combination
metal	metallic
mobile	mobility
oppose	opposition
perspire	perspiration
inspire	inspiration
prepare	preparation
translate	translation

Introduce/Model — *Small Groups*

- Use the whiteboard DVD or the CD word cards to introduce in context any word that may be unfamiliar.

- Model sorting several base words and derivatives. Then have students sort the words into pairs. Help students note that each derived word has a suffix that changes the vowel sound in the base word.

- Reread the sort, emphasizing the accented syllable. Have students identify which vowels changed sounds.

- Tell students that listening carefully to the accented syllable in one word may help them spell an unaccented vowel sound in a related word.

Practice the Sort — *Independent/Partner*

- Have students use the Student Book or whiteboard DVD to say each word and use the grid to sort the words into related pairs and identify the vowel that changes.

- Have students check and explain their sorts.

Apply — *Independent/Partner/Small Groups*

- Read aloud the directions on Student Book p. 40. Have students complete the activity.

- **Game** Allow time for students to play Flying Home, which is on the CD.

Extend the Sort

Vocabulary **W**ord **O**f the **W**eek:

oppose/opposition Ask students what the words *oppose* and *opposition* mean. Provide students with sentences, such as *The king was not used to having anyone oppose his ideas. He rarely faced opposition.* Explain that *oppose* is a verb that means "to be in conflict with" or "resistant to," and *opposition* is a noun that means "the act or condition of being in conflict."

Alternative Sort: Accented Syllables

Have students sort the words by number of accented syllables they hear in each. Have them sort into two categories: one accented syllable and two accented syllables. Have students check their answers using a dictionary.

ELL English Language Learners

Have students repeat each word after you. Encourage them to mime words such as *combine, invite, oppose, perspire, inspire,* and *prepare.* Then have students illustrate or use the remaining words in sentences.

Adding the Suffix -ity: Vowel Alternation (/ə/ to Short)

Objectives

- To recognize how the suffix -ity affects words with the unaccented final syllable /ə/
- To sort and spell words with a final -al or the suffix -ity

Materials for Derivational Relations

Whiteboard Activities DVD-ROM, Sort 11

Teacher Resource CD-ROM, Sort 11 and Think Time Game

Student Book, pages 41–44

Words

/ə/	Accented
individual	individuality
general	generality
brutal	brutality
personal	personality
neutral	neutrality
original	originality
fatal	fatality
formal	formality
national	nationality
mental	mentality
normal	normality
inequal	inequality

Introduce/Model
Small Groups

- Use the whiteboard DVD or the CD word cards to introduce in context any word that may be unfamiliar.

- Model sorting several base words and derivatives. Draw students' attention to the -al and -ity patterns at the ends of words. Lead students to notice that the suffix -ity changes an adjective into a noun and that it means "state" or "quality."

- Read the sort, emphasizing the accented syllable. Have students identify which vowels changed sounds.

- Guide students to see that adding -ity to a base word changes the unaccented /ə/ to an accented short vowel.

Practice the Sort
Independent/Partner

- Have students use the Student Book or whiteboard DVD to say each word and use the grid to sort the words into related pairs and identify the vowel that changes when accented.

- Have students check and explain their sorts.

Apply
Independent/Partner/Small Groups

- Read aloud the directions on Student Book p. 44. Have students complete the activity.

- **Game** Allow time for students to play Think Time, which is on the CD.

Extend the Sort

Vocabulary **Word Of the Week:**

neutral/neutrality Write these sentences on the board: *The King tried to remain neutral to avoid fighting in the war. When the country was invaded, however, neutrality became impossible, and he had to choose a side.* Have students guess what *neutral* and *neutrality* mean and then consult a dictionary (*neutral* means "not supporting or favoring either side in a war, dispute, or contest"; *neutrality* is the state of being neutral).

Alternative Sort: Parts of Speech

Have students sort the words by part of speech: noun, adjective, and both. Provide example sentences for *individual* to illustrate how a word can be both a noun and an adjective. Have students check their sorts using a dictionary.

ELL **English Language Learners**

Pronounce each word slowly and clearly and have students repeat aloud after you. Have students mime or tell what each word means using their own words, and use the word in a sentence. Allow them to check definitions in a dictionary.

Adding Suffixes: Vowel Alternation (With Spelling Change)

Objectives

- To recognize how words ending in -m, -n, or -e change with the addition of suffixes -ation or -ption
- To sort and spell words ending in -m, -n, and -e and their derivatives ending in -ation and -ption

Materials for Derivational Relations

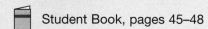

Whiteboard Activities DVD-ROM, Sort 12

Teacher Resource CD-ROM, Sort 12 and Spelling Pattern Match Game

Student Book, pages 45–48

Words

Base -*m* or -*n*	Derived -*ation*
proclaim	proclamation
explain	explanation
reclaim	reclamation
acclaim	acclamation

Base -*e*	Derived -*ption*
presume	presumption
consume	consumption
receive	reception
resume	resumption
conceive	conception

Introduce/Model
Small Groups

- Use the whiteboard DVD or the CD word cards to introduce in context any word that may be unfamiliar.

- Have students begin by sorting base words and derivatives. Then display the headers Base -*m* or -*n* *exclaim*, -*ation exclamation*, Base -*e assume*, and -*ption assumption*. Have students match each base word to its related derived word.

- Read the sort, pointing out spelling changes. Discuss how adding -*ation* and -*ption* to verbs changes them to nouns.

- Lead students to understand that this type of spelling change is infrequent but occurs between words in the same spelling-meaning family, and there is a predictable pattern when it does occur.

Practice the Sort
Independent/Partner

- Have students use the Student Book or whiteboard DVD to say each word and use the grid to sort the words into related pairs and identify the vowel that changes when accented.

- Have students check and explain their sorts.

Apply
Independent/Partner/Small Groups

- Read aloud the directions on Student Book p. 48. Have students complete the activity.

- **Game** Allow time for students to play Spelling Pattern Match, which is on the CD.

Extend the Sort

Vocabulary **Word Of the Week:**
proclaim/proclamation Share the following sentences: *I proclaim a red school day! Because of my proclamation, you will wear red on that day!* Ask students to guess what *proclaim* and *proclamation* mean. Explain that *proclaim* means "to declare or announce officially and publicly," and a *proclamation* is something that is announced officially or proclaimed.

Alternative Sort: Vowel Sound

Have students sort the base words and derived words according to the vowel sound in the second syllable: ē, ĕ, ū, ə and ā. Ask students to pair the base and correlating derived words as they go.

ELL **English Language Learners**

Have students practice pronouncing each word, focusing on articulating each sound clearly. If necessary, describe or demonstrate how to move the mouth and tongue and how to breathe in order to create the sound. Provide a mirror for students to monitor their own mouth and tongue movements.

Sort 13
Adding the Suffix *-ation*: Vowel Alternation (With Spelling Change)

Objectives

- To recognize how words ending in *-ify* or *-iply* change with the addition of suffix *-ation*
- To sort and spell words ending in *-ify* and *-iply* and their derivatives ending in *-ation*

Materials for Derivational Relations

Whiteboard Activities DVD-ROM, Sort 13

Teacher Resource CD-ROM, Sort 13 and Around the Dock Game

Student Book, pages 49–52

Words	
Base	**Derived**
-ify/-iply	*-ation*
identify	identification
justify	justification
multiply	multiplication
simplify	simplification
verify	verification
magnify	magnification
notify	notification
clarify	clarification
purify	purification
qualify	qualification
unify	unification

Introduce/Model   *Small Groups*

- Use the whiteboard DVD or the CD word cards to introduce in context any word that may be unfamiliar.

- Have students first sort the words into two categories: base words and derived words. Read aloud all of the base words. Lead students to notice that the base words all end in *-ify* or *-iply,* and that *-y* always has a long *i* sound.

- Display the headers Base *ify/-iply classify* and Derived *-ation classification.* Have students match each base word with its related derived word.

- Lead students to see that *-y* is changed to *i* and *c* is added, and the long *i* sound spelled by *y* in the base word changes to a short *i* sound.

Practice the Sort   *Independent/Partner*

- Have students use the Student Book or whiteboard DVD to say each word and use the grid to sort.

- Have students check and explain their sorts.

Apply   *Independent/Partner/Small Groups*

- Read aloud the directions on Student Book p. 52. Have students complete the activity.

- **Game** Allow time for students to play Around the Dock, which is on the CD.

Extend the Sort

Vocabulary 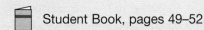 **W**ord **O**f the **W**eek:

justify/justification Ask students to guess the meanings of *justify* and *justification* from sample sentences, such as *She could justify every dollar she spent. Her justification was that she only bought supplies that she needed for school.* Explain that *justify* means "to show or prove to be just, right, or valid." *Justification* can mean "the act of justifying" or "something that justifies."

ELL **English Language Learners**

Have students repeat after you as you pronounce each word. Then pose questions that require students to choose the correct sort word and to explain their answer, such as *If you have a good reason for doing something, can you justify/multiply what you did?* (justify) *Why?*

Teacher Tip

Whenever possible, share important information with students by using multiple media or modes of communication. For example, along with oral and written explanations of a word's meaning, you could also provide illustrations or videos.

Examining Multiple Alternations

Objectives

- To recognize that there can be many related words in a family
- To sort and spell words that come from the same root or base

Materials for Derivational Relations

- Whiteboard Activities DVD-ROM, Sort 14

- Teacher Resource CD-ROM, Sort 14 and Catching Fireflies Game

- Student Book, pages 53–56

Words

diplomat	diplomacy	diplomatic
punish	punitive	impunity
academy	academic	
syllable	syllabic	
impugn	pugnacity	pugnacious
diverse	divert	diversion
defame	defamatory	
copy	copious	
allege	allegation	
trivial	triviality	

Introduce/Model   *Small Groups*

- Use the whiteboard DVD or the CD word cards to introduce in context any word that may be unfamiliar.

- Model grouping together *diplomat, diplomacy,* and *diplomatic.* Help students sort by spelling-meaning families, putting words they think go together in groups. Have students name the words in each group and discuss how the words are related in meaning.

- Read the groups of words, pointing out prefixes, suffixes, and spelling and pronunciation changes.

- Lead students to understand that recognizing a root or base word will help them know the meaning of many related words.

Practice the Sort   *Independent/Partner*

- Have students use the Student Book or whiteboard DVD to say each word and use the grid to sort the words into related groups and identify the spelling and pronunciation differences.

- Have students check and explain their sorts.

Apply   *Independent/Partner/Small Groups*

- Read aloud the directions on Student Book p. 56. Have students complete the activity.

- **Game** Allow time for students to play Catching Fireflies, which is on the CD.

Extend the Sort

Vocabulary **W**ord **O**f the **W**eek:

diverse Ask students to guess the meaning of *diverse* from a sample sentence, such as *The crowd was made up of students of all ages and their opinions were quite diverse.* Explain that *diverse* means "different" or "unlike."

Alternative Sort: Which Affix?

Have students sort the words by affix (*-ity, -ic, -ous, -ion, im-, de-*).

ELL **English Language Learners**

Have students repeat after you as you pronounce each word. Then pose questions that require students to choose the correct sort word and to explain their answer, such as *The diplomat suggested we try to solve the problem with allegations/diplomacy first.* (diplomacy) *Why?*

Sort 15

Greek and Latin Number Prefixes *mono-, bi-, tri-*

Objectives

- To identify the prefixes *mono-*, *bi-*, and *tri-* and understand how they influence the meanings of words
- To sort and spell words with the prefixes *mono-*, *bi-*, and *tri-*

Materials for Derivational Relations

🖥 Whiteboard Activities DVD-ROM, Sort 15

💿 Teacher Resource CD-ROM, Sort 15 and Spin and Win Game

📖 Student Book, pages 57–60

Words

mono-	bi-	tri-
monologue	biennial	tripod
monopod	bisect	tricolor
monopoly	binary	trilogy
monorail	bicameral	trigonometry
monotone	biweekly	tricentennial
monotony	bimonthly	triathlon
	biceps	triplets
		triennial

Introduce/Model
Small Groups

- Use the whiteboard DVD or the CD word cards to introduce in context any word that may be unfamiliar.

- Model sorting several words according to prefixes. Have students complete the sort.

- Ask students what *monthly* means. (It means "done once a month.") Point out how the meaning of base words such as *monthly* are changed by the addition of prefixes such as *bi-* and *tri-*. (*Bimonthly* means "once every two months" and *trimonthly* means "once every three months.")

- Discuss with students what the prefixes *mono-*, *bi-* and *tri-* mean. (*Mono-* means "one," *bi-* means "two," and *tri-* means "three".)

Practice the Sort
Independent/Partner

- Have students use the Student Book or whiteboard DVD to say each word and use the grid to sort.

- Have students check and explain their sorts.

Apply
Independent/Partner/Small Groups

- Read aloud the directions on Student Book p. 60. Have students complete the activity.

- **Game** Allow time for students to play Spin and Win, which is on the CD.

Extend the Sort

Vocabulary **Word Of the Week:**

tripod Ask students to guess the meaning of *tripod* from a sample sentence, such as *All three legs of the tripod must be solidly on the ground to hold the camera steady.* Explain that *tripod* means
"a three-legged stand to hold a camera or other device."

ELL **English Language Learners**

Have students repeat after you as you pronounce each word. Then ask students to supply any other words they know that begin with one of these prefixes. (*tricycle, bicycle, monorail*)

Teacher Tip

Ask students to search books and magazines for new words with the prefixes *mono-*, *bi-*, and *tri-*. Have them write the words on sticky notes and include them with the other words from the sort.

260 **Derivational Relations**

Objectives

- To recognize how the prefixes *inter-, sub-,* and *over-* change the meaning of base words
- To sort and spell words with the prefixes *inter-, sub-,* and *over-*

Materials for Derivational Relations

- Whiteboard Activities DVD-ROM, Sort 16
- Teacher Resource CD-ROM, Sort 16 and Mail Route Game
- Student Book, pages 61–64

Words

inter-	*sub-*	*over-*
international	subfloor	overflow
intercept	submerge	overlook
Internet	subway	overstep
interact	subhead	overthrow
interchange	subtitle	overwhelm
interconnect	suburban	overreact
intersect	sublet	overeager
interfere	subtotal	overripe
intermediate	subdivide	oversee
		overtake

Introduce/Model
Small Groups

- Use the whiteboard DVD or the CD word cards to introduce in context any word that may be unfamiliar.
- Model sorting several words into prefix groups. Have students complete the sort.
- Help students develop definitions for the prefixes: *inter-* means "between" or "among"; *sub-* means "under" or "close to"; *over-* means "above," "excessively," or "completely."
- Guide students to examine how adding prefixes changes the meanings of words, such as *national* meaning "of or about a nation" and *international* meaning "between or among two or more nations."

Practice the Sort
Independent/Partner

- Have students use the Student Book or whiteboard DVD to say each word and use the grid to sort the words into prefix groups.
- Have students check and explain their sorts.

Apply
Independent/Partner/Small Groups

- Read aloud the directions on Student Book p. 64. Have students complete the activity.
- **Game** Allow time for students to play Mail Route, which is on the CD.

Extend the Sort

Vocabulary **Word Of the Week:**

overthrow Ask students whether they have heard the word *overthrow*, and if so, when and where. Provide a sample sentence, such as *The rebels secretly planned to overthrow the government.* Give students time to guess the meaning of the word from context and then clarify that *overthrow* means to "throw over" or "overturn."

Alternative Sort: Base Word or Word Root

Have students sort by whether each word contains a base word or a word root. Remind students that word roots, unlike base words, cannot stand alone when prefixes and suffixes are removed.

ELL English Language Learners

Review with students the pronunciation of each word and meaning of the prefixes. (*Inter-* means "between" or "among"; *sub-* means "under" or "close to"; *over-* means "above," "excessively," or "completely.") Then ask students to identify any words that they still find difficult or confusing, and why. Work with students to clarify understanding.

Number Prefixes *quadr-, tetra-, quint-, pent-, dec*

Objectives

- To identify the prefixes *quadr-, tetra-, quint-, pent-,* and *dec-* and understand how they influence the meanings of words
- To sort and spell words beginning with *quadr-, tetra-, quint-, pent-,* and *dec-*

Materials for Derivational Relations

Whiteboard Activities DVD-ROM, Sort 17

Teacher Resource CD-ROM, Sort 17 and Spin and Win Game

Student Book, pages 65–68

Words

quadr-	*tetra-*	*quint-*
quadrant	tetralogy	quintuplets
quadrangle	tetrarchy	quintessence
quadruplets	tetrapod	quintessential
quadruped		
quadrennial		

pent-	*dec-*
pentangle	decathlete
pentathlon	decimate
pentathlete	decathlon
pentarchy	
pentad	

Introduce/Model   *Small Groups*

- Use the whiteboard DVD or the CD word cards to introduce in context any word that may be unfamiliar.
- Model sorting several words according to prefixes. Have students complete the sort.
- Ask students if they have heard of *quadruplets.* Explain that *quad-* means "four" and that *quadruplets* are four children born at the same time to the same mother. Tell students that the prefix *quint-* means "five." Challenge them to define *quintuplets.*
- Lead students to develop definitions for *tetra-, pent-,* and *dec-.* (*Tetra-* means "four," *pent-* means "five," and *dec-* means "ten.") Point out that some of these sort words no longer carry the numerical meaning of the prefix.

Practice the Sort   *Independent/Partner*

- Have students use the Student Book or whiteboard DVD to say each word and use the grid to sort.
- Have students check and explain their sorts.

Apply   *Independent/Partner/Small Groups*

- Read aloud the directions on Student Book p. 68. Have students complete the activity.
- **Game** Allow time for students to play Spin and Win, which is on the CD.

Extend the Sort

Vocabulary **W**ord **O**f the **W**eek:

pentathlon Ask students to guess the meaning of *pentathlon* from a sample sentence, such as *The winner of the pentathlon was not announced until much later since all the athletes had to complete five contests each.* Explain that *pentathlon* means "an athletic competition that requires five different sports."

ELL **English Language Learners**

Have students repeat after you as you pronounce each word. Then caution students that some of the words in this sort no longer carry the numerical meaning of the prefix (*decimate, quintessence, quintessential*).

Monitor Progress ✔ **Spell Check 2**

After completing Sort 17, administer Spell Check 2. See p. 245 in this Teacher Resource Guide for instructions.

Latin Word Roots *spect, port*

Objectives

- To recognize how the roots *spect* and *port* combine with other elements to create derived words
- To sort and spell words with *spect* and *port*

Materials for Derivational Relations

📺 Whiteboard Activities DVD-ROM, Sort 18

💿 Teacher Resource CD-ROM, Sort 18 and Root Work Game

📓 Student Book, pages 69–72

Words

spect	port
inspection	support
perspective	portable
speculate	deport
spectator	import
prospect	transport
inspector	report
spectacle	portfolio
spectacular	heliport
spectrum	opportunity

Introduce/Model
Small Groups

- Use the whiteboard DVD or the CD word cards to introduce the words, but do not discuss the meaning of any words yet.

- Guide students to notice that the words contain either the root *spect* or *port*. Then display those headers and have students sort according to the roots.

- Help students develop definitions for the Latin word roots: *spect* means "to look" or "*see*" and *port* means "to carry."

- Display *inspection* and provide its meaning, "examination" or "the act of inspecting." Guide students to see that *inspection* is made up of the prefix *in-* (meaning "into"), the root *spect* (meaning "to look at"), and the suffix *-ion* (meaning "the act or result"). Continue in a similar manner for other words.

Practice the Sort
Independent/Partner

- Have students use the Student Book or whiteboard DVD to say each word and use the grid to sort the words into Latin root groups.

- Have students check and explain their sorts.

Apply
Independent/Partner/Small Groups

- Read aloud the directions on Student Book p. 72. Have students complete the activity.

- **Game** Allow time for students to play Root Work, which is on the CD.

Extend the Sort

Vocabulary Word Of the Week:

prospect Provide a sentence using *prospect*, such as *The prospect of nice weather caused the family to plan a camping trip.* Give students time to guess its meaning from context. Then have a student look up *prospect* in a dictionary and share with the class that it means "something anticipated" or "an expectation."

Teacher Tip

Point out that Latin or Greek roots may show up in a word but not be an actual root. For example, have students consult a dictionary to find that *sport* looks like it contains the word root *port* but actually comes from the French *desporter*, meaning "to divert." Have students check a word's etymology in a dictionary if they are unsure about its root.

ELL English Language Learners

Pronounce each word and have students repeat the words aloud after you. Have them summarize what they have learned about *spect* and *port*. Then ask students to tell in their own words what each sort word means. Clarify understanding as needed.

Sort 19
Latin Word Roots *dic, aud*

Objectives

- To recognize how the roots *dic* and *aud* combine with other words or word parts to create new meanings
- To sort and spell words with the roots *dic* and *aud*

Materials for Derivational Relations

🖥 Whiteboard Activities DVD-ROM, Sort 19

💿 Teacher Resource CD-ROM, Sort 19 and Word Building Game

📖 Student Book, pages 73–76

Words

dic	*aud*
predict	auditorium
contradict	auditory
unpredictable	audience
verdict	audiotape
dictionary	audible
dictator	audition
diction	audiovisual
	audit

Introduce/Model *Small Groups*

- Use the whiteboard DVD or the CD word cards to introduce the words, but do not discuss the meaning of any words yet.

- Guide students to notice that the words contain either the root *dic* or *aud*. Then display those headers and have students sort according to the roots.

- Help students develop definitions for the Latin word roots: *dic* means "to say" or "speak" and *aud* means "to hear."

- Display *unpredictable*. Show students how after *un-* and *-able* are removed, the base word *predict* remains. *Predict* means "to say before"; put *-able* back on and discuss what *predictable* means. Put *un* back on and discuss what *unpredictable* means.

Practice the Sort *Independent/Partner*

- Have students use the Student Book or whiteboard DVD to say each word and use the grid to sort the words into Latin root groups.

- Have students check and explain their sorts.

Apply *Independent/Partner/Small Groups*

- Read aloud the directions on Student Book p. 76. Have students complete the activity.

- **Game** Allow time for students to play Word Building, which is on the CD.

Extend the Sort

Vocabulary **W**ord **O**f the **W**eek:
verdict Ask students whether they have heard the word *verdict,* and if so, when and where. Provide examples of people making a verdict (a jury declaring a person "not guilty" or race officials watching a videotape to say who won a close race). Ask students what they think *verdict* means. Clarify that people make a verdict by examining facts as best they can to decide and state what is true.

Alternative Sort: Parts of Speech

Have students sort the words by parts of speech: nouns, verbs, and adjectives. As this sort is finished, challenge students to remove words that can be either a noun or verb. (*audition, audit, audiotape*)

Teacher Tip

Have students draw a character with its mouth wide open and write words that contain the root *dic* in a speech balloon. Instruct them to underline *dic* in these words. Then have students draw a large ear and write words that contain the root *aud* in a funnel of sound waves. Instruct them to underline *aud* in these words.

Objectives

- To recognize how the word roots *rupt, tract,* and *mot* combine with other words or word parts to create derived words
- To sort and spell words with *rupt, tract,* and *mot*

Materials for Derivational Relations

☐ Whiteboard Activities DVD-ROM, Sort 20

◉ Teacher Resource CD-ROM, Sort 20 and Analyze It! Game

📖 Student Book, pages 77–80

Words

rupt	*tract*	*mot*
erupt	subtract	remote
rupture	contract	promotion
abrupt	distract	demote
disrupt	traction	promote
corrupt	attraction	emotion
bankrupt	extract	motivate
interruption	tractor	motor

Introduce/Model   *Small Groups*

- Use the whiteboard DVD or the CD word cards to introduce the words. Ask students what they notice about these words.

- Guide students to identify the word roots *rupt, tract,* and *mot*.

- Have students sort the words according to the word root. Encourage them to predict the word roots' meanings.

- Help students develop definitions for the Latin word roots: *rupt* means "to break," *tract* means "to draw out or pull," and *mot* means "to move."

Practice the Sort   *Independent/Partner*

- Have students use the Student Book or whiteboard DVD to say each word and use the grid to sort the words into Latin root groups.

- Have students check and explain their sorts.

Apply   *Independent/Partner/Small Groups*

- Read aloud the directions on Student Book p. 80. Have students complete the activity.

- **Game** Allow time for students to play Analyze It!, which is on the CD.

Extend the Sort

Vocabulary **Word Of the Week:**

extract Ask students whether they have heard the word *extract,* and if so, when and where. Provide an example sentence to clarify meaning: *The vet extracted the dog's infected tooth.* Ask students what they think *extract* means. Clarify that *extract* means to "pull out" or "remove."

Alternative Sort: Prefixes

Have students sort the words by prefixes: *sub-, dis-, re-, inter-, ex-.* As this sort is finished, challenge students to tell what the prefixes mean.

ELL **English Language Learners**

Have students practice pronouncing each word, focusing on articulating each sound clearly. Encourage students to use the words in sentences.

Latin Word Roots *ject, man, cred*

Objectives

- To recognize how the word roots *ject, man,* and *cred* combine with other words or word parts to create derived words
- To sort and spell words with *ject, man,* and *cred*

Materials for Derivational Relations

🖥 Whiteboard Activities DVD-ROM, Sort 21

💿 Teacher Resource CD-ROM, Sort 21 and Lucky Draw Game

📕 Student Book, pages 81–84

Words

ject	*man*	*cred*
reject	manipulate	credit
eject	manage	discredit
subject	maneuver	credentials
projectile	manuscript	credible
objection	manufacture	
rejection	manicure	
injection		

Introduce/Model *Small Groups*

- Use the whiteboard DVD or the CD word cards to introduce the words. Ask students what is alike and different about the words.

- Guide students to identify the word roots *ject, man,* and *cred*.

- Display the headers *(ject inject, man manual, cred incredible)*. Have students sort the words according to the word root.

- Help students develop definitions for the Latin word roots: *ject* means "to throw," *man* means "hand," and *cred* means "to believe."

Practice the Sort *Independent/Partner*

- Have students use the Student Book or whiteboard DVD to say each word and use the grid to sort the words into Latin root groups.

- Have students check and explain their sorts.

Apply *Independent/Partner/Small Groups*

- Read aloud the directions on Student Book p. 84. Have students complete the activity.

- **Game** Allow time for students to play Lucky Draw, which is on the CD.

Extend the Sort

Vocabulary **Word Of the Week:**

projectile Provide a sample sentence using *projectile,* such as *Wearing a seat belt protects a person from becoming a projectile during an accident.* Have students predict what *projectile* means. Clarify that any object or person can be a projectile if it is thrown, hurled, or shot by a strong force and goes on moving until another force stops it.

Alternative Sort: Nouns and Verbs

Have students sort the words by the categories noun, verb, noun or verb, and oddball. Challenge students to explain why they placed the words in the categories they did. (*Manicure, credit,* and *discredit* can be either a noun or a verb; *credible* is the only adjective.)

ELL English Language Learners

Model and have students echo repetitive sentences using *credit,* such as *I give her credit for trying. The new player is a credit to the team.* Personalize the sentences to be appropriate to your students and your school.

Objectives

- To recognize how the word roots *vid/vis* and *scrib/script* combine with other words or word parts to create derived words
- To sort and spell words with *vid/vis* and *scrib/script*

Materials for Derivational Relations

- Whiteboard Activities DVD-ROM, Sort 22

- Teacher Resource CD-ROM, Sort 22 and Clue In Game

- Student Book, pages 85–88

Words	
vid/vis	**scrib/script**
revise	inscription
television	description
visionary	transcribe
vista	subscribe
supervise	prescribe
video	prescription
visible	inscribe
visit	transcript
televise	postscript
improvise	subscription
provide	scribe

Introduce/Model
Small Groups

- Use the whiteboard DVD or the CD word cards to introduce in context any word that may be unfamiliar.

- Display the header *vid/vis vision* and have students sort all appropriate words in this category.

- Organize the remainder of the words into a column and ask students if they see a pattern. Display the header *scrib/script describe*. Then have students read the columns of words aloud and predict the word roots' meanings.

- Clarify that *vid/vis* means "to see," and *scrib/script* means "to write." Explain that these word roots come from the original Latin verbs in which the sound changed in different forms and therefore the spelling changed as well, similar to what happens with many English verbs: *think/thought, sleep/slept.*

Practice the Sort
Independent/Partner

- Have students use the Student Book or whiteboard DVD to say each word and use the grid to sort.

- Have students check and explain their sorts.

Apply
Independent/Partner/Small Groups

- Read aloud the directions on Student Book p. 88. Have students complete the activity.

- **Game** Allow time for students to play Clue In, which is on the CD.

Extend the Sort

Vocabulary **Word Of the Week:**
subscribe/subscription Provide a sample sentence using *subscribe* and *subscription*, such as *Mom wants to subscribe to that magazine, but the subscriptions are for five years.* Have students predict what *subscribe* and *subscription* mean. Have a student check the dictionary for the definitions.

ELL English Language Learners
Model and have students echo the sort words and volunteer sentences using the words: *The school will provide the sports equipment.*

Alternative Sort: Verbs Changed to Nouns

Have students sort the *scrib* and *script* cards into three categories: verbs, nouns with a base-word spelling change, and other nouns. Challenge them to reorder the nouns so they are beside their verb base word.

Latin Word Roots *jud, leg, flu*

Objectives

- To recognize how the word roots *jud, leg,* and *flu* combine with other elements to create derived words
- To sort and spell words with *jud, leg,* and *flu*

Materials for Derivational Relations

📺 Whiteboard Activities DVD-ROM, Sort 23

💿 Teacher Resource CD-ROM, Sort 23 and Sailing Safety Game

📖 Student Book, pages 89–92

Words

jud	leg	flu
judgmental	illegal	flume
judge	legalize	fluctuate
judicial	legislate	fluent
prejudge	legacy	fluency
misjudge	privilege	flush
prejudice	legitimate	influence
	legislator	influenza

Introduce/Model   *Small Groups*

- Use the whiteboard DVD or the CD word cards to introduce in context any word that may be unfamiliar.

- Display the header *jud/judgment* and have students sort the appropriate words into this category.

- Ask students what is alike and different about the remaining words. Guide them to see the *leg* or *flu* pattern in the words and then sort the words. When the sort is complete, have students predict the meanings of the word roots.

- Explain that *jud* means "to judge," *leg* means "law," and *flu* means "to flow."

Practice the Sort   *Independent/Partner*

- Have students use the Student Book or whiteboard DVD to say each word and use the grid to sort.

- Have students check and explain their sorts.

Apply   *Independent/Partner/Small Groups*

- Read aloud the directions on Student Book p. 92. Have students complete the activity.

- **Game** Allow time for students to play Sailing Safety, which is on the CD.

Extend the Sort

Vocabulary **Word Of the Week:**

judgmental Help students deduce the meaning of *judgmental* by having them talk about the meaning of each word part. Then provide a sample sentence, such as *The artist welcomed helpful suggestions but not judgmental comments.* Have a volunteer consult a dictionary and clarify that *judgmental* describes having or making statements of opinion.

Alternative Sort: Words and Connotations

Place *illegal* and *fluent* in different columns and lead students to see that you sorted by "words that connote negative feelings" versus "words that connote positive feelings." Let them identify where the other words belong and explain why.

ELL **English Language Learners**

Give extra support and practice for pronouncing the roots within the sort words. Help students softly clap out syllables as they read each word and identify when a letter in the root changes sound or goes with the next syllable.

Greek and Latin Elements *-crat/-cracy, -arch/-archy*

Sort 24

Objectives

- To recognize how the elements *-crat/-cracy* and *-arch/-archy* combine with other elements to create meaning
- To sort and spell words with *-crat/-cracy* and *-arch/-archy*

Materials for Derivational Relations

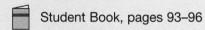

Whiteboard Activities DVD-ROM, Sort 24

Teacher Resource CD-ROM, Sort 24 and Word Search Game

Student Book, pages 93–96

Words

-crat	-cracy	-arch	-archy
aristocrat	aristocracy	oligarch	oligarchy
democrat	democracy	anarchist	anarchy
bureaucrat	bureaucracy	hierarchical	hierarchy
plutocrat	plutocracy	patriarch	patriarchy
technocrat	technocracy	matriarch	matriarchy

Introduce/Model   *Small Groups*

- Use the whiteboard DVD or the CD word cards to introduce the words.
- Display the headers *-crat autocrat, -cracy autocracy, -arch monarch,* and *-archy monarchy.* Have students sort the words according to word elements.
- Help students develop definitions for the Greek and Latin elements: *-crat/-cracy* and *-arch/-archy* mean "form of government or one who follows that government."
- Guide students to refer to dictionaries to determine the meanings of *auto, bureau,* and *monarch.* Discuss how those word parts are combined with the elements *-crat/-cracy* and *-arch/-archy* to create *autocrat/autocracy, bureaucrat/bureaucracy,* and *monarch/monarchy,* and determine their meanings.

Practice the Sort   *Independent/Partner*

- Have students use the Student Book or whiteboard DVD to say each word and use the grid to sort.
- Have students check and explain their sorts.

Apply   *Independent/Partner/Small Groups*

- Read aloud the directions on Student Book p. 96. Have students complete the activity.
- **Game** Allow time for students to play Word Search, which is on the CD.

Extend the Sort

Vocabulary **Word Of the Week:**
aristocrat Help students deduce the meaning of *aristocrat* by providing a sample sentence, such as *The wealthy aristocrat thought everyone should look to him for how to behave.* Have a volunteer consult a dictionary and clarify that *aristocrat* means a person of high birth or wealth.

ELL **English Language Learners**
Give extra support and practice for pronouncing the sort words. Help students see that the first part of these words can help them with other words they might come across: *techno—technology, technician, high-tech.*

Teacher Tip
To help students remember the definitions of this sort's words, set up a classroom chart. List the words in the chart. Then ask students to find the definitions of each word and include them in the chart.

Sort 25

Latin Word Roots *spire, sist, sign*

Objectives

- To recognize how the word roots *spire, sist,* and *sign* combine with other elements to create derived words
- To sort and spell words with *spire, sist,* and *sign*

Materials for Derivational Relations

🖥 Whiteboard Activities DVD-ROM, Sort 25

💿 Teacher Resource CD-ROM, Sort 25 and Stepping Stones Game

📓 Student Book, pages 97–100

Words

spire	sist	sign
inspire	insistent	assign
transpire	insist	signature
perspire	consistent	designate
aspiration	resistance	resign
conspire	assist	design
	persist	insignia
		cosign

Introduce/Model   *Small Groups*

- Use the whiteboard DVD or the CD word cards to introduce the words. Ask students to suggest how the words can be sorted.

- Display the header *sist resist* and have students sort the appropriate words into this category.

- Guide students to see the *spire* or *sign* pattern in the remaining words and have them sort the words. When the sort is complete, have students predict the meanings of the word roots.

- Help students develop definitions for the Latin word roots: *spire* means "to breathe," *sist* means "to stand," and *sign* means "to write one's name or mark."

Practice the Sort   *Independent/Partner*

- Have students use the Student Book or whiteboard DVD to say each word and use the grid to sort.

- Have students check and explain their sorts.

Apply   *Independent/Partner/Small Groups*

- Read aloud the directions on Student Book p. 100. Have students complete the activity.

- **Game** Allow time for students to play Stepping Stones, which is on the CD.

Extend the Sort

Vocabulary **W**ord **O**f the **W**eek:
conspire Share a sample sentence for *conspire,* such as *A girl's friends will conspire to surprise her with a party.* Allow students time to define the word. Clarify that *conspire* means "to plan secretly." Have a student consult a dictionary and share that the Latin word parts of *conspire* mean "to breathe together."

Alternative Sort: Schwa Review

Help students recall that the vowel sound in unaccented syllables of words such as *amaze, distant,* and *decorate* is different from short and long vowel sounds. Have students sort to find words with and without the schwa sound.

ELL **English Language Learners**

Explain that one common American usage of *resign* has nothing to do with giving up a job. Model this use in a sample sentence, such as *You must resign yourself to staying in bed when you are sick.* Explain "resign yourself" as "to quietly do something without complaining." Prompt students to add more examples by completing the sentence, *He had to resign himself _____.*

Greek and Latin Elements *cap, ped, corp*

Objectives

- To recognize how the elements *cap, ped,* and *corp* combine with other elements to create meanings
- To sort and spell words with *cap, ped,* and *corp*

Materials for Derivational Relations

- Whiteboard Activities DVD-ROM, Sort 26
- Teacher Resource CD-ROM, Sort 26 and Clue In Game
- Student Book, pages 101–104

Words

cap	ped	corp
captivity	pedal	corporate
captive	pedestal	corporal
capitol	expedition	corpse
decapitate	peddler	incorporate
captivate	centipede	corps
captain	pedicure	
	peddle	

Introduce/Model   *Small Groups*

- Use the whiteboard DVD or the CD word cards to introduce the words. Ask students what they notice about the words.

- Display *capitol* and *captive.* Guide students to identify a pattern. *(cap)* Have them sort the appropriate words into this category.

- Explain that *cap* has a Greek and Latin meaning— "head" and "to take."

- Have students sort the remaining words according to the *ped* and *corp* patterns. Explain that *ped* means "foot" in this sort (it can also mean "child") and *corp* means "body."

Practice the Sort   *Independent/Partner*

- Have students use the Student Book or whiteboard DVD to say each word and use the grid to sort.

- Have students check and explain their sorts.

Apply   *Independent/Partner/Small Groups*

- Read aloud the directions on Student Book p. 104. Have students complete the activity.

- **Game** Allow time for students to play Clue In, which is on the CD.

Extend the Sort

Vocabulary **Word Of the Week:**

capitol Help students deduce the meaning of *capitol* by providing a sample sentence, such as *We hurried up the steps into the capitol to see our state congress in session.* Have a volunteer consult a dictionary and clarify that *capitol* means a building where a legislature meets.

Alternative Sort: Parts of Speech

Have students sort the words by the categories nouns, verbs, and others. When students have finished the sort, challenge them to use one of the nouns and verbs together in a sentence.

ELL **English Language Learners**

Give extra support and practice for pronouncing the sort words. Help students remember the difference between the similar words: *corps* and *corpse.* (a group of soldiers and a dead human body)

Greek and Latin Word Roots *sect, vert/vers, form*

Objectives

- To recognize how the root words *sect, vert/vers,* and *form* combine with other elements to create derived words
- To sort and spell words with *sect, vert/vers,* and *form*

Materials for Derivational Relations

📺 Whiteboard Activities DVD-ROM, Sort 27

💿 Teacher Resource CD-ROM, Sort 27 and Find the Formula Game

📖 Student Book, pages 105–108

Words

sect	vert/vers	form
bisect	revert	formal
insect	convert	conform
intersect	divert	inform
sector	invert	reform
section	advertise	format
	conversion	formulate
	reverse	uniform
	universe	landform

Introduce/Model
Small Groups

- Use the whiteboard DVD or the CD word cards to introduce the words. Ask students if they see any words that may be related by meaning. *(sector, section; convert, conversion; revert, reverse)*

- Display the headers *sect dissect, vert/vers version,* and *form formula* and point out that ancient Greeks and Romans sometimes used slightly different spellings for words, as with the roots *vert* and *vers*. *Have students complete the sort.*

- Ask students in what way they think the words in each column reflect the meanings of the roots.

- Invite students to predict the meanings of the word roots. Clarify that *sect* means "to cut," *vert/vers* means "to turn," and *form* means "to give shape."

Practice the Sort
Independent/Partner

- Have students use the Student Book or whiteboard DVD to say each word and use the grid to sort.

- Have students check and explain their sorts.

Apply
Independent/Partner/Small Groups

- Read aloud the directions on Student Book p. 108. Have students complete the activity.

- **Game** Allow time for students to play Find the Formula, which is on the CD.

Extend the Sort

Vocabulary **Word Of the Week:**

conform Share sample sentences that relay the different contexts of *conform: Students should conform to school and class rules. We need to write sentences that conform to usual sentence patterns.* Have a student consult a dictionary and clarify that *conform* means either "to be in accord or agreement" or "to agree with what is usual."

Alternative Sort: Schwa in Unaccented Syllables

Have students sort the words by the categories accented first syllable and accented second syllable. Then have them identify the vowels in unaccented syllables that stand for the /ə/ sound.

ELL **English Language Learners**

Draw a large circle and explain that it's a big pizza. Illustrate cutting it up and serving it. Use target sort words *(bisect, sector, section, intersect)* to describe what you are doing.

Objectives

- To recognize how the root words *onym* and *gen* combine with other elements to create derived words
- To sort and spell words with *onym* and *gen*

Materials for Derivational Relations

Whiteboard Activities DVD-ROM, Sort 28

Teacher Resource CD-ROM, Sort 28 and Word Roots Game

Student Book, pages 109–112

Words

onym	gen
antonym	genesis
anonymous	progenitor
patronymic	generic
pseudonym	genre
eponym	progeny
acronym	genetic
homonym	hydrogen
	regenerate
	gene

Introduce/Model
Small Groups

- Use the whiteboard DVD or the CD word cards to introduce in context any word that may be unfamiliar.
- Help students notice that the words contain the roots *onym* and *gen*.
- Display the headers *(onym synonym, gen generator)*. Have students sort the words accordingly. Ask students what they think the roots might mean.
- Help students develop definitions for the Greek and Latin elements: *onym* means "name" and *gen* means "to be born" or "to become."

Practice the Sort
Independent/Partner

- Have students use the Student Book or whiteboard DVD to say each word and use the grid to sort the words into Greek and Latin element groups.
- Have students check and explain their sorts.

Apply
Independent/Partner/Small Groups

- Read aloud the directions on Student Book p. 112. Have students complete the activity.
- **Game** Allow time for students to play Word Roots, which is on the CD.

Extend the Sort

Vocabulary W**ord** O**f the** W**eek:**

pseudonym Share a sample sentence to give a context for *pseudonym: The reporter used a pseudonym so that he could keep his identity hidden.* Have a student consult a dictionary and clarify that *pseudonym* means "false or made up name."

Alternative Sort: Where's the Root?

Have students sort the words by the categories beginning, middle, and end to show the part of the word containing the root. Then have students generalize what they can tell about these roots in these words. (Some roots are at the beginning or ending of a word most often, but they can appear anywhere.)

ELL English Language Learners

Have students repeat after you as you pronounce each word and discuss its meaning. Then have them choose words from the sort to complete this sentence: *The _____ is biography, but the author's name is not given; the writer is _____. (genre, anonymous)*

Greek and Latin Word Roots *voc, ling, mem, psych*

Objectives

- To recognize how the root words *voc, ling, mem,* and *psych* combine with other elements to create derived words
- To sort and spell words with *voc, ling, mem,* and *psych*

Materials for Derivational Relations

Whiteboard Activities DVD-ROM, Sort 29

Teacher Resource CD-ROM, Sort 29 and Which Root? Game

Student Book, pages 113–116

Words

voc	ling	mem	psych
vocalic	linguini	remembrance	psychiatry
vocabulary	multilingual	commemorate	psycholinguists
advocate	linguaphile	memorandum	psychopathology
provocative	psycholinguists	memorial	
invocation	sociolinguist	immemorial	
invoke			
provoke			
provocation			

Introduce/Model
Small Groups

- Use the whiteboard DVD or the CD word cards to introduce in context any word that may be unfamiliar.

- Display *vocalic* and *vocabulary* following it. Ask students if they notice a pattern. *(voc)* Have them sort the appropriate words into this category.

- Guide students to see the *ling, mem,* and *psych* patterns in the remaining words and then sort the words accordingly.

- Help students develop definitions for the Greek and Latin elements: *voc* means "voice," *ling* means "tongue," *mem* means "worthy of being remembered," and *psych* means "soul." Ask students in what way they think the words in each column reflect the meanings of the roots.

Practice the Sort
Independent/Partner

- Have students use the Student Book or whiteboard DVD to say each word and use the grid to sort.

- Have students check and explain their sorts.

Apply
Independent/Partner/Small Groups

- Read aloud the directions on Student Book p. 116. Have students complete the activity.

- **Game** Allow time for students to play Which Root?, which is on the CD.

Extend the Sort

Vocabulary **Word Of the Week:**

multilingual Share a sample sentence to give a context for *multilingual: The transfer student was truly multilingual; he spoke Spanish, English, and French with ease.* Have a student consult a dictionary and clarify that *multilingual* means "to know several languages."

ELL **English Language Learners**

Pronounce the words slowly, emphasizing each sound, and have students repeat them. Check that students are correctly saying each word. Emphasize that in related word pairs, the same letter may represent a different sound.

Teacher Tip

If students have difficulty remembering the definitions of some of the sort's words, have them use those words in context as they sort. For instance, they can write a sentence using each word as practice.

Prefixes *intra-*, *inter-*, *intro-*

Objectives
- To recognize how prefixes *intra-*, *inter-*, and *intro-* combine with other elements to create derived words
- To sort and spell words with the prefixes *intra-*, *inter-*, and *intro-*

Materials for Derivational Relations

📋 Whiteboard Activities DVD-ROM, Sort 30

💿 Teacher Resource CD-ROM, Sort 30 and In the Game Game

📒 Student Book, pages 117–120

Words

intra-	*inter-*	*intro-*
intravenous	international	introspection
intranational	interpersonal	introversion
intrastate	intercept	
intracellular	interregnum	
intragalactic	Internet	
intrapersonal		

Introduce/Model *Small Groups*

- Use the whiteboard DVD or the CD word cards to introduce the words. Ask students what they notice about the words. (They begin with the prefix *intra-*, *inter-*, or *intro-*.)

- Display the headers *(intra- intramural, inter- intermural, intro- introvert)* and have students say the words aloud and then sort them according to prefix.

- Give students time to discuss what each prefix might mean.

- Explain that *intra-* means "within or inside of," *inter-* means "between, among," and *intro-* means "into, within, inward."

Practice the Sort *Independent/Partner*

- Have students use the Student Book or whiteboard DVD to say each word and use the grid to sort.

- Have students check and explain their sorts.

Apply *Independent/Partner/Small Groups*

- Read aloud the directions on Student Book p. 120. Have students complete the activity.

- **Game** Allow time for students to play In the Game, which is on the CD.

Extend the Sort

Vocabulary 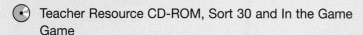 **Word Of the Week:**

introspection Share a sample sentence to give a context for *introspection: After her moving speech, we all needed time for introspection.* Have a student consult a dictionary and clarify that *introspection* means "looking inside oneself."

Alternative Sort: Words with Same Base Word

Have students find three pairs of words that share the same base word. (*international, intranational; intermural, intramural; interpersonal, intrapersonal*) Ask students to create a sentence for one of the pairs that shows the difference in meaning.

ELL English Language Learners

Have students repeat after you as you pronounce each word, focusing attention on the prefixes. Then have them tell the difference in meaning between the two most similar prefixes: *inter-* (between) and *intra-* (within).

Predictable Spelling Changes *ceiv/cep, tain/ten, nounce/nunc*

Objectives

- To recognize how some words change in predictable ways when *-tion* is added to form derived words: *ceiv/cep, tain/ten,* and *nounce/nunc*
- To sort and spell words with spelling changes *ceiv/cep, tain/ten,* and *nounce/nunc* when *-tion* is added

Materials for Derivational Relations

📺 Whiteboard Activities DVD-ROM, Sort 31

💿 Teacher Resource CD-ROM, Sort 31 and Word Match Game

📔 Student Book, pages 121–124

Words

ceiv/cep	tain/ten	nounce/nunc
deception	retention	pronunciation
preconceive	detain	renounce
preconception	detention	renunciation
perceive	attain	denounce
perception	attention	denunciation
	sustain	
	sustenance	
	abstain	
	abstention	

Introduce/Model
Small Groups

- Use the whiteboard DVD or the CD word cards to introduce in context any word that may be unfamiliar.

- Display the headers *ceiv/cep deceive, tain/ten retain,* and *nounce/nunc pronounce).* Model pairing words that are related by meaning and sorting several words to show the spelling change. Have students complete the sort. Then challenge students to sort the words again, matching base words and their derived words.

- Explain to students that *ceiv/cep* means "to take," *tain/ten* means "to hold," and *nounc/nunc* means "to report."

- Help students recognize and pronounce the sound changes that go with these spelling changes: *ceiv/cep* (/ē/ to /ĕ/); *tain/ten* (/ā/ to /ĕ/); *nounce/nunc* (/ou/ to /ŭ/).

Practice the Sort
Independent/Partner

- Have students use the Student Book or whiteboard DVD to say each word and use the grid to sort.

- Have students check and explain their sorts.

Apply
Independent/Partner/Small Groups

- Read aloud the directions on Student Book p. 124. Have students complete the activity.

- **Game** Allow time for students to play Word Match, which is on the CD.

Extend the Sort

Vocabulary **W**ord **O**f the **W**eek:

sustain Share a sample sentence to give a context for *sustain: Knowing help was on the way sustained our spirits during the flood.* Have a student consult a dictionary and clarify that *sustain* means "to keep up" or "to keep going."

ELL **English Language Learners**

Have students repeat after you as you pronounce each word, focusing attention on the change in the pair of words. Ask students to give a sentence using the words.

Alternative Sort: Speed Sort Alphabetically

Have students sort the words into alphabetical order. Have them note the time it takes to accurately sort the words. Encourage them to increase the pace while maintaining accuracy.

Adding Suffixes -ent/-ence, -ant/-ance #1

Objectives

- To identify the suffixes *-ent/-ence* and *-ant/-ance* and understand how they influence the meanings of words
- To sort and spell words ending with the suffixes *-ent/-ence* and *-ant/-ance*

Materials for Derivational Relations

⊡ Whiteboard Activities DVD-ROM, Sort 32

◉ Teacher Resource CD-ROM, Sort 32 and Rocket Ride Game

▤ Student Book, pages 125–128

Words

-ent	-ence	-ant	-ance
different	difference	abundant	abundance
prominent	prominence	dominant	dominance
dependent	dependence	fragrant	fragrance
resident	residence		
obedient	obedience		
excellent	excellence		
patient	patience		

Introduce/Model
Small Groups

- Use the whiteboard DVD or the CD word cards to introduce the words. Begin the sort by having students match each base word with its derived form. Have them say the word pairs aloud.

- Display the headers *(-ent confident, -ence confidence, -ant brilliant, -ance brilliance)*. Model pairing words that are related by meaning and sorting several words to show the spelling change. Have students complete the sort.

- Read the sort, discussing the meanings of the words.

- Help students recognize that words with *-ent* and *-ant* are adjectives and that *-ence* and *-ance* are noun suffixes.

Practice the Sort
Independent/Partner

- Have students use the Student Book or whiteboard DVD to say each word and use the grid to sort.

- Have students check and explain their sorts.

Apply
Independent/Partner/Small Groups

- Read aloud the directions on Student Book p. 128. Have students complete the activity.

- **Game** Allow time for students to play Rocket Ride, which is on the CD.

Extend the Sort

Vocabulary **Word Of the Week:**
dominant/dominance Share sample sentences to give a context for *dominant/dominance: The _____ color in the room was red.* Then have a student consult a dictionary to clarify meanings.

ELL **English Language Learners**
Have students repeat after you as you pronounce each word, focusing attention on the sound of the suffixes. Make sure that students can produce the different sounds.

Teacher Tip
During class discussions, point out that the words *dependent* and *patient* have multiple meanings. Have students find these words in a dictionary and write multiple sentences, using a different meaning for *dependent* and *patient* in each sentence.

Sort 33

Adding Suffixes -ent/-ence, -ant/-ance #2

Objectives

- To identify the suffixes *-ent/-ence* and *-ant/-ance* and understand how they influence the meanings of words
- To sort and spell words ending with the suffixes *-ent/-ence* and *-ant/-ance*

Materials for Derivational Relations

Whiteboard Activities DVD-ROM, Sort 33

Teacher Resource CD-ROM, Sort 33 and Spell Check

Student Book, pages 129–132

Words

-ent	-ence	-ant	-ance
adolescent	adolescence	abundant	abundance
inconvenient	inconvenience	defiant	defiance
incoherent	incoherence		
adherent	adherence		
inherent	inherence		
impertinent	impertinence		
iridescent	iridescence		

Introduce/Model
Small Groups

- Use the whiteboard DVD or the CD word cards to introduce the words. Have students match each base word to its derived form and say the word pairs aloud.

- Display the headers *(-ent imminent, -ence imminence, -ant irrelevant, -ance irrelevance).* Model pairing words that are related by meaning and sorting several words to show the spelling change. Have students complete the sort.

- Read the sort, discussing the meanings of the words.

- Help students recognize that words with *-ent* and *-ant* are adjectives and that *-ence* and *-ance* are noun suffixes.

Practice the Sort
Independent/Partner

- Have students use the Student Book or whiteboard DVD to say each word and use the grid to sort.

- Have students check and explain their sorts.

Apply
Independent/Partner/Small Groups

- Read aloud the directions on Student Book p. 132. Have students complete the activity.

- **Game** Allow time for students to play Spell Check, which is on the CD.

Extend the Sort

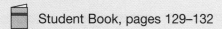

Vocabulary **Word Of the Week:**
impertinent/impertinence Share sample sentences to give a context for *impertinent/impertinence: The _____ two-year-old folded her arms and shouted "No!" Her _____ encouraged others to defy the teacher.* Have students choose the words to complete the sentences. Then have a student consult a dictionary to clarify meanings.

ELL **English Language Learners**

Have students repeat after you as you pronounce each word, focusing attention on the sound of the suffixes. Make sure that students can produce the different sounds and understand the change in meaning.

Alternative Sort: Speed Sort

If students need an extra challenge, have them repeat the sort as before, but arrange the words in alphabetical order as well. Have partners make note of the time. Encourage students to sort the words as quickly and accurately as possible.

Adding Suffixes -*able*, -*ible*

Objectives

- To recognize that the suffix -*able* is usually added to base words and the suffix -*ible* is usually added to word roots
- To sort and spell words ending with suffixes -*able* and -*ible*

Materials for Derivational Relations

- Whiteboard Activities DVD-ROM, Sort 34

- Teacher Resource CD-ROM, Sort 34 and Spin and Spell Game

- Student Book, pages 133–136

Words

Base + -*able*		Root + -*ible*	
dependable	laughable	edible	legible
breakable	punishable	audible	horrible
agreeable	adaptable	visible	tangible
predictable	decipherable	feasible	compatible
remarkable	preferable	terrible	gullible
profitable	favorable	possible	invincible

Introduce/Model
Small Groups

- Use the whiteboard DVD or the CD word cards to introduce the words. Ask students what they notice about the words.

- Model sorting several words into -*able* and -*ible* categories. Have students complete the sort.

- Read the sort, discussing the meanings of the words. Invite students to read aloud each word and the base word or word root within it.

- Help students recognize the pattern across the words and suffixes: base words end with -*able* and root words end with -*ible*.

Practice the Sort
Independent/Partner

- Have students use the Student Book or whiteboard DVD to say each word and use the grid to sort them into groups.

- Have students check and explain their sorts.

Apply
Independent/Partner/Small Groups

- Read aloud the directions on Student Book p. 136. Have students complete the activity.

- **Game** Allow time for students to play Spin and Spell, which is on the CD.

Extend the Sort

Vocabulary **W**ord **O**f the **W**eek:

audible Ask students to share any prior knowledge they have about the word *audible*. Then use *audible* in a sample sentence, such as *He whispered so softly that his words were barely audible.* Allow students time to guess the word's meaning from context and then explain that *audible* means "that is heard or that can be heard."

Alternative Sort: Which Syllable?

Have students sort the words again by whether the first or second syllable in each word is accented. Have them use a dictionary to check the words.

ELL English Language Learners

Remind students that words with the suffix -*able* or -*ible* are adjectives—words that modify or describe a noun. Have students work with partners to look up each word's definition and brainstorm things or situations that each adjective might describe.

Sort 35 Adding the Suffix *-able* (With *e*-Drop and No Spelling Change)

Objectives

- To recognize when and why the *e* remains or drops from base words when the suffix *-able* is added
- To sort and spell words with suffix *-able* (with drop *e* and no spelling change)

Materials for Derivational Relations

Whiteboard Activities DVD-ROM, Sort 35

Teacher Resource CD-ROM, Sort 35 and Slap Jack Game

Student Book, pages 137–140

Words

e-Drop	No Change
desirable	noticeable
reusable	manageable
lovable	knowledgeable
comparable	replaceable
excusable	exchangeable
consumable	salvageable
pleasurable	changeable
believable	rechargeable
disposable	traceable
adorable	
removable	

Introduce/Model *Small Groups*

- Use the whiteboard DVD or the CD word cards to introduce in context any word that may be unfamiliar.

- Display the headers (*e*-Drop and No Change) and challenge students to sort the words accordingly.

- Encourage students to look closely at the base word in each word and look for a pattern in the words' spelling.

- Guide students to see that base words ending in *-ce* and *-ge* tend to keep the *e* when *-able* is added, because if dropped, the soft *c* or *g* would become hard consonant sounds.

Practice the Sort *Independent/Partner*

- Have students use the Student Book or whiteboard DVD to say each word and use the grid to sort them into groups.

- Have students check and explain their sorts.

Apply *Independent/Partner/Small Groups*

- Read aloud the directions on Student Book p. 140. Have students complete the activity.

- **Game** Allow time for students to play Slap Jack, which is on the CD.

Extend the Sort

Vocabulary **Word Of the Week:**

consumable Provide sample sentences such as *The puppy tried to eat everything, even items that were not supposed to be consumable.* Suggest students think about the related words *consume* and *consumer* and guess *consumable's* meaning. Clarify that the base word, *consume,* means "to take in as food; to use up; to waste or destroy" and that *consumable* means "something that can be consumed."

Alternative Sort: Speed Sort

Have students do a speed sort. Have them note the time it takes to accurately sort the words by drop *e* and no spelling change. Challenge students to increase the pace while maintaining accuracy.

ELL English Language Learners

When pronouncing words aloud for students, make sure to emphasize each stressed syllable clearly. This will be particularly helpful for those accustomed to hearing different placement of stress in the pronunciation of cognates in other languages.

Monitor Progress **Spell Check 3**

After completing Sort 35, administer Spell Check 3. See p. 245 in this Teacher Resource Guide for instructions.

Prefix Assimilation: Prefixes *in-, im-, il-, ir-*

Objectives

- To identify *in-* and its variations of spelling meaning "not"
- To sort and spell words with suffix *in-, im-, il-,* and *ir-*

Materials for Derivational Relations

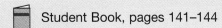 Whiteboard Activities DVD-ROM, Sort 36

Teacher Resource CD-ROM, Sort 36 and Which Prefix? Game

Student Book, pages 141–144

Words

in-	*im-*	*il-*	*ir-*
inactive	immoral	illegal	irremovable
inescapable	immeasurable	illiterate	irrational
injustice	immature	illogical	irresponsible
inaccurate	immortal	illegitimate	irregular
insecure	immigrate		irresistible
incapable	immodest		

Introduce/Model
Small Groups

- Use the whiteboard DVD or the CD word cards to introduce in context any word that may be unfamiliar.

- Display the headers *(in- incorrect, im- immobile, il- illegible, ir- irreplaceable)* and have students sort the words accordingly.

- Explain that the prefixes *im-, il-,* and *ir-* actually derived from *in-*. Guide students to see that over time, the prefix *in-* has been assimilated, or absorbed, so it is easier to say with a root or base word.

- Ask students what all these prefixes mean ("not") and have volunteers provide a definition and context sentence for some of the words.

Practice the Sort
Independent/Partner

- Have students use the Student Book or whiteboard DVD to say each word and use the grid to sort.

- Have students check and explain their sorts.

Apply
Independent/Partner/Small Groups

- Read aloud the directions on Student Book p. 144. Have students complete the activity.

- **Game** Allow time for students to play Which Prefix?, which is on the CD.

Extend the Sort

Vocabulary **Word Of the Week:**

immoral Ask students whether they have heard the word *immoral*. Provide a statement such as *Stealing is immoral besides being against the law in our country.* Ask students to tell what *immoral* means in the sentence. Have them consult a dictionary and share the idea that if something is immoral, it is very wrong and very much against what people believe is right, fair, or kind.

Alternative Sort: Suffixes

Remove all adjectives that don't include suffixes and have students sort the remaining adjectives into three categories: suffix *-al,* suffix *-able,* and other suffix. When students have finished the sort, challenge them to tell situations in which they are likely to use some of the words in each column.

ELL English Language Learners

Write the suffixes, prefixes, and base words that appear in this sort. Have students practice building words. When necessary, have students cover the *e* before adding a suffix.

Objectives

- To identify *com-* and its variations of spelling meaning "together"
- To sort and spell words with *com-, col-,* and *con-*

Materials for Derivational Relations

🖥 Whiteboard Activities DVD-ROM, Sort 37

💿 Teacher Resource CD-ROM, Sort 37 and Word Building Game

📖 Student Book, pages 145–148

Words

com-	col-	con-
combine	collide	concert
combination	collision	connect
commit	collate	congress
committee	collaborate	congestion
compete	collect	constellation
competition	collapse	conclude
company	colleague	conference
companion	collateral	congregation

Introduce/Model *Small Groups*

- Use the whiteboard DVD or the CD word cards to introduce in context any word that may be unfamiliar.

- Display the headers *(com- common, col- collection, con- conspire).* Model sorting several words according to the prefix *com-, col-,* or *con-.* Have students complete the sort.

- Read the sort, discussing whether the base word changes when the prefix is added.

- Guide students to see that over time, the prefix *com-* has been assimilated, or absorbed, so it is easier to say with a root or base word. Explain that the prefixes *col-* and *con-* actually derived from *com-.* Ask students what all these prefixes mean. ("together")

Practice the Sort *Independent/Partner*

- Have students use the Student Book or whiteboard DVD to say each word and use the grid to sort them into groups.

- Have students check and explain their sorts.

Apply *Independent/Partner/Small Groups*

- Read aloud the directions on Student Book p. 148. Have students complete the activity.

- **Game** Allow time for students to play Word Building, which is on the CD.

Extend the Sort

Vocabulary W̶ord O̶f the W̶eek:

collaborate Tell students that you will list things people collaborate to do (research about community history, raise money for a good cause, practice spelling words), and have them predict what *collaborate* means. Have a volunteer consult a dictionary and share that to collaborate is to work together.

Alternative Sort: Likely Applications

Have students sort the words by broad subjects in which they think they are likely to use the words: math, science, music, current events. As they sort each word, have students explain how they would use it in the subject context.

ELL English Language Learners

Have students repeat each word after you. Have them choose one word they find difficult and then draw a picture and write a sentence to help them remember its meaning.

Objectives

- To identify *ob-, ex-, ad-, sub-* and their variations of spelling
- To sort and spell words with *ob-, ex-, ad-,* and *sub-*

Materials for Derivational Relations

Whiteboard Activities DVD-ROM, Sort 38

Teacher Resource CD-ROM, Sort 38 and Lucky Three Game

Student Book, pages 149–152

Words

ob-	ex-	ad-	sub-
oppose	erosion	attachment	subject
offend	eject	affiliate	supportable
obstinate	extract	accountant	subtraction
obstruct	emotion	affix	suffix
		arrange	
		aggressive	
		advice	
		appetite	

Introduce/Model   *Small Groups*

- Use the whiteboard DVD or the CD word cards to introduce in context any word that may be unfamiliar.

- Display the headers *(ob- object, ex- exchange, ad- attractive, sub- suppression).* Model sorting several words according to *ob-, ex-, ad-,* and *sub-.* Have students complete the sort.

- Read the sort, discussing the meanings and different forms of the prefixes. Explain that the prefix *ob-* means "against," *ex-* means "out of" or "beyond," *ad-* generally suggests "to" or "toward," and *sub-* means "under" or "below."

- Guide students to see that over time, the prefixes *ob-, ex-, ad-,* and *sub-* have been assimilated, or absorbed, so that they are easier to say with a root or base word. Explain that variations in their spellings will occur.

Practice the Sort   *Independent/Partner*

- Have students use the Student Book or whiteboard DVD to say each word and use the grid to sort.

- Have students check and explain their sorts.

Apply   *Independent/Partner/Small Groups*

- Read aloud the directions on Student Book p. 152. Have students complete the activity.

- **Game** Allow time for students to play Lucky Three, which is on the CD.

Extend the Sort

Vocabulary **Word Of the Week:**

obstruct Ask students whether they have heard the word *obstruct* before. Offer this sentence to clarify meaning: *The trees obstruct our view of the beautiful sunset.* Ask students what they think *obstruct* means in this sentence. ("to block" or "get in the way of") Have a student consult a dictionary to verify meaning.

ELL **English Language Learners**

Have students repeat each word after you. Have volunteers choose one word and write a sentence using the word.

Monitor Progress ✔ **Spell Check 4**

After completing Sort 38, administer Spell Check 4. See p. 245 in this Teacher Resource Guide for instructions.